THE FRANKFURT SCHOOL CRITIQUE OF CAPITALIST CULTURE

REVISED AND EXTENDED EDITION

The Frankfurt School Critique of Capitalist Culture
A critical theory for post-democratic society and its re-education

Revised and extended edition

RONALD JEREMIAH SCHINDLER

Routledge
Taylor & Francis Group
LONDON AND NEW YORK

First published 1998 by Ashgate Publishing

Reissued 2018 by Routledge
2 Park Square, Milton Park, Abingdon, Oxon, OX14 4RN
52 Vanderbilt Avenue, New York, NY 10017

Routledge is an imprint of the Taylor & Francis Group, an informa business

Copyright © R. J. Schindler 1998

All rights reserved. No part of this book may be reprinted or reproduced or utilised in any form or by any electronic, mechanical, or other means, now known or hereafter invented, including photocopying and recording, or in any information storage or retrieval system, without permission in writing from the publishers.

Notice:
Product or corporate names may be trademarks or registered trademarks, and are used only for identification and explanation without intent to infringe.

Publisher's Note
The publisher has gone to great lengths to ensure the quality of this reprint but points out that some imperfections in the original copies may be apparent.

Disclaimer
The publisher has made every effort to trace copyright holders and welcomes correspondence from those they have been unable to contact.

A Library of Congress record exists under LC control number: 97076932

Typeset by Alison Anderson, Philadelphia, Pennsylvania

ISBN 13: 978-1-138-34363-4 (hbk)
ISBN 13: 978-1-138-34364-1 (pbk)
ISBN 13: 978-0-429-43904-9 (ebk)

Contents

Foreword by Mihailo Marković — vii
Preface to the revised edition — xi
Acknowledgements — xxiii
Introduction — xxv

1 The dialectical intelligence: Its origins in German philosophy — 1

2 Toward a metatheoretical reconstruction of Marxism — 36

3 Philosophy and critico-practical activity — 64

4 Habermas's historical materialism and semiotic phenomenology — 80

5 Contemporary modalities of alienated consciousness — 102

6 False consciousness: Ideology and mental pathology — 133

7 Materialist phenomenology of language — 149

8 Work and communicative competence — 159

9 Whither critical theory and its exponents — 172

10 Hermeneutics and political visions for the universities — 194

11 Toward a post-Auschwitz ethics 211

12 Conclusions 251

Postface 267
Appendix 1: Black nationalism and emancipation 271
Appendix 2 280
Appendix 3 by Stephen C. Zelnick 282
Afterword by David Lamb 285
Bibliography 289

Foreword

Like many other interesting cultural events in an age of transition, Ronald Schindler's impressive book is a contradictory cultural phenomenon. It has obvious practical intentions but, since it cannot rely on any American practical movement, it remains almost purely theoretical. It addresses almost every existing contemporary school of thought, yet it does not belong to any of them and would not be recognized by the epigones of any one of them, since it lacks most of those external signs which demonstrate adherence to the club. The book is exceptional in the present day American philosophical culture and yet it reflects some of its new tendencies.

What *prevails* in present day American philosophical culture is still a clear-cut division among philosophical trends and disciplines. Analytical philosophy still dominates; the majority of those who oppose it seek a clear identity as phenomenologists, hermeneuticians, Marxists, or pragmatists. Philosophers are still specialized: they teach and write on logic, or philosophy of science, or history of philosophy, or ethics, or metaphysics (whatever it might mean once it was coopted by logicians). Schindler's book defies any classification of that sort. His basic sympathies lie with critical theory, but he is critical of both Marx and Habermas, sympathetic of hermeneutics, and tends to identify his standpoint as one of 'critical phenomenology'. He deals with a variety of topic areas, from methodology and epistemology to critique of science and ideology, ethics, politics, and psychology of education theory.

A remarkable erudition is another exceptional characteristic of Schindler's book. Those hundreds of books listed in the bibliography have been carefully studied by the author, who has never attempted to learn the technique of 'speed reading'. In American culture, strangely enough, erudition is not a highly regarded merit. A virtue has been turned into a vice in order to justify a style of life in which there is not enough time for reading. Universities are being turned into business-corporations in which high paying students require a lot of attention: teaching is more demanding than anywhere else. Intellectuals, socialized into being achievers of power and/or wealth, waste a good deal of their best energy in departmental power struggles. Building true friendships has been replaced by a very extensive socializing which produces fragile, easily perishable human links in exchange for precious time which could have been spent with a book, or in some meaningful social engagement. Even the greatest erudites of our epoch, people like Ernst Cassirer or Ernst Bloch, fared poorly in the New World, and the Frankfurt School itself made no impact on American academia during its time of exile from Nazi Germany and temporary stay in New York. Of course a certain repulsion for erudition is not only a special case of *mauvaise foi* generated by a special style of academic life but also a consequence of analytical methodology. Vast knowledge is required for a historical approach to problems. It is much less relevant for a mere clarification of concepts, for a play with logical possibilities, no matter how brilliant it could be.

Another idiosyncrasy of Schindler's work is his 'dialectical' language. Fredric Jameson, quoted in the Postface of this book, is right when he says: 'Nowhere is the hostility of the Anglo-American tradition toward the dialectical more apparent than in the widespread notion that the style of these works is obscure and cumbersome, indigestible, abstract, or, to sum it all up in a convenient catchword, *germanic*'.

An arrogant superficiality tends to condemn all true thinking, all creation of original complex symbols, all openings of new difficult problems, by raising clarity to the level of a supreme criterion of evaluation. This does not mean that an effort to truly communicate to an audience is not a matter of human decency, of respect for other human beings. Obscure, mystifying thought conceals itself behind an obscurantist language. Other conditions being equal, clarity is a legitimate criterion of evaluation. But other conditions are not equal. A conformist thought can rely entirely on a very clear and simple, descriptive terminology. A thought that questions and challenges given institutions and patterns of life must explore the realm of the non-visible, non-behavioral, not immediately testable; it must speak about deep structure, about possibilities which can be tested only under very specific conditions. A radical thought goes beyond the observable, easily conceivable specifics; it examines universal aspects of social life, the totality of human condition; thus it must be more abstract and condensed in its multidimensionality. Since its purpose is not only to inform but also to express preferences and to translate pure theory into practical engagement, it will need many more metaphors and value-laden concepts. With increasing maturity, more complex messages will require more complex symbolic means. And, vice versa, deliberate simplifications and pauperization of language reduces culture to an increasingly infantile level.

While Schindler's book is exceptional in relation to the academic establishment and the dominant positivist tradition, it reflects some new trends in American philosophical culture. There is a growing malaise within analytical philosophy itself. To be sure, analysis of concepts will remain one of the lasting tasks of any good philosophy. But all those specific features which used to characterize philosophical analysis as a particular philosophical school are crumbling. Since Kuhn and Feyerabend, the historical approach to knowledge is no longer neglected. The emotivist approach to values, to ethics and aesthetics, is under attack. Some analytical scholars have become critics of society. Bridges are being built toward European schools of thought: hermeneutics, phenomenology, Marxism, structuralism, existentialism. Students demand courses in continental philosophy; bookstores are full of books on Nietzsche, Marx, Heidegger, even Hegel.

In spite of an amazing shallowness of being and an unconcealed anti-intellectualism among most people, a restless, rebellious spirit is at work. Discrepancies between appearance and reality are glaring and the trends thinking people discover are scary: approaching collective suicide of humanity; mindlessness of waste of precious human and natural resources; accelerated destruction of the only natural environment we have; reduction of all senses and all interests to the one of consumption; growing gaps between levels of consumption and production; reversal of all trends toward greater fairness and justice; growing misery of people excluded from work, from social space, from socially recognized life.

Official society does not want to hear the truth about itself. It fills the atmosphere with false optimism, shallow patriotism, medieval fundamentalism, and arrogant self-righteousness. Critical voices risk being treated as subversive voices. But the hypocrisy of the situation is that they would not be judged for the harshness of their criticism or even for its allegedly unacceptable political implications. Of course, it would be a poor style in a free society to dismiss free thought for the freedom it takes. They would be dismissed for being 'over-educated', 'over-intellectual', abstract, utopian, unintelligible, 'germanic'.

With all their talent and knowledge and academic qualifications, people like Ronald Schindler have nowhere to teach, nowhere to do research, nowhere to make a living. They are welcome to the club of the street people.

That is the American tragedy of the Nineties.

Mihailo Marković

Preface to the revised edition

This revised edition of *The Frankfurt School of Capitalist Culture* addresses the decisive emergence and triumph of plutocratic capitalism from the wreckage of state democratic capitalism. We are a democracy only in political terms. The economic substance of the American middle class has been gutted. The Frankfurt School proponents of our day cannot fathom this phenomenon. I undertake to understand why capitalism's structural-systematic requisites and communicative cultural dynamics led to this destruction of the Age of Reason itself.

The book reviews the general social science literature and the Frankfurt School's critique thereof. That critique is witheringly caustic and on the mark. There have been two generations of the Frankfurt School. The first had a general theory to attack capitalism in its imperialist phase as it came to a climax in Nazi Germany. Its leading exemplars were Adorno and Horkheimer. Unfortunately, they did not develop a praxis to engage the very besieged proletariat with whom they had no political contact. The second generation arose as a response to the Cold War. It was unable to predict the collapse of the Soviet Union, the fragmentation of the bipolar balance of power and the re-emergence of toxic nationalisms, and the specific mechanism that might regulate current global conflicts and the impending Armageddon with the runaway proliferation of nuclear devices. Habermas's disciples in the twenty-first century will be the third generation.

Jürgen Habermas is the current generally accepted spokesperson of the school. There are contradictions internal to the school's theory itself and its own privileged class position in society, particularly in its tenured cloisters at the universities, which it attacks. In the end, there is no political engagement with a program to deal with the wrongs their theoreticians identify and what results is an abstract legitimated utopia with a call for socialism by democratic discursive will formation without a content. The theory has an elaborate linguistic analysis of the sundry schools of social theory and their respective shortcomings. It presents basically a counter-discourse to fashionable methodological disputes and trends at the universities, especially the elite ones. All the contestants understand that their overreaching goal is the self-preservation of their own professorial positions in the name of the ideological smokescreen of free speech, but without the ethical, inwardly determined compulsion to commit themselves to the corresponding social responsibilities of what they advocate.

We can call this phenomenon of intellectuals: critique without risk. Habermas claims their theories, in the final analysis, cannot supersede the very status quo they deconstruct because it is in the nature of their dialogue that they accept the grounding normative premises and empirical conditions which give rise to these meta-critiques, not only in the physical sanctuary of the Academy, but in the notional Enlightenment tradition itself, which produces only reasonable gentlemen politely engaged in the civilized colloquy of how to form theories consensually, while preserving their bases of power from the competing claims of other legitimate interest groups.

Furthermore, in his recent writings in the legal domain Habermas mistakes the rule of law in bourgeois capitalist society as the precondition for general emancipation. No. It leads to the administration of the masses in a proto-fascist social order. The laws of corporate property have abolished the status of the individual as the building block of the Enlightenment. As Marx knew too well, this individual with individual rights is a fiction in terms of being politically efficacious and economically viable.

The Frankfurt School also falls into a metaphysics of pure reason with echoes of neo-Kantianism. Habermas argues for the unforced force of the best argument to prevail in debates at the universities and the larger society. Unfortunately, he does not understand a negative dialectics in which, as in totalitarian polities where there is a basic asymmetrical distribution of power, the will to will of someone who chooses to be irrational and violent destroys a disarmed and naive opponent. Too, it is human second nature to lie. This situation holds most true in the universities, where there is no accountability because the structure of power does not hold individual miscreants accountable. There is a sad and bizarre debate happening in Germany about when German responsibility for the Holocaust ends. It never will. Habermas understands the reasons why, but he cannot persuade his opponents in the debate who for reasons of nationalism argue to the contrary and deliberately misread the historical record. The Germans did behave worse than the Russians in World War II; they reaped what they sowed in the genocidal destruction of the Jews, and to a lesser extent other groups and their own people, willingly and with premeditation. It is the worst type of bad faith to argue that the Germans, too, were the victims of Hitler. Setting aside for the moment the blatant war criminals, there were the 'little hitlers' who, as long as things were running efficiently and successfully did not protest. Today Germans consider themselves 'victims', as if Hitler materialized as a demigod. To Habermas's credit, he has kept pricking the neo-Romantic consciences of Germans to remember. That has been his greatest contribution to modern political discourse. If the Germans bury in their political unconscious the fact that the Holocaust is their unique contribution to the chronicles of humanity, they will be bound to repeat their shameless history. To learn from history, there must be a collectively experienced and empathized guilt and remorse, but in a personal framework so as to effect individual responsibility.

In addition, the very class privileges of the Frankfurt School and its proponents belie its call for the emancipation of the species. These theorists have no mediatory links to the larger world and its disinherited. Their very cosmopolitanism with its closed 'guild' mentality is elitist and undemocratic and could not possibly relate to a mass movement for historical change. Their agent of history is the intelligentsia on the left/liberal wing, who lead very respectable bourgeois lives. Hence there is a serious lack of a sense of urgency to resolve by personal intervention the critical issues they raise. In a leisurely manner, over the past three decades, they have been exchanging papers and attending conferences. This clinical detachment is part of the problem of social critics; by default, they potentially give tyrants the political field. Thus the tomorrows of dealing with exigencies in their situational context become the past present. Unfortunately, intellectuals in the social sciences and humanities are isolated within their own institutions and have only marginal utility to the real lived experience of the dispossessed of the world, for whom they claim to speak without any authority derived from them by actual speech acts.

What gives the intelligentsia special powers of empathy to represent the dispossessed? There is an ideological arrogance in this self-appropriation of causes to which they partake of no direct observation or participation. In short, their critiques resound with hypocrisy and jargon because their hidden agenda is to attain the very power at the universities which they find corrupts the will to truth. At its nadir, we see the mischief wrought by well-meaning but reverse discriminatory affirmative action programs which have only further stereotyped minorities as 'naturally' handicapped, while forcing the architects to compromise the public general interest for tactical, political gains of dubious merit and longevity. The June 12, 1995 U.S. Supreme Court decision in *Adarand Constructors v. Pena* validates in part this interpretation.

If intellectuals were in power, might they be unable to resist the forced force of the 'best argument' if they could silence their benighted opponents by expulsion? After all, what has historically happened to individuals who could not be persuaded to see the adversary's point of view? This kind of silencing happened sixty years ago in Nazi Germany and Stalin's Soviet Union without even a whimper from the well-placed victims at the universities. At best, their colleagues maintained an opportunistic silence. As for the Frankfurt School and its followers, there is evidence of a potential brutal will to power in the very eschatology of efforts to redeem humankind. Paradoxically, there is a totalitarian germ dormant in the 'linguistic turn' of the school, despite its claim to be representative of democratic socialism in its programmatic form, given this quasi-substantive emphasis on procedural consensus formation blindly issued without first determining concrete goals with respect to groups and factions extrinsic to the school itself. Implicitly, they want a blank check to write an ad hoc new history in their millennial Reich of Theoria, because they have abstracted a pseudo-consensus from the people in whose name they speak because the latter are speech-less. No, thank you. Hitler and Stalin, too, exploited the idealism of intellectuals who generally lived in the historical vacuums of teaching and research institutions where traditionally trained scholars, initially in their climb to power, successfully blurred the line between consensus and pseudo-consensus formation in the name of morality and laws of *das Volk* or class.

What is to be done? Aside from unmasking critical theory's limitations, I point out pragmatic steps to make the universities more pertinent, first in being true to themselves and then in the practical world in the post-democratic era. Plutocrats plunder the treasuries of corporate America and avoid taxes, while internecine multicultural strife provides a smokescreen to distort the collective consciousness about the loss of popular sovereignty and consensus on legitimating values. These values are needed, at levels of analysis from private lifestyles to effective public policies for the middle class, to anchor even a minimal liberal society, let alone a socialist one. The political act of criticism and self-criticism is also therapeutic insofar as the learning process purges one of illusions. One can then venture forth into the world armed with the reality principle in terms of life affirming concepts which can be applied to human beings who must struggle in distressed environments and at the same time face irremediable existential dilemmas of the human condition. Both problems in their totality await a prophetic message. The particular elements of that critical theoretical arsenal, with an intent to implement major policy decisions, are not that decisive; what is affirmative and ultimately definitive is the process of critical thinking itself, whereby how one poses the proper questions in the appropriate collective context will help determine in their own uniqueness the basic outlines of our future life forms.

The purpose of this book is to demonstrate the tension between understanding and explanation in treating various modes of alienation in our administered capitalist political culture. In articulating social science theory, we must be made cognizant of a type of lived false consciousness which obstructs the development of thought. Through a phenomenological hermeneutics, we can constitute our selves with a semiology of the political 'text' so as to be able to make visible the conflicting interests at play in the underworld of politics. The revealed contents of these contradictions will liberate logical forms so that social science theory can assimilate itself to a critique of its own generative context. Then we can rationally engage in a discourse with the intent of achieving a universally derived consensus on values regulative of the polity and its potential for reform or even revolution.

In order fully to grasp particular features of a wide range of problematics, we shall examine the Frankfurt School theorists who have advanced a 'depth grammar' of contemporary capitalist society and the mythifications enveloping the fetish commodity form of production as they hypostatize social relations and even the commodification of literary theory itself. So, contrary to the optimism of mainstream social science theory, three generations of this tradition as we go into the twenty-first century have always stated unequivocally that the high valence of ideology is characteristic of capitalist culture. The nature of this discrepancy in analysis must be researched if we are to evaluate the validity of the predications of social science paradigms. Complementarily, if false consciousness is the defining attribute of capitalist culture, in what political space, then, does reason survive to address itself, through critique, to the human predicament?

In idealist fashion, the dialectical intelligence found a full exposition in modern times through reworking the efforts of Hegel in the *Phenomenology of Mind*. He treats reality as wholly accessible to rational consciousness. Alienation and contradiction interpenetrate (conceptually, not ultimately in accomplished human history), leading to the split between subject and object, the ideal and the real, and idea and existence - the whole woof and warp of the Unhappy Consciousness of contemporary political philosophy. Modern social science theory and critique have therein an archetypical model for understanding and explanation, in inverted form, when we examine the Master/Slave relationship of the *Phenomenology*.

For our purposes, a paradigm of 'liberation' will be developed with the counterexample of a failed attempt at Western universities, particularly American. A moment of truth arose during the civil rights era and the Vietnam War. The New Left not only did not conduct itself according to a strategic plan, actually became part of the problem by dissolving into sectarian bands in the theater of the surreal. Today they are often the dominant force at prestige universities. Their inherent character flaws, mainly the self-indulgence of a clinically definable narcissistic personality, led to cooption rather easily. Hence they were playing at rational change. That adolescent frame of mind depicts the current state of higher education in the Ivy League institutions. Unresolved Oedipal conflicts are sublimated into policy. So, greed is good. Money is power.

More, power is money. Affirmative action programs are no less than extortion because there is a war of each against all where the public good has not been defined.

I suspect that there is a 'natural selection' process in the publishing of books in this country, biased by those who have an ideological axe to grind. That means that truth is an exchangeable commodity for barter in the power struggles. I have wondered, why do I have to publish abroad? Obviously, my themes are deeply disturbing to the new status quo in the cloistered halls of academia. Quite frankly, the answer is that I am not for sale. That fact makes me dangerous. I am a mutation in the academic world of racketeering in currently fashionable 'isms'. However, I have been converted to the point of view that there is a remote potential for the women's movement to be a focal point for a world transvaluation of all values if the groups involved can ever reach a consensus on an executable political agenda with a legitimate and authoritative leadership. However, the coefficient of resistance of Islamic fundamentalists, the Roman Catholic Church, and the Republic of China's totalitarian criminals dictate that the struggle will dominate the whole of the next century.

From a Marxist point of view, the crisis of the universities for the next century is a collective effort at preserving knowledge from being corrupted to mere use value: the crusade by the New Left of the quaint 1960s provided a blatantly aborted test for the political implementation of critical theory. But the impetus to reconcile the theory and practice of critical theory propagated by the Frankfurt School has been dissipated by the public spectacle engendered by the consciousness industry of capitalism. The writings of the Frankfurt School themselves have become commodities in the university marketplace, more talked about than read or understood. Their books are somewhat radical chic which a 'cultured' person must have on a bookshelf. Nonetheless, we will show how critical theory, in spite of certain conceptual shortcomings, has enough residual strength to be able to address itself to legitimacy problems of present-day late-state capitalism. Indeed, with the virtual 'apostasy' of even Jürgen Habermas to a hermeneutic, linguistically inspired phenomenology with a strong positivist bias toward critical legal studies, we now must understand that for any so-called radical left group to be viable in the political field, it must first conceptually retool. To the degree that universities are integrated into the corporate structure of capitalism, then any reforming movement has barely the potential to develop in a shrinking public domain. I explore, consequently, how sundry alienated states of collective consciousness displace critically minded intellectuals to a peripheral role in society because they can develop no stable constituency for a historically effective power base.

The book, in consequence, examines Hegel's historicism in the light of Marx's re-evaluation. This shift from Mind to Nature issued in a major theoretical revolution which actualized the Idea through the mundane mediation of politics, thereby creating new dimensions for philosophical and social science inquiry. Marx took up this theme and saw the proletariat as the agency of a revolutionary historical change to the promised land of human freedom and equality. This idea is employed throughout the unfolding arguments in an effort to show how political attempts at 'liberation' have demoralized intellectuals and the masses from performing either theoretical research or the mass organization work to actualize a transformation of the entire global community, given the rather poor subjective set of conditions. The objective circumstances for a massive change in our lifeworlds is at hand; there is just not the will. However, the specific Marxian idea of human liberties manifested internal contradictions linked to historical debacles and impasses and this led to a radical reevaluation by three generations of the Frankfurt School. They conceived a critical theory of the epistemological premises which cover the entire range and depth of social theory, and, in the line of Hegel, they made the last collective endeavor at a speculative *Weltanschauung* suggestive of an Absolute Knowledge. As we shall attempt to demonstrate, Marxian concepts can no longer rationally accommodate sociopolitical realities. For example, the immiseration of the proletariat, the labor theory of value, and the mechanistic base-superstructure dichotomy, are inadequate to the reality addressed. In time, they might only be an antiquarian residue - ideological in form and with no substance. Indeed, to the degree that these concepts fail to survive in existing virulent and reified ideological and state bureaucratic forms, it is not extreme to say that human survival is at stake, for the new false consciousness of our era not only has dire implications for geo-political collectivities but menaces the whole biological species. To meliorate, however marginally, the obstacles to overcoming our lived Unhappy Consciousness, I will peruse in the format of this text, more novel and adaptable philosophical forms and ideas and come to understand the time frames and structural levels at which they interconnect. But it will be argued that the *Phenomenology of Mind* still presents the image of the problematic, and that image survives in appropriate historical forms and theoretical constructs. We therefore study selectively this recent history of dialectical philosophy in order to understand the human condition and any dormant possibilities for the realization of human freedom and equality. Is there, in this context, a moral imperative to political action and commitment within such a philosophy?

Marx had a novel concept of knowledge almost diametrically opposed to Hegel's. The difference goes to the very heart of what the 'dialectical method' can accomplish as a theoretical project which outlines the possibilities for transcendence at any given moment of history. By Marx's reasoning, knowledge is a 'totality' progressively evolving but conditioned by the mode of production which historically generates a particular social organization. But this kind of argument makes knowledge appear to be technocratic and reason positivist: such is the unintentional nature of truth that Marx elaborated. He failed to grasp the antinomy between the lived alienated experience and the instrumentalist thrust of his basic thesis that institutionalized reality has been inverted by the subversion of Enlightenment reason through the invasion of everyday life by organized forms of domination through the mechanism of fetish commodities. We will show how fetish commodities objectify human experiences by reducing human vision in an existential and ontological sense. This can be attributed to the lowered horizon of the conditioned consumption of devalued goods and services. The human world is consequently rendered atemporal and derealized as we reflexively, and not critically, react to sights and images which imitate conformist patterns of predictable behavior. The general culture supports this semiotic galaxy - a galaxy which the critical character of this document attempts to rise above and proposes to demythologize. We live in a public space which has been rationalized to the point where human solidarity is disrupted. Certain key words, to be enumerated, mime the fetish character of the production of commodities and its modern depiction as rational subjectivity. Intellectual systems rigidify into apologetic ideologies for the isolated, dedifferentiated individual locked into the status quo. We must, then, show how capitalist society has lost that space of freedom for political expression formally allotted between civil society and the state, and how the republic has lost its democratic virtues through bureaucratic domination and the over-rationalization of every aspect of life. This we can attribute to a reifying division of labor whose rationale serves not only production but also corporate power elites whose interests are not only in profits but in the legitimation of their hegemony through control of consciousness, will, morality, and the collective ethos. Marx's 'dialectic', ensnared in a metaphysics of the political economy of the nineteenth century, foundered in that he saw only one dimension of this problematic - the fact that the working class was denied its political efficacy by the appropriation of its surplus labor. Consciousness of class was derailed from pursuing its true interests by bourgeois democratic mystification encoded into belief value systems (e.g., constitutions) to be systematically disseminated.

Marx literally invented the Myth of the Proletariat as the universal agent of history to counter the bourgeois antithesis of the Invisible Hand. Both myths were impaled on a methodological essentialism belied by the actual historical tendencies from which they abstracted certain properties in order to serve axiological prejudices only to infer erroneous political norms from the abstract system. The historical logic of these reified theories will be examined, and the theme of the relation of science and ideology will be developed. How, for example, did intellectuals from the bourgeoisie come to be the revolutionaries who embodied the interests of the proletarians? Indeed, we will argue that the locus of the principal contradictions has shifted from the 'base' to the 'superstructure' where systems of ideals and intellectuals can exercise a degree of cultural autonomy of their own in modifying reality relatively independently of concerns of production. Indeed, we will argue that this conclusion holds more truth the greater the level of material development of a society under study. If knowledge is indeed conditioned in the social sense understood by Marx, then even Marxists are left vulnerable to an epistemological relativism and ontological dualism (between the subject and the real objects subtending the historical dynamic). This ultimate reality created by Marxism is consequently created ex nihilo, and that is not compatible with the Marxist intention of founding a theory of praxis. Here lie the difficulties of a practically dialecticized reason where action and thought no longer can be synchronized. Furthermore, in such a case there is no way of properly ordering norms and values practically because the spatio-temporal disorder obliterates the necessary and telic forms of things. Human imagination, play, and education are de-historicized to the extent that the de-naturalizing of concepts splits them off from the context of their growth out of immediate experiences 'for consciousness'. Among other tasks, I will attempt to illuminate false consciousness engendered in such a situation for the phenomenal and noumenal division which partially degrades critical conceptual thinking itself into a mystifying discussion of what is and is not 'in-itself'.

Because everyday life has assumed the ultimate form of lived alienation, we need to examine what conditions of our *Zeitgeist* led reason to be equated with the rational administration of things. To fathom the reality in which we partake of and reflexively act out our designated roles, we must find features of consciousness which are immutable yet dynamic if the concept of truth is to be more than a montage of illusions and ultimately to have a liberatory thrust. This is a methodological necessity if we are even to have a project which assumes that truthfulness can not only be ascertainable by universally acceptable standards but even somehow be enacted in an open society of communicants all equidistant from a constitutive collective consciousness. Such an understanding of truth will be shown to be amenable to constant revision not only for the substantive issues but for the very nature of the cognitive standards which will be developed in the formative first four chapters. These standards can be grasped in the face-to-face contacts which form a matrix of power in the tissues of any society. We will attempt in the subsequent chapters to demonstrate that the more one-sided the relationships, the more repression must be engaged to inform behavioral codes and taboos. In this context, extreme repression (psychological intimidation combined with the background threat of police disciplinary actions) often is the other side of an existing state of anomie. Motivation decreases, and capitalism suffers a legitimation crisis often quite independent of the material level of the common weal.

Questions must be posed, then, in the last two chapters, about the very meaning of a life where work and the nature of its experience and self-determination are severed and absorbed into the leveling impelled by political acculturation. Metaphysical problems about authenticity and anguish are raised to a general level of discourse. Ultimately, in the political sense, a counter-cultural response arises to contest the regnant order. We must investigate why the work ethos is subject not only to question but to vilification. These intertwined 'radical' questions and issues are obviously beyond the purview of the 'authoritative' writings of Marx. Hence, as this century expires, we must look at these Marxisms without Marx.

Only the Frankfurt School, among all the philosophies of the social sciences attempting to address and reprove modern society, developed to the limit a 'negative dialectics'. The limit condition is that after so much critique there must be radical engagement with the identified social issues. The root of alienation was rightly unraveled in culture - in the last instance. But the methodological correctness did not lead to political commitment once Hitler's threat became evident. Rather, a malaise set in. The same analysis holds true for the former Soviet Union. We can only conclude that the concepts of this movement succumbed to a type of skepticism in which its concepts fell short of englobing reality. The totalitarian threat did not elicit a theoretical auto-critique which might stay ahead of the events. This de-temporalization and intellectualism of the Frankfurt School undermined the whole dialectical enterprise. Severed from ties to any mass movement, the theoreticians of this school declined into a Gnostic grouping of intellectuals celebrated for their recondite writings and basic failure of nerve. But this very exotic quality, paradoxically, once appealed to the infantilism of the now best forgotten New Left in America.

Even Habermas, the leading current representative of Frankfurt School critical theory, cannot relate his abstract ideals of pragmatic universal communicative competency (an action theory) to concretely mediated forms of societal interaction. There is no historical materialism in his exposition at this juncture of his development, and for that reason he communicates only to an initiate in a scholastic manner. We thereby must come to understand how it is that social thought is severed from political engagement at the very junction where the thought enjoins action. The theory consequently mutates into an arid scholasticism. Lacking political commitment, a result of mistaken premises in his theoretical structure, Habermas has estranged fellow communicants who are broadly sympathetic to his intellectual apparatus. But we must explore how his concept of truth lodged in *Logos* is nonetheless redeemable to the extent that we can project how a free society would need to operate in a given historical situation to obtain a procedural consensus. On this consensus a new world free of the pathologies of ideology, false consciousness, and charismatic leaders might subsequently be built through mass political action. The key to interpreting the mysterious ciphers of ideology lies in the concept of critique in its contemporary theoretical setting. Social science theories will be shown to be second degree constructions of primary socio-political realities (the parts substituting for the whole) where ideas follow social formations of conflicting interests (complexes of interrelated values, exuding a pseudo-concreteness) ultimately tied into power elites and their challengers. So, truthfulness is largely an ideal to be approximated by clearing communication channels. These channels will have to be constituted outside the corrupting power struggles if lived reality is to undergo therapeutic de-alienation. Their first step toward this general elucidation of truth consists in establishing the meta-critical bylaws for methodological consistency to be expounded within definite problematics.

One problematic will be to set standards for this realm of freedom where necessity will only be the limits of the human mind and not the debased human passions and ambitions striving for political domination over the Other. So we will very cautiously begin to propose elements of a philosophical anthropology. In its most degenerate form, debased necessity takes on the face of compulsion-ridden rituals bereft of the celebration and festival peculiar to humanity that make human life worth living and unique among the species. Ontogenetically, the obsession with the Medusan stare of the Other obviates the profundity of human sociability.

To the extent that, through discourse, we can identify and grow with this Other, it will interpenetrate empathetically with our own self-conception. The duality will be dissolved into a One-ness which presupposes that the need to find expression through aggression and hostility will have been overcome. Given these spelled-out presuppositions, the social organization of this ideal can only be actualized by politics. So we must further investigate what possibilities loom in the human condition to even give us a basis for hope. For we learned that fear, even the fear of a nuclear apocalypse, is not sufficient for praxis to be initiated. In this manner, we must at least begin to sketch a social democratic libertarian utopian vision to be posited after the forces of production have been set free from interest groups and ideologies which currently struggle for domination. In the meantime, social antagonisms multiply in the technical and social division of labor in American society. The egoism inherent in the present social organization of the means of production (the corporate ownership and private appropriation of wealth in our two-class society) is no longer compatible with the universalism of the forces of production (science, properly understood). American democracy is now in form only; the substance is plutocratic. In the body of the text, by pointing to the loci of contradictions in social science theory and its alienated social reality, we strive to initiate a dialogue which furthers the possibility of therapeutically engaging these processes of social formation that deny human potential for praxis and poiesis.

Indeed, the process of outlining the dialectic implicates immanently the contradictions of our lifeworld whose evaluation simultaneously defines the problematics to be tackled by social science theorists. We attempt to begin to sketch a critical hermeneutics which extends beyond Marx and his purview to bring to the surface and explore most concretely the existential questions not just of capitalism and socialism but of the broader category of modern urban civilization. By binding our existential roots to tradition and demystifying our lived history, we try sensibly and prudently to prefigure horizons in the realm of desired freedom. In this sense, there is an attempt to step beyond the arts to posit a substantive transcendence of alienation. This elitism was another factor driving the Frankfurt School to sectarianism and hence removing it from a mass following.

So we see that Marxism is conceptually dated by the still illusory presence of Marx as embalmed in the Marxist literature and long since deceased Communist Party canons of the erstwhile Soviet Union. We must exorcize Marx by transcending critical theory in order to redeem the progressive thrust of the humanist side of Marxist movements based on legitimate aspirations for equality. In addition, the text posits the critical hermeneutic orientation (as yet, only a partial transcendence) to reveal what reasonable political prospects can be expected from the variety of situations confronting humans and how they articulate their discontents to arrive at a normative appraisal of life contexts and any radically desired social changes to be redeemed in actualizing freedom.

Acknowledgements

I would like to acknowledge my overwhelming debt to Dr. Mihailo Marković, President of the Serbian Academy of Arts and Sciences, for teaching me the intricacies of Hegel studies and its relation to historical materialism. His level of scholarship is unsurpassed. I thank him for befriending me.
   This work originated from a doctoral thesis. At that time, 1978, Dr. Mark Blitz of the Political Science Department of the University of Pennsylvania supervised the work with ingenuity, intellect, and integrity. I bear witness to his inordinately high standards of humanity and fair play.
   Dr. Alison Anderson typed, edited, and criticized with great astuteness, graciousness, intelligence, and perseverance. We have a range of political philosophical differences which I hope to work out with her over the coming years as further works are produced in a cooperative effort. I feel privileged to know this charismatic feminist human being.
   I fully appreciate Dr. Stephen C. Zelnick of the Intellectual Heritage Program at Temple University, who gave me employment in a time of 'political correctness' and scarcity of jobs. His program truly allows for diversity of opinions in a community of friends. He has the most original mind in higher education today because he can combine theory and practice with an uncanny organizational genius to reconcile what would otherwise be unmanageable interest groups stuck in the muck of parochial power struggles. Temple University is Dr. Zelnick. Too, I thank my undergraduate students for having received my ideas so resoundingly well as I register top ratings for teaching. Students clamor to be on Schindler's List.
   I, LOVING, am deeply indebted to my PARENTS for their very gracious sacrifices afforded to me over the decades. Their insights into National Socialist Germany, as Jewish refugees to the United States from München,

inspired my first curiosity as why people hate and why people care. As Freud said, Eros and Thanatos are locked in mortal combat in an eternally recurring pattern. With my parents as a model, I have learned to accept, in consequence, life's limits and fundamental unfairness. Yet there is hope that springs from a faith that there is, remotely conceivable, an ultimate purpose to the universe.

Introduction

It has been almost two decades since I wrote the original version of *The Frankfurt School Critique of Capitalist Culture*. The main assertions remain truer than ever. Namely, an auto-critique of the critical terms of the Frankfurt School leads by its exercise to the vitiation of the possible application of its concepts with respect to practical concerns and their solutions in the polity. Too, how objective can a critique be when it is reserved for review solely by its proponents who have a vested interest in their own propagation? In short, the 'critique industry' protests through the protective screen of its own closed membership in the universal academy. Abstract theory absorbs praxis. In its first political test, the first generation of theorists were unable to deal concretely with the urgent crisis of survival of the Jewish culture supportive of these theorists against Nazi Germany and its ruling mafia.[1]

In its second test, the next generation was not equal to the totalitarian challenge of the ascendancy, decline, and collapse of the Soviet Union. In his time Leon Trotsky had been more accurate in his Cassandra-like forecasts of the ultimate outcome, mainly because he himself had been part of the forging of a totalitarian society. The Russian Revolution sacrificed the 'best and the brightest' and then imploded, catching off guard virtually every Western Sovietologist, who diagnosed the communist polity as developmentally stable and politically legitimate, with a status of moral equality with Western representative democracies in the struggle for the minds of the Third World.

While the Frankfurt School's critique of the hegemonic capitalist social science ideologies has been devastating since its 'linguistic turn', its major scholars have nothing programmatic to offer for engagement in the vacuum of academic philosophy. Hence its social democratic allegiances have no concrete recommendations to educate the reified consciousness of the mass electorate in our global village. The liberated consciousness of a vanguard intellectual elite stands ineffective against the Lenin-style politicos in the second and third worlds with their organized state violence to discipline their respective societies. This state of self-reflective contemplation is the logical outcome of original Frankfurt School principles, but in its very adherence to the unforced force of the best argument in an open competition of ideas, speech acts mediate merely abstract values, mirroring an already subjugated polity. The already saved need no further persuasion, and those in need do not matriculate at institutions of higher learning. Or, if they do, their character structures generally prove unamenable to purely disinterested dialogue and personal criticism. People have private agendas geared to attaining or using power and do not surrender its achievement for ideal, uncorrupted ends. Too, there is an attachment to power because it is enabling and therefore axiomatically has survival interest for the individual. Truthfulness and the 'will to will' within the black hole of power can be at odds. In fact, lying and political duplicity are normative if one is to prevail by the forced force of the most obscurantist argument. Truthful and untruthful statements are simply variations of positive and negative inflections put on information. Which side shows its face depends on the context of a debate and what is at stake. I never met a man (or woman, in the age of affirmative action) who did not lie through his teeth if there were enough gain to be achieved. Lying is a phylogenetic survival trait and might have benefits for the public good at times. As for truthfulness and the Big Lie, one is a universal and abstract realization of sincere speech acts, the other often the negation of truthful dialogue through organized state violence in the name of particular and concrete interests that defy public delineation. The great aporias of the human condition are to reconcile these opposites. Our social science concepts are not yet adequate to the task. We must have a revolution in language in its institutional embodiment to overcome these limits.

The Frankfurt School exhibits a utopian model for a small community of the elect in a distant and indeterminate future. By necessity, this community of scholars would be the antithesis of the political because there is no connection to a territorial domain, *Realpolitik*, or a mass movement with an agenda. We have the *theoria* of despair. The Hegelian dialectic is the reverse of Kant. The political steps to mediate any type of transition to social democracy could be progressive but are not practical at this state of Frankfurt School history. Whether Critical Theory can reproduce another more activist and personally involved, hands-on generation in the next century to address concretely a political praxis is highly problematic. Its main contribution has been to critique superstructural aspects of society and the state, namely, 'higher' culture, or, really, the absence thereof in both East and West. The conformism, bureaucratism, and routinization of life have led the academy to betray its role as a voice of dissent and renege in its obligation to create new social forms of resistance to the daily insults practiced on our society by the 'powers that be'. These powers need to reduce individuals to the status of mere cogs in the machinery of production to induce an artificially conditioned mass consumption. The academy has become the superstructural, normative apologist for those powers, while simultaneously being coopted.

In 1978 when I concluded my initial work, I had foreseen that the circumscribed utility of Critical Theory would be to the limited sphere of highly specialized and elitist universities with minimal critico-practical impact on the everyday world. I was much too optimistic, if not outright naive, about the anticipated progressive role to be played by universities and a radicalized student body as the imputed agents for historical change in the United States. Independent scholars, who lead an anomic existence, do not by their pariah status have support groups to advance their minimal interests. 'Political correctness' has resurrected the Jewish Question in a post-Auschwitz celebration of Jew baiting. Jews, once again, are subjected to quotas in the name of an abstract justice in affirmative action/reverse discrimination programs without ethical grounding. A generation of intellectuals have had their rightful place in the tenured ranks denied due process in the name of an illusory racial, sexual orientation, and gender equality. Affirmative action and the goal of equality are antitheses as practiced at the major Ivy League institutions. There is a strong suspicion that affirmative action has resulted in reverse discrimination which has not had the effect of bringing about equality but rather the injury of other groups of individuals who have comparable or superior qualifications. The real issue of quotas has not been answered forthrightly. That is not equality or fairness. Even equality will not be a panacea for society's ills if it is not connected to a work ethic. Those extremists on the right and left who demand 'equality' (really affirmation of their groups' parochial political goals) undermine democracy because the government does not have the capability, let alone the constitutional obligation, to process all demands discriminately.

The extreme left levels society, encouraging a narcissistic flood of demands for entitlements beyond our productive capacity to meet. You cannot make something from nothing. There are no documented miracles. The extreme right with its white supremacist agenda wants government 'off its back' to effect an annihilation of all legitimate sources of authority. The false freedom for which the right struggles negates civilization. The apocalyptic events of April 19, 1995 in Oklahoma City are but symptomatic of an infantile aggression (a primal rage) emerging from within our collective political unconsciousness - indeed, very psychotic and beyond conventional political remedy as understood by ordinary citizens. Such egalitarian policies create rancorous divisions and new sets of historical wrongs which have to be righted in the future. Politically correct policies are based on group, tribal warfare. We must restore unique individuals to the center of focus and examine their empirical qualifications to do the work independently of capricious and leveling political criteria. If we do not have the courage to do that, then we will only mirror the injustices endemic to our society. There is even the possibility of taking these injustices to a higher level because of the dialectical skills of intellectuals to take any point of view and give it a theoretical justification in this age of new historicism where anything goes and has its attendant theoretical, ideological rationalization. We can even apply Habermas's concept of the ideal speech community to assess counterfactually how to adjudicate the antithesis between equality and affirmative action. Habermas says that in order to have general validity speech acts must be rendered by communicatively competent speakers. Thus we have the choice between the ideologically charged particularistic interest group ideologues in academia and the universal class of the dispossessed intellectuals in the Diaspora. Who is more representative of truthfulness, imagination, selflessness, and rationality in presenting their respective world views to a common humanity, loving freedom and equality without the political compromises, bureaucratic constraints, and ideological baggage?

For example, the University of Pennsylvania, my alma mater, has been in perpetual crisis for two years over issues of free speech. The First Amendment has been sacrificed to political expediency. Whoever dissents from the administration's guidelines risks punishment and ostracism. Lives are disrupted and careers derailed if you become publicly identified as the Other. The quintessential outsiders of the past have become the establishment but without a transcendence to achieve a general emancipation for all. Rather, historically conditioned injustices are multiplied. The master-slave relationship continues because political careers in their nexus with vested economic interests are in collusion to legitimize the status quo with the incorporation of new ideological ingredients. Political expediency displaces academic freedom, truthfulness, and a meritocratic society based on achievement and performance. Democracy itself has been put on trial at such elite institutions. Corporate individuals, not the common folk, exercise the sovereignty, for they monopolize society's scarce resources and staff the personnel of the state with its monopoly of the means of violence.

Of course, these aforementioned activist interest groups have quite legitimate single issue complaints with general implications for the larger society and polity. Still historically applicable to this day, Marx said that only the Jews, and by extension the global class of the dispossessed intellectuals, as the vanguard of the proletariat not conscious of itself or its historical responsibilities, because of their chosen and exceptional status as the generalized Other, in their historically totalized suffering for all humankind, embody a universal class because they enjoy a privileged epistemic position encompassing all other oppressed minorities and their generalized representation. In post-modern society the Jews cum intellectuals have made their case universally through the universities. The shaming and ostracizing of these now nameless individuals have shattered lives because their high calling has been forever put beyond their reach and what has resulted is the involuntary migration into the purgatory of the business world to live out lives of quiet desperation wherein their use values of excellence to teach and do research have been debased into the exchange value of the mere objective of making a living. There is the odor of the Nuremberg Racial Laws in these machinations to create a false consciousness by the hydra-headed hegemonic class that historical wrongs have been rectified by multiplying the number of new victims. What results is a lose/lose strategy for society. A win/win strategy is to open the universities to all by federalizing them and making students, teachers, and administrators employees of a *Rechtsstaat*. That policy would make the system's need for scapegoating Jews redundant. We have sacrificed a generation of the Jewish intelligentsia violently and needlessly. Asian American students and scholars are now too being punished for being too successful by the traditional, time-honored standards of merit performance and the employment of the venerable work ethic. We must listen to their cries of racism.

By 1995 Critical Theory has broken down into a quasi-religious righteousness which, when interacting with political correctness, has deeply divided not only the left but the campuses themselves. What was erstwhile radical has become often reactionary, trite, and mundane. Theory has devolved into what it once witheringly critiqued. There is a normatively driven, legitimate need for an independent left in post-industrial society to organize strata of the oppressed masses. But in what form? Obviously, the political dimensions of such a need have not become manifest. The sectarian left has spent its intellectual capital in bombastic rhetoric. The right is too parochial and mean-spirited in its world view to assume a responsible global leadership role. A resurgence of tribal nationalisms and Islamic fundamentalism disturbs the coherence needed in an interdependent polity of nations. Neither configuration of ideologies on the left or the right can rise to meet the needs of universal disarmament; peaceful coexistence; a just husbanding and redistribution of finite global goods, assets, information networks, and social services; the reconciliation of political freedom and social equality; conservation of the environment; the transcendence of caste, gender, and class prejudices; and, ultimately, an institutionalized consensus on the due processes of an open-ended, evolving, normative political discourse at a supra-national level. While technical reason has flourished, moral sensibility has not been able to tame its consequences when unscrupulous nation-state despots misuse knowledge in contradiction to the general interests and needs of our species-being. We can have hope when leaders and natural elites of talent are informed instinctually to a selflessness in the service of a commonly crafted good fully cognizant of an exercisable option toward the transcendence of now prevailing dysfunctional political units. The education of these 'aristocratic' individuals oriented toward excellence should be a fundamentally public school matter with only secondary recruitment from the elite private schools.

The reverse is true, hence undoing this potential for liberation from our reified second natures. Of course, scarce resources are differentially allocated by the wealthy; hence public policies favor private school education. Why? It is not only to preserve existing privileges but to assure the proper selection of the 'fittest' to be the next generation of rulers. That is why affirmative action ultimately fails. It makes cosmetic changes out of pity and self-interest, while maintaining the same power elite and its capitalist ethos of production as an end in itself and devoid of humanity or any sense of community ethics. Affirmative action coopts the elite members from marginal groups in order to defuse revolutionary energies within the masses. Affirmative action in this sense has a genocidal thrust. Cooption is displacing natural black leaders into a subservient status in either academia or commercial society. To play this white man's 'game' is to betray one's own people and the memory of their four hundred continuous years of suffering.

Malcolm X in his *Autobiography* saw right through the hypocrisy white and black intellectuals play. Change, he said, had to be a combination of economic and political conditions at a fundamental, revolutionary level in which attitudes are re-educated within the communities. You cannot have equality where there is not equality of economic circumstances and life opportunities. Unfortunately, he confused his thinking with the gobbledygook of Elijah Muhammad for twelve years. This faker with his fraudulent religious tenets of how whites were grafted from a prehistoric African race through genetic engineering deceived Malcolm X into a white- and Jew-baiting political stance counterproductive to the collective well-being of the black people. Only in the last year of his life did he realize his errors in thinking. His ideological turnabout led to his assassination. In a sense, his unfortunate phrase about Kennedy's death (that the 'chickens came home to roost') applied even more to him. Nonetheless the soul force of Malcolm X, in conjunction with Martin Luther King's efforts, reshaped race relations permanently for the better. At least, black men thought of themselves thenceforth as men because they understood they were just as much human beings as Caucasians.

In the Malthusian underworld of the inner cities, population growth outstrips the resources of the ghetto to provide the needed jobs. It is only black entrepreneurial leaders who can create jobs with their imagination, capital, and economic connections. Affirmative action by design severs these vital ties. The masses then revert to a state of war in a self-fulfilling prophecy in which stereotypes and realities converge to deny a people's humanity. Affirmative action fosters, unintentionally, a culture of dependency on fickle white policy makers who pander to 'ignorant' white voters, for the intelligent ones have not been going to the polls in the last generation. The few elect of a black elite are 'showcased' and the remainder are damned. There is a double bind at work here. For when you make it, you do not, since the 'average' white person assumes that it is a consequence of political brokering, disregarding blacks' natural abilities. The more things change, the more they remain the same. Only the political semiotics changes to fit new circumstances.

Black people, particularly the bourgeoisie, have the illusion that the totemic sacrifice of their ethnic identity and their extended family networks (emanating ultimately from the ghettos and the rural South) to the white power structure in exchange for the cold cash nexus of a 'democratic' marketplace has made all equal. But the equality is only in the fact of their wage slavery, and there is still a significant wage differential between the races for equal work. A vicious master-slave dialectic works to subvert both equality and freedom in our society. The penultimate problem concerns harnessing the primacy of political power to responsibility and limits.

While such concerns are reviewed in the forum of universities, the school of life has another, more compelling rationale. In an idealistic thought experiment, a first step may be taken on the initiative of privileged universities. Redeemable letters of credit can be provided on demand to serve the members of the often impoverished neighborhoods in which they reside and too often act as predatory landlords, abusing their legal weapon of eminent domain. By teaching the untutored, giving job training, gentrifying the local neighborhoods instead of colonizing them, and sharing their wealth of information and financial assets, corporate universities could assimilate these alien and hostile milieus into feasible political cooperative units. Then we can have real world micro-models for systems building. The dialectical multiplication and application of such a local empowerment movement could revolutionize the consciousness of the species in preparation for implementing a workable global paradigm politically consonant with popular grassroots sovereignty in a stable world order.

This thought experiment has no historical example except as a remote possibility. But speech acts can beget political embodiment. For example, from the violent rhetoric of the committees of public safety during the French Revolution issued a constitutional republic. Its armies carried the ideas of liberty, equality, and fraternity across a monarchically institutionalized Europe and changed its character, though igniting modern nationalism, imperialism, and racism in the train of an emergent *Realpolitik* which no longer recognized moral limits to wars. Wars became total, with civilians now at the forefront of each struggle. The politics of necessity has become universally totalitarian. We are beyond good and evil. In the epoch of Thanatos in late capitalist society we forget history's lessons and repress our inability to accept individual and social responsibility toward others, whom we demonize in America's paranoid style of politics by denying our 'dark' side and then projecting our worst attributes onto helpless and hopeless scapegoats. In this fixated historical development, only the dead can bury the dead. The living are *Musselmenschen*.

Georg Lukács and Martin Heidegger defined mid-twentieth-century politics in central Europe in terms of an ideological critique. Historicity opposed Being. Soviet troops and historicity prevailed in a totalitarian totality. So Lukács ideologically prepared the post hoc intellectual justification for Stalin becoming the factual embodiment of Hegel's Absolute. This happened not in an ideal world but in the empirical lives of everyday people who had no interest in experiencing, like Pavlov's dogs, this transcendental politics of immanence. Stalin created a false totality and the concomitant super-structural consciousness. By violence, he forged the material base to vindicate Leninist-Stalinist ideology. Thus we see the distilled essence of the primacy of the political in everyday life.

Of course these policies of state inverted Marx's reasoning, while apotheosizing his ultimate value of socialism and communism, however much cut off from his empirical analysis of capitalism's true historical possibilities which had held Russia in the lowest regard. As Maurice Merleau-Ponty pontificated, humanism and terror gave civilization its highest avatar of praxis in this dictator. Historicity and Being are the two major concepts hypostatizing the subject and object of totalitarian movements. Totality is identarian violence in which gangster dictators literally annihilate their peoples. The polity traumatizes the masses to be phobic of public space. All power, then, stands in antithesis to the lowest common denominator of the alienated citizen. Heidegger protests, but in the name of *Dasein*. If it fails, then we can appeal to God.

Lukács justified the progress inherent in the dictatorship of the proletariat even if its constituent members have no idea how they are to be its proactive participants. Totalitarian leaders produce ineffable fetish commodities in the doublespeak of a fragmented language in portraying political life through arcane legal and linguistic codes, which are reserved for the ruling elite's interpretations, and whose constitutive elements are made relative to situationally dictated needs to maintain and expand power. Public space and justice are obscured, then denied to their subjugated citizens. Intellectuals voluntarily honored tyrants in the Soviet Union and Germany in order to achieve power, material rewards, and status, thus giving their idle words efficacy on the world historical stage. In every intellectual lurks a hangman.

Two of the most notorious bootlicks are the celebrated German professors Carl Schmitt and Martin Heidegger. This phenomenon might be called the perpetual return of the repression of consciousness in the service of the nationalistic Id. 'World historical hypotheses' degenerated into apology and the enthusiastic endorsement of criminal public policies. *Schadenfreude* saturated their motivations, that is, a Manichean delight in the plight and intense suffering of human beings, in part due to their own bad will and personal participation. Yet in many circles renowned scholars separate the personal anti-Semitic biases of Schmitt and Heidegger in their respective worship of the State and *Das Volk* from their public political philosophies. It cannot be done, for writings issued by a bad will are intrinsically debased since they promote a vision of a distorted reality emanating from a perverted and evil interior dialogue which is arbitrary and hence anti-scientific, contra-empirical, and, in the end, anti-democratic.

The spoken word in private underpins the written text and in Jewish mysticism, for instance, supersedes it as primal, authoritative, and originary. So who a person is will invariably be embodied in the texts that issue forth from the persona to the printed page. The printed page becomes at times the template of public policy. For example, if celebrated writers cannot uphold values of democracy and truthfulness, we would live in a world where anything goes, including Auschwitz and the Gulags. The postulate of liberation is most certainly forsaken in the totalitarian devaluation of counter-factual, plural possibilities. We arrive at the real moment in time when the actuality of regimes of terror, with their reductionist and nihilistic decisionism, results in their sheer horrorful, imposed facticity. Political existence consumes whole essence. These existentially exhausted men and women of our post-modern society prepare us for the millennium of the advent of the Antichrist. Might we be approaching ground-zero possibilities in terms of entertaining any principle of hope for a better day? We wonder whether the praxis of the Big Lie precludes emancipation and today is forever. Perhaps the hopes of transcendence have collapsed into the immanence of the sheer administered inertia of our all-encompassing institutions. Even our thoughts, dreams, and wishes are dictated and screened by the consciousness industry.

Jürgen Habermas with his theory of communicative action oriented to a common strategic understanding tries to transcend this perversion of language and consequent usurpation of state power by ideologues and fools. He succeeds only partly. Being a prescient man, he has come to realize that humanity is always reinventing itself. By necessity, this cannot be done by totalizing political agendas but rather by pragmatic engagement in concrete tasks of limited scope. Hence there is no climax to history. Its realization is in the enlightened process of opening up the public space to new avenues for human development. This applied practical reason is an outcome of the eighteenth-century Enlightenment.

In a sense, Habermas exemplifies the best of post-modernist German philosophy by wedding empirical techniques to the rational explication of concrete tasks. Nonetheless, his highly technical linguistic theory cannot be grasped by the everyday concrete agents of history in its unfolding in situ. He assumes a degree of actual enlightenment not to be found in the masses. His utopia deposes reality. If anything, the level of democratic cultural consciousness and its discourse has been falling away from praxis in this last decade of this most violent century in the development of the species. Critical reason and science exist in an adversarial relationship. Habermas has taken Critical Theory to a quasi-transcendental level from philosophy of history to a materially and linguistically mediated philosophy of consciousness. The quasi-transcendental does not bring heaven to earth but nurtures insightful normative discourse in the forms of social life in order to bring to birth discursive will formation and liberate humankind from reified public institutions. The immanence of the latter process lies in speech acts. Speech acts are institutionalized and reified in the text where the historical process ends if there are not consequent social enactments. Theory by itself reifies, absolutely, in its mass production of itself. Habermas attempts in this way to transcend 'class struggle' with the emergence of a species-being capable of seeing for-itself the in-itself of subjectivity reconciled to an objectified reality in nature and the Other.

This species-being of subjectivity operates through the mechanism of a theory of communicative action. Habermas projects himself as a godhead who is the embodiment of the species-being to come, with Habermas 'the Man' as will and representation of the millennium. He and his circle of recruited imitators make questionable methodological assumptions about the inherent rationality of human nature which contradict a significant part of social science research. Their claim to being the historical signifier of a hypostatized rationality actually takes us into the realm of the supernatural rather than the quasi-transcendental, for one can never stand outside one's own interests and claim at the same time to be neutrally propagating universal values for humankind. One can learn from the past and reconstruct it, but not make counter-factual deductions from an idealized future state of an emancipated humanity. The data are by and large non-existent and rather in the realm of wishful thinking.

History is littered with the delusional good intentions of prophets who would be gods. A critical reading of history will make one think twice before making public statements about either philosophy or programs for social democracy. The pursuit of personal self-interest has merits insofar as its will is exercised with moderation. This theory of communicative action with a pragmatic intent fails to explicate fully how communication among strategically interdependent actors evolves into a liberating praxis in the interstices of mundane, empirical life. In particular, how does one re-appropriate a reified world if consciousness is false? If the maintainers of the madhouse are insane, what next? And where is the revolutionary and politically committed mass movement to direct the dynamics of history to nobler intermediate ends without creating a tyranny in which everyone feels entitled to a mere pecuniary restitution? Even cold-blooded mass murderers now claim discrimination in a society devoid of moral sensibility, feelings of shame, and the need to cleanse the self by atonement through good works.

Critical theory's explication sounds more like a collective ontological-theological psychoanalysis for well-meaning, progressive university professors, who themselves are privileged and basically rendered unaccountable by the institutional atavism of tenure. Professional academics act as if the circles in which they themselves labor do not have provincially particularistic and specialized interests antipodal to the common good. Another question, then, is how we generate a new ethical set of values to change material circumstances and their outmoded interests along more equitable and progressive lines.

There is definitely a conflict of interests at work in which by faith alone the man or woman in the street would be led to believe that these self-proclaimed agents of liberation in the universities are acting on our behalf. Ideologically, we can call this immature belief the American dream, or one component part of it. They would have more moral credibility if in a good faith show of solidarity they offered to share their power, money, perquisites, time, and status to serve both their students and the army of systemically produced, unemployed intellectuals, who they irresponsibly educated and degreed and who are now running footloose in the streets. Have these educators heard of the laws of supply and demand? What is the ethical basis for producing doctorates, the epitome of academic achievement, if the net result is redundancy on a truly world historical scale? The ultimate test of their sincerity would be the revolutionary act of renouncing tenure, the archaic totem of an outmoded institution. There comes a time to step down from a throne, pass power to one's disciples, and bring new blood and ideas to academia.

The Big Business curriculum has coopted talent with promises of material rewards which are redeemable, hence real and tangible. So we have to investigate the sado-masochistic relationship of teacher to student. These ritualistic sacrifices defy common sense and certainly call for a clinical study of this repetition compulsion, which mimics paternal homicide in an Oedipal-like, tragicomic drama.

The past twenty years have seen no progress in theory formation or revolutionary paradigms to reinvigorate the moribund social sciences. The Western canon is now subject to an unprecedented politically motivated attack in order to open up the readings to those with multicultural credentials. What results is a double standard in looking at excellence. The intention is probably well meaning. But it opens a Pandora's box whereby through political bargaining trafficking begins in recruiting authors and books which have no legitimate reason to be on the reading list of an Ivy League institution. The result is an atavistic spoils or patronage system where outside pressure groups can subvert the authority of tradition.

In short, there can be radical change while traditional texts are still honored and modernized to talk to our generation. After all, the major criterion for being part of the Western canon is timelessness. This updating of the canon by progressive inclusion would make texts more sensitive to issues of class, race, gender, and sexual orientation. The new and the old can fuse their horizons in the manner of Gadamer.

However, you do not do so by destroying your historical memory and thinking. You cannot start the updating of academic excellence ex nihilo. Realistically, academia is precisely where human beings are wolves to their fellow human beings, for there are no consequences of being irresponsible. In fact, we have a modern day Diaspora. The humanity and sincerity of a moral educational elite can be judged directly by their willingness to help the least advantaged constituents of both society and academia and their own progeny, those who have been 'romantically' called 'gypsy scholars.' The gypsy scholar is to academia what the field slave once was to the plantation: a marginal if not ultimately expendable commodity. But it is in the nature of power to be indefeasible. If power were held in common, we would have effected a radical transformation of both the universities and the society which supports them. Hence we are dealing with a purely counter-factual condition which is merely academic, yet instructive enough to show the hypocrisy to which people can adapt. In fact, there is a schizophrenia in the universities in terms of how they function and how they prove themselves false within the rationale of their own structures. The administration is stocked by personnel who have to meet objective criteria of performance, while tenured faculty members enjoy an unrestrained ascribed role more akin to the guilds of the Middle Ages than to the rationalized nature of a modern capitalist corporation. In that sense, there is a profound alienation in effect in the Academy with respect to systemically serving Big Business. Hence its putative set of values claims to adhere normatively to a universal and democratic, populist ethos, while in reality serving its master in parochial departmental or private, administrative interests. Such is the stuff of the legends which make for the 'false consciousness' Marx identified so well in the nineteenth century as the mark of Cain of the epoch of capitalism. Lukács developed this theme in the twentieth century further in his *History and Class Consciousness*.

We have an analogue here for the deracinated Jewish and Gentile intelligentsia if we compare their status to the plight of the helpless Jews before the Second World War. Then, we must ask, who are the agents who speak on behalf of these disowned intellectuals in a sincere way? The abuses of persons in academia rival the Big Business practices of the Fortune 500. But the insult runs deeper because the professorial role, as built into the very teleology of the university, purports to transmit the standards of the good, the true, and the just. Without the onus of political pressure, Friedrich Nietzsche forsook his tenured post at the University of Basel in order to overcome his own personal limitations experienced in the technical division of labor in academia and arrive at the ethos of a Dionysian, biologically driven freedom of the unleashed human animal will to power. He was the last heroic intellectual of note to do so. We have a historical example of a 'superman' who defied a society's conventions in Oskar Schindler, with his rescue program of Jews during the Second World War. All Righteous Gentiles fall into this category of the superman or -woman who worked against war crimes and crimes against humanity. But in going against a system at great personal risk, the transgressor of the order of things loses his or her innocence. The ultimate hero is the martyred murdered individual, who by the very innocence of his or her sacrifice achieves a posthumous atonement or transcendence in the act of dying with 'clean hands', unpolluted and virtuous.

There is a dubious assumption of an infinite moral improvement of society through time-in-itself. This narcolepsy-inducing prejudice is deeply rooted in the Enlightenment and its problematic legacy. Universities have been undermined by the cash nexus in which social relations between individuals have devolved into the 'natural attitude' of the relationship between things. Knowledge is transformed into personal power. De-differentiation of the higher purposes of the academy into a mere assimilation process to corporate American commercial practices and opinions suborns students from the day of matriculation to that of the literal signing of their death certificates. It is the corruption of malleable youth that is unconscionable. Knowledge decomposes into fetish commodities with only monetary value and strictly instrumental application for the pursuit of profits. The human dimension has been 'suspended' in this Darwinian 'survival of the fittest' at our finest institutions so as to guarantee the perpetuation of capitalism's access to the brightest students, cooption of university faculties, the use of behavioral technologies for social control (*Gleichschaltung*), and the wholesale appropriation of scientific discoveries by industry for strictly private and venal profit motives. The radical evil is the corruption of the young. In Dante's nine concentric circles of Hell, the lowest rung is reserved for those who betrayed a trust. While only allegorical, it is morally instructive enough to suggest the need for a foundational change in the power relationships of our academies of higher learning.

In fact, Canadian universities are now seriously discussing a basic reevaluation of tenure's legal status. The state should intervene to make faculties part of an accountable civil service with compulsory retirement with full pay and benefits after twenty years, that is, a generation. The United States military serves as a workable model. This regulation by receivership would be compatible with universally recognized standards of fairness and update the academy's world view to the achievement criteria of a modern society.

Let us suspend judgment momentarily on these blatant contradictions for the sake of furthering Habermas's argument. He has a methodological problem with respect to levels of analysis. He underestimates how power-hungry the people are who are strategic actors comporting themselves in a predictable manner in late capitalist society. Max Weber and his 'iron cages' comes to mind. Weber's limitation is that he believes humankind has reached a point where reified subjectivity determines individual actions to the detriment of freedom. Habermas the post-modernist theorist also undervalues how powerless people are in a highly articulated and routinized social division of labor. Namely, he is not fully aware of how his own class privileges influence his bias toward 'reducing' humanity to a fundamental goodness and rationality which is highly problematic. Readings of the Marquis de Sade, Machiavelli, Sorel, Lenin, and Hobbes, among others, might have leavened his political philosophy toward a more balanced perspective. Know thy enemy! In a historical irony, Marx's 'the administration of the masses' emerges not in a classless society of communism but in late capitalist society with a professional class of managers in the economy and the entrenched civil servants and political consultants, who are fundamentally above traditional popular and party loyalties in the polity.

As for who's who in society, there is a socioeconomic elite, trained in the best business schools in the United States, who exercise an ideological and cultural hegemony over its validating symbols, who own the means of production in the form of the key centers of industry and communications, and who dominate the forces of production with respect to the appropriation of the yield of science and the attendant cooption of its gatekeepers, such as department heads and senior professors of the major universities, directors of research institutes, heads of foundations locked into industrial enterprises and their board memberships, and the professional civil service. Administrators are phasing out 'uneconomic' programs and projects in the humanities and the social sciences. The cost-benefit analysis spreadsheets of the Wharton School of the University of Pennsylvania have become a universal normative standard.

How could a school of Critical Theory expound a public interest without an independent material base? Hence the balance between the forces of reification and freedom has become unhinged to the disadvantage of the latter, injuring democratic ideals and their material realization. In that sense, Habermas is correct to say there is a 'crisis of legitimacy' in which the state is asked to reallocate the perceived scarce goods and services of society to the denied majority. The state does not have the means to accomplish these 'egalitarian' ends; it can barely maintain itself. Too, equality should not just be equated with opportunity to move up the social ladder. It is about economic power in which the question is, who owns the means of production and to the exclusion of whom? The means of production, of course, now includes the apparatus of the information revolution.

In the United States, the system's failure to perform to the level of society's general expectations, particularly for the middle class, augurs a decline in the willingness of citizens to commit themselves for the long term to an American ideology, which in itself falsely reflects, while nonetheless affirming, the material conditions which generate its inverted formulation of socio-political reality. The dangers lie then in a frustrated people confronting a plethora of problems with no imminent solution and indulging themselves in a mindless, addictive consumerism; organized criminal gangs; African American baiting of the Jews[2]; the uprooting of the middle class from their achieved social status by punitive and regressive tax policies; the relentless waging of class and caste warfare from above, particularly in the U.S. Senate; the corruption of civilized discourse in the public space, accompanied by the denigration of the written word for the catharsis of emotive verbal and physical violence; alienating their better selves to charismatic cult leaders. Most general is simple secession by individuals, who spurn the electoral process, which has been unable to produce a reconciling higher order political unity beyond the vulgar coalitions of calculating single-issue interest groups. They turn to the new and ugly phenomenon of 'attack politics' with its appeals to mob actions to intimidate legitimately constituted authority.

These latter manifestations of political alienation create a power vacuum in which a collective 'bad will' could climax in an authoritarian oligarchy, and which most certainly has already been happening in society's most archaic subsystems, ironically most ruthlessly manifested in the universities. The academy, however, is too inefficient in its modes of operation, and its highly ideological and political style, to model the successful structures and functions of Big Business. In a sense, academia neutralizes otherwise very intelligent people who could be a threat to the system's domination of the reproduction of personnel, legitimacy, and the informational infrastructure necessary for Big Business to adapt effectively to higher levels of complex organization for attaining the goals of a rational capitalism. But the academic community fails at resolving certain basic societal conflicts by its chronic inability to develop coherent policies with a world view that is just and universally accepted in its commonly formulated values. Tenure, affirmative action, racial and gender warfare, escalating tuition rates, politically correct curricula, constraints on free speech, and forced segregated living quarters on campuses have hurt the honest working multi-cultural and multi-racial middle class who do not demand entitlement programs. There is a residual work ethic in the broader center of America. They made their voice heard in the November 1994 elections. The people spoke. They wanted fundamental reforms, not in a racist reaction to affirmative action but in response to reverse discrimination. The traditional, historical route of mobility through higher education has been blocked by the false totality of blocs of minority groups and highly politically motivated college administrators with their parochial interests in maintaining a self-serving, self-recruiting power base. They act in such a way as mimetically to amass power, not to challenge but to invite an alliance with the power elite. Granted, there is an overlap between the two groups, but this power of the academic bureaucracy is illusory since their financial sustenance is almost wholly from outside their own domain. It is difficult to be politically autonomous when economically dependent. Hence the theater of the absurd in academia masks from the public view how power generates itself and dominates the larger society.

Where is Critical Theory at this moment of crisis? The particular has triumphed over the universal in a relentless 'negating' dialectics of despair. Ironically, from a Marxist frame of reference, the bourgeois, constitutional, liberal democracies have won the day because by incremental reforms we are left with a simulacrum of hope for a better day which has never come in communist regimes. We can no longer indulge ourselves by thinking in terms of the millennium. We will be most fortunate if we can save our collective selves on an individual by individual basis from today to tomorrow. Hopefully, the thrust of this aggregate emancipation of individuals will climax in the kind of emergent novel life forms which have also been most cogently thought out by Habermas in a theoretical realism, one without content. He does not bring us guarantees, for history has its own woof and warp unbeknownst to its weavers. This limited point of view, however, vouchsafes our freedom from the intellectual terrorists with their politically charged world views, such as Heidegger and Schmitt, who can only operate in a revolutionary climate, which they and their followers helped to foment and where they could influence public policy. Nonetheless, other 'toxic' ideologues currently have been having an effect in near and remote parts of the world, in regions breaking down into their component nationalistic and even village loyalties, where the masses mechanically follow charismatic leaders and warlords. The 'will to will' has collapsed into itself.

Yet the project of a viable, limited United Nations police force still testifies to the primacy of politics. The creative force of applied violence through the international law of collective security supersedes superannuated ideologies to give us a newly conceived vocabulary of an outraged world opinion. With it comes the potential for consequent healthy world frames of reference and their embodied institutionalized promise of a peace of all loving all. To be effected, love must be willed and, paradoxically, force must be applied multilaterally and collectively against outlaw states and organizations which blatantly commit crimes against humanity. With the United States in the vanguard, a multi-national alliance ousted the Iraqis from Kuwait in 1992 at minimal cost. So blatant aggression by a regional power can be undone with the perpetrators punished, though the issue of retribution for war crimes and crimes against humanity was left outstanding. Wilsonian idealists and neo-liberal conservatives could have an interesting interlocution with social democrats over the arch-values of a future polity at peace with itself.

In 1994 Jordan and Israel signed a peace treaty, auguring a new ethical model of international politics. At the same time, Bosnian Serbs were massacring their Muslim countrymen and Russians were indiscriminately killing their Chechen brethren. These eternally recurring patterns of random actions and inevitable counteractions make the future the past and the past the future with a day on the horizon where, if the iron-clad cycle cannot be broken, the species will either self-liquidate or find an equilibrium in which collective violence is no longer the norm and is institutionally contained by the rationally arrived at consensus of a responsible world order.

In the final analysis, we are left with hope for a better day. There are certainly political instruments at hand to transfigure enlightenment hope into an actually experienced reality. The problem is that there is not a universal consensus on what are the bedrock values to inform those policy makers with these political tools in our post-modern society, in which we are told to be value-free since each person's opinion is equal to the other's. What we obtain, then, is a war of all against all, since an ideology of pseudo-equality leads to multiple inabilities to compromise, postpone immediate gratification, sacrifice for the common good, or cooperate socially. If we are to recognize our higher responsibilities for the survival and overall health of our species and the biosphere, we must have the courage of our newly discovered convictions to surrender part of our egoism for the public weal. Hence the empirical manifestations of the 'quasi-transcendental' lie in the collective subjective sovereignty which would reclaim lost nature and revitalize our ossified second nature through a self-reflective praxis constantly open to new information, inter-subjective dialogue, and novel forms of politically structuring higher level functions of the world system. The quasi-transcendental would integrate the canonical truths of the living past with the emancipators' promise of a future open to negotiated solutions to problems from a position of strength and power. Might wisdom tame excess? Perhaps hope alone breaks the historically sealed solipsism of history's recurring patterns of random acts of nihilism where we cannot transcend the limits of good and evil. Like the inevitability of death may be the inevitability of resigning ourselves to historical determinacy while freeing ourselves individually of the illusions of grand theoretical designs for human behavior. Capitalism's limit is that it is built inherently on personal and selfish interests of a communicatively distorting kind and so must justify self-serving actors with their toxic will to power.

Whether we can evolve beyond capitalism to socialism poses the ethical and practical questions of our day. Most people do not care because they are not educated to be critical. We all know Soviet-style communism was an unmitigated failure. However, it would be as much a fallacy to equate totalitarian communism with democratic socialism as it would be to say that the National Socialism of Germany naturally was the culmination of late capitalism in its imperialist phase. How does one then materialize a future for which there is no successful model? The answer, in part, lies in the community of critical inquirers, where how questions are formulated will determine the dynamic character and the clearly worked through conscious quality of our commonly shared human condition. A citizenry in a world republic would have its open public space to achieve a fluid self-definition, much like the United States during its formative period of nation-building, initially under the Articles of Confederation.³

The hint of ultimate success with these epochally defined macro-problems goes hand in glove with a politics of scale. The larger the scale, the greater the risk. Let us take the leap and make the future past open to the constructions of novel life forms where everyday citizens are the creators. Then, the 'last man' will finally be first and the Enlightenment creed executed critico-practically and its contradictions resolved.

Notes

1. There is a problem with second order constructs of concepts of theory formation insofar as how they can instruct us to take a position of political engagement. For instance, I was profoundly moved to empathy at a liberating instinctive rather than intellectual plane by the movie *Schindler's List*, produced and directed by Steven Spielberg. Gut experience replaced the 'authenticity of jargon' which always sanitizes the ineffably evil. The ambiguous protagonist, Oskar Schindler, a convinced National Socialist before the outset of the war, spent the fortune he corruptly made to save a 'surplus' of 1000 Jews who were working for him as slave labor. By 1942 he was a double agent working with Jewish agencies in Budapest, Hungary, to document the destruction of Eastern European Jewry. No other Nazi underwent such a personal transformation of the soul so successfully. His vices in the end proved to be the vehicle to negotiate with the SS for Jewish lives at a global level. To paraphrase his equally heroic wife Emilie, he was an 'angel from hell.' His Jewish workers saw him as a savior and reserved judgment on his personal life. In the end, Schindler used his venal war profits to redeem himself by buying the lives of these *Schindlerjuden*. With their depositions, these same Jews saved Schindler from a war crimes trial for his part in the preparation of intelligence reports that led to the 'rape of Czechoslovakia' before the war. Overall, by the logic of his ideology, he was acting irrationally and illegally. What he did violated Nuremberg Racial Laws and

his personal oath to Hitler, for which violations he could have been summarily executed at any moment. He acted on an intuitive, instinctive level. When asked after the war why he did what he did, he simply exclaimed 'it was the right thing to do!' While there are tinges of Kantian moral axioms in this declamation, Schindler had no formal training in dialectics. Hence there can be 'Righteous Gentiles' outside formal university schooling.

Ironically, several among those tried at Nuremberg and subsequent trials had doctorates from major specializations of education. Philosophers, lawyers, and medical personnel had the worst record. These were the world's best and brightest, yet hubris and fascination with instrumental reason shut the eye of the mind to blind these elites toward any perspective on the human consequences of their actions. For example, the medical profession euthanized 100,000 physically and mentally 'unfit' Germans during the 1930s. Hitler saw in this action a model to exterminate the Jews. The legal establishment provided the statutes. The philosophers spun out nihilistic rationalizations. Corruption and mass murder always originate in the 'moral' and state leadership by producing the sanctions to do the unthinkable. Obviously their formal university training had only ritualistic dimensions to initiate these individuals to take power when their opportunistic moment arrived, leaving in its wake deformed characters with the obsessive repetition compulsion to repeat the errors of history in killing authority figures or the hopelessly weak with no voice, while displacing them shamelessly with themselves and their transvalued values in the anonymous horde to justify not assuming personal responsibility for criminal actions. They refused to see the 'big picture.' Even on the scaffolds, the condemned, after legal due process, never assumed personal responsibility or expressed contrition. Trivializing the enormity of their actions, they felt scapegoated by a 'victor's justice.' Their nihilistic and relativistic claim is that the winners in war always rewrite the history books.

Unfortunately, this generic type of thinking prevails at the academies of higher learning, where new in-groups of highly ideologically charged coalitions of minority groups re-script the curricula. There had been a century of consensus on the core curriculum: the necessary courses to develop a functional, humane, and universal adult citizen of the world. But administrative control in the severely circumscribed reality of higher education does not spell political power or social status in the larger society, and the really tough issues of class, gender, and caste have not been seriously examined because such an undertaking would first require a social and political revolution in the larger society in which there would be a constitutional shift of power underwritten by an economic bill of rights. But randomly inspired acts of beneficence initiated by individual contact across the races and classes at least could fashion by the sheer force of numbers a moral revolution in public manners as a prelude to general changes in the material world of state and society into the very mode of production.

The point is that Schindler underwent just such an internal revolution in values, and so affected countless lives for the better. However, he always intuitively knew what to do as right. He never had to consult any ultimate authorities other than his own conscience. If we all act in good faith, there emerges a general truth insofar as all human beings have an innate capacity to comport themselves with dignity and honor even in the most extreme situation. We can all choose to be personally responsible after an aesthetic, practical evaluation of any set of given circumstances. So a sense of beauty can give rise to conscientious acts in defiance of the pathological dictates of a totalitarian state. Political human beings, above all, act in conjunction with judgments which are ultimately derivative from these aesthetic sensibilities. Art, including music, and politics can be in alliance.

Frankfurt School theorists would do well to center us on an explanation of why people take the courses of action they do. What has surprised me about the documented instances of Righteous Gentiles is the many ordinary people, who are supposed to be powerless and hopeless, but who, violently or passively, did not accede to Hitler's Behemoth and intervened to disrupt the bio-political order. Of course, as Carl Schmitt so avidly defended on the lecture podium and in his writings, Hitler's scheme of things was legitimate within the framework of the Weimar constitution: in a purely formal sense. While an investigation into authoritarian versus democratic personalities has significance, more questions are begged than answered as to individual, human actions and their motivations when theoreticians, in particular, have real world responsibilities as historical actors. There are numerous substantial deviations from what would be expected in terms of those ordinary individuals who conducted themselves in contradistinction to regnant paradigms of party loyalties, personality types, national identifications, and ideological training and predispositions. Particularly in times of revolutionary flux in social structures and power alignments, individuals have an opening in reified Being to act justly no matter how heavy the burden of domination. After a rigorous Socratic self-examination, Aristotle believed that the 'just man', who is the norm in the properly ordered polis, 'naturally' on rational grounds of the *zoon politikon* prefers to do good no matter what tyrant must be opposed, or what the opinion of the masses dictates. Justice can and does have a grounding in discursive will formation which can be indefinitely tenable and ongoing. Hence we escape the Charybdis of the nihilism of relativism and the Scylla of the absolutes of metaphysics. We are thrown toward our existential freedom where we can collectively define our horizons. Our possibilities are embedded in the very radicalness of our being thrown into the world which becomes concentric circles of friends and acquires a proximate character according to our chosen projects. Too, our possibilities are just as much defined by will as by the struggle to overcome the truth/Big Lie dilemma.

2. African Americans need not overly concern themselves with the spectacular success of Hebrew Americans and the first generation of Asian Americans, the latter group having asserted their presence in unprecedented numbers in the prestige schools of the country. The recent history of these two groups belies the rote cry of 'racism' leveled by political demagogues and professional academics who, being 'politically correct,' promote the view that African Americans on their own cannot radically improve their economic conditions because of a devil theory of whites. Nor is there merit in the charge of the Nation of Islam that the Jews initiated and profited inordinately in the slave trade. The bigger the lie, the more gullible are the 'dumb' *lumpenproletariat* to its simplifying appeal. The Big Lie may unify the black masses, but at the expense of removing them one degree farther from the true centers of power. The Jews now have access to that power in the communication and educational subsystem and as a pariah/parvenu group can have some understanding of the African American condition. Jewish financial power, with its philanthropic inclinations, and black numbers could make a difference in the quality of life, particularly at the neighborhood and university levels where they co-habit and by the nature of their respective situations should have the same underlying values as to what is the good life and the political means to realize it. African Americans most certainly can make major changes, and in a manner that is a win/win strategy for all Americans. See my 'Black Nationalism and Emancipation' in Appendix One.

3. There is a way to teach in which you can create a sense of community in a Leviathan, inner city school. We can bring heaven to earth through interdisciplinary studies which involve investigating scientifically multiple cultures, world views, and research paradigms. Along the way, we can extinguish the flames of hell from the eschatology of university over-specialization, where by a kind of conditioned reflex teachers cynically promote and students take careerist-oriented courses. This overspecialization entails a rank positivism where critical thinking cannot develop because the students know everything about nothing; this is what we denounce routinely as professionalism, yet avidly practice out of naked but quite stupid self-interest. See Appendix Two.

1 The dialectical intelligence: Its origins in German philosophy

Introduction

Without Hegel's *Phenomenology of Spirit*, the historical materialism of Marx would have been stillborn. With this new genre of critique, philosophy and politics in a revolutionary age developed together both coherently and in problematic contradiction - the 'lag' in the 'superstructure' took an unexpected institutional materialization, becoming a transformative force in history in its own right. The question of the significance of history for the *Phenomenology* and the particular nature of its own historicity remain problematic. The idiosyncratic historicity of the *Phenomenology of Spirit*, as exhibited in the 'Preface', in the concluding sections of the work, and more particularly in the overall movement of this development evidenced in conjunction with Hegel's full life's work, has motivated philosophy to query, more fastidiously, in what sense the antinomy of a 'history of the Absolute' tested against a lived reality is conceivable, justifiable, and, ultimately, adaptable by other scholars in a general schema. Marx, of course, owed much to this dialectical form.

There is a difference between an 'immanent' disquisition, which endeavors to interpret the *Phenomenology* without displaying any philosophical tendentiousness, and an 'assimilative' account. Present-day examples of such assimilation can be discerned in the projects to interpret the *Phenomenology* - or sections of it - from a phenomenological, ontological, Marxist, existentialist, or history-of-Being vantage point. As was already the case with Marx, the majority of these assimilations are conceived by the needs of the time and undertake to effect a basic transfiguration of humanity and reality. Lukács, Kojéve, Bloch, and Habermas are some of the more prominent figures on this 'highway of despair'.

In the 'history of consciousness' of German classical philosophy, Hegel found 'knowledge' unfolded up to the point at which - in the Absolute - it arrives at insight into the identity of subject and object and, hence at a denial of the opposition between knowing and objecthood. We do not simply start from a self-restriction of the primary intellectual intuition, but from a curtailment of 'spirit', which becomes 'other to itself' and alienates itself in order to find itself again in otherness, in which process the aspect of otherness, namely objectivity, then makes a more compelling presence.

The construction of subject-object identity in German Idealism is rooted in Kant's idea of 'transcendental apperception', the idea that the pure subject, forged as a structure of fundamental logic acts, employs its synthesizing power of conception to confer logical form on the universe confronting it. The subject is hence the genesis of an a priori identity of cognition and objectivity, in the modality Kant delineated in his *Critique of Pure Reason* as the 'supreme principle of all synthetic *a priori* judgements': '... the conditions of the *possibility of experience* in general are likewise conditions of the *possibility of the objects of experience*' (A158/1965, p. 194).

Kant writes in the *Critique of Pure Reason*: 'The transcendental unity of apperception is that unity through which all the manifold given in an intuition is united in a concept of the object' (B139/p. 157). That is, transcendental apperception, pure subjectivity of the pure self, is what constitutes objectivity, in that it brings the manifold of intuition into the necessary relation with the concept. This necessary conjunction of the concept 'is', for Hegel's design, ultimately the transcendental apperception of the self, that is, 'of' the concept. He thereby interprets Kant's insight into the structure of transcendental apperception. The unifying oneness of the self which fulfills itself as concept is the basis of the universal and necessary association with objectivity. In the dialectic, the subject can find itself again in the other - in the sphere of objectivity it has 'grounded'. The analogous process will occur in the 'Idea' of the *Phenomenology*: consciousness must forsake the idea of an objectivity independent of its knowledge and recognize everything else is 'permeated' by categories of the self; the concept (conceiving in its 'otherness', insofar as it is 'thought') remains at home with, and is identical with, itself.

To Kant, pure self-consciousness in its centripetal motion was of import for the possibility of synthetic judgements a priori, that is, ultimately, for generating the basis of the empirical knowledge of natural science and its 'objectivity'. The problem for German Idealism, for Hegel in particular, was more rudimentary. For Hegel subjectivity was the movement which 'logicizes' the whole of Being, not just natural science. It therefore has the significance that the *Logos* had possessed for Greek philosophy. For post-Kantian philosophizing, the knowing subject is the source of the order of the categorialized objectivity of the objects which are mediated by the concept. Hegel remains faithful to this 'conversion'. For him the concept, the *Logos* expressing itself as subject, constitutes the order and intelligibility of everything which exists. Here the term 'subject' certainly does not refer to human or even individual knowing. It includes also the order mirrored in the forms and laws of nature, the ordering objective spirit of ethical life, and the 'Absolute Spirit', which presents itself in the hierarchized structures of art, religion, and philosophy. Human cognition does not produce all these orders but rather plumbs their genealogy with comprehension. Because this logicization has always taken place already, knowing is not, as in Kant, a bestowal of form to what was previously primeval, but a becoming manifest to itself of the movement of the concept which, as *Logos*, governs everything. The concept reaches a condition of being completely manifest to itself once it has interpenetrated everything 'other' to it and 'sublated' this medium to itself. The path of this ever mounting self-permeation is the dialectical movement which occurs in the distinction between the knowing and knowingly acting self and its 'object'. This whole presentation is no less than the 'phenomenology of Spirit'.

Within the traditional sense of *Logos* by which Hegel is inspired lie further determinations which have also become operative in the *Phenomenology*. The *Logos* by tradition signifies more than the identity of thinking and Being (in modern terms, subjectivity and objectivity). Even for the Greeks it already had the import of an order (a value-laden structure) which - at least potentially - must be obvious to those initiated into dialectical discourse. The *Logos* as thought or thinking continues to preserve this illumination in *Nous* - 'spirit' or 'reason', which is light-imparting principle. Thinking, as *noesis*, the possibility bestowed on human beings for intuitive apprehension which evokes insight, is infallible. The realization of Logos and *dianoia* - 'understanding' - occurs as a knowing which apprehends, judges, infers, induces, deduces, and is able to conjugate definitions and determine essences.

For the Greeks this power of *nous* and *Logos* culminated in a philosophy which was grasped as an ontology, as a quest for the ultimate categorical determinations of the existent, *theos*, insofar as ontology was always at the same moment theology. Aristotle considered the most important category in the ontological order to be that of *ousia*, or substance, which was articulated into a plethora of types, particularly that of *telos*, or goal. It is crucial to keep this determination of *telos* in mind, because the thought of an 'attained goal' or a 'fulfilled purpose', which from the beginning refers everything back to itself, could thereby lend a definite sense of 'necessity' both to what is individually and to the association of all that is, the *cosmos*. The limitations of Kant prepare us for the Copernican revolution in dialectical exposition made possible by the interplay of Hegel and Marx in the nineteenth century, a revolution which transformed critique into a mode of radical political criticism and a ground for revolutionary commitment to radical social change.

The emergence of dialectical reason - the 'Creation'

Subject and object, Hegel claimed, should not be conceived of as stable entities but, on the contrary, as two moments in the single process of becoming. Hegel's concept of 'becoming' needs meticulous elucidation. Becoming alludes to an epistemological structure in which both subject and object undergo an irreversible and coalesced process of self-transformation. The knowing subject and the known object continually dissolve and refashion themselves, and in the process of this dissolution and re-creation the 'moments' thoroughly interpenetrate each other. The reunification of subject and object is conceivable because in the ultimate reconciliation the two are identical. External objective reality must be comprehended as a continually changing consequence of activities by the thinking subject. Conversely, the thinking subject breaks through to reality only by activities which continuously create and re-create the objective world.

Because of this understanding, Hegel sharply rejects the Kantian distinction between the knowing subject (Kant's theoretical reason) and the acting subject (Kant's practical reason). Thought and action, theory and practice, can be separated neither empirically nor analytically. Likewise, the object of knowledge is necessarily also the object of moral action or human practice. Therefore the process of knowing must not only trace the process of 'becoming' of the object of knowledge but actually collaborate in the movement of that process.

The effort of reason (i.e., the knowing subject) to comprehend the process of becoming is what Hegel calls dialectic. Hegel in his *Logic* cultivates the dialectical method in the context of a general theory of logic which analytically separates several interlocking steps of cognition:

> In point of form Logical doctrine has three sides: (a) the abstract side or that of understanding; (b) the Dialectical, or that of negative reason; (c) the Speculative, or that of positive reason. (1975, p. 113)

The dialectical mode of cognition makes conceivable a deeper and more encompassing penetration of the objects than 'understanding' can adequately comprehend:

> In the Dialectical stage these finite characterizations or formulae

> supersede themselves, and pass into their opposites. ... In its true and proper character, Dialectic is seen as the very nature and essence of everything predicated by mere understanding - the laws of things and of the finite as a whole. ... By Dialectic is meant the indwelling tendency outwards by which the one-sidedness and limitation of the predicates of understanding is seen in its true light, and shown to be the negation of them. (pp. 115-6)

This deeper fathoming of the universe comes about through three interrelated thought processes: negation, contradiction, and totalization. Negation decomposes the fixity of the object by conceiving it as a complex configuration of alternative potentialities, some of which stand in direct opposition to each other. Hegel evaluates all real entities as the unification of opposites; hence his frequent reference to a thing turning 'suddenly into its opposite'.

Contradiction focuses on the recognition of an internal dynamic propelling the object of knowledge away from whatever its present finite condition might be:

> For anything to be finite is just to suppress itself and put aside. ... Wherever there is movement, wherever there is life, wherever anything is carried into effect in the actual world, there Dialectic is at work. ... The finite, being radically self-contradictory, involves its own self-suppression. ... [Dialectic's] purpose is to study things in their own being and movement and thus to demonstrate the finitude of the partial categories of the understanding. (pp. 116-7)

Dialectical reason refuses to comprehend the objects of knowledge as distinct categories and entities, conceiving them as moments of a totality in the process of becoming.

Totalization alludes to the process by which thought supersedes separation and fashions a conceptual unity out of what had appeared at the level of understanding as distinct, self-sufficient existence. Totalization envelops not only the entire sequence of transformations undergone by the known object, but also the self-transformation of the knowing subject. Hence the subject/object dualism posed by Kant's theoretical reason is banished.

The concepts Hegel employed occur in pairs which I shall refer to as dialectical categories. Every stable entity must be dissolved into a process before its existence can be coherently apprehended. The dialectical categories illuminate the internal logic of the process into which stable entities have been dissolved. The concepts occurring in such pairs are both opposing and complementary. The process to which the dialectical category is applied cannot be apprehended as a whole except as an interpenetration or synthesis of the opposing concepts which identify the category itself. We develop here four dialectical categories intended to render the fundamental methodological dicta of negation, contradiction, and totalization more concrete and available to the 'initiate' for the purpose of understanding Hegel's political theory: (a) subjectivity-objectivity; (b) universality-particularity; (c) freedom-necessity; and (d) rationality-positivity.

The *subjectivity-objectivity* category has been illustrated above. The *universality-particularity* category concerns the relationship between any concept or idea, on the one hand, and a finite instance of the concept, on the other. In another sense the universality-particularity category focuses on the concept and its historical incorporation in space and time. Insofar as an entity to which a concept refers encompasses only those facets necessarily implied by the concept and nothing more, it manifests universality. Conversely, insofar as the entity contains other facets in addition to the ones implied by the concept, it evidences particularity. The universality or essence of a concept can only acquire concrete existence in the real world through particular entities, whereas the meaning or identity of one of these finite particulars only becomes apparent through the universal concept it elaborates.

One manner of conceptualizing the relationship between *freedom and necessity* is through the notion of authenticity. The unity of freedom and necessity pertains to the realization of the authentic nature (that is, the genuine essence) of an entity. The authentic nature of an entity is the self-determined unraveling of its concrete potentialities, in comparison to those facets imposed from without. Authenticity incarnates freedom because it engenders self-determination rather than external causation. Authenticity embodies necessity because it rejects arbitrariness in any form, expressing instead the indubitable requirements of determinate being.

Authentic human beings, for example, are those who comprehend their essential being and real potentialities and always remains true to this ideal. A particular individual, while fully partaking of all the delights of the senses, is shielded by particular interests and not dominated by capriciousness or spiteful whims, false needs, or impulsive desires. On the contrary, protected by a strictly defined status hierarchy, the individual can self-consciously choose to act in congruence with those true needs which flow through one's own essential and vital being, and to act in a manner true to the real potentialities of the specific historical situation. The actions of the authentic person embody the basic unity of freedom and necessity. Finally, *rational* individuals materialize their potential in the *positivity* of making empirically engendered history.

The combined interests pursued by those enjoying their authenticity in freedom form the collective universality organized by the State, especially the mechanism of a bureaucracy, constituted by an 'interest-free' mandarin 'class' independent even of the major branches of government, to assume 'rationality' within the terms posed by necessity.

Hegel defines freedom as human self-consciousness, and comprehends the realization of freedom as the absolute aim of world history. Therefore in the *Philosophy of History* he construes world history as the development of the consciousness of freedom.

> In the history of the World, only those peoples can come under our notice which form a state. For it must be understood that this latter is the realization of Freedom, *i.e.*, of the absolute final aim, and that it exists for its own sake. It must further be understood that all the worth which the human being possesses - all spiritual reality consists in this, that his own essence - Reason - is objectively present to him, that it possesses objective immediate existence for him. Thus only is he fully conscious; thus only is he a partaker of morality - of a just and moral social and political life. (1956, p. 19)

The emerging categorically bound self-consciousness of freedom, therefore, approximates itself best through the concrete political structure of individual nations, which are to date the most complete embodiments of the unfolding essence of humanity.

> ... all the worth which the human being possesses - all spiritual reality, he possesses only through the state. ... The state is the divine Idea as it exists on Earth. (p. 39)

The state will, moreover, coincides with the will of a hypothetical individual perfectly harmonized with the institutions and culture of society conceived as dynamic processes and stripped of all particularizing, egocentric traits. Such an individual can only be a theoretical abstraction, but an abstraction which finds historical incarnation in the potential of all concrete members of society to reconcile their socio-political differences.

In a very abbreviated examination, we can say that Hegel's view of the state as the sublime and superordinate incorporation of freedom by no means implies that the state will advance the desires of the majority. The existence of the state embodies the capacity for individuals to act collectively. The state mobilizes the potency for action - the potential power - which resides in the holistic human community. Without the supervision of the state (that is, under conditions of lawlessness) the exercise of the human will would be stymied at every turn. Sustained collective actions would be totally inconceivable, while the uncharted interaction of individual wills would make precarious even those actions conceived on a smaller, subcollective scale. The state will provides the basis for the exercise of individual will. The state will fashions the crucible for the very existence of individual wills.

Consider, for example, the first dialectical category, universality-particularity. Hegel perceives the state as a representative of the universal facts of social life. The state, at least in principle, encompasses the totality of society and its generalized interest and acts as steward of the values and interests implicit in this totality. Under stress (class conflict), successive historical eras will appear in the form of particularities; that is, the state, without canceling its essential universality, will appear as an agent for a particular class. Such situations often generate vapid critiques of the state, critiques which are misinformed because they fail to understand the universal essence beneath the particular appearance. Only an analysis catalyzed by profound historical consciousness can fathom reality when the seeming particularism of a situation is mere display or an alienation of statehood and not an element with persuasive ethical value.

Although an identity holds between individual will and state considered on the conceptual level, the real historical relationship between individual and state is mediated by specific social institutions. The most crucial such institutions identified by Hegel are property; the domains of ethical life, namely the family and civil society; and class structure. Hegel posits these institutions as universal constituents of any social order. Without them any historical society would dissolve of its own accord. Nonetheless, property, family, civil society, and class structure are historically specific in that their forms and functions change over time and across social segmentations.

Hegel considers personality to be the inner subjective manifestation of freedom and treats the domains of family and civil society as representative of the historical development of the principle of personality. He identifies property as the external objective manifestation of individual freedom. Property is different and separable from the individual, yet it functions as an extension and objectification of the individual ego. Through property the individual compels others to recognize the individual's concrete existence and confirms a domain where personal, not state will is ultimately sovereign.

Hegel holds property to be a particularly momentous mediation between individual and state because it permits a format and even an agenda for relations between the two. Every social formation in which private property appears announces a major corpus of law emanating from the institution of property. Property law specifies the rights and obligations attributable to property, the procedures which must be followed in transactions between the state and the property owner, and sometimes even the class position of the property owner. Property provides an autonomous power base enabling the ego to confront the state from a position of self-reliant dignity rather than subaltern weakness. Hegel's analysis should not be derogated as a mere ideological defense of private property. Indwelling in his analysis is a critique of the propertyless *condition*, not an attack on the personal worthiness of a person without the means to obtain property. Hegel's stance implies a muted antagonism toward a society which condemns most of its members to the propertyless condition. His defense of property is at least as much a critique as a justification of capitalism: he fully acknowledged the ethical impoverishment entailed by misery imposed on the masses by new techniques of production.

Hegel's position becomes more evident if we recognize that he is actually justifying the property of petty bourgeois producers, not capitalists. The virtues he imputes to property stem from the direct, concrete identification of owner and property in a strong correlation of subjective and objective attributes; they require that the owner of property actually use the property, labor on it, and be familiar with its idiosyncrasies. For Hegel, property was not yet alienated to a degree that could be said to resemble reification. He had no real idea of the full scale division of labor and the development of automated assembly lines. So the notion of property with which the owner has an abstract, generalized relationship, which is simply an instrumentality for the expansion of 'property value and the 'massivity of wealth' (i.e., capitalist property) can at most find only scanty exaltation in Hegel's schema.

Social classes are groups with common interests, common needs, and common types of work synthesized from the complex and interrelated components of production and exchange in their dynamic manifestations. Hegel states in the *Philosophy of Right*:

> The infinitely complex, criss-cross movements of reciprocal production and exchange, and the equally infinite multiplicity of means therein employed, become crystallized, owing to the universality inherent in their content, and distinguished into general groups. As a result, the entire complex is built into particular systems of needs, means, and types of work relative to these needs, modes of satisfaction and of theoretical and practical education, *i.e.*, into systems, to one or other of which individuals are assigned - in other words, into class divisions. (1967a, p. 19)

Although class fissures arise through the process of production, social classes themselves have a deeper reality. The essence of class, like the essence of state, is common will. Hegel considers any entity capable of social action as, conceptually speaking, a form of will. This interpretation provides a direct though often overlooked tie between Hegelian idealism and the positions of more recent social scientific action theorists like Talcott Parsons. If the dialectical categories mentioned above are denuded of their 'dialecticity', they bear a remarkable resemblance to Parsons's pattern variables.

For Hegel, a social class exists as a potentiality for corporate organization and as a distinctive mode of consciousness sifted from participation in the activities of production and exchange. The class will is far less comprehensive than the state will, but it is a manifestation of universalism within the context of civil society Through their membership in social classes, individuals attain a partial transcendence of egoistic particularism. The existence of a social class transfigures the pursuit of private interests into the pursuit of group interest, enclosing thereby a circumscribed universalism. In contradistinction to Marx, Hegel does not regard class structure as historically variable. Since the inner reality of class is that of mode of consciousness and common will, which are in turn forms of the Idea, it should be possible to abstract the notion of class structure from that of civil society. Civil society is an invariable component of modern society, so, class structure must display a similar fixity. With empirical documentation, Marx regards the state, private property, and civil society as the domain of *universal* aberration par excellence. In these corporate entities the autonomous ego of Hegel has been leveled by capital and the social and technical distinction of labor. The essence of contradiction is to be found not in logical categories but in the confrontation of real material interests.

For Hegel, the existence of a universal class does not lead to the revolutionary dissolution of the other domains of society. The family and civil society must persevere as institutionalized mediations which protect the individual from domination by the state and, even more important, from an estranged sense of political impotence. When individuals relate to the state directly without mediating institutions, Hegel contends, they become conscious primarily of their own vulnerability. This consciousness is rampant in systems of government based on direct political representation.

The principle of mediation Hegel had in mind may require a more reticulated organizational structure than he imagined. A class organization too may confront individual members as an overbearing power and induce the same sense of impotence as did the state. But the basic precept remains unchanged; the situation would simply necessitate subclass organizations. The precept invokes a structure of organizations, starting with the individual and consummated with the state, such that a few simple conditions are satisfied. Individuals must experience their own efficacy within the lowest level organization in which they participate directly. Each organization within the structure must be subject to influence by the lower level organizations which form its constituency and must exert influence on the higher level organizations in which it is involved. If these conditions are secured, the processes of identification and mediation will beget meaningful linkages between individual and state, and the state will appear as the actualization of individual freedom. Hegel does not indict social structure as the antithesis of freedom but celebrates it as an instrumentality necessary for the concrete maintenance of that freedom.

Hegel's dislike of revolutionary movements must be perceived in the context of his reaction to the Jacobin excesses in France. Recall that Hegel understands the ultimate content of history as the efflorescing consciousness of freedom. The idea of freedom actualizes itself subjectively in the individual consciousness and objectively in the form of social institutions, especially the state. The nexus between the abstract concept of freedom and the freedom actualized in the consciousness and institutions of a concrete social formation is always intricate, and under certain circumstances it can be adulterated and tampered with. Such perversions are particularly destabilizing if they emanate from a misapprehension or limited perspective of what freedom entails. Hegel chastised the French revolutionaries on two grounds: (1) they equated negative freedom with the totality of freedom; and (2) in the footsteps of Rousseau (particularly *The Social Contract*) they confounded will conceptualized at the individual level with that emerging holistically at the state level.

Hegel's concept of will has three moments: negative, positive, and self-determining freedom. *Negative freedom* is essentially the will's capacity to determine its own content. The will is not dominated by what exists here and now. No matter what the individual's present cognitions and state of mind, the will can conceive alternative cognitions and alternative states of mind. Hence the will can distinguish its own existence from that of every determinate state of mind and can dissolve in thought (or even action) every concrete stricture. Negative freedom embodies the totally unrestricted facet of the (annihilatory) will, its ability to transcend every given content; it is the element of pure indeterminacy which issues forth from the very existence of the will.

Positive freedom incorporates the capacity of the will to forge a definite content and to exist blissfully within the confines of its creation. Positive freedom emerges through the cancellation of negative freedom. It affirms certain contents as non-translucent, as a permanence to be identified in the flux of the infinity of activities engendered by absolute knowledge. *Self-determining freedom* is the capacity of the will to coalesce negative and positive freedom. It energizes this outcome by apprehending its own ability to dissolve all indeterminate contents, and by recognizing that accepting a determinate content embodies a phase of the will's authentic self-determination.

According to Hegel, the French revolutionaries understood themselves as a manifestation of the universal will striving to realize absolute freedom. But pure universality can exist only as an abstract idea and never in the form of a particular state. When the universal will, in the form of a revolutionary movement, becomes manacled by a misdirected desire to exist as a concrete historical state, it betrays an exaggerated passion to wipe clean everything but itself, and advances to annihilate all structures which mediated between the individual and the state. The result is a reign of terror which ultimately feeds on the revolutionary movement itself.

The revolutionaries' second misapprehension of freedom was their uncritical acceptance of Rousseau's social contract theory, which makes the state derivative from individual consent and thereby subordinates state will to individual will (in the case of the populist leaders of the Jacobin clubs outside Paris, even the sum total of all the members was a distinct minority). By accepting the private ideas of freedom current among contemporary French intellectuals, they ignored the concept of freedom as unfolded in the movement of world history. These private notions of freedom, though pervasive in their culture, had no basis within either the development of the French consciousness conceived as a self-determining process or the prior evolution of French social institutions. These notions confronted French reality as an abstract, alien force which could be brought to bear only through the dissolution of the preexisting state (for Hegel, the embodiment of concrete freedom) and the massive institutionalization of terror. Because for Hegel the dynamic of development ultimately results from the internal logic of the concept which animates a historical epoch, he construes the tragic errors which undercut the French Revolution - exclusive emphasis on negative freedom and the substitution of human for state will - as shortcomings inherent to the concept of revolution itself. The Jacobin 'reign of terror' was no accident. On the contrary, it flowed naturally from the very notion of revolution and issued in a dire warning to all would-be revolutionaries.

Yet in some matters Hegel treats the state as a functional surrogate for revolution. The classic conception of revolution treats it as simultaneously historical product and historical intervention (i.e., as a process transcending the subject/object duality), which, in times of social dissolution, reasserts the claims of universality (society as a whole) against the disruptive particularisms (conflicting social interests) which previously dominated society. This conception closely parallels what Hegel perceives as the function of the state. The state is related to but independent of civil society. The state embodies the claims of universality and contains the sphere of action of particularism. It is the instrumentality through which society mobilizes itself to handle collective problems. Hence, when faced with pervasive poverty, conflict, imperialism, and the like, Hegel does not (as would Marx) embrace revolution as the agency of a transforming corrective universalism. Instead he embraces the state itself as that collective will which rises above class divisions and incarnates whatever realistic hopes history may offer for the palliation of existing evils. Unlike revolution, the state vouchsafes the existence of mediating social structures.

Without institutions like the family and class structure to mediate between the individual and the state, Hegel contends, the social order would simply deteriorate to the disadvantage of all.

In his *Critique of Hegel's Dialectic*, Marx critiques Hegel in summary fashion on all fronts:

> The appropriation of man's objectified alienated faculties is thus, in the first place, only an appropriation which occurs in *consciousness*, in *pure thought*, i.e. in abstraction. It is the appropriation of these objects as *thoughts* and as *movements of thought*. For this reason, despite its thoroughly negative and critical appearance, and despite the genuine criticism which it contains, ... there is already implicit in the *Phenomenology*, as a germ, as a potentiality and a secret, the uncritical positivism and uncritical idealism of Hegel's later works - the philosophical dissolution and restoration of the existing empirical world. (Marx, 1964a, p. 201)

Marx objects to the incorporation of alienation in the very dialectic itself:

> ... this [dialectic] process must have a bearer, a subject; but the subject first emerges as a result. This result, the subject knowing itself as absolute self-consciousness, is therefore *God, absolute spirit, the self-knowing and self-manifesting idea*. Real man and real nature become mere predicates, symbols of this concealed unreal man and unreal nature. (p. 214)

But his most indelible criticism concerns the negation of the negation, which ends up affirming rather than negating what exists. As used by Hegel, negation of the negation involves a series of negations or supersessions which lead from a relatively specific to a highly abstract mode of existence but which are played out on the conceptual level. Within this sequence of negations each notion is negated, but, since Hegel conceives the result as a totality, that is, a recapitulation of the entire process, each notion must nevertheless persist and be preserved in the final totality.

> The act of *supersession* plays a strange part in which *denial* and preservation, denial and affirmation, are linked together. Thus, for example, in Hegel's *Philosophy of Right*, *private right* superseded equals *morality*, morality superseded equals *the family*, the family superseded equals *civil society*, civil society superseded equals the *state*, and the state superseded equals *world history*. But in *actuality* private right,

morality, the family, civil society, the state, etc. remain; only they have become 'moments', modes of existence of man, which have no validity in isolation but which mutually dissolve and engender one another. *They are 'moments' of the movement.* (p. 211)

Hence the Hegelian dialectic unfurls itself as a logic of totality rather than a logic of process. It proves far more adaptable for posing questions relating to the existence of complex and seemingly inconsistent moments within a simple totality than for posing and answering questions pertaining to the dynamics which propel a historical sequence of social totalities. Hegel certainly does not intend his dialectic as an equilibrium of opposing forces; rather, equilibrium emerges as a negative totality in which conceptual opposites figure as moments unified through a process of conceptual negation. These moments, in the words of Marx, simultaneously 'dissolve and engender one another', creating a total effect virtually indistinguishable from the notion of equilibrium, which pervades most subdivisions of 'bourgeois' science.

For Hegel the state is the totality which cannot be interpreted as the agent of any specific sector. Marx dissects the state as a creature of civil society whose actions reflect the interests and tensions within that society. Although Marx does not postulate a complete isomorphism between ruling class interests and state policies, he does analyze the state as the guardian of a historically specific social formation which necessarily produces and reproduces a pyramidal class structure. The state is also guardian of this class structure and protector of the ruling class (or at least the politically hegemonic and activist parts of it). It is bound by its own long term interests to reproduce the means of production and legitimacy of this class, and to maintain the functional requirements of the system of which the plutocratic minority is the principal beneficiary. Paradoxically, such blindness can generate a clash between state and the ruling class, a clash which if observed only on the surface obscures the true relationship between the two. It is here that the modern rift between political and private ultimately concerns not only the scope of the realm of freedom but its very substance.

The Marxian materialization of Hegel's absolute knowledge: A schema for developing critico-practical reason

It is necessary to explore further the epistemological/ontological roots of the Hegelian system if we are to arrive at the radical political philosophy which is the achievement of Marx. This section will endeavor to trace these roots, primarily in Hegel's *Phenomenology of Mind*. Marx used the phenomenological matrix of relationships unfolding there to analyze empirically class conflict and conformity in capitalist societies. This analysis provides the scaffolding for the present day radical political philosophy and ethics which, in some instances, lead to individual commitment to be a 'Marxist'. The term has become so abused as to be no longer self-explanatory as Marxian terminology has undergone so many permutations by scholars, literary figures, and politicians with conflicting interests and aims.

Alienation is the key transitional concept which serves as a common denominator between Hegel the objective idealist and Marx the historical materialist. It was Marx's study of Hegel's alienation of the Subject to Nature (by externalization and reappropriation) that induced him to see Labor as the embodiment of the concrete universal force characteristic of species-being and the free play of its faculties; capital, from this perspective, is the alienation of all human activities, for in classical capitalism generic humanity must submit to scarcity, exploitation, and necessity. The essential problem will be to study how Marx derived his basic assumptions of practical action through the 'demystification' of Hegel's understanding of an 'Unhappy Consciousness' stemming from the march of the World Spirit through *progressive* History - for humanity, in Marx's eyes, had substituted fictions and a demonology of capital for a holistic and authentic interpretation of the complex meanings of the human situation. The dialectical convolutions performed by the 'unhappy consciousness' seeking its return and reconstruction to its essence leads to the overcoming of alienation in toto, but in Hegel only ideally, in absolute knowledge.

Hegel, from his perspective, has logically (through universal categories) shown that the multiversity within evolving philosophy is not a source of despair and ruin but a primal value and a necessity - it is no less than the modes of Truth being unraveled, posited, and, consequently, *aufgehoben* and accessible to the penetration of totalizing reason. Hegel not only demonstrates that the major philosophic positions which have been brought together in the course of the action of the World Spirit reintegrate parts or aspects of an integral, rational chronicle of human events, he also claims to know the manner in which this occurs: through the agency of the roil and toil of conflicting and contradictory quasi-systems which can ultimately embrace only one scientific truth.

The key to Marx's 'activist' constitutive reorganization and 'setting on its feet' of Hegel's thought resides in Marx's concept of *praxis*, a term used consistently and coherently throughout his writings. This notion is a linchpin for his ultimate goals and values. The key (in his Hegelian transposition) to grasping his 'early' philosophical evaluations, it reaches its height in the scientific and dialectical exposition in *Capital* of the serialized stages of capitalism. It is fundamental for interpreting and explaining the deplorable human condition he envisages, and for coming to terms with his understanding of the 'nature' of human nature as implanted in the ensemble of social relationships with their linkages to production and all its mechanisms. It is the crux for understanding what Marx meant by revolutionary practice (in a programmatic form which has yet to be actualized on the global scale he intended). Even communism, by his definition, is merely the beginning of history in its real essence. He declined to make futuristic projections, realizing from the predictions of the utopian socialists that the course of human events cannot be extrapolated and projected in terms of highly specifiable factors after the model of the natural sciences. Marx condemned the institutions and technological rationalism of his own day as a pervasive form of predatory 'barbarism'.

The point is that praxis in its dialectical import not only constitutes a critique of the Hegelian *Geist*, it is also its cancellation, preservation, and transcendence. Hegel's Geist attempts to integrate two independent but mutually sustaining ideas. The first is that of Reason, or *Nous*, especially as the concept had its incubation period in the classical era. The second is that of God as Spirit. Hegel's 'God' is described as an omniscient, all-encompassing, activist Being who renders himself tangible to human intelligence within historical processes (for instance, in finitude, through the Incarnation of Jesus Christ) and engineers history in the form of 'pneumatological' Providence (that 'good infinity' of human events and institutions climaxing in the 'divinely willed' Prussian state).

What Hegel meant by Reason is not an entity in permanent flux like the Marxian truths, which ebb and flow with capitalist crises and encroach on Nature to fashion civilization. Hegel's Reason is objectified in, and ultimately reconciled to, Nature through a process of objectification in the Speculative Mind, what Marx denounced as metaphysical persiflage to mask the one-sidedness and rank inequalities of the human condition. This point is basic. Reason is a kind of processional self-actualization in that its thrust, when grasped in a holistically emerging way, constitutes the highest instance of a theoretical exposition which interprets a reality revealed in a topography of dialectical categories. This reality is grasped when human rationality is shown to be indivisible from it. For Hegel, therefore, reason is not metaphorical; it literally saturates the world. For Marx, this argument is too cunning; the human element has been abstracted senselessly, leaving us with a purified phenomenology of the Mind denuded of human social activity and generic potentialities.

Geist, then, which combines reason and God in dialectical categories through its substantive manifestations and its latent meanings awaiting actualization, turns out to be the efficient and final cause in the world; it is therefore also formal and material in essence. Carefully nurtured, it reconciles the objective precipitating agents and subjective insights which fuse the moments of the natural and supernatural realms to give us the Logic of Existence. History, objectified one-sidedly, engenders the efficient cause, for, apparently through the cunning of reason, it wends its way in a tortuous manner through the reefs that compose human passions. It entails the formal cause because, as *Logos*, it is the wellspring of the rational structure of the world. It comprises the final cause because Geist 'programs' history to its completion in the realm of ('abstract') freedom.

Hegel is divining that if one figure, a solitary hero, assumes by force a world historical orientation, that one will uncover an inner Logic hidden in the apparent chaos of happenings which elude immediate systematization. This Logic has an eschatological purpose. In the 'mad' genius in the *Phenomenology of Mind*, Hegel boldly acclaims that the time has arrived to demonstrate conclusively that philosophy can forgo the mere claim to love wisdom and eventually *become* actualized wisdom (culture). Philosophy is finally sublated through the emergence of its scientific dimension; it displays the necessity and virtuosity of the truth of the Geist. Spirit makes peace with itself, particularly after externalizing itself in Nature and returning therefrom with both entities the richer for the experience.

The process by which this reconciliation is arrived at initially meets formidable resistance. Development through Nature becomes in Spirit an arduous, infinite series of internal and external confrontations between Mind and Nature, using the contradictions - the objectifications of subjective intentions - which alienate certain possibilities to the advantage of civilization. Geist is 'eternally' (a very ahistoric term if taken in this light) undergoing 'mitosis', that is, rupturing itself, struggling for and against itself mercilessly and relentlessly, with the element of necessity providing the impetus. The struggle is not purely in itself, meaningless, viscous, impenetrable. Only by means of this life and death interplay can Geist be transported to the kingdom of reality and freedom. Geist returns Phoenix-like from the ashes, renewed, that is, refurbished in an amplified consciousness. The logic of the development of Geist is definitively dialectical, as Geist grapples strenuously with what appears to be 'other' than itself - a circumscribing parameter or limit to be surpassed.

This process, of course, is unmistakably deterministic. Marx empties the Hegelian contents and saves the forms (the 'kernel'); the 'System' is thereby transformed to describe and explain a reality which immanently affects the lives of masses of people in a very direct but discordant way. In Hegel, Geist 'returns to itself' where it dissolves by assimilation the specific domain of largely pre-selected objects - sense certainty, perception, and understanding - on its pathway to Reason. In each successive stage consciousness ferrets out direct and immediate knowledge of the object it encounters; consciousness strives to gratify itself and ground itself on stable moorings. In each ascending stage, contradictions and conflicts arise in the quest for immediate certainty which compels one to reach for a higher, richer plane. Hegel demonstrates no less than that the so-called 'hard objectivity' of facts is largely an illusion that because of its actual fleetingness can be absorbed into pure subjectivity. The realization comes about that consciousness, the undertaking to know an 'other' (recognition through subjugation) - an 'other' indeed autonomous of one's own individuated consciousness - is also a knowing of itself.

Hegel gives a new twist to the notion of 'critique'. In the *Phenomenology* it denotes reflection on a humanly produced system of strictures (not just Kant's conditions of knowledge): distorting pressures to which individuals or a group of individuals or the human race as a whole succumb in their process of self-formation. Critique in this sense probably has its origins as early as the Hegel's Jena period (1804). In the *Phenomenology of Mind* he develops a concept of reflection which presents the idea of a liberation from coercive illusions. This idea is perhaps most convincingly and archtypically elaborated in the section which treats of the relationship of Master and Slave.

Hegel depicts the experience of the Slave as the overcoming of a resistance. The Master-Slave relationship is to be grasped in terms of its connection with material things. (It also has become a text-analogue to serve as a design or paradigm for a materialist hermeneutics, as can be seen in the opposition of capital and wage-labor in Marx's follow-up studies on capitalism. Marx, in his methodology, also attacks the problem of fetish commodities, in which the human mind is lost in an 'inverted' reality.) At the outset, the Master, having obtained possession of the Slave's labor, tries to reduce the Slave to a mere instrument of his will, a tool he interposes between himself and nature so that he is shielded from direct encounter with the negative side of things, that is, qualities in things by virtue of which they are experienced as sources of resistance and constraint. This opposition precludes an ideal speech situation because the other party is totally denied access to discourse. It represents the epitome of alienation and the absence of community informed by the search for truth. It is a reflexive and de-dialecticized situation where practical actions degenerate into repetitive compulsive reactions; thought and objects dissolve into each other in fragments; and sociopolitical tensions lie dormant just beneath the surface.

Yet, paradoxically, it is exactly the constraint imposed by the Master on the Slave that opens up for the latter the possibility of growth beyond the given conditions of his existence. It is true that the life of the Slave remains warped to the degree that his aims are limited by the dictates and 'private language' of the Master; he lives in a false reality which has largely been de-symbolized and so 'alienated' of its inherent diversity. Nonetheless, the Slave comes to perceive the objects on which he works no longer merely as the fixity of resistance. By working on them he has brought his human capacities to the forefront for his positive self-evaluation. As the objects are forged by his will and cognition they come back *praxically* to him in his appreciation of his own humanity, which he is able to convey to the alter egos which share his situation. His own labor transforms Nature, and thereby himself, for he now embarks into a world which incarnates his self-assertion as a subject. Here the ways the Slave appraises his situation and acts within it belong inextricably together. A shift in the Slave's 'theory' about his 'human condition' brings about a change in his 'practice', his action within the given context.

The lesson is a general one, since the Master-Slave relationship is for Hegel an avatar of a universal dimension of human life and thought. This facet is what he calls 'negative' - subversive of relations of dominance. The 'negative' connotes those historical forces which conflict with a certain labile form of sociopolitical experience and which act on it destructively, forces which nonetheless stem invariably from the particular social structure they negate and overcome in an individualized and specified 'moment'. So the parts in relation to the merging whole are definitively accessible to the informed mind. Human rationality has a history which comprises the criticism in life and thought of these structures foisted on people by the totality of all specific historical manifestations in a given epoch. The comprehension of critique intimates a particular narrative structure in which the potentialities for development of a given mode of thought or social condition are latent within the very structurization of the initial terms. We have then a 'negation of the negation': even tyranny, however well entrenched, can never suppress the emancipatory interest which a priori always gives the offended party a rational (albeit not necessarily realistic) alternative to be weighed.

Hegel's discussion of self-consciousness, which we will discuss at length, gives as one element this analysis of the Master-Slave relationship, so often alluded to in many genres of argument which mar good human fellowship. We have introduced these materials now because, it turns out that self-consciousness cannot accomplish self-fulfillment without recognition of the 'other' in the other's own orbit of self-consciousness, and this recognition is distorted by violence. But recognition, as Hegel sees it, involves subservience, which devalues and de-structures the relationship in the ethico-social sense, indeed, at the very moment one 'surrenders'. Epistemologically, the very nature of knowing implicates this perverted power relationship in all its one-sidedness. Through labor the Slave masters necessity; through being a parasite the master's sensibilities and cultivation steadily deteriorate into studied arrogance and indifference. In conjunction with Nature, and in coalition with others of his kind, the Slave can grapple with raw Necessity. He is then at the threshold of Freedom because his numbers, informed by understanding, can qualitatively reverse the bondage relationship. This 'logic' involves the change of quantity into quality (a new era of emancipated human relationships).

Here again the power of negativity comes to the fore. Every 'limited' social relationship gives rise to its opposite in the form of the Idea. In the maelstrom of social conflicts, contradictions clear the way toward Freedom. For Hegel, Freedom and Absolute Knowledge coincide asymptotically. The conditions for Unhappy Consciousness will have been banished. In the science of experience, then, the epistemological rupture between subject and object will fuse in an absolute with no 'black holes' between the two moments to substantiate alienation.

To condense a point, self-consciousness persists through a being-in-itself in the social medium in which one is being one-sidedly acknowledged by another self-consciousness of comparable stature (at least initially, for heuristic purposes) at the genesis of the primeval social interaction. Master and Slave thus find their first determination in this combat of social antagonisms, in which each tries to objectify the 'other' totally, in a state of some scarcity of goods, services, or the symbolic insignia of status and class. A fundamental division then arises: the winners and losers are concerned with the 'right' to recognition and the regalia and institutions implied by the situation.[1]

Marx both agreed and disagreed with various points raised by the above discussion. He grasped the dialectic but saw the phenomenological schematic as the very constitution and negative confirmation of class differences and basic structural conditions which required an 'interventionist' theory of knowledge: a praxis to accommodate change by way of self-correcting standards and working rules. For one must ask what is the ontological premise in this deadly quarrel. It can be seen that the 'gaze' of the 'other' limits the Master's sense of self-sufficiency so that he must make this alien genuflect to his will. In exaggerated form, this type of thinking leads to psychopathological consequences, in which the group is made vulnerable by crises so that the 'other' is transmogrified into the 'enemy', who through the mechanism of projection takes on in distorted form the attributes of the false consciousness of the accuser. And only through risking life can one's freedom be validated existentially.

But the first part of the syllogism, with its evaluation put on 'natural' force, is for Marx a notorious hubris, factitiously installed in humanity not because of any cultivated virtues but rather by the resort to violence. This Master-Slave dialectic, as Hegel describes it, produces an interesting turnabout. At the very moment (almost confronting his abstract negation in death) that the Slave is most nearly reduced to nothingness, where he empties himself in the form of the objects which he in a dissociated manner labors on and produces for the leisurely consumption of the Master, he becomes acutely cognizant of the fact that he really has a mind and a creative will of his own: that he is not merely a thing-in-itself, that his essential being in the world is not exhausted by the artifacts he is compelled to produce. It seems that fear, when it reaches a certain limit, often causes a reaction whereby feelings of self-disgust and inadequacy are not internalized but denied and projected onto one's persecutors in such a way that a resolute will (along with all the skills learned during the institutionalization of terror and forced labor) can draw out a solution that brings about liberation - being *für sich* while in consensus with like-minded people. After all, the Slave comes to respect himself again in and through his creative work, in context, with other oppressed Slaves who recognize each other's humanity and pragmatic interests. Also, through time, the Master is enervated by an emergent dependency for his needs on a class coming to self-enlightenment through self-reliance and self-transformation.

Marx transposed this dyadic archetype empirically to the place of class conflicts, and from the resulting analogue made inferences similar to Hegel's. This 'positivist' rendering clarifies the problem of alienation immensely. What has happened is that in the locus of labor, where there seemed to be merely the mind and ideas of an alien superimposed on the truncated personality of the Slave, the latter becomes sensitized sensually and sensuously, so that he rediscovers and rehabilitates himself to the extent of critically measuring the quality of his own mind in common with his muscular power - taking measure of the real order of things. The nub of the matter is that Geist informs one to understand its concrete 'working through' in the very materiality of the world itself, which is not impenetrable to scientific inquiry even by the laboring masses.

Here the Marxist finds a solution to the problem of alienated labor, but only at the level of critical insight, not that of mass action. This becomes the task of the Leninist-type Communist Party, depending on a plethora of yet unexamined factors and interpretations.

It is clear from the Master-Slave paradigm that to categorize Hegel point blank as an arrant idealist with hopeless metaphysical flights into the realm of rarefied fancy is to make an absurd misrepresentation of his system. Marx was more familiar with this idiosyncrasy of Hegel's than he openly conceded: it was heuristically and politically practical to set Hegel up as a foil in order to rationalize his forerunner's thoughts, and he had enough good sense and respect never to carry them to a reductio ad absurdum. He felt no such compunctions, however, with opponents of the ilk of Proudhon and Bakunin. Eventually Marx's discourse of the living with the dead will lead us to his preoccupation with the tension between theory and practice. But Marx and Hegel, in their peculiar ways, were deeply concerned with this schizoid separation, and with respective variations posed an organic unity of the passions and reason, a union characteristic of the Spirit of the age of alienation. Indeed, Hegel, in his *Philosophy of Right*, brilliantly illuminates the nature of the perennial problem, for 'The owl of Minerva spreads its wings only with the falling of dusk' (1967a, p. 13).

Simply assessed, this statement means that philosophy and radical political philosophy must follow the contours of actuated reality with its real actions and agents - ideas being the emanation of the substantiality of a concrete world of, interweaving events, things, and processes. It also signifies that philosophy is in the rearguard of historical events and can only 'lecture' as to its aftereffects. At best, political philosophy can be a prefigurement of ripening events. After the events philosophy can try to redeem the artifacts for culture in order to enhance the intrinsic difficulties in any type of totalitarian planning, whose justification can never rise above the level of the ideological. This whole theme is recapitulated by Theodor Adorno in his *Negative Dialectics*, which views the Holocaust as an unmitigated disaster, rather than a historical event with human agency - and an act done in misinformed good faith, at that. Philosophy is the apprehension of the *Logos* intrinsic in praxis, given that praxis is the crankshaft for Geist. There is an ultimate unity of theory and practice, a wholeness which becomes clearer when one realizes that Geist is in one aspect praxis and in its self-reflective manifestation *theoria*.[2]

Hegel would have been the first to insist that, if one pontificates on unresolved antinomies and conflict, this impasse is a certain indication that one has not yet arrived at an authentic rational account of where one is. Marx's 1843 assault on Hegel in the *Critique of the Philosophy of Right*, a dialectical critique of his 'mentor', could only be executed by one who identified with the Hegelian voyage into rational understanding. The method Marx deploys is one he appropriated in part from Feuerbach as the 'transformative method' (the conversion of objective idealism into a dialectics of historical materialism or dialectical humanism).

According to Feuerbach, Hegelian philosophy embodies a systemic mystification because it inverts the subject-predicate relation. It is crucial that Hegel always transmuted the idea into the subject and the particular, actual subject into the predicate. Geist, or Reason, is not truly a subject because it is not a genesis of agency. It is a predicate, the consequence of real, active subjects. The real subjects have been mistaken by Hegel to be the effects of a *perpetuum immobile* in the Spirit. For Marx this grandiose dialectical sweep of the Spirit is a sham, misrepresenting human needs and interests. Hegel's description of the development of Geist with all its divine attributes, which climaxes in the solution of freedom, is nothing but the negative of the delineation of the development of a mythologized subject with idealized and therefore truncated human traits. The succeeding forms of the self-alienation

of Geist turn out to be nothing but the forms of human alienation.
There has been a relocation of consciousness in Marx's writings when compared to Hegel's. Consciousness in the world can never be anything other than sensuous, free, creative human activity, or praxis. This conceptualization differs from Hegel's mainly in that it is radically rooted in an empirically verifiable picture of humanity in the mode of production. Hegel abstracted consciousness from any particular era to place it above any specifiable society, such as capitalism, in order to portray it ideally in culture. The very nature of his *concepts* put the emphasis on epistemology and ontology. Marx undertook a philosophical anthropology in his 'early' writing which he later discontinued, although certain assumptions about 'false consciousness' remain more or less constant. Lukács and Gabel in this century have, in the Marxist humanist tradition, renewed this effort at a philosophical anthropology. For Marx, consciousness has to be understood as an aspect or moment of praxis itself. Furthermore, the forms consciousness takes in society are defined by the parameters of social practices.

The distinction between objectification (*Vergegenständlichung*) and alienation (*Entfremdung*), which embodies a historical form of this 'objectification', is an extremely important qualification for Marx. It is the basis for his conviction that an alienated condition can be overcome by revolutionary praxis. But his assertion that Hegel failed to make such an authentic distinction is very tenuous, for Hegel nowhere asserts that all manners of objectification are alienation. In any event, the Speculative Mind will prevail. With respect to despair over alienation and its perniciousness, Marx is closer to the above-mentioned stance, particularly in his analysis of fetish commodities and surplus value. But in his dialectical hermeneutics he sets Hegel and his writings up as a 'text' in order to demonstrate some of his methodological presuppositions on political economy. Moreover, a question also arises between them concerning how to redeem these 'forsaken' objectifications alien to human will. Here Marx and Hegel have a confrontation that is apparent to third parties.

Marx is especially hostile to Hegel's conceptualization of Nature as accreted Spirit (also an unalterable objectification in Marx's sense). Nature is rather the inert fountainhead of the objects human beings appropriate and employ or consume to fulfill their needs and wants. Therefore there is nothing absolutely intrinsic to the nature of production which would result ineluctably in alienation, although alienation can be deemed an objectification, especially if embedded in fetishistic forms. The key to Marx is the matter of social organization. For objectification is fundamentally seen as an excrescence of a given sociohistorical formation rent with class contradictions over the matter of the ownership of the means of production. It is only because people exist in a social situation where the objects they produce and the 'system' in which the objects are exchanged and distributed are such that people are plagued by a reversed duality of subject and object toward their own goods, producing that inverted objectification which is alienation par excellence. Alienation is not grounded in any basic ontological category, for it is also a historical condition, and one of Marx's main undertakings was to lay open the structures of the historical scenarios in which objectification culminates in alienation.

With Hegel the comparable situation will give us the skeptical consciousness, which brings the sense of alienation at this level to the fore through demonstrating the power of the negative. Marx vividly depicts this process as it occurs in a capitalist society in his 1844 *Economic and Philosophic Manuscripts*, summarizing his argument with the idea that

> In the viewpoint of political economy this realization of labor appears as the *diminution* of the worker, the objectification as the *loss of and subservience to the object*, and the appropriation as *alienation* [*Entfremdung*] as externalization [*Entäusserung*]. (Marx, 1967, p. 289)

Glimpsing a kernel of the solution, he proposes that:

> Suppose we had produced things as human beings: in his production each of us would have *twice affirmed* himself and the other. (1) In my *production*, I would have objectified my *individuality* and its *particularity*, and in the course of the activity I would have enjoyed an individual *life*; in viewing the object I would have experienced the individual joy of knowing my personality as an *objective*, *sensuously* perceptible, and *indubitable* power. (2) In your satisfaction and your use of my product I would have had the *direct* and conscious satisfaction that my work satisfied a *human* need, that it objectified *human* nature, and that it created an object appropriate to the need of another *human* being. (3) I would have been the *mediator* between you and the species and you would have experienced me as a reintegration of your own nature and a necessary part of yourself; I would have been affirmed in your thought as well as your love. (4) In my individual life I would have immediately *confirmed* and *realized* my true *human* and *social* nature. (p. 281)

So one can perceive alienation primarily as a social category, not an epistemological/ontological one. Alienation can be provisionally deemed to be a set of conditions where negativities characterize the political, social, and economic domains in their very large areas of contextual interpenetration.

For Marx the psychological factors were largely derivative from social structures; here Hegel at certain points evidenced a deeper sensitivity to the anthropological peculiarities of human nature. For the 'early' Marx, human nature is entwined in its anthropological peculiarities and historically articulated by what the teleological mechanism of the species sets as limits to the growth of socio-political organizations. For Marx, then, human nature is a universal classification of generalized human activities with an open-ended, empirical status to be developed by political means as the ultimate ontological guarantee of the *Gattungswesen*. Technology, therefore, will be the means of salvation in gaining hegemony over the 'catastrophic demons' in nature. Marx said this only implicitly, for of course the other side of the coin is that nature could be humanized and humanity naturalized to enjoy the full play of the senses. He did, however, show an underlying tendency which, in his lapses at least, could be construed as seeing the world as being fought over by the forces of good and evil. There is no past golden age to be resurrected. Rather there are future possibilities to be achieved through present revolutionary praxis. In this praxis, collective consciousness radicalizes the world to the extent that what is universal is social and immanent to the senses and an intelligibility innate to humanity is liberated through multilateral, self-determining expressions when necessity no longer inflicts havoc on the species-being.

Here I refer the reader back to the earlier discussion of communism and praxis and Marx's lucid 1843 criticism of Hegel. Marx there clarifies some of the prevailing dogmas of the time with a challenge to speculative philosophy:

> The weapon of criticism obviously cannot replace the criticism of weapons. Material force must be overthrown by material force. But theory also becomes a material force once it has gripped the masses. Theory is capable of gripping the masses when it demonstrates *ad hominem*, and it demonstrates *ad hominem* when it becomes radical. (Marx, 1967, p. 257)

No more than Hegel did Marx come to believe that people are paramountly or fundamentally driven solely by willed, rationalized deliberations. For both of them, history is the playing out of humanity's most profound inclinations and acquired drives. The reason for criticism's efficaciousness is the fact that it informs, exhorts, and caters to those passions. Criticism has the power not of descrying some utopian norm but of bringing people to understand critically what, how, and why they are suffering.

The full complexity of Marx's understanding of Capital has been obscured by academicians who claim he portrayed the human race unidimensionally as purely *Homo economicus*. I will show in later chapters how the label *Homo symbolicus* would be equally appropriate. Political economy actually embodies a holistic approach, for it consists of condenses and distilled substantiations of species activities assimilated to the various facets of praxis.

To think of a pure economic category is to think 'fetishistically', that is, to fall into the fallacy of pars pro toto. Capitalist society values not human character traits in their totality but only the modality of 'having'. For instance, it mis-identifies the virtue of an individual by reductionalistically looking at that individual in a reified market context where the seller must make money, not only in order to survive but to partake individualistically and selfishly of a rationalized status. This type of fetishism holds a person dear because of the person's money-making ability, which is the essence of Capital, not of *Homo sapiens*.

The consequences of Hegel's thought are evident in the text of *Capital*; its very methodology, with historical materialist trappings, is borrowed from him. The purpose of the argument is to demystify all ordinary forms of value in order to perceive in depth how much socioeconomic and political reality has been rendered fraudulent by the capitalist mode of production. This classical critique of capitalism is not a reification of economic laws, but the converse: a demonstration of the malleability of all so-called economic laws, which are really only central statistical behavioral tendencies of the masses, the vogues and modes in which they emerge, the internal dynamic contradictions they conceal, and the ways they are transcended. *Capital* is therefore Hegel's *Phenomenology* concretized, the net intellectual product being an understanding of labor power as materializing Spirit. This is the heart of the argument. So there are really no irreconcilable 'logical' differences between Hegel and Marx, ceteris paribus (though their political conclusions certainly sometimes clash at a deep level). They can almost be thought of as comrades in arms if we envision humanist inspiration from the Enlightenment as motivating both.

Marx usually gives credit where it is due, conceding in his *Economic and Philosophic Manuscripts* that

> The great thing in Hegel's *Phenomenology* and its final result - the dialectic of negativity as the moving and productive principle - is simply that Hegel grasps the self-development of man as a process, objectification as loss of the object, as alienation and transcendence of this alienation; that he thus grasps the nature of *work* and comprehends objective man, authentic because actual, as the result of his *own work*. (1967, p. 321)

This is the phenomenology of praxis. For Marx, this means, in the end, that commodities are social products and that the Value they incorporate (the labor value and its ideological parameters) is nothing more than a materialized form of labor activity. In *Pre-Capitalist Economic Formations* he remarks:

What requires explanation is not the *unity* of living and active human beings with nature, and therefore, their approximation of nature; nor is this the result of a historic process. What we must explain is the separation of these inorganic conditions of human existence from this active existence, a separation which is only fully completed in the relationship between wage-labor and capital. (1964b, pp. 86-87)

The idea of a human species, as found in Marx's early work, is one where all human impulses to perfection inherent in an 'ideal' mixture of genetic constitutional, and environmental conditions are brought forth in a dialectical matrix in order to map out clearly the topography of existence with all its pitfalls. This matrix for examining the terrain of reality can be roughly equated with Hegel's Absolute. Radicalizing this 'Idea' even further in *Capital*, Marx is fairly explicit about passing beyond the vagaries of species-being to class as a natural category. There is a shift in emphasis here from ethical to empirical projects in order to identify the problematics to be remedied by study and action. The alienated human condition is measured (by both Marx and Hegel), not against a transhistorical human nature or a human potentiality trammeled inexplicably by the very phenomenon of alienation, but against the standard of an immanent human potentiality - albeit a potentiality which appears at first in an estranged set of contingencies, permitting one to visualize a previously unrecognized possibility of ultimate polyvalent human self-enrichment.

Marx's thrust, in the end, proved to be the demand for workers' self-management along the lines of the commune to initiate an effective communal form of radical democracy. He praised the Paris Commune of 1871 for its unprecedented revolutionary initiatives arising from the self-organization of the populace. He understood that the failure of the Commune did not arise from within its own constitution. His *Critique of the Gotha Programme* in fact provides another source of specific elements in human nature which could conceivably be included in a 'communist democracy'.

For Marx, then, human alienation is an objective social condition. A critical understanding of the roots and causes of this alienation can provide a foundation for ascertaining real, indeed measurable human possibilities and for envisioning a hitherto unforeseen chance for ultimate human self-transformation. The metaphysical and epistemological ramifications of Hegel's position, on the contrary, resonate with the more classical perspective, which maintains that only by understanding what humanity is - actuality - can one appreciate what humanity can become - potentiality. This is so for Hegel despite the fact that his actuality, contrary to Aristotle's notion, is not transhistorical.

Human alienation, even with the scientific interpretation rendered by Marx, cannot in good faith be deemed a wholly objective 'thing-fact' insofar as the phenomenon is not a brute datum. It is not something directly or even indirectly observed by a 'spectator' at a distance so as not to be affected by the experienced situation. A rather profound methodological note arises here. One might wish to say that certain 'value-free' (*wertfrei*) traits are observed, collected, and classified as alienation, allowing for rendering a logically interdependent value judgment about alienating conditions and how they come to be experienced. These value judgments are determined by class relations. They emanate from vanguard theoreticians of the bourgeoisie who see history as necessity for revolutionary action.

Now this notion of estranged human powers is suspect from the bourgeois perspective of a ruthless empiricism, with its dogmatic staking out of markets for the domains of a tangible reality which can be directly appropriated through conditions simulating 'experimentation'. But it is this very sterile idea of scientific observation and, more comprehensively, the appraisal that cognitive categories are value-free, which Marx and Hegel incisively and persistently opposed as false and damaging, not only to the truth and its very integrity but to the types of action one is willing to embark on. In his unique way, Marx is combating the myth of the given - the idea that one can critically cull what is immediately given to one in cognition from what is built, deduced, inferred, or explained. There is thus a tight affinity between what Marx is laying claim to and what has been claimed by a number of present-day philosophers of both analytic and phenomenological persuasions. Marx would concur that all observation is theory-bound; he would propose that the 'reality' dispensed to one is conditioned by the variations in life forms which have evolved in and through human social institutions.

In order fully to develop our understanding, we must elaborate on Hegel's discussion of self-consciousness, as developed in *The Phenomenology of Mind*, where the alienated contents of objectified human activities have been recovered by the subject and can be freely assimilated in a manner known through the subject's own experience; the subject then need not bow to necessity but can cooperate with others to fulfill common projects to the advantage of all. The culmination of the dialectic of consciousness, then, shows that what was taken as 'other' and 'truly objective' is evidenced to be nothing but a crystallized social-natural form of consciousness itself, one which apprehends itself as the consummation of its own concept. Along with this realization is the conviction that the subject-object polarity does not apply to consciousness and to something other than consciousness, but to two moments (the social and the natural) *within* consciousness. There is then the advent of self-consciousness (*Selbstbewusstsein*).

The initial phase of self-consciousness is the self's certainty about its own self. At this launching pad of self-consciousness the self is embodied as pure and voracious desire and strives to certify its autonomy by the gratification of its desires. From the internal perception of this phase, the world is discerned merely as a source of egoistic gratification. The self endeavors to maintain its integrity by negating all objects, by appropriating them as objects for itself, for its own monadic mediation. The individual is thereby called to the realization not of being self-sufficient in this inauthentic expression of 'autonomous' being, but rather of being dependent on the existence of objects which are 'other' from what the individual is or can hope to be. These objects (which are also individuals with countervailing ambitions) condition the individual, who discovers that the form of consciousness presently achieved is really a highly contingent one. The immediate conclusion in the dialectic of self-certainty is found where the self has undertaken and failed to achieve authentic freedom and autonomy. Herein lies the subverting base for the introduction of the Master-Slave contradistinction we have already discussed.

The ultimate impasse reaches into the epiphanies of the Unhappy Consciousness. But one must not forget that each emergent manifestation seeks a more embracing and substantive freedom grasped by us and for us. (It is 'for' us in that a layer of the Geist, and hence humanity, has been lived through, with all the concomitant traumas which make for a further expansion of the World Mind.)

Skeptical Consciousness, the next decisive stage, incarnates the representation of negative freedom. The skeptic's power and freedom are apparent only in the nihilistic act of defiance and abstracted negation, for freedom here is only freedom in pure, spiteful opposition to something, however venerable or creditable. All institutions, all objects, anything that appears to be permanent, affixed, determinate, must be annihilated. This freedom is anarchy of a simplistic kind which reduces complexity to its rudimentary elements, hence the sense in which revolutionaries must work through this necessary stage.

Unhappy Consciousness makes its debut when there is a tendency toward becoming aware of the contradictory condition which is at the heart of skepticism. Even the condition which was split into two individual self-consciousnesses in the unprincipled struggle between the Master and the Slave is now internalized, in Hegel's understanding, into a single consciousness. Unhappy Consciousness is conceived in an individual's full sensitivity and self-awareness as a contradictory being. So it is 'the alienated Soul which is the consciousness of self as a divided nature, a doubled and merely contradictory being' (1967, p. 251). In the Unhappy Consciousness, then, the self which lives and works through this dialectic is itself sensitive to its own disruption of its substantiality and consequent failure to differentiate in complexity its subjectivity to radically shifting objective circumstances. All the phases of self-consciousness are now relocated in the *Lebensraum* of Unhappy Consciousness, but there is a significant difference in this field of transactions from previous ones. Unhappy Consciousness - or the highly individuated experience of it - is now itself one-sidedly conscious of what we have been observing extrinsically - that it incarnates an alienated soul. Hegel says (with Marx taking it in the spirit of a basis for an epistemological/ontological restructuring of the nature of reality and how it is to be registered), 'It is itself the gazing of one self-consciousness into another, and itself is both, and the unity of both is also its own essence - is not yet the unity of both' (p. 251).

For Marx, the 'Unhappy Consciousness' is the antagonistic and contradictory relationship to which the proletariat finds itself bound in its project to overthrow the bourgeoisie - the 'other' who is legitimacy and respectability. For Hegel it epitomizes the meaning of alienation. Alienation, therefore, for Hegel, is not simply a sundering, a self-deception, or even an affective dissonance of orientation toward something which stands implacably opposed to one. It is the coming to a self-realization by a highly individuated consciousness of one's integral humanity, a humanity in which one is cursed through one's relationship to another like-minded, clashing, contradiction-ridden ego, in a situation of manifold scarcities. Yet this wounded ego needs to undertake the mission to palliate and pacify this inner duality, and to synthesize it with its strident components of denial of the unity of theory and praxis. So the self, in its alienated state, has not yet surmounted its own inner contradictions, particularly between prideful desire and the conditions of scarcity.

This intrapsychic divisiveness is why the praxis of the Marxian solution provides a topography for achieving freedom which is an alternative to the reputed pseudo-solution of the phenomenological realism of the Hegelian method or 'logic'. Hegel's understanding is better mapped out in its detailed schema, but on such a rarefied level of analysis that concretely only individuals who loom large in world history can achieve it, figures like Caesar and Napoleon, who acted momentously on a world historical stage. The average individual does not have such an opportunity. The proletariat, for Marx, want to usher in a qualitatively new era, one whose operational conditions are hidden from view since humanity knows only the conditions of its prehistory. Marx asks us to take a leap of faith in the assumed absence of self-consciousness, *momentarily*.

In the *Phenomenology* itself, Hegel is not strongly preoccupied with applying categorical distinctions to historical movements. Tactically, he digests historical material heuristically in order to portray the developing multitudinous dispositions of consciousness (with the generic implication always assimilating these particularities). The general structure of Unhappy Consciousness is that of a single consciousness sensitized to itself as being both immutable or universal in its input and radically contingent, or individual. Simultaneously,

Unhappy Consciousness strives to negate itself as particular and exigent; it (partially) denies itself as unchangeable; and reason undertakes to mediate this opposition by unveiling the immutable in the embodiment of the highly focused and concretized particularity in the Unhappy Consciousness itself.

This aspiration signals the transcendence of both the stoic and the skeptical approaches. The answer in Hegel lies in unadulterated Reason absolutizing reality and bringing these antinomial matters to resolution. The following passage from the *Phenomenology of Spirit* systematically points out the nature of this solution in the trailblazing mediations from the Unhappy Consciousness to a Reason which captures the vision of alienation succeeded by freedom. Although extensive, the passage gets to the heart of this volume in a rather authoritative fashion.

> With the thought which consciousness has laid hold of that the individual consciousness is inherently absolute reality, consciousness turns back into itself. In the case of the unhappy consciousness, the inherent and essential reality is a 'beyond' remote from itself. But the process of its own activity has in its case brought out the truth that individuality, when completely developed, individuality which is a concrete actual mode of consciousness is made the negative of itself i.e., the objective extreme; - in other words, has forced to make explicit its self-existence, and turned this into an objective fact. In this process it has itself become aware, too, of its unity with the universal, a unity which, seeing that the individual when sublated is the universal, is no longer looked on by us as falling outside it and which, since consciousness maintains itself in this its negative condition, is inherently in it as such its very essence. Its truth is what appears in the process of synthesis - where the extremes were seen to be absolutely held apart - as the middle term, proclaiming to the unchangeable consciousness that the isolated individual has renounced itself, and to the individual consciousness that the unchangeable consciousness is no longer for it an extreme, but is one with it and reconciled to it. The mediating term is the unity directly aware of both, and relating them on one another; and the consciousness and thereby to itself, is the certainty and assurance of being all truth.
>
> From the fact the self-consciousness is Reason, its hitherto negative attitude towards otherness turns round into a positive attitude. So far it has been concerned merely with its independence and freedom: It has sought to save and keep itself from itself at the expense of the world or its own actuality, both of which appeared to it to involve the denial of its own essential nature. But *qua* reason, assured of itself, it is at

peace so far as they are concerned, and is able to endure them; for it is certain its self is reality, certain that all concrete actuality is nothing else but it. Its thought is itself *eo ipso* concrete reality; its attitude towards the latter is thus that of *Idealism*. To it, looking at itself in this way, it seems as if now, for the first time, the world had come into being. Formerly, it did not understand the world, [and] it desired the world and worked upon it; then withdrew itself from it and retired into itself, abolished the world so far as it was concerned, and abolished *qua* consciousness - both the consciousness of that world as essentially real, as well as the consciousness of its nothingness and unreality. Here, for the first time, after the grave of its truth is lost, after the annihilation of its concrete actuality is itself done away with, and the individuality of consciousness is seen to be in itself absolute reality, it discovers the world as its own new and real world, which in its permanence possesses an interest for it, just as previously the interest lay only in its transitoriness. The subsistence of the world is taken to mean the actual presence of its own truth; it is certain of finding only itself there.

Reason is the conscious being of all reality. This is how Idealism expresses the principle of Reason. (1967, pp. 272-3)

There is then the revelation that Reason is the conscious appraisal of itself as being apodictically all reality (Absolute Knowledge). What is rational is real, and what is real is rational. In other words, Reason is both omnipresent and omniscient.

Using the transformative method, Marx takes this elaborate structure of reality and fills it dialectically with the scientific components empirically adduced from his study of political economy. Geist is transmogrified into revolutionary praxis where history marches to the cadence of practical activities which serve as the guideposts to theory so that they mesh. When the theoretical design stands corrected, it improves on the revolutionary movement, such that a historically conditioned 'absolute' in communism can be tentatively postulated and identified as one among several possibilities for the staging ground of real history, humanity being in unity with the predication of all its essences, but yet only at the elementary threshold of breaking these new grounds and with no certainty as to the outcome. In this scenario the forces of production in science and technology have only use value to assure that the cycle of exploitation and social stratification does not start anew. Given the finely balanced nature of the ecosystem, continued exploitation can only bring humanity catastrophe if the very biological conditions which sustain production and reproduction are destroyed. The nature of the legitimation crisis of capitalism with its annihilatory relationship to nature calls for the system's very supersession, since the state cannot institutionalize controls of these monopolies but rather rationalizes their devastating aftereffects by putting itself at their service. In a world with finite resources, Reason calls attention to the fact that zero hour is fast approaching and that these institutional 'lags' in controls are intolerable.

Given this grim picture, social democracy, to the degree that it has and will be discussed in this volume, can be an alternative system to capitalism. Marx would have had no truck with any of its modern totalitarian trappings because, in his socialism, improvised and flexible democratic institutions can work on palliating alienation to the optimal extent compatible with the new level of material organization belonging to the public, while still preserving the degree of anxiety necessary to be a creative being distinct from the masses yet contributing to their culture.

This tendency will be expedited by the vehicle of the so-called 'democratic directorate of the proletariat' (a term with radically different connotations for Marx in his day) in a conciliar world republic. One who has read Marx perspicuously will see that this vehicle subsequently undergoes its own transformation, culminating in the whole annexing the realm of freedom. Thus Necessity is transvalued to a free association among producers with a happier consciousness working for the commonly defined 'good', which will have international effects.

Moreover, this higher materialized mass culture would not repel the intellectuals, who could finally acclaim that they were 'at home'. In this state of affairs, Marx assumed that any Party would be superannuated, for many types of individuals could be persuaded morally rather than by means of cajoling and coercing. Through acculturation, the public could then intelligently and sensibly form an equable historical bloc with a high enough degree of initiative that it could be said that a 'new Man' has indeed come to be the primary factor in the administration of things. The reigning principle will be individuality in the masses or diversity in unity. Only time will reveal whether this formulation offers historical merit or merely escapism into utopian fantasizing of a self-canceling character. But the capitalist alternative, without the element of fantasizing, exudes this self-canceling character even more strongly, into either barbarism or global genocide.

Epistemologically, this chapter has brought us into contact with the concept of Critique as it made its mark on German classical philosophy. The discussion has involved two senses of the word. The first deals with the conditions of possible knowledge. The second is complementary: an interest in expunging those coercive illusions and structural constraints which place systemic and ideological hindrances in the modes of production and thereby obstruct the human self-transformation and capacity to transcend alienation. This is a task as much for politics as for philosophy. Critique wends its tortuous way through the history of philosophy to the concerns of Critical Theory and beyond, originally under the aegis of the 'Frankfurt School' but long since diversified in its problematics among several schools. My conceptualization of 'critique' provides the consistency, coherence, and substance to this volume. My purpose is to follow the development of critique in the twentieth century, introducing a further elaboration of Marx's views at appropriate points.

The next chapter examines how the critical theorists of the Frankfurt School reached the conclusion that Marx did not anticipate that his transformative method could be turned *against* him at a meta-level of interdisciplinary critique. In the historical problematic of late capitalism, both the weaknesses and the strengths of dialectical critique are made evident as portrayed by the role of reason in history and shaped by conflicting philosophical heritages. We must unravel these esoteric heritages and sort out the interests they protect if we are to attain a concrete modality of communicative competency in telling the truth and a liberatory mechanism for living in a realm of freedom. The thrust toward liberation must be global to overcome once and for all the 'external recurrence' of the aggressive 'desire of the Other' which degenerates into mutual suspicions unwarranted by the material condition and ontological imperatives of everyday life.

Marx faltered here in that his theoretical use of reason came up against the historical limits of his era. Our critique, then, must address Marx's construction of critique, which addressed only political economy. To understand alienation dialectically, we must investigate other fields of reified human activity and thought. The result is a meta-critique in which we find alienation in our very mode of linguistic expression. We must therefore examine not just the basis of the modes of production but also the more amorphous superstructure, where communicative competency has been so disrupted that even reflection on the truthfulness of a statement becomes impossible in the face of resistance from the sheer inertia of over-rationalized institutions. The next chapter, then, examines the nature of the problematic as seen in Habermas, who first perceived in depth the issues raised by conflicting Marxist schools of thought. The shift in time perspectives is sharp but necessary. Theoretical, dialectical clarity about the conceptual unity and polyvalence of critique is essential if we are to deal with alienation as a collectively and individually disorganized experience of reality.

In short, I will use an interdisciplinary approach to examine the conditions for human emancipation, freed of ideological distortion. Ultimately, my thought-experiments will pivot on my own unhappy consciousness as I have seen bourgeois democracy die in the universities along with the decline of the polity. The past generation, with the emergence of a corporate hegemonic ideology, recognizes the interests of the new while sacrificing the public good to private appropriation.

Notes

1. I acknowledge the contribution here of Mark Blitz in a private interview on the dissertation on which this volume is based, Philadelphia, May 1975.

2. This unity can be dialectically transformed into freedom by Hegel and Marx along their respective paths, a point which need not be belabored further for the present discussion.

2 Toward a metatheoretical reconstruction of Marxism

As can be seen in the concluding paragraphs of chapter 1, one thrust of this work is that Marx's theory contains an internal, unresolved tension between the dialectical character of his theory of historical materialism and the critique of political economy, on the one hand, and the quasi-reductionist bent of his fundamental anthropological and epistemological tenets, on the other.[1] Some major thinkers, notably Louis Althusser, believe that in his later works Marx forsook his earlier humanistic thrust in order to develop a naturalized human science which could be explained monistically through vulgar materialist precepts. This internal tension between tiers of Marx's theory is a key for understanding certain ambiguities in the theory; for appraising (though not explaining historically) the degeneration of Moscow-inspired 'Marxism' after the collapse of the Second International; and for reconstructing the basic intentions of the sundry elaborated forms of neo-Marxism which have developed since the 1920s in opposition to Marxism in its official, bureaucratized guises.

Significant work has been done at some critical epistemological and ontological points in the development of Marxist thought, in particular, on the problems contained in Marx's conception of labor and the connection of this work with Jürgen Habermas's recent 'linguistic' refashioning of the primary assumptions of historical materialism.

Friedrich Engels's version of 'dialectical materialism' differed substantially from Marx's. In Engels the inclination to interpret historical materialism and the critique of political economy according to the methodological paradigm of the materialist science of his day became quite explicit. With not the French but the Industrial Revolution as a fundamental working model, he interprets literally the movement of socialism from utopia toward science. He elaborates the perspective that scientific socialism would offer a general knowledge of the laws governing historical and social processes - knowledge which would make scientific control over social processes conceivable in the sense in which the knowledge acquired by the natural sciences renders the control and manipulation of natural processes possible.

This 'naturalization' of history is also the real essence of Engels's 'dialecticization' of nature, that is, its 'historicization'.[2] His working assumption in constructing his dialectical materialism is that human nature operates on principles isomorphic to those in nature, so that a single encompassing science would eventually subsume both 'moments'. In contradistinction to Marx's historical materialism, Engels's dialectical materialism is a 'reversal' of Hegelian dialectics.

For Engels as for Hegel, dialectics is the principle of movement for a 'substance' which undergirds the unity of the world and, in particular, the unity of nature and history in their interaction, to give the development patterns of growth under the impetus of capitalism (for Hegel the *Weltgeist*). Engels's naturalization of history imparted a positivist influence to his theory which resulted in a vulgarized mechanistic materialism in which ideas and their organization are simply a reflux from the base. History is then hypostatized into a rigid case whereby subjectivity is reified. Thus for Engels this 'substance' - as the principle of unity - is 'matter' rather than any configuration of mind and spirit. Engels's version of the dialectic now becomes a science concerned with the general laws of motion and development of nature, history, and thought, with no differentiation of levels of analysis.

This ontological interpretation of dialectics can, under materialist presuppositions, lead only to a naturalization of history not to a historicization of nature. We thus have the project of humanity trying to liberate itself from the contradictions of capitalism, which reduces essential human wholeness to one alienated aspect in the quantum of exchange value. Dialectical materialism declines into a naturalist metaphysics which can never be a praxiology for liberating humanity to at least a minimally accepted state of universal communicative competency across cultures. Indeed, it cannot even be practically useful for developing rational, standard rules of operation for a simple society so that all can participate equally in arriving at a working consensus of egalitarian goals within a state of self-determining freedom. Furthermore, this materialist 'dialectics' leads back to a naive-realistic (i.e., pre-dialectical) epistemology. This genre of epistemology we attribute to Engels reached its epitome in Lenin's *Materialism and Empirical Criticism* as a picture-theory of knowledge.

The uncritical, ontological conception of dialectics in Engels's theory no longer supports a critical notion of 'ideology'.[3] 'Ideology' is bound to degenerate into a notion designating the contents of consciousness in their abstract generality. As Habermas indicates, 'the dependence of consciousness on social being becomes a special case of a general ontological law according to which the higher is dependent on the lower and ultimately everything is dependent on its material "substratum"' (Habermas, quoted in Wellmer, 1976, p. 236). Consequently the concept of ideology loses the unique strategic import it has in Marx's theory, that of signifying a 'false consciousness' which in its falseness adequately articulates and expresses the reflection of a 'false' social reality. This is Engels's concept of ideology; it betokens the general relationship between matter and 'spirit' rather than the particular nexus between critique and revolution. Engels then makes a travesty of dialectical materialism by overgeneralizing in such a way that specific details of alienated capitalism are lost in a univocal ontology which has faulty epistemological implications for a general theory of knowledge about the sociopolitical nature of capitalism. If such is the case, theory is divorced from any historical facticity.

Engels's dialectical materialism, although it is a 'reversal' of Hegelian idealism, no longer represents a 'critical' assimilation of Hegelian dialectics; rather, it is a regression to a pre-Kantian ontology. In other words, the nature of the practical reason Engels is working with is explicated in an undifferentiated materialistic medium where human events unfold mechanically and where the human actor/agent is rendered virtually superfluous in the whole of the personality/characterological structure. The real subjects of history are dissolved into the alienated objectifications of a naturalistic theory of knowledge. For Marx, by comparison, dialectics is essentially a historical-anthropomorphic concept; that is to say, dialectical materialism is essentially the product of Engels, who took the liberty of validating it through upstaging Marx's historical materialism. For Marx, the concept of dialectics would not be applicable to nature-in-itself but only to nature-in-relation-to-humanity, the moment which makes history truly dialectical.

Whereas Marx believes his historical materialism embodies a demystification of the dialectics of Hegel, Engels's dialectical materialism is a remystification of materialism. Materialism has become metaphysical again in the process of 'naturalizing' the subject of history and denying agency, will, and praxis to that subject. Engels's materialist metaphysics ultimately rests on the hypostatization of the methods of the natural sciences applied to the study of humanity. Thus Engels mimes the natural sciences, which sacrifice a critico-practical activity which could culminate in the individuated self-consciousness. In an 'ontological disguise', his theory also articulates the epistemological consequences which ensue if the anthropological primacy of the concept of labor in Marx's own theory is taken over-seriously or one-sidedly. Indeed, there is a subliminal relationship between the epistemological reductionism implicit in Marx's conception of labor and Engels's more explicit materialist ontology. The manifest correlates of this materialist ontology are 'objectivist' and 'determinist' interpretations of historical materialism and the critique of political economy - objectivist and determinist interpretations which were actualized practically among socialists during the period of the Second International.

Such objectivist misinterpretations of Marx's theory, where they come to prevail, have almost invariably been indicative of a degeneration of socialist practice. As a rule, they demonstrate that the tie between theory and practice has been severed, and that the theory itself has assumed the ideological task of legitimating the bad politics pursued by a party and its leadership. Paradoxically, objectivist misinterpretations of Marxian theory can be employed to legitimate two radically opposed though equally inadequate forms of 'socialist' practice. The interpretation of this theory as a 'scientific' theory exhibiting the 'iron laws' of development of history in general and capitalism in particular is intrinsically ambiguous. It can signify either that revolutionary politics is unnecessary (because the breakdown of capitalism is unavoidable) or that a technocratic revolution is at hand - that is, that management by an elitist political 'vanguard' is possible, for the domain of freedom will be automatically constituted once the capitalist form of property is abolished and the forces of production developed far enough.

In a nutshell, scientistic misinterpretations of Marx's theory can be used to legitimate opportunism or quietism as well as technocratic activism or Stalinism. Naturally, we cannot hold Marx responsible for the egregious objectivist misinterpretations of his theory in the era of late capitalism with its very different problematics, nor for an absence of practice or a misapplication in policy because of misunderstandings of what he intended. But misconceptualizations can be so gross and ethically reprehensible as to serve to legitimate a poorly conceived socialist practice. An elucidation of the genuine epistemological bases of historical materialism would be in order so that the relationship between social structure and its temporalization can be coherently rendered. This is a task for dialectics.

Marx's theory, critically reviewed, also evinces a systematic ambiguity with respect to the conceptualization of the different forms of 'rationality' which are characteristic of capitalist and socialist forms of production. It appears that the endeavor to resolve this ambiguity must lead in one of two directions. The first is a revision of the categorical framework of historical materialism - a revision which would restore the distinction between technical and practical reason. The second is a modified theoretical construction which restates the manner in which history unfolds by qualifying the differentiation of 'necessary' states with qualitative breakthroughs to mark the unique characteristics of each society as a 'special' instance of the dialectical totality. We will discuss the second possibility and its drawbacks first.

According to the 'inauthentic' interpretation, the 'revisionist' (Bernsteinian) one, the revolutionary construction of a classless society would have to be perceived as a continuation of the process of 'rationalization' which takes place under conditions of capitalist production. This process of rationalization is close to an internal limit of the legitimacy and productive capacity possible under capitalism, with its private ownership of the means of production underwritten by the 'interventionist' state and the employment of state powers to maintain the stability of the economy. But thereby the 'expropriation of the expropriators' and the so-called democratic transition of the dictatorship of the proletariat could turn out inadvertently to be the recurrence of this process of rationalization. And now, beyond the limits set by private ownership, socialist rationalization comes to mean the centralization of planning and an increase in the productivity of labor, with administration of things replacing rule by the people.

This type of socialization process would allow a much lower tolerance for the exercise of rights than found today in constitutional, bourgeois democracies. The importance of these bourgeois rights - testified to by the fact that they are upheld by the courts - is that they have opened up a space of personal autonomy and disalienation between the political domain and the marketplace, thereby permitting demands to be articulated in a radical fashion: nonviolence without the fear of police-type sanctions. Consequently, according to this projection of Marxian theory, the transition from capitalism to socialism could easily accelerate the process of rationalization and bureaucratization from the sphere of production to the whole society (even though late capitalist societies are undergoing a similar but less systematized process). Even the realm of culture would be subsumed. Overall, such socialism would lower political consciousness to a level compatible with totalitarian controls. Yet it is this very projection which empirically spins off from Engels's image of a scientific administration of the social process.

The novel types of events which have occurred between the time of the formulation of the 'Marxist classics' and the present, and the interpretations of these events, show the futility of such a base-superstructure dichotomy. Because of the seemingly independent trajectory taken by the rationalization process in all areas of life, even in what passes for socialism, the perpetuation of alienation is much more likely than the implementation of Marx's genuine humanistic visions and his ideas on participatory democracy. Yet it seems that the categorical framework underlying Marx's theory of historical materialism does not itself support the distinctions which would be necessary decisively to preclude such a 'technocratic' conception of the idealized transition from capitalism to socialism. For example, Marx simply did not fully foresee the distinction between 'reflective' and 'productive' knowledge, or between technological rationalization and rationalization as democratization and emancipation. So theoreticians must be inventive in projecting what Marx would have said if he could have anticipated the present configurations of the sociopolitical modes of production, where the principal contradiction is now in the forces of production which have lost their emancipatory thrust.

Most attempts at this sort of projection are themselves inadequate because for them 'productive labor' is the basic anthropological and epistemological category. The resulting theory is apparently insufficient even as a basis for an adequate conceptualization of the very problems which have been created by the 'deceptive' victories of socialism and the destructive successes of capitalism in our century. In particular, such theory does not provide a basis for analyzing the ideological role science and technology themselves have played in the production of industrial societies, including the radical reconceptualization of what is the very nature of life and its 'right' organization.

These ultimately unsuccessful theoretical attempts begin with Max Weber, who worked under the assumption that the human race is doomed to reified conditions of institutionalized existence. His arch-positivist presupposition was that science, supposedly a means to human ends, had triumphed over the craftsmanship of politics by assimilating the latter to its own modus operandi. But this perception overlooks the fact that science itself is a social form of organization. It has 'autonomy' only where it is hypostatized by academicians who cannot properly conceive that scientific paradigms emerge in part from human experience and are profoundly value-laden and dependent on tradition and culture. Because of Weber's understanding of the dominance of science as disengaged from the societal totality, he grimly predicted that a socialist revolution could only lead to a new triumph of bureaucratic rationality and hence of 'massification' of human existence. Human beings would then be condemned to an apparently impregnable 'shell of bondage' which becomes human destiny.

Weber's prediction is astounding, not because it truly expresses the sweeping force of historical necessity, but because it formulates an antithesis to Marx's conception of socialism while not being unambiguously identifiable as an antithesis. For it is not convincingly clear in Marx himself that technical rationalization, especially where 'authentic', is not full socialist rationality. Thus Weber in his analysis of the process of rationalization and bureaucratization in modern European history, its internal logic of progress, and its dialectical interdependence with the process of democratization, elaborates a problematic which, in one form or another, was to become a focus of attention for neo-Marxist thinking after the early 1920s. What first appeared as merely a return to the 'true' Hegelianized Marx ultimately led to new conceptions regarding the relationships between the critiques of idealism and of materialism, conceptions in which the critique of instrumental reason as an ideology began to play a preponderant role.

With Lukács, the critique of 'technology and science as ideology' begins to replace the critique of the ideology (and moralism) of the theorem about the exchange of 'equivalents' and 'values' (the materialized labor power of present and dead generations of workers) on the 'free' market (the sphere of generalized, estranged labor), which had gradually lost its function as an ideological legitimation of capitalism. Correspondingly, the critique of political economy is now being integrated into a critique of instrumental reason.

Lukács adopted the concept of rationalization from Weber and strove to reinterpret it in the currency of the critique of political economy. The internal dynamics of the capital/labor nexus, which had its genesis in the 'commodification' of labor and which leads to a universalization of commodity relationships, becomes the 'secret essence' and the instrumentality of the process of rationalization. Once a society has learned to satisfy its needs 'in terms of commodity exchange', remonstrates Lukács, 'the principle of rational mechanization and calculability must embrace every aspect of life' (1971, p. 91). The attendant reification of consciousness becomes an essential constituent in the reproduction of capitalist society against the better (but uninformed) sense of its members. Lukács is the first within the Marxist tradition to critique the universalization of 'formal' rationality, not only as grounded in an ultimate irrationality of the system as a whole, but also as a form of ideology which screens as well as legitimates the power relations underlying the tie between capital and wage labor. The individual laborer does not meet the prospective employer as a peer since the lack of equality of condition makes the relationship discontinuous and asymmetrical. In general, social status is quasi-inherited and not improved upon from one generation to the next.

But Lukács's attempt to integrate Weber's analysis of the process of rationalization into the critique of political economy remains ambiguous. On the one hand, he criticizes the specific constraints to which the concept of rationality is subjected in Weber's theory - prohibitions by which questions concerning ultimate 'values' are in principle excluded from possible 'rationalization' or from rational/sensible discourse in an open public forum. From this vantage point, Weber's concept of rationalization can only in an ironical sense be directly related to that of 'reification'. In a discursive analysis, ideology and its embeddedness in particularized material power groupings is best articulated by the critical concept of reification. It exemplifies the extreme subrealist tendencies abstracted from the accentuated consequences of an overdeveloped division of labor which can no longer effectively engage even the forces of production in science and technology which imparted the original impulses toward drastic social change. (Witness Taylorism in its ideology and implementation on a national scale in capital-intensive industries.)

On the other hand, for Lukács the restriction of that peculiar rationality which, by the process of rationalization, becomes a universal form of life, manifests itself paramountly through the incoherence of the system as a whole, that is, by the very lack of integration of the rationalized subsystems into a systemized whole. For Lukács still expects that ultimately an economic crisis will make the incoherence and irrationality of the capitalist subsystems evident for all to decry, and that it will thereby fashion the communalized objective possibility of surmounting the capitalist mode of domination by a kind of voluntarism: an extreme exertion of the will, often with a deep disrespect of objective material circumstances. Like Marx, however, Lukács at this juncture remains muddled about how 'substantive' rationalization (the very life forms and their abstracted organization) could be distinguished from the extension of formal rationalization (bureaucratic rules and regulations which might obstruct the further development of all the forces of production which provide for the multifarious needs of any national society) to the whole of society, especially in its normative ordering. Integrating Weber's analysis simply into the critique of political economy does not give Lukács the forceful countertheses needed to be engaged against the pessimistic conclusion Weber himself drew from his analysis of the dialectical integration between 'democratization' and 'bureaucratization', to wit, that the progression to socialist democracy would be the final triumph of concentrated power among an elite separated from the rest of the population. Lukács's endeavor to assimilate Weber to Marx alters the dialectic into a quasi-positivist pessimism, if not outright skepticism, which imparts to humanity a tragic destiny. It is with some cause that Lukács renounced his 'youthful' *History and Class Consciousness*. It trammeled the mind and will with loosely formulated abstractions while slighting the material conditions under which a viable historical subject was to emerge.

That Lukács's theory foundered is an ironic autocritique related to the fact that his philosophical restoration of Marxism was one which his objective idealism struck down from behind. To the degree that Marx's historical materialism is objective idealism 'put on its feet', the problems created by the latent reductionism of Marx's basic anthropological and epistemological assumptions cannot be resolved by a return to objective idealism. It rather appears that the former reflects a structural flaw which allows the entry of the latter. This interpretation would mean that the positivist elements in the Marxist legacy are intimately interwoven with an idealist heritage which has not yet been overcome in its limitations. Furthermore, according to Lukács, the progressive reification of consciousness reflects the universalization of the commodity form in capitalist society. This universalization of the commodity form corresponds to the internal logic of the capital/labor nexus.

Lukács was one of the first Marxists to emphasize not only the production side of the capitalist phenomenon but its consumer dimension, which itself has undergone commodification, thereby undermining the 'potential consciousness' in class struggles. Because of *political intervention* by the state, the forces of production emerged as the primary process in late capitalism for the generation of capital-intensive labor. There was also a strong element of voluntarism in his thinking about the future of the communist movement (Stalin feared the idea of 'permanent revolution' crystallizing in Lukács's thought, for it threatened the Soviet state in its infancy). Furthermore, Lukács had a strong contempt for the Party and the type of privileges that accompany any hierophantic order.

It appears that at the time Lukács wrote his magnum opus (1927), the conception of an autonomously developing economic 'base' was generally considered archaic by the standards of Western Marxism. Because of the increase in state intervention and the growing interdependence of scientific research and technology and the disaccumulation of capital in the period of late capitalism, the particular configuration of economics and politics which had been characteristic of liberal capitalism had changed. Weber's analysis already referred to a situation in which the mutual penetration of economic, political, and scientific subsystems had become clearly visible. With this new conspecification of 'base' and 'superstructure', the presuppositions of the critique of political economy ceased to be authoritative or even informative.

The new *étatist*-inspired increase of 'formal rationality' which ensued from this new complex, and the threat it contained for the chances of socialist movements, could hardly be analyzed on the basis of those presuppositions about base/superstructure reflexes. To attempt to do so would have led to a sterile methodological operationalism. In particular, Lukács's endeavor to relate the process of reification directly to the universalization of the commodity form prevents him from fully apprehending the peculiar novelty of the technocratic ideology he criticizes, and its peculiar function in a post-liberal phase of capitalism. The ideology of false consciousness is now contrasted to older forms of legitimation, including the bourgeois ideology of just exchange, in that it separates the criteria for legitimating the organization of social life from any regulation of interaction, hence depoliticizing them. Technocratic consciousness does not, like traditional forms of legitimation, have the capacity to control the breakdown of ethical life without a massive influx of corrective policies by the state. The technocratic consciousness can paradoxically thrive under the conditions of anomic breakdown in the civil spheres of society because the state employs its organs for the regulative function of coercing and cajoling the labor force to accept the conditions of a dual patronage, but with the state now the ultimate mediator of conflicts to guarantee that the capitalist interests do not work at cross purposes. Ironically, even policy decisions can be broken down into exchange value. According to Habermas, his revivified bourgeois ideology indicates the 'repression of ethics as such as a category of life' (Habermas, 1970a, p. 112).

The ideological core of this technocratic consciousness is, in Habermas's reckoning, the elimination of the distinction between 'technical' and 'practical'. This consciousness, therefore, can no longer be understood simply as justifying a particular class's interest in emancipation. Rather, as Habermas understands the matter, it affects the 'human race's emancipation interest as such' (1970a, p. 110).[4] The theory of knowledge of both Marx and Habermas contains an essentialism which drives both to assert types of human values which simply cannot be validated by standard, scientific criteria. Correspondingly, the critique of this ideology can no longer simply direct itself to unraveling its particular class content. It rather has, first of all, to restore the very aspect of the 'practical' which all former ideologies still presupposed. In this vein Habermas enriches the theme:

> The new ideology consequently violates an interest grounded in one of two fundamental conditions of our cultural existence: in language, or more precisely, in the form of socialization and individuation determined by communication in ordinary language. This interest extends to the maintenance of intersubjectivity of material understanding as well as to the creation of communication without domination. Technocratic consciousness makes this practical interest disappear behind the interest in the expansion of our power of technical control - thus the reflection that the new ideology calls for must penetrate beyond the level of particular historical class interests to disclose the fundamental interests of mankind as such, engaged in the process of self-constitution. (1970a, p. 113)

Habermas posits implicitly a quasi-transcendental measure to give us an improved picture of the human condition with human beings potentially agents to dissolve the embedded element of destiny from their own historicity.

Unlike Lukács, the first generation of Frankfurt School philosophers were aware that the transformation of the critique of political economy into a critique of instrumental reason reflects the historical progression of liberal capitalism into organized capitalism. They have in common the perspective that, with the emergence of organized capitalism, a closed universe of 'instrumental reason' or 'one-dimensional rationality' was being fashioned which not only overcomes the chances of emancipatory political movements but also threatens the chances for the emancipatory thrust of the suppressed masses as such. Lukács looked at the universal 'reification of consciousness' (the progressive instrumentalization of reason) as not only the expression of an economic crisis (the mechanism of which, while it is approaching its catastrophic denouement, subjects all domains of social life of the commodity form) but also the articulation of a political reorganization of the capitalist economy which successfully fends off its self-destructive inclinations. If so, then the threat posed for emancipatory movements, and for the emergence of 'class-consciousness', will be much more severe than Lukács himself was ready to concede. It would then appear that the political emancipation of the masses, rather than being the 'logical' consequence of the unraveling contradictions of capitalism, would have to be carried out against the internal logic of the development of capitalism.

But for Lukács the Frankfurt School's alternative thesis is problematic. In part, it naturally reflects differences in the historical situation in which Lukács, on the one hand, and Adorno, Horkheimer, and Marcuse, on the other, were writing. But, in part, the emergence of this alternative also seems to indicate an unresolved problem which the above-mentioned theories seem to share with those of Lukács and Marx. For Marx, for example, 'instrumental reason' (i.e., natural science) is the paragon of true, nonperverted reason; for the Frankfurt School philosophers it is the paradigm of perverted reason. For Marx the internal logic of the process of industrialization points toward emancipation; for the Frankfurt School philosophers toward a new manifestation of servitude in technocratic 'liberalism'.

This somewhat perplexing relationship apparently reflects not only the 'outer' historical changes from liberal to organized capitalism but also the 'inner' fact that the latent reductionism of Marx's philosophy of history has been resurrected (although, as it were, with inverted signs) in the Frankfurt School philosophy. Both external and internal nature submit to the knout.

This thematic comes to the fore in Adorno's and Horkheimer's *Dialectic of Enlightenment* (1944). Here 'instrumental reason' becomes the category by which both facets of the world historical perspective are conceived: the revolutionary changes in external nature (technology, industry, the domination of nature) and the transfiguration of internal nature (de-individuation, repression, forms of everyday social domination). Western democratic culture is at a threshold where even bourgeois freedoms become alienable bargaining chips exchanged for security. Given this anthropological and epistemological slant toward 'monism', the philosophers of the Frankfurt School seem to be more radical than Marx in binding institutionalized exploitation to in-depth, psychological variations of self-estrangement. For even if the transformation of external nature fashions the objective possibility of a liberated society, the simultaneous 'revolution' (inversion) of internal nature is likely to destroy the subjective possibilities for any emancipatory practice, since objective conditions must be matched to a real predisposition toward action. The 'reification of consciousness', the price tolerated for the subjugation of external nature, threatens finally to debase the subjectivity of the very subjects who by 'humanization' of nature had intended their own emancipation. To date, then, this kind of 'humanization' needs a reconceptualization to do justice to human potentialities and then optimize them accordingly.

In an ironical way, the latent reductionism of Marx's philosophy of history is here brought to its ultimate consequences. Liberation can now only be formulated as a radical breakthrough of the continuum of instrumental reason. As the negation of instrumental reason, it would be the rehabilitation of external and internal nature as well as the onset of a novel history of human creation of humanity in the fullness of self-consciousness. Marx's theory has a tendency to blur the historical discontinuity which would separate a liberated society from the universe of instrumental reason, whereas the philosophy of the Frankfurt School is in danger of losing historical continuity. This is particularly so with the Enlightenment tradition, which alone could make for a socialist humanism in a practical historical project. Liberation becomes an eschatological injunction, in Adorno, for instance, an injunction to leap across Rhode, because the present is so unamenable to Frankfurt School reasoning. And the past simply cannot be flushed away by rhetorical flourishes.

Habermas explicitly introduces into the theory of historical materialism a categorical qualification which Marx, in his materialist analysis, had always implicitly presupposed. Marx distinguishes two aspects of his epistemology dealing with the self-transformation of the human species: a cumulative process of technological development (forces of production, the labor process) and an emancipatory process of critique and class struggle (production relations). He shows that this distinction can be elevated to a meta-level if an ideal type in 'communicative competency' is abstracted from the moments of 'instrumental' and 'purposive-rational' action to search for a consensual community based on freedom.

To introduce this distinction means to split Marx's construct of 'sensuous activity' into two dynamics which are not reducible to each other: human as tool-making animal and human as speaking animal. Only if we make this distinction, by Habermas's account, can we reconstruct the interdependent historical processes of technological and institutional development in a way which will not blur the differences between technical progress and political critique. Only then can we adequately grasp the peculiar 'dialectic of Enlightenment' (targeted in a series of negativities by Adorno and Horkheimer) by which scientific rationality, which in its historical genesis was a vehicle of critique and emancipation from dogmatically reified structures of domination, ultimately has become a threat to practical reason as such.

To put the point another way, Marx's qualitative distinction between the forces of production and the relations of production has to be renovated in a way which makes the epistemological meaning of his notion of 'sensuous activity' clear by avoiding the implicit reductionism of his theoretically 'working through' the omnipresent conception of labor. Only then will it be conceivable to ascertain the ideological content of Max Weber's concept of 'rationalization'.

Corresponding to Habermas's distinction between instrumental and communicative action, we would have to distinguish between two historically interdependent yet categorically veridical processes of 'rationalization'. In the dimension of communicative action, 'rationalization' would mean processes of emancipation and individuation as well as the extension of communication free of domination. There are cross-currents at work within this problematic. In no uncertain terms, Habermas imparts to us this rich insight:

> While instrumental action corresponds to the constraints of external nature and the level of the forces of production determines the extent of technical control over natural forces, communicative action stands in correspondence to the suppression of man's own nature. The institutional framework determines the extent of repression by the unreflected 'natural' force of social dependence and political power, which is rooted in prior history and tradition. A society owes emancipation from the external forces of nature to labour processes, that is to the production of technically exploitable knowledge (including the 'transformation of the natural sciences into machinery'). Emancipation from the compulsion of internal nature succeeds to the degree that institutions based on force are replaced by an organization of social relations that is bound to communication free from domination. This does not directly occur through productive activity, but rather through the revolutionary activity of struggling classes (including the critical activity of reflective sciences). Taken together, both categories of social practice make possible what Marx, interpreting Hegel, calls the self-generative act of the species. (Habermas, 1971, p. 53)

Again, there is a certain essentialism to this analysis which current social science and ethnological research do not necessarily bear out. The 'self-generative act of the species' calls on our sympathies intellectually. The terminology as it stands is clearly definitional and not explanatory in nature.

Habermas's distinction between 'instrumental' and 'communicative' action is part of an overall attempt to clarify the meaning and the epistemological bases of historical materialism. This project has become necessary as a response to a new historical configuration in which science has not only become a necessary and primary productive force but in which science and technology themselves have assumed the opaque character of an omniscient ideology. The categorical distinction between 'instrumental' and 'communicative' action is meant to reinstate within the theory of historical materialism the division between *technē* and *praxis*, between 'instrumental' and 'practical' reason, between 'productive' and 'reflective', and finally between two different meanings of 'rationalization' and 'emancipation'. The outcome of the previous discussion is that historical materialism is inconceivable without an adequate theory of language.

Habermas's reformulation of the theoretical 'blueprint' of historical materialism has epistemological implications, but let us here indicate in a general way how this approach is tied to the Marxian program of a simultaneous critique of idealism and materialism. A 'linguistic' reformulation of historical materialism must be intimately interwoven with a critique of positivist materialism if new theoretical ground is to be broken. The study of contradictions in capitalist society must be shifted from the means of production to its primary locus in the forces of production, where science and technology have been reduced to instruments of the corporate structures of the state and culture in producing a submissive consciousness through the most subtle and advanced methods of manipulation. Marx of course had no idea of the 'political economy' of the mind (in particular the unconscious, which can be harnessed by the state to serve its often perverse purposes), which today puts a special emphasis on public education to prepare individuals for the travails of the highly technical division of labor.

It must still be demonstrated through linguistic studies that the above-mentioned theoretical reconstruction is hospitable to historical materialism, that is, that the approach indicates a critique of idealism as well. In actuality the critique of idealism takes place in two interlocking steps. The first step has already been implemented once the problematic of a philosophy of consciousness has been changed into that of a philosophy of language. The importance of the study of language lies in what it reveals about the substantive forms of social reality which provide the material infrastructure for a communicative competency. Distorted communication, where comprehensibility, veracity, and truthfulness are denied or distorted, will belie the false consciousness of the reigning ideology of a falsified reality so that legitimacy questions about state and corporate economic policies can be raised in an intelligent manner. This transformation is an achievement not of historical materialism but of twentieth-century philosophy, perhaps its most perdurable achievement.

We must now refer to a tradition which goes back to some of the neo-Kantian philosophers at the end of the nineteenth century and was continued by hermeneutic, phenomenological, and linguistic philosophers in the twentieth. These philosophers held in common the belief that the natural and 'cultural' sciences build on different methodological and epistemological bases. Habermas's dualistic interpretation of Marx's conception of 'sensuous activity' directly mirrors this epistemological fault. But his life project has been to transcend this variation in theory formation by first affirming a meta-level to redefine the terrain to be covered in a new conceptualization of the problematic.

According to Habermas, the distinction between instrumental and communicative action signifies two different, quasi-transcendental frames of reference in which reality is 'constituted' and knowledge's boundaries extended. Instrumental action, considered as an epistemological category, embodies the cognitive interest in 'nomological' knowledge. In the orientation of communicative action, reality is constituted as a community of actors and speakers who seek a commonality of polyvalent practices for forming rules and norms which govern behavior at every level of the society in such a way that through an open circuitry of feedback even the internal perception of each actor is changed to resonate a greater degree of 'truthfulness'. While instrumental action coincides with the polarity of subject and object, communicative action corresponds to the reciprocity of ego and alter ego. As epistemological categories, consequently, 'instrumental' and 'communicative' action embody the distinction between nomological and epistemological knowledge, on the one hand, and hermeneutic and reflective knowledge on the other. Together they also reflect the methodological distinction between 'natural sciences' and *Geisteswissenschaften*. This distinction was first expounded by Wilhelm Dilthey and some of the neo-Kantian philosophers at the end of the nineteenth century. Habermas has drastically modified some of their ideas to fit his purposes in the formulation of explanatory principles within his own ideational construct.

In manifold ways, Dilthey and the neo-Kantian philosophers strove to achieve for the historical sciences what Kant had achieved for the natural sciences. They undertook to develop a 'Critique of Historical Reason' which would adumbrate the conditions of the possibility of a science of history. These endeavors, none of them conclusive, had one guiding beacon. They made it understandable that a critique of historical reason cannot succeed from within a philosophy of consciousness, since the outcome can never be better than a critical idealism. Hence Dilthey, the most important of these philosophers, moved in his later writings from a psychological toward a hermeneutic theory of the *Geisteswissenschaften*. The neo-Kantians in contrast, particularly Heinrich Rickert, undertook to retain the vantage point of transcendental philosophy and to import Kant's critique of knowledge to the field of historical methodology. This project made it clear that an extension of Kant's method of critique to the province of historical knowledge is ill-conceived, even if we assume that Kant provided an appropriate solution with respect to the natural sciences. The object of the historical sciences cannot be construed as being constituted in a sense analogous to that in which for Kant the basis of the natural sciences is constituted by a transcendental object. Kant posited a universal ego which ideally knows the object world through a priori categories as essential and necessary for the very nature of that phenomenal naturalism in its being 'grounded'. For in history, as Hegel postulated, the 'transcendental' subject of this constitution itself is posited penultimately in an empirical realm.

That this statement is paradoxical from the standpoint of a transcendental theory of knowledge is certainly not a decisive counterthesis against dialectical reason, but it does outline the limits of transcendental philosophy. Rickert's attempt to surpass Kant and yet maintain the standpoint of a transcendental critique of knowledge was bound to fail, for reasons similar to those which affected Husserl's later attempt to reconstruct the transcendental constitution of the alter ego and the human 'lifeworld'. Both endeavors ultimately took for granted what Hegel in his critique of Kant had already spurned as an inadequate and uncritical epistemological presupposition, to wit, that a solipsistic transcendental consciousness and its acts can provide the ultimate ground for a theory of knowledge.

The 'transcendental consciousness' of Kant that irked Hegel was the dualism which split science and culture into different entities, one knowable through empirical methods and the other through a medium which placed a premium on subjective moralism and gave rise to logical antinomies. A critique of historical reason cannot be premised on Kant's distinction between the 'transcendental' and the 'empirical', since, in the sphere of historical facts, the 'empirical' itself assumes a transcendental signification and the 'transcendental' in turn assimilates an empirical meaning. The transcendental subject is pinpointed as a moment of 'superstructurally' *derived* truth, implying a fissure in social reality, rather than as the ground of empirical intersubjectivity, where all the involved subjects can *objectively* posit and determine the values which have embodied their circumstances in definable, materialist terms: terms which can be subjected to reevaluation and structural modification in an ever widening circumference of the public realm.

Hegel's Geist reconciles the subject/object dichotomy, particularly between humanity and nature. His *Philosophy of Nature* has Nature as a primary, not a subordinate element in the dialectic. In Marx, humanity finds essentiality in nature inadvertently, by exploiting it through institutionalized forms of violence which plunder its resources and create social stratification. Here Marx succumbs to a historical positivism which finds this exploitation historically necessarily in the name of progress; hence we have the 'second nature' in its opaque givenness to humanity through the 'gift' of socialization and civilization. A dialectical reason would reconcile the two by existentializing nature, so that humanity would be at home in a world where 'Apollonian principles' prevailed.

Overcoming the aggressiveness impelled by reified institutions would allow the formulation of a correct praxiology; a 'third nature' would emerge which would allow human self-determination with this 'reconciled' and totalized realm of freedom.

From the perspective of a transcendental critique of knowledge, we have here at first glance an unresolvable dilemma. Two ways out have become prominent in the history of philosophy: the Hegelian and the empiricist. Hegel redeems the Kantian intentions toward a transcendental critique of knowledge by overcoming transcendental philosophy as it was designed by his other notable precursors (Fichte, Schelling, et al.). 'Absolute consciousness' becomes the ground of Kantian 'nature' as well as of empirically derived intersubjectivity, that is, of history made by human beings themselves, not by impersonal forces. The empiricists save the moment of historical contingency which is separable from human subjectivity and voluntarism by reintegrating the transcendental subject into Kantian 'nature'. Hegel immolates the contingency of history because consciousness can never be happy; the empiricists dispense with history since dealing with it means exploring its indebtedness to past generations and their contributions, which are still ongoing in that they are always in a certain sense present to us. Hegel saves the critique of knowledge (including the subject); the empiricists save the object of this 'otherness' of knowledge by sacrificing the critique of knowledge and the subject which is immersed in the very formulation of its object domain. Hence, in this transcendental sense, the concepts of the empiricists are never really adequate to the object they claim they are investigating validly and dispassionately.

The first step toward a solution is already assumed once we make the transition from a philosophy of consciousness toward one of language. The peculiar relationship between subjectivity and intersubjectivity, between the 'transcendental' and the 'empirical', which for transcendental idealism remains an unattainable objective, becomes comprehensible once we grasp these dissonances in the unique structure of communication in ordinary language and in actual speech situations where there is a working consensus. The critique of historical reason consequently has to be nurtured in terms of a theory of ordinary language where conflicting problematics find a univocal denomination in order to redeem expectable and reasonably derived promises derived from a pragmatic universal competency among the participants.

The development of Dilthey's thinking (from a psychological toward a hermeneutic theory of the *Geisteswissenschaften*) and that of neo-Kantian philosophy (e.g., Cassirer) and phenomenology (Heidegger) clearly show the internal necessity of this transition toward a philosophy of language for any post-Hegelian philosophy of language (and consciousness - conscience, morality, and ethics) once the problems of history and historical knowledge had moved into the center of attention. It is equally clear that a critique of historical reason could not be developed from within the tradition of analytical philosophy until the empiricist and 'constructivist' conceptions of language had been subjected to trenchant criticism and a philosophy of ordinary language had emerged (Wittgenstein).

Habermas's categories of 'instrumental' and 'communicative' action provide two quasi-transcendental frames of reference in which reality is constituted and knowledge accumulated. Since the possibility of a transcendental critique of historical reason has been questioned, this notion needs amplification. A transcendental interpretation for instrumental action appears to have had a fairly lucid signification, a meaning Marx hinted at in sporadic glosses, particularly in his *Theses on Feuerbach*, and which has been developed systematically by Charles Peirce in his pragmatist reinterpretation of Kantian philosophy. If so, it becomes clear that the relationship between instrumental and communicative action, considered as epistemological criteria, must be an asymmetrical one. For, while the category of instrumental action has a transcendental significance in the Kantian sense, this outlook cannot be equally applicable to that of communicative action. The 'constitution' of a world in the behavioral system of instrumental action is essentially mediated by a process of material production, but the (transcendental) constitution of 'nature' is not at the same time the *production* of nature. Communicative action, on the other hand (i.e., symbolically mediated interaction), signifies not only a transcendental frame of reference in which historical reality is constituted as an object of knowledge, but also the empirical process by which this historical reality is literally generated (constituted, in the ontic sense) as historical reality.

To be more exact, instrumental and communicative action indicate two different dimensions in which the evolution of the human species occurs. The constitution of society and of nature as objects of knowledge is at the same time the creation of an experienced world: the world of historical reality. This statement has two immediate consequences. Against the grain of Kant, the epistemological constitution of the world is one moment of a historical process. Against the empiricists, it is an essential structural feature (not just an empirical facet) of human societies that they have a conception of the world, themselves, and their praxiology, a conception which makes each of these dimensions unique as it tries to actualize idealizations of the future by embodying the hopes of humankind found in the cultural repository of its symbols.

Habermas finds new uses for the term 'transcendental' which separate him from the older philosophical traditions. The term must be considered an epistemological articulation of historical materialism. Although, as we have indicated, it presupposes the transition from an transcendental-idealist toward a hermeneutic or linguistic critique of historical reason, the second step in the critique of idealism has yet to be taken. This is the critique of hermeneutic and linguistic idealism. Hermeneutic and linguistic philosophers have denied the (epistemological) possibility of developing a theory which would allow us to reconstruct historical developments and social changes by systematically transcending the self-interpretation of a society and its de-totalized individuals. They have denied the possibility of reconstructing historical processes as processes taking place 'behind the backs' of individual agents who systematically deceive themselves about their mutual social relations and the meaning of their own actions. In brief, they have questioned the legitimacy of the constructs of 'ideology' and 'false consciousness', which in fact are fundamental ideas of historical materialism. This attitude would ultimately mean that we are not responsible for making our own future after it has transpired but can attempt to recall it.

Their fundamental thesis would run approximately along the following lines. Since social and historical reality is essentially 'symbolically mediated', that is, a linguistically organized reality, the objects and data of social and historical analysis are meaningful in themselves, and are given as objects and data only insofar as they are meaningful. It is precisely their intrinsic meaningfulness which constitutes them as possible objects and data of analysis. This pre-given, inherent meaning of the objects and data of social analysis is determined by their place in a specific 'language game'. Hence, in the last instance, the only adequate method of analysis is that of 'hermeneutic understanding' and of linguistic analysis respectively. The ultimate standard for such an analysis is the very 'language game' which is under investigation. With regard to the understanding of social reality, there is thus no appellate court beyond what the individuals concerned could say about themselves in terms of the motivations, perspectives, attitudes, and even biases which result in very stylized conformations for each individual. The idea is then to tease these materials and individuals together to make a dialectical society.

It is certainly possible to think that this hermeneutic position in the more recent controversies, which can be identified with Hans-Georg Gadamer, Michel Foucault, Jacques Derrida, Jean-François Lyotard, and Richard Bernstein represents a radical empiricism in disguise. Bernstein, deeply influenced by the American pragmatic tradition, advocates a more tolerant debate. Let us see whether he himself will expand his horizons to unknown scholars who are not 'politically correct'.

It will be all the more paradoxical, then, if hermeneutic empiricism is critiqued as a form of idealism. But this is Habermas's strategy. By his reasoning, the idealism of the hermeneutic position consists in the fact that it itself is the expression of an inadmissible idealization, to wit, that the linguistic organization of social relations and of the motivational base of social exchange has supposedly reached a state of 'perfection'. The assumption Habermas critiques here is that the linguistic organization of social interaction gives an intrinsic ideal norm. The actual structure of social relations (communicative interaction in his terminology) in any given historical period has deviated to a greater or lesser degree from this norm, so abstractly and idealistically that the theoretical import of fundamental societal upheavals has been ignored. The direction of history is then a product of its vectors of facticity and essence. To paraphrase Marx's dictum that all previous history has been a chronicle of class conflict, we could now say that all previous history has also been a process of recording events of 'distorted communication'.

Such a claim and the corresponding critique of hermeneutic philosophy could ultimately only be vindicated through a general theory of knowledge, a theory of language which would have to be a theory of 'undistorted' as well as 'distorted' language and the concomitant power struggles. The critique would have to reveal the conflict of interests in the relations of production which necessitates mystification of whatever legitimizes the order, for instance, of a confabulated ideology.

Habermas has been working on variations of such a theory as his life project, while still acknowledging a certain indebtedness to Marx, who is not a dead dog. Habermas has been developing a critique of hermeneutic idealism to transcend the methodological dualism of 'natural science' and the *Geisteswissenschaften* in order to integrate them into historical materialism. At this juncture we should be able to understand that instrumentalism has been an oppressive manifestation of a systematic misuse of the forces of production, one which has permitted the capitalist class to distort communication at the social cultural level through ideology. There is as well the false consciousness of a primary sort which emanates from the inverted reality of everyday capitalist work and life experience.

The 'theoretical practice' of the social sciences has never been in congruence with either the methodological paradigm of the natural sciences or a pure 'hermeneutic' discipline. Correspondingly, philosophically oriented social scientists as well as philosophers of social science have with cause eschewed the alternatives which they were offered by radical empiricists on the one hand and radical 'hermeneutic' philosophers on the other. We must explore why these tendentious alternatives are rejected by existing social science practice and what this rejection means for the competing claims of hermeneutic and empiricist philosophy. We can then explore its consequences for actual social science practice.

According to Habermas the hermeneutic position rests on a mistaken idealization concerning the linguistic organization of social relationships. This idealization can be 'unpacked' in three ways, as concerning (1) the consistency and comprehensibility of communication; (2) the potentialities of communication; and (3) the character of the basic agreements operative in communication. These senses convey the idea of the mystification of objective reality and the way philosophers as actors report certain intentions in their own scholastic communities which cannot be properly organized through their socialization process. Taken together, these three idealizations elevate the existing self-interpretation of groups and individuals to a position where they cannot be questioned; furthermore, they block questions concerning the truth of basic beliefs in the justice of fundamental norms from ever being raised by the hermeneutically geared social sciences. There are manifest and latent 'meanings' which (as Habermas would elaborate) are systematically excluded from public discourse and which therefore can appear in communicative interactions only as shards of an abused text, tailored to fit the reigning orthodoxy.

Mihailo Marković once told me that he feared to use terms like 'historical materialism' and 'dialectics' because he would then be denied access to academic audiences in the United States (1976). If one is forced to speak in value neutral terms, then a good part of the tradition of Western philosophy will be relegated to extremist sectarian groups which will give it a 'bad press'. Inconsistency and incomprehensibility of 'communicated' meanings indicate a systematic inhibition of communication. This occlusion of communication is in turn indicative of a deceptive appearance of consensus about the beliefs and norms considered valid and adequate in a society. That beliefs are taken for true and norms for just seems to imply the idea of free consent. But consent cannot be free if it is based on a systematic inhibition of communication, because either political institutions or the social setting exhibit antagonism toward any 'deviance' which could remotely precipitate new levels of demands on corporate entities or government organs (which share essentially the same outlook on policy making and pool of personnel and other resources). We may rather assume that, under conditions of systematically 'distorted' communication, basic beliefs and norms, that is, the basic 'rules' of the 'language game', serve in part to hinder as well as legitimate the very distortion of communication which makes a non-enforced (i.e., 'rational') consensus about beliefs and norms impossible.

It is precisely because of the internal relationship every society has to the idea of truth that social science can question the self-interpretation of groups and individuals and expose both the delusion and the 'rational' function performed by false consciousness: ideology as rationalization. If Western Marxism can undergo de-occultation at a structural level, then hermeneutic philosophy could be integrated into a historical materialist perspective which could be authentic critique. Naturally, the social phenomena of domination, exploitation, and repression will not be miraculously transformed into merely linguistic realities. Nor will they, as forms of distorted communication, have that label written on their face. Rather, they must be rooted out and purged. This overall theme would then have to be carried over into a sociology of power elites if we are to have any clues as to the character of the relationship between controlled institutions of communication and the kind of politics which sustains the bond.

Empiricist materialism and hermeneutic idealism both rest on tacit assumptions concerning the structure of social reality which are equally inadequately conceived in the light of their role as partially rational subsystems of thought. The empiricist assumes that human history will move within the sealed circuitry of animal behavior, the hermeneutic idealist that history already corresponds to the *imago* of a fully formed humanity (this latter evinced in the spoken and written words which give us clues to the nature of the reality in which we find ourselves immersed). Neither can come to an adequate conception of history. Both, for complementary reasons, can be shown to take the human condition as given once and for all, as it could have been consummated only at the beginning or the end of history.

Herein lies the reason the empiricist and hermeneutic conceptions of the social sciences each contain just a part of the truth. Hermeneutic analysis is necessary because any historical reality is inherently meaningful in that it takes place in an ordered, working social ensemble, juridically operative in some political time and space. The objectifying methods of causal and functional analysis are necessary because the meaning of history still condenses 'behind the backs' of the agents who are making it, while leaving behind a spectrum of artifacts which influence others to render some kind of judgment since their lives have been restructured. To the extent that these others are compelled to be inquiring, new actors are thus brought into the playing scenario.

Historical materialism, properly articulated, is only the philosophical germ of the above 'truths'. Their many-sidedness will be explicated later in this volume. The rich connections between natural science, with its instrumental perversion of reason, and humanity's aborted psycho-biological needs will be examined in the chapters below. The discussion will also address the psychopathology of everyday life in late capitalist society and how the proliferation of reifying theories in the professional academic world accentuates the alienation of this falsified reality veiled by ideology.

The scientific objectification of social reality treats the latter as a kind of 'quasi-nature' which cannot of its own accord purge itself of the interpretive procedures of a hermeneutic analysis. Since the elemental data of social analysis are constituted as meaningful-in-themselves, they are accessible only as units within the totality of a 'language game' accessible to a universe of actor/agents. If this game is a parochial one - as is invariably the case, for instance, in cultural anthropology - then hermeneutical analysis is a necessary first step in the identification and classification of data. But this peculiar dependence on the objectifying methods of the social sciences, on hermeneutic principles and the social scientists' level of previous understanding respectively, does not unequivocally establish the meaning of the scientific objectification of social reality. For this objectification (i.e., causal, statistical, fundamentalist, or systems analytic analysis) can still be partially understood by analogy to the objectifying methods of the natural sciences.

Social science then offers a knowledge which can be used 'technologically' for the purposes of social engineering. In the latter case the objectification is a finalized one. The practical application of theoretical and empirical knowledge presupposes a separation between two classes of individuals: social engineers who treat society as quasi-nature and the people who are possible objects of their social engineering. This possible meaning of scientific objectification of social reality manifestly corresponds to Engels's vision of social science as an instrument for controlling and steering social processes. On the other hand, the scientific objectification of social reality can also be understood as a tool for a hermeneutic interpretation which rises above the self-interpretation of the 'objectified' individuals to gain access to meanings of their conduct which have been suppressed and hence are hidden from public view, that is, the buried 'depth grammar' of their modalities of interaction. This depth grammar is exemplified, for instance, in the internalized relationships between capital and wage labor as crystallized around the explication of authority relationships in the family and the concomitant socialization and training of a unique individual for the purpose of reproducing that society by the dictates of a historically specified social and technical division of labor. In this reified social context a quasi-natural collective force emerges over the life processes of the members of the society. It adumbrates a distortion of communication belied by the 'surface grammar' of their behavior: an element of violence and repression has been injected into the society so that individuals by force of economic necessity must submit to a process beyond their understanding and control. In this instance the exposure of quasi-causal mechanisms operating behind the backs of individuals does not serve an interest in social control or social engineering but rather in the abolition of such mechanisms. It serves the 'de-naturalization' of history (if 'nature' is understood in a narrowly Kantian sense as the being of a thing insofar as it is regulated by general laws), as the self-conscious objectification of social reality from a quasi-transcendental position wherever this serves an emancipatory interest.

This type of objectification is essentially critical theory which penetrates the armature of the surface grammar of a language game to unravel the quasi-natural forces incarnated in its depth, that is, definitely patterned grammatical relationships and norms indelibly imprinted on the individual psyche and collective mind. One such manifestation is the need to consume conspicuously to make one's status evident while at the same time suffering from deep insecurities. These possibly compensate for the 'wounds' inflicted in the Oedipal power struggle in the bourgeois family, in which the child submits only to emerge as a neurotic adult whose drives are harnessed to the generator of capitalism with its manipulable instrumentalities. When the provenance of these relationships and how they come to be warped is made manifest and explicit, their aura of sanctity can be grappled with in a more tangible fashion. Critical theory has an indigenous *telos*: to enhance individuals' consciousness to their situated and estranged reality in an attempt to cancel social domination and repression. It purports to achieve a communication free of domination. Such a critical social theory can become 'practical' in an authentic sense only by initiating processes of self-reflection, a self-reflection which would be the first step on the road toward practical emancipation. The truth claims of a critical social science will ultimately only be substantiated to the extent to which the emancipated individuals can still recognize their own past in the objectifying analyses obtained from social scientific theories.

From the point of view of the Marxian linguistic reformulation of social science as critique, the project arises of interpreting the critique of ideologies as the materialist equivalent of the idealist critique of knowledge. Clearly the critique of knowledge in both the Kantian and Hegelian sense signifies more than a mere surpassing of false consciousness. It also, paramountly, means a reflective, inward looking rebuilding of authentic knowledge with liberatory potential. To be sure, Marx hoped to overcome the 'problematic' of the idealist critique of knowledge once and for all by transforming it into that of a materialist critique of ideologies. But his elaboration of the categories of historical materialism is faulty exactly at the juncture where he is blind to the dimension of a self-reflective rebuilding of knowledge together with the idealist presuppositions of the critique of political economy. Marx's categorical lens only divulges to us that history is not the history of Mind (objective and subjective Mind would be impossible without an internal history). To elaborate the epistemological infrastructure of historical materialism consequently implies the demand genuinely to transform rather than forsake the problematic of an idealist critique of knowledge by uncovering it as a dimension of historical materialism itself.

A materialist theory of knowledge can be negatively heralded by the demand to avoid the shortcomings of both empiricism and transcendental and absolute idealism, while retaining the respective truths of these disparate and mutually antagonistic positions. Roughly speaking, this materialist theory of knowledge will have to assimilate three critiques: Kant's of empiricism, Hegel's of transcendentalism, and the empiricists' of absolute idealism. Reconstituted in this manner, Marx's programmatic demand for a naturalism which is teased out from both idealism and materialism (and comprises their unifying truth) now looms as the extraordinary demand for a materialist version of the *Phenomenology of Mind*.

To produce this materialist version has been the life work of the Italian Marxist Enzo Paci. Reflection on the epistemological bases of historical materialism impels us to fashion a novel conception of the programmatic significance of historical materialism. If the critique of knowledge is to be assimilated to a materialist theory of history, historical materialism has to be developed as a materialist phenomenology of the Mind (an issue treated in chapter 1). It would be a materialist theory insofar as it deals with the irreducible empirical constellations of conflict which delineate the starting point and boundary conditions of the evolution of the human species. It would be a phenomenology of mind in that it takes into account the fact that the reproduction of the human species is mediated by language, that is, by the ideal of truth, and thereby its cultivation would be intertwined with an internal progression of a concrete, historical 'consciousness of freedom' while exploring the optimal conditions for imparting to it a specificity for all in the public realm where all could partake of a freely determined 'communion'.

Borrowing a bit from Noam Chomsky, Habermas has elaborated on the idea of a 'universal pragmatics' which would provide the metatheoretical basis for the reconstruction of both individual and social processes for development. Insofar as 'genetic' explanations mean a rational rebuilding of the implicit knowledge of adults, they assume an epistemological meaning as well, as genotypes for an empirical phenomenology of the mind. If this is so, then the theoretical articulation and genetic reconstruction of the implicit knowledge of adults can no longer be located in the inter-relationship of theory and metatheory. Strictly speaking, neither can be articulated independently of the other. While this arrangement may not create a major difficulty for developmental theories of individuation, it does pose a problem for the materialist reevaluation of cultural evolution.

Habermas's theory of pragmatic universals tries to explicate the universally valid pragmatic rules which every 'competent' speaker-actor has mastered. Not least, it tries to offer a linguistic articulation of the traditional notions of truth, freedom, and justice, an explication which strives to demonstrate that these ideas are operative in any symbolic interaction. Correspondingly, the theory of pragmatic universals also provides a transcending of the idea of 'systematically distorted communication', an idea of basic importance for Habermas's reinterpretation of historical materialism. If a systematic reconstruction of cultural evolution, a materialist phenomenology of mind, is to be possible at all, then it must be possible to develop such a theory. But it is not clear how far it can be developed as a quasi-transcendental pragmatics of communication prior to and independent of the work of actual historical reconstruction.

In this context, historical materialism remains a project for political action-orientation theoreticians, an impulse, to some extent utopian, to liberate the 'global village' from the endemic recurrence of escalating levels of violence and impotence which to date have denied humanity sovereignty over the contours of its future. Pragmatically, this vision would have to be implemented on a world scale to assure the even dispensation of justice. Although the plan could be institutionalized in federated regions and communes, one major problem to its even being reasonably proposed is the pernicious 'residues' and 'derivations' of nationalism, which have an even more divisive international effect than class conflict.

If Habermas's 'hunch' is right (and not just ethically attractive), this project of liberation springs forth from deep wells of aspiration in the evolution of the human species, as an interest in emancipation, transmitted from generation to generation, which, like an invisible but latently explosive force, is operative in the very reproduction of human societies and the novel ways they can be designed. To say that it is an interest in emancipation means that in the linguistic organization of social relations reason functions as a material force for the revolutionary self-transformation of humankind. To say that it is an interest in emancipation means that human needs and interests, once they have become symbolically interpreted needs and desires, are necessarily brought into a pragmatic relationship with the liberatory ideas of truth, freedom, and justice in a world and nature without domination and exploitation (see Leiss, 1976). Thus 'Absolute Spirit' would fulfill the thrust of a critique toward self-reflection and reconstruction of world institutions so that the human species would subjectively know its own ultimate limitations and then lay rightly conceived plans to optimize objectively the possibilities of the human condition (Marković, 1976).

Notes

1. An example of this kind of tension can be found in the *Grundrisse*:

> The communal substance of all commodities, i.e., their substance not as material stuff, as physical character, but their communal substance as *commodities* and hence *exchange values*, is this, that they are *objectified labour*. The only thing distinct from *objectified* labour is *non-objectified labour*, labour which is still objectifying itself, *labour*

as subjectivity. Or, *objectified* labour, i.e., labour which is *present in space*, can also be opposed, as *past labour*, to labour which is *present in time*. If it is to be present in time, alive, then it can be present only as the *living subject* in which it exists as capacity, as possibility; hence as *worker*. The only *use value*, therefore, which can form the opposite pole to capital is *labour (to be exact, value-creating, productive labour)*. This marginal remark is an anticipation; must first be developed, by and by. Labour as mere performance of services for the satisfaction of immediate needs has nothing whatever to do with capital, since that is not capital's concern. (1973, pp. 271-2; emphasis in original)

2. Engels in *Dialectics of Nature* gives us an example of his version of dialectics modeled after the sciences:

Probably the same gentlemen who up to now have decried the transformation of quantity into quality as mysticism and incomprehensible transcendentalism will now declare that it is indeed something quite self-evident, trivial, and commonplace, and so they have been taught nothing new. But to have formulated for the first time in its universally valid form a general law of development of nature, society, and thought, will always remain an act of historic importance. And if these gentlemen who have for years caused quantity and quality to be transformed into one another, without knowing what they did, then they will have to console themselves with Molière's Monsieur Jourdain who had spoken prose all his life without having the slightest inkling of it. (1940, pp. 33-4)

3. Engels's rank positivism comes to the fore in a rather blatant ideological fashion in a passage in *Socialism* when he attacks Kant:

This 'thing in itself' is beyond our ken. To this Hegel, long since, has replied: If you know all the qualities of a thing, you know the thing itself; nothing remains but the fact that the said thing exists without us; and when our senses have taught you that fact, you have grasped the last remnant of the thing in itself, Kant's celebrated *Ding an sich*. To which it may be added, that in Kant's time our knowledge of natural objects was indeed so fragmentary that he might well suspect, behind the little we knew about each of them a mysterious 'thing in itself'. But one after another these ungraspable things have been grasped, analyzed, and, what is more, *reproduced* by the giant progress of science; and what we can produce, we certainly cannot consider as unknowable. (1935, pp. 14-5)

4. Habermas pursues this theme ingeniously:

> For the interest of self-preservation cannot aim at the reproduction of the life of the species automatically and without thought, because under the conditions of the existence of culture this species must first interpret what it counts as life. These interpretations, in turn, orient themselves according to ideas of the good life. The 'good' is neither a convention nor an essence, but rather the result of fantasy. But it must be fantasied so exactly that it corresponds to and articulates a fundamental interest: the interest in that measure of emancipation that historically is objectively possible under given and manipulable conditions. As long as human beings must sustain their life through work and interaction subject to instinctual renunciation, in other words under the pathological compulsion of deformed communication, the interest of self-preservation necessarily takes the form of the interest of reason, which only develops through critique and confirms itself through the practical consequences of critique. (1971, pp. 288-9)

3 Philosophy and critico-practical activity

Karl Marx: Contemporary social science and his 'early' writings

Now that we have an understanding of the range of problems to be theoretically de-reified in our broadened historical context, we can return to Marx and Marxian theory with the advantage of these new theoretical weapons to critique capitalism on a broader front. To overcome Marx's limitations a meta-critique must be developed.

Marx notes approvingly that the demand has been articulated to abolish philosophy because of its ineffectiveness in the resolution of practical problems. But the demand is wrongly stated as Marx put it in his 'Contribution to the Critique of Hegel's *Philosophy of Right*' because '*you cannot abolish philosophy without realizing it*' (1972a, p. 17; emphasis in original). This comment can serve multiple purposes in explicating Marx's understanding of philosophy. *First*, it focuses on his interest in certain traditional philosophical preoccupations and his belief that for the most part philosophy does not contribute to a practical solution of these problems. Marx's concern with the conditions of human self-development is intimately related to Kant's interest in a possible realm of ends or Hegel's discussion of universal recognition. But Marx denies any claim that traditional philosophy in and of itself could help us reach this goal: it offers theoretical solutions to practical problems and practical problems need practical means. In Marx's terms, the proletariat must be set in motion so it can solve its own problems and those of humanity: 'Material forces can only be overthrown by material force; but theory itself becomes a material force when it has seized the masses' (1964a, p. 53).

What is required, therefore, is a theory which can and will convert itself into practice and hence realize the goals of philosophy. Still, if philosophy must be realized in order to be sublated and if the theory which can accomplish this is philosophical, then Marx's theory must be a form of philosophy, at least in part. This is not to imply that there is no substantive difference between Marxian philosophy and other traditional perspectives. Nor, according to Marx, does it mean that the theory which is to bring out the realization and abolition of philosophy is itself philosophical and ought to be comprehended as such, though to recognize even this facet requires forsaking the idea, presupposed in many approaches to Marx, that his theory is opposed to these traditions and fundamentally disparate from any value the traditions enjoy.

Since the raison d'être of Marxian philosophy is that reality is only imperfectly rational if measured by the standard of human self-actualization, an important element in this orientation is its critical posture: 'Criticism has plucked the imaginary flowers from the chain, not in order that man shall bear the chain without caprice or consolation but so that he shall cast off the chain and pluck the living flower' (1964a, p. 44). The theory is critical in several senses. First, it takes other philosophies and philosophy in general to task for their historical failure to play a positive practical role and their conservative or ideological function in support of the status quo. Second, it rebuffs a bourgeois society for its failure to meet human needs and actualize human aspirations. It criticizes classical economic theory for its portrayal of capitalism as both intrinsically good and quasi-natural, indeed so natural that it identifies money, a fetish, as a real attribute of human virtue. (Indeed, from this perspective, it is difficult to apprehend how one would want to pass beyond a historical state in which most individuals are alienated, especially if one does not understand the circumstantial and historical nature of being.) Third, Marxian philosophy is self-critical, since awareness of its own relationship to the social context is necessary if the theory is to summon change in this context.

Marxian philosophical anthropology, of which only the most fragile outline can be sketched here, is a theory of humanity in terms of human activity, which varies as a function of the social context. Impressed by Aristotle, Marx held that man is a *zoon politikon*, a social being, who exists within or with respect to a social milieu. Human relationships to others, their needs, and their projects are mediated through their activity, as an outcome of which individuals produce their products, themselves as definite individuals, their social relations, and the entire human world. To needs correspond potentials and the activity which mediates their interaction. Marx distinguishes two forms of needs: reproductive needs, which humanity holds in common if individuals are to continue to exist, and human needs, which are non-reproductive and derive historically from the social context. To needs which can be met, there must correspond appropriate potentials. The human species is differentiated from other animals by the general capacity for human needs, sometimes called 'species-being' in the earlier writings, and even by the capacity for 'play', which supersedes conventional norms to anticipate a better future where sensibility and reason are reconciled.

Even from these brief details, some general conclusions about the relationships between the more coherent aspects of Marx's position and the philosophical heritage may be drawn.

Three distinctive traits of Marxian philosophy are monism, a categorical scheme, and philosophical anthropology, all of which are general features of nineteenth-century philosophy. *First*, Marxian philosophy is monistic because of its relativization of the subject/object relationship, signifying an explicit repudiation of Cartesian dualism. On the one hand, human beings as natural beings exist alongside other beings in nature. On the other, through their activity they engender themselves as individuals, their products and cultural artifacts, and their social world. The above is not to deny that Marx apprehends the existence of an independent given, that is, nature; rather it is to assert that human beings and their social milieu comprise a unity (what Lukács keenly called an identical subject-object) out of which both they and their world emerge. This attitude humanizes nature and vice versa.

Second, Marx's theory incorporates a categorical approach. The most extensive discussion of this theme is to be found in the *Grundrisse*. Here Marx suggested that there are only two approaches to experience. One can begin with concrete or real existence, then progress to abstract relations, in order finally to reconstitute the real in terms of abstracts. Conversely, one can begin from abstract categories such as population, in order to reconvene the real directly. Because of his critical pose with regard to Hegel, Marx contended that the latter methodology is the right approach. The difference is that for Hegel the categories, although merely thought-out categories in the abstract, are immutable in the relationships generated. In Marx's perspective, categories are locked into real social conditions and how these conditions are patterned, and must be recomposed as society changes in its underlying characteristics. It follows that no absolute categorical framework can be anticipated in its details, because to do so would be to deny human freedom. Philosophy hence forfeits its special status as absolute knowledge and becomes instead a contingent categorical analysis of a mutable social reality, an analysis which must be constantly reviewed to mirror changes in social reality.

Third, philosophical anthropology is another important tie between Marxian philosophy and the German heritage. An explicit notion of humanity as human individual is notably absent in Kant's thought, although several partial perspectives out of which one might fashion such an outlook are engrained in his understanding of the subjects of sundry fields of human endeavor, such as knowledge and ethics. Yet it was Kant who authored a work of philosophical anthropology, *Groundwork of the Metaphysics of Morals*. Beginning with Fichte, although the major avatars of German idealism include a more explicit concept of humanity in their theories, their major emphasis is on the human epistemological capacity. This is so even for Hegel, whose *Phenomenology* may be read as an answer to how knowledge is possible if the conditions and process for its attainment are indistinguishable. Marx's assessment of humanity through the problematic of alienation, on the other hand, is the preoccupation with the early writings which directly influenced his overall development. After this early period, the epistemological element fades into the background, as it is no longer of interest for its own sake. Hence, although Marxian philosophy includes a theory of humanity, its change in epistemological emphasis somewhat loosens its tie with German classical philosophy.

In terms of the overall goal of Marx's theory, it is clear that its conceptual or philosophical aspect needs to be supplemented by an objective or empirical analysis of the social forces which govern human social interaction. He notes in the early essay, 'The German Ideology',

> The first fact to be established, then, is the physical organization of these individuals and their consequent relationship to the rest of nature. (1967a, p. 409)

This fact suggests two aims for what may be called the objective side of the theory. First, there must be an apprehension of the structure and function of the contemporary, but alienating and hence non-fulfilling, social context. From Marx's perspective, this requires a theory of the genesis of society, since what is can be understood only through an understanding of how it came to be. Second, there must be an analysis of the practical conditions which would be needed for a change to another and potentially more rewarding form of social behavior. Since the Industrial Revolution, social forces have been organized principally as a function of underlying economic relationships. It follows that the real social forces which govern human interaction can best be understood and studied on the politico-economic plane, to see how corporate industrial interests have created a new character structure, largely incompatible with a democratic outlook on life.

The key to the entire analysis/synthesis in Marx's works is the explanatory power of the commodity-fetish thesis. Commodity fetishism personifies the productive factors of capitalism and hypostatizes the social, human activities which make the system possible. Hence Marxian politico-economic theory in general can be fully accounted for in terms of two constituents drawn from Marxian philosophy, the general categorical approach and the specific category of activity, which derives from his philosophical anthropology. The notions of exchange and use value then show us how the basic purposes of humanity as *zoon politikon* at whatever level of development are subverted by this reificatory process in capitalism. The production and exchange of commodities is an essentially circular process which can be expressed in the formula C-M-C' (commodity-money-commodity), where the commodity value is both the initial and the terminal point of the process. The circular process described by this schematic is the dual condition of bourgeois society's continued existence and self-development. Through this process capitalism produces and reproduces its own necessary conditions for self-perpetuation, while at the same time the constant interconversion between commodities and money results in the expansion of capital through the accumulation of surplus value. He points out in *Capital*:

> Capital-profit [profit of enterprise plus interest], land-ground rent, labor-wages, this is the trinity formula which comprises all the secrets of the social production process. (1967b, vol. 3, p. 814)

Marx's categorical scheme begins presenting a series of categories adequate for the interpretation of any and all facts of capitalist economy. Then it defines the inner composition of the categories in terms of external controls. Accordingly, in the first of the *Paris Manuscripts* Marx indicates that private property, arguably the linchpin of bourgeois society, emanated from alienated labor. He further remarks that from these two factors all other categories of political economy can be sifted:

> As we have discovered the concept of *private property* by an *analysis* of the concept of *alienated labour*, so with the aid of these two factors we can evolve all the *categories* of political economy. (1964a, p. 133)

This strongly suggests that alienated human activity in work is the central category of Marxian political economy, the category in terms of which the balance of the theory both must and can be validated. Since the concept of work is arrived at by studying the forms of human activity in the logically prior philosophical anthropology, Marxian 'science' is premised on Marxian philosophy.

The above point was made most persuasively in the *Manuscripts*. An analogous conclusion follows if we consider the final form of Marxian political economy as discussed in *Capital*. Here work is the logically antecedent category both from the perspective of bourgeois society, the system of social relations which owes its existence to commodity production, and from that of the worker whose existence is contingent on it. In terms of commodity production, Marx observed simply that value is work. In the end, such an analysis/synthesis entails plumbing the whole production process. Furthermore, work is the logically primitive category within the 'trinitarian formula' above. Although land can be embodied in terms of capital, capital itself is constituted and accumulated as the crystallization of work expended within the mechanisms of production. But, even in *Capital*, Marxian science is based on Marxian philosophy. This conclusion should not be taken as a demonstration that Marxian political economy is nonscientific because of its philosophical association, but rather as a proposal that the scientific side of the theory must be grasped in terms of an underlying philosophical tendency.

Marx's theory can be delineated as an enterprise to comprehend the real possibility of human social development and self-actualization through a theory of human capacities and their consummation through goal-oriented human activities. Since the rupture between concept and object and theory and action can never be fully overcome, its possibilities must be examined at two levels. Empirically, Marx studied the social forces which condition the contextual manifestation of human activity and provide the locus for human self-expression. The conceptual side of the theory needs to be confirmed by massive empirical studies, particularly in the realm of power elites, but politico-economic analysis is conceivable only in the currency of a philosophical theory. The two facets of Marx's position are fused through his concept of human being as activity.

Let us return to two related points, the radicalism and novelty of Marx's position. As stressed earlier, Marx's intention is enmeshed in the relative innovations of his position. His concern with human affirmation of generic capacities comes from a major leitmotif of the nineteenth-century German legacy. In his theory of humanity as activity, he further articulated an approach whose proximate source is the philosophy of Fichte.

Marx's position is unique in two critical respects. First, it integrates philosophical and scientific, conceptual and empirical approaches to experience within a single *Weltanschauung* to an extent not found elsewhere in the tradition. Other philosophers like Fichte and Hegel have a politico-economic facet, but no other presentation in the German tradition combines philosophy and science to the extent that Marx's does. Second, Marx's theory is future-oriented in an extraordinary manner in that his 'realism' was so empirically bound that he could not be accused of indicting 'utopianism' in the sense Joseph Gabel finds so repellent. Whereas Hegel's perspective, for instance, at times appears metaphysically optimistic, Marx's empirical analysis of real conditions offers a more substantial basis for the changes he expected for theoretical reasons. Much of the novelty in Marx's stance can therefore be inferred from its radical premises projected into a concrete universal 'dream' for humanity.

It is regrettable that tyrants like Stalin used Marx's name in vain in their recipes for creating an 'instant millennium' *now*, as they ignored the real historical contradictions which dictated moderation for the 'democratic' dictatorship of the proletariat. This behavior parallels the 'magical' thinking of much of schizophrenic thought. At the collective level the result is a kind of mass delusion which checks people's responsibility to take their places in their own history-making in the face of the 'bad will' objectified in an all-knowing, all-seeing Party which revolves around the whims of one man, charismatic but psychopathic.

Karl Marx: Contemporary social science theory and his 'mature' writings

Beyond classical German philosophy, Marx engaged in the critique of political economy to validate the discipline of historical materialism in which a sociology of knowledge about the fetish mode of commodity production has a practical import.

In Karl Mannheim's perspective, what is perceived as knowledge within a society is constitutive for what the society as a whole perceives as its reality. Although Mannheim's later orientations have been rightly criticized by other social theorists, this transposition from epistemology as a category of inquiry to knowledge as a potentially dialectical category simultaneously appropriating description and critique is crucial. There are various modalities in the transposition from epistemology to knowledge. The question concerns that of the validity of our knowledge of the social order. Mannheim employed the term 'constellation' for the structure of knowledge as it appears in a particular epoch. A contemporary constellation, for example, deals with approaches considered in the context of the interaction of language, symbol, and society.

The real subject matter of the present volume begins with Marx, and his presence underlies the argument throughout. The terms alienation and fetishism appear often at strategic places in Marx's corpus, the latter eventually replacing the former. If the task of the sociology of knowledge is to understand the source, character, meaning, and distribution of knowledge in society, the transition is not unimportant; hence the attention paid to it in this chapter. By plumbing the depths of alienation and fetishism, we can specify not only that which gives cohesion to the social order but also that which enables a certain linguistic specificity about the forms or totality of culture. To make this proposition tenable requires a definition of 'symbol' and illustrates its relationship to language. Symbols provide the context in which ordinary language is a social form: the former provides the basis for the belief structure in society, the latter is simply the representation of that belief structure.

The phenomenological theory of language, given its propensity for factors of subjective appropriation and constitution, has argued against structuralism that the real meaning of language is to be found in the subjective act of constituting linguistic forms when language is appropriated by the subject. In this sense, it has not merely undertaken to argue that language is a medium of human intention and desire. It has also claimed, against both structuralism and analytic philosophy, that the human use of language means more than the scheme of environmental determinism which can be derived from those positions. It has wanted to claim that the 'essence' of language is something more than either 'game' or 'grammar', that language has meaning in relationship to the phenomenological subject. To make this claim, it has distinguished between ordinary and symbolic modes of human usage. It has contended that the ground of ordinary language usage is to be found not only in the appearance of the language itself but in the symbols which are at the base of culture and which in turn unify in a common meaning the meanings articulated in the culture.

In order to ground this thesis, its proponents have turned to poetic and literary (Heidegger), religious (Ricoeur), and social (Schütz) forms of symbolic expressions for documentation. Hermeneutic methodologies (which help reveal the real signification beyond immediate appearance) have shown that behind ordinary linguistic appearance is a latent value structure which provides the ground for the structure of meaning as it is available for subjective appropriation. In relation to Marx, there is a desire to ascertain a level of meaning beyond the immediate and the relative, and in this sense it is possible to conclude that Marx does not engage in analysis comparable to language-game theory (analytic philosophy). One could contend that language game theory, since it presupposes social determination, would be analogous to Marx's theory of the materialist determination of consciousness. To a degree such an analysis can indeed be made. At this level Marx would spurn the relativity of language game theory in linguistics. A like analogy could be made with respect to structuralism. Here Marx's position would eschew the assumption that the material base (or in this case the structural or grammatical base) functions in total independence of consciousness.

But phenomenology, under the illusion that consciousness is free for subjective appropriation, operates in the absence of an adequate social theory. As stated, this is the presupposition of the so-called free individual in civil society, that is, the individual subjectively free and objectively determined.

Therefore great caution is needed to suggest that the quests for meaning in Marx and in phenomenology are analogous. They are so to a certain degree. The phenomenology of language makes a distinction between ordinary language, language as a mere tool (Ricoeur), language as monovalent (Eliade and Ricoeur), language in the common sense world (Schütz), and the symbol as a latent multivalent cultural form which gives cohesion to the social order. Alfred Schütz perhaps perceived this most clearly when he contended that symbolic forms are the unity experienced between the sundry regions of meaning: common sense language and experience, scientific experience, poetic experience, and religious experience. In Hegelian/Marxist terminology, given that perspective, the symbolic embodies the totality of meaning inherent in the social orbit. But phenomenology could only make symbolic forms a matter of subjective appropriation. Because of this tendentiousness, as Marx would say, it would not examine the 'base' from which the symbol is secreted. Equally, it could not, because of its commitment to idealistic epistemology, make a historical decision regarding the symbolic structure which was to be the center of meaning in a particular society.

The terms alienation and fetishism are not symbols but, respectively, a term referable to experience and a critical term attached to a particular attitude within a society. The symbolic structure Marx eventually decided was representative of the total social order was the commodity-form, that central term with which the first volume of *Capital* begins, that form which articulates the totality of cultural meaning and also can be the focus of critical-practical activity. The term alienation originates in Hegel. Marx read it through Feuerbach, who provides an intermediary between Hegel and Marx and who, by applying the term to religion, let Marx move beyond him to apply it to secular culture per se. Hence it is possible to see a developing line of criticism, from religion as the embodiment of meaning (Hegel), to religion as the assimilation of meaning (Feuerbach), to secular culture as the incarnation of the alienation of human meaning (Marx's early perception), to Marx's later determination of the exact symbolic form which portrayed that alienation.

Marx had begun to throw off the ballast of Feuerbachian criticism as early as his 1843 'Critique of Hegel's *Philosophy of Right*': 'For Germany, the *criticism of religion* has been largely completed; and the criticism of religion is the premise of all criticism' (1972a, p. 11). The category of political economy is added to what Marx would later call the 'secular base' as the underpinnings of civil society. It is of some significance that this early dissertation on the commodity-form is associated with the term 'alienation' or 'estrangement':

If then the product of labour is alienation, production itself must be active alienation, the alienation of activity, the activity of alienation. In the estrangement of the object of labour is merely summarized the estrangement, the alienation, in the activity of labour itself. (1972b, p. 60)

To make the case that alienation is the basic articulation of human activity, Marx needed an originary anthropology, an expression of a situation in which alienation would *not* occur. (It is necessary here to stress that alienation is a derivative or negative term.) Most crucial for this apperception is the Feuerbachian perspective of the human individual as an embodiment of the species-being. According to this profile, the reality of individuals must be taken into account in and through their expression as members of the species or in relation to other people. The activity which best demonstrates this relationship is that of production, producing to meet the needs for survival and producing new needs and correlative credos. Herein lies the normal process of objectification arising from the creation of the objective world, that is, a world which becomes objective through the interaction of people and nature, the humanization of nature. In social and political terms, this points to the origin of institutionalization, for in this activity people fashion the institutional orders which are the representation of this activity. It can equally be said to be the genesis of culture:

> It is just in the working-up of the objective world, therefore, that man first really proves himself to be a *species being*. This production is his active species life. Through and because of this production, nature appears as *his* work and his reality. The object of labour is, therefore, the *objectification of man's species life*: for he duplicates himself not only, as in consciousness, intellectually, but also actively, in reality, and therefore he contemplates himself in a world that he has created. (1972a, p. 62)

There is a false derivation from normal objectification: the alienation found in the 'tearing away from man the object of his production', what will in Marx's later work be identified as the separation of labor from the means of production under the category of commodity production. We may ask what conditions make possible this separation, which leads to the illusion of the free individual in civil society. We see that alienation at this juncture not only takes on an imaginary form in production but is also perpetuated by the political form of civil society. This in turn is based on the legitimation of private property and hence private interest, which will expunge the social foundations of human actuality. If we assume from Marx's critique of Hegel's *Philosophy of Right* that the criticism of religion has already been duly secularized, then the spawning beds of alienation must be found at the depths of secular culture itself. In one of the most profound of all Marx's statements, in his 'Theses on Feuerbach', he finds the root of the problem most fitly described by the conflict of forces and ideas raging at that particular historical moment:

> Feuerbach starts out from the fact of religious self-alienation, of the duplication of the world into a religious, imaginary world and a real one. His work consists in resolving the religious world into its secular basis. He overlooks the fact that after completing this work, the chief thing still remains to be done. For the fact that the secular basis detaches itself and establishes itself in the clouds as an independent realm can only be explained by the cleavage and self-contradictions within this secular basis. The latter must itself, therefore, first be understood in its contradiction and then, by the removal of the contradiction, revolutionised in practice. Thus, for instance, after the earthly family is discovered to be the secret of the holy family, the former must then itself be criticised in theory and revolutionised in practice. (1972c, p. 108)

The question then is what in the symbolic depth of secular culture gives industrial society its basic cohesion. The question itself clearly requires a highly sophisticated command of methodology, for Marx must not only make this symbolic totality manifest but also expose it as a falsification, as the irrational expression of social cohesion in secular society. He not only characterizes capitalist culture but critiques it at its root.

Marx had resolved, along with some of his Hegelian colleagues, that Hegel's conception of philosophy was a false one. That philosophy should or could be the explication of what was implicit in religion, the rationality of religion; that reason should ultimately find its confirmation in the development of the state; these were assumptions with which Marx came to differ. This dissonance led to a double critique, of religion on the one hand and of civil society on the other. Yet the critique was really not conceivable apart from Feuerbach, who found religion to be the expression not of reason but essentially of irrationality, an irrationality which could be made intelligible only as alienation. Marx would make a further decision, that in capitalist society the source of alienation could no longer be identified with religion. Rather, alienation was rooted in the irrational form of production, which, because of the structure of civil society, falsely attributed the right of control to ownership, to the holder of property - a most sacred institution. This assumption led to the critique of idealism and materialism along with empiricism.

In the beginning there was the commodity. Marx decided that the commodity-form is that form through which all the meanings of capital society are to be mediated. The need to study the commodity as the symbol of meaning in capitalist society becomes further apparent when one considers the options from which Marx had to choose. The classificatory system of political economy would have given cost or price as the basic element of value, and would not have unearthed the structure or meaning in capitalist society as a whole. In Marx's terms, it would not have revealed the 'base' of the society which could then be criticized. The categories of *Geist* (or subjectivity or self-constitution), from the perspective of idealism, had already been denigrated as manifestations of the consciousness of civil society. Religion, the negative object of Feuerbach's materialism, had been spurned in the name of development in the history of the very society he chose to analyze. That is, the analysis was no longer necessary because society was secularized already. Finally, the utopianism of French socialism lacked historical perspective: it failed to understand the actual historical development of production in capitalist society. So the choice of the commodity as that which expresses capitalist society as a whole was the most strategic theoretical choice. Marx in this instance impressed on the world for all time *his* theory of capital.

The first three volumes of *Capital* follow this choice consistently. The first volume begins with a discussion of commodities and their characteristic as use-value and exchange-value in capitalist society. It endeavors to demonstrate how commodities are transmuted into money through a process of quantification which results in making all commodities equivalent (equal to a third form). Once quantified, commodities can be transformed into capital through the generation of surplus-value. For surplus-value to become the property of certain individuals or a class, it is necessary that labor itself be turned into the commodity form of wage-labor. Finally, for capitalism to grow, the commodity which is transformed into its money form must be subject to greater and greater accumulation and concentration, leading to greater exploitation and the imposition of market conditions on 'colored folk' in need of 'Christianization' abroad. So the three volume tour de force of dialectical exposition on the state of the political economy is the centerpiece of classical Marxism, to which Marx himself had reservations as to its 'coming'.

The project in volume 2, manifestly the description of the process of circulation of capital, is to demonstrate how that circulation is only conceivable on the basis of repeated renewal of capital investments in the process of commodity production, that is, productive capital. For money to circulate, it must be transformed back into commodities, into wages and materials, into labor power using human capital and the cost of the means of production, so that new commodities are created through the bringing together of the means of production and labor power. This buildup creates a surplus value through the metamorphosis of the commodity back into money, which allows the circuit of capital to proceed anew. Furthermore, no matter from what vantage point the circuit of capital is studied, the reproduction of capital at higher surplus value is its reason for being. No matter whether it is from production, from circulation, from the perspective of money-capital or commodity-capital, the end result is the alienation of labor power from its 'rightful' possessors or creators.

Volume 3, which endeavors to detail the 'process of capitalist production as a whole', attends to the thesis that for capitalism the rate of profit is the motive power:

> The capitalist does not produce a commodity for its own sake, nor for the sake of its use-value, or his personal consumption. The product in which the capitalist is really interested is not the palpable product itself, but the excess value consumed by it. (1967b, vol. 3, p. 41)

Because Marx chooses to challenge political economy on the ground of its concentration on price and profit, which excludes considering the overall picture of the economy, he presents the commodity as the basis of capitalist production, the rate of profit, and the rising rate of exploitation. The direct discussion of commodity production and its centrality is reserved in that volume for the keystone chapter, 'The Trinity Formula':

> In the case of the simplest categories of the capitalist mode of production, and even of commodity-production, in the case of commodities and money, we have already pointed out the mystifying character that transforms the social relations, for which the material elements of wealth serve as bearers in production of these things themselves (commodities) and still more pronouncedly transforms the production relations into a thing (money). All forms of society, in so far as they reach the state of commodity-production and money circulation, take part in this perversion. (1967b, vol. 3, pp. 826-7)

It is important to note that these 'things themselves' are commodities, and to add that the point of the trinity formula is an open assault on the capitalist assumption that it is money, not the activity that is invested into the production of a commodity, which generates value.

Most important, the commodity begins as a singular phenomenon in volume 1 and has a paramount centrality in the entire work. Although it will metamorphose into alienation, it is a cultural form visible with its material content; yet it is the progenitor of the mystification elaborated in the entire society. The entire embodiment of meaning in the foundations of the society is located in the commodity. Full analysis will show not only that the commodity expresses and embodies this meaning but that perceiving the commodity reveals the meaning. To apprehend this significance as elaborated in the commodity will be to grasp the totality of contradictions within the society. In the beginning, the first commodity is 'innocent' in appearance, but Marx reveals the real world behind it, as evidenced in the process underlying its conception:

> A commodity appears, at first sight a very trivial thing, and easily understood. Its analysis shows that it is, in reality, a very queer thing, abounding in metaphysical subtleties and theological niceties. So far as it is a value in use, there is nothing mysterious about it, whether we consider it from the point of view that by its properties it is capable of satisfying human wants, or from the point that those properties are the product of human labour. It is as clear as noonday, that man, by his industry, changes the forms of the materials furnished by Nature, in such a way as to make them useful to him. The form of wood, for instance is altered, by making a table out of it. Yet for all that, the table continues to be that common, every-day thing, wood. But, as soon as it steps forth as a commodity, it is changed into something transcendent. It not only stands with its feet on the ground, but, in relation to all other commodities, it stands on its head, and evolves out of its wooden brain grotesque ideas, far more wonderful than 'table-turning' ever was. (1967b, vol. 1, p. 71)

If we consider this statement from the perspective of *Capital* as a whole, we must weigh two factors. The commodity-form is the basic form of capitalist society, yet it takes on a totally mystical facade. It is from that material-symbolic structure that apparent meaning will appear, and it is from exactly that structure that the critique of appearances will emerge. It is conceivable to claim that in this mainstream of Marx's ideas he is now bearing out in actuality an enterprise he had already sketchily formulated in his fourth thesis on Feuerbach. There he made the decision that it was not sufficient to criticize religion, since culture was already secular: it was necessary to criticize its secular substratum. The commodity-form itself is said to show the origin of its mystification. That is, when in capitalist culture something that ordinarily is used becomes a commodity, it is mystified or fetishized:

> The 'equality' of all sorts of human labour is expressed objectively by

their products all being 'equal values'; the measure of the expenditure of labour powers by the duration of that expenditure, takes the form of the quantity of value of the product of labour, and finally, as the mutual relations of the producers, within which the social character of their labour affirms itself, take the form of a social relation between products. (1967b, vol. 1, p. 72)

The key to this quotation is the process of equalization. Equalization will lead to quantification (i.e., the meaning of equalization will be quantity). The aspect of equalization will lead to a fundamental transfiguration of value from the social character of labor to the social character of products. Herein lies the key movement, the basic alteration, the process of becoming the social relations between things. On the surface, human beings have become assimilated to nature, namely, the 'second nature' that is reification. In civil society, this perversion of the subject/object dialectic will evolve into the condition for the perception of what is taken for real.

The sociology of knowledge was made possible by a drastic adjustment in theoretical perspectives from epistemology to knowledge. Mannheim knew this well, as is demonstrated by his argument against Max Scheler in the discussion alluded to earlier in this chapter. If one were to endeavor to comprehend the cohesion of the social order from an epistemological orientation, the outcome would merely be appropriation of knowledge limited to acts of appropriation by individual subjects. Speaking of Scheler's phenomenology, Mannheim in his essay 'The Problem of Knowledge' defines this perspective as 'one involving nothing but straight description of the given, disregarding all aspects, which are connected with its genesis' (quoted in Rasmusssen, 1975, p. 53).

As a consequence, epistemological knowing is limited to the activity of the knowing subject without regard to the actual historical genesis of the object known. As a result, that perspective is limited in social thought by what can be characterized as an 'epistemological residue', knowledge left unknown regarding both the historical genesis and the validity of the object known. There is a transformation in emphasis in Marx's thought from alienation to fetishism precisely at the juncture of the transposition from epistemology to the sociology of knowledge, putting to the fore the limits of an epistemological frame of reference.

The term 'alienation' was abstracted from social contract theory, where it signaled that one surrendered or 'alienated' certain of one's own natural rights in order to enter into the communion of the social contract. The social contract itself was a highly speculative proposition premised on an anthropology of humans in a 'state of nature'. In the Hobbesian perspective, one alienated virtually all rights in the state of nature, a state of individual freedom where individuals were brought into conflict when following their individual impulses and a war of each against all ensued. This general formulation was followed with thematic variations by social contract theorists such as Locke and Rousseau. In Hegel the term was further modified, assimilating negation and the externalization of human activity. In late twentieth-century thought, under the influence of existentialism, alienation has come to be synonymous with the experience of negation. But in its classical context it applies to an act of exchange. The two primordial subjects in the social contract relinquish (lose or gain) to a third agency something in exchange for something else, access or denial to property, for example, or more exactly, money for property, goods for services, freedom for protection. Theoretically all stand more or less equal before a sovereign.

Behind this primeval act of mutual appropriation and alienation lies the idealistic subject of modern society, the subject which was necessary for constitutive knowledge associated with the development of idealistic epistemology. Marx never ceased to point out that, so long as attention was limited to this act of exchange between individual subjects, it would appear to demonstrate the basic value structure of modern society, namely, freedom, equality, the right to personal security (the guarantor of property and power), leaving the individual stranded at a meta-level. In addition, valid knowledge could be demonstrated from an epistemological perception as long as the framework was restricted to this limited set of interactions. 'Alienation' could describe the experience of individuals within a society, but could not depict the experience to the society in terms of the whole.

In sum, the theoretical launching pad for Marx is commodity fetishism. It embodies the movement from epistemology to knowledge and the sociology thereof. Exploration of the commodity reveals relationships in the society as a whole. Critical social theory thereby grasps knowledge in its coherence and plenitude. The result is a key changeover for social thought through the commodity-form, which directly implicates the whole social and technical division of labor and the prescribed anti-democratic performatory roles. This conceptual breakthrough, linking practice to theory through an instrumentalized reason by the commodity-form, an integral part of Western social science theory, is equally applicable for Third World countries in the throes of freeing themselves from the 'bondsman' mentality of colonialism. Indeed, there are 'colonial enclaves' in industrial countries for which Marx has a message. In many senses we must move beyond Marx conceptually to maintain a check on the powers-that-be of the establishment if there is even to be a critique of the whole society.

4 Habermas's historical materialism and semiotic phenomenology

In the first three chapters, we have seen methodologically and empirically how a perverted dialectic can absorb the concept of alienation and the constitutive nature of consciousness into a materialism that reifies theory because matter is rendered a primary substance. Subjectivity then becomes secondary and subject and object are made foreign to each other. To recover the dialectic of subject and object we need to fashion a new tool, a phenomenology of the contemporary positivist mind which has suppressed the human processes of spontaneity, creativity, and imagination. Modalities of alienation can be found not just in the production process. Human beings are also symbol-forming creatures, and distorted communication processes have decentered the human structure of subjectivity. With language theory and hermeneutic techniques, we can aspire to regain the suppressed layers of meaning which lie beneath the surface of the reificational institutions of industrial society. Humanity can then engage in praxis so that political interests will no longer mechanically serve the forces of domination. Jürgen Habermas is the foremost 'Marxist' authority on this slant to the philosophy of social theory.

Conflict of science and lifeworld: Deriving theory

Habermas's point of departure for reading the history of social theory is the so-called classical doctrine of politics. This latter finds its takeoff point in Aristotle, with its penultimate depiction as 'practical philosophy', the art of right living through the medium of politics. The interpretive scheme developed in social theory is derived from the Aristotelian distinction between *epistémè* and *phronesis*, between science and prudence. The great advantage of phronesis, from this perspective, is that it enables one to preserve the domain of political activity inspired by categories of direct calculation from rigorous science. The course of action determined on the basis of phronesis defies categorization by scientific nomenclature. Instead, practical activity is required to determine the ends of political action, praxis, to find in the end the 'good' life' (by Habermas's standards, not Aristotle's). In Habermas's perspective, although we no longer directly partake of the tradition of classical politics, this distinction must be maintained if social domination itself is to be superseded.

This foundation in the tradition of classical politics permits an interpretation of the development of modern social philosophy as one which has lost sight of the primacy of phronesis translated into practical political activity. Instead, modern social philosophy with few exceptions has been inclined to find its model in the new science of nature. This science strove to appropriate, analyze, and directly govern society on the basis of scientifically derivable rules of action, rules which could orchestrate the overall motions of society. Social philosophy, mimetically designed positivistically after the new science, would lead to a theory which imparted priority to categories of social domination, that is, the legitimation and orchestration of social activity by an elite few, who would seek to engineer society as natural science sought to do with nature.

In the end, this positivism ran against the grain of Enlightenment reason by inverting the standard of rationality into one of irrationality, reifying theory and closing off subjectivity from the public realm. This event happened because the contradiction between the social nature of production and ownership was absorbed by the privileged few in total command of the means of production, which have become a constraint on the further development of the forces of production to the detriment of human reason and intelligibility.

For Habermas it was Giambattista Vico (judged from a cynical vantage point by Critical Theory) who not only first unearthed this fundamental style of modern social philosophy but also first reacted adversely to it. Vico, as Habermas interprets him, was cognizant of the limitations of technical science when applied to practical action and put forth a modern solution to the problem of social domination which reintroduces the classical idea of prudence under the heading of the art of rhetoric. For Vico, rhetorical activity allows for the prudent achievement of consensus independent of the generally conceded limitations of the categories of so-called rigorous science. The peculiar resemblance between Habermas's interpretation of Vico and his own solution to the dilemmas of modern social science theory appears not to be accidental. The theory of communicative competence finds one of its sources in Vico's reaction to the development of the new science.

According to Habermas, the other major exception to the dominant trend in the history of modern social theory is Marx. In this interpretation it is Kant, perhaps even more than Hegel, who provides the foundational concepts for Marx's analysis by conceiving the nexus between philosophy and science in essentially critical terms. Habermas's analysis, as well as his relationship to Marx (to the extent that he at this time feels indebted to the latter), is an area of ambivalence fraught with methodological traps. In his reading, Marx should be interpreted not only as reinstating the Kantian notion of critique but as extending that notion from self-reflection to society itself. His critical reaction or disposition, by Habermas's account, is ultimately to be subsumed by his enthrallment with the burgeoning developments of his day. Evidence for this claim is found in Marx's concentration on the category of production as motive force in historical development.

This basic criticism of Marx runs through Habermas's work. Marx, reconsidered in this way, is a victim of the preoccupation which dominated modern social philosophy since the Renaissance, the assumption that science itself would provide the ground for the messianic resurrection of modern society. From this analysis come two corollary conclusions. First, the interpretation given to Marx by orthodox Marxism is only partly correct in the extent to which it interprets Marx's works tendentiously on grounds befitting a dialectical science. Second, Marx's analysis runs parallel with some of the developments of nineteenth-century positivism.

Habermas's appraisal deems Marx's analysis unsuccessful because of its dependence on the new science. But Marx's critical analysis of capitalist society, his continuation of the tradition of social theory, and his erroneous endeavor (again, this is the evaluation of a rather contentious Habermas) to vindicate a technocratic mode of analysis which would eventuate in human liberation are all aspirations Habermas posits to varying degrees as interests worth pursuing according to his own theoretical paradigm. In light of the tendentiously posited failure of Marx's analysis, Habermas must continue the search for a critical theory of society which will result in human liberation. There is something very subtle about the general thesis which emerges from the corpus of Habermas's work. Accepting his critique of the history of social theory could persuade one to accept the solution tendered (the theory of communicative competence) as the one prospect for human social liberation.

Facile as this argument may seem, it has deep, serious basic flaws which threaten the general framework of analysis. One fault relates to the distinction between *epistémè* and *phronesis* endorsed from his reading of the history of social philosophy. This distinction induces an epistemological dualism between modalities of interpretive activity and results in a merely descriptive account of types of science without providing a ground for the unity of knowledge. This shortcoming strips the critique of science, whether in its classical, modern, or positivist form, of its basic integrity. The second, related fault is associated with the interpretation and critique of Marx's thought. Habermas's unique reading of Marx's work as a contribution to positivism rather than a critique of it overlooks the basic transfiguration in Marx regarding the modern problematic of the relationship of theoretical knowledge and social activity. Marx strove for a unified ground for theoretical knowledge in social activity itself, in order not to be impaled on an epistemological dualism. Habermas, by interpreting Marx in the light of orthodox Marxism, overlooks his real contribution to a modern theory of society. As a consequence, Habermas must persuasively establish the tie between positivistic and non-positivistic ways of knowing. He fails to do this, in the main, by ignoring Marx's explicit condemnation of capitalist society, which reifies the lifeworld in an englobed domain of fetish commodities and so alienates the power of human agency.

Habermas since his 1975 *Legitimation Crisis* has been trying to reconcile two positions which are at first glance dissonant with each other: system and lifeworld. This enterprise discloses an underlying idealist-materialist dilemma which preoccupied Habermas in one way or another for the period of his mature work. Constructing social theory from a purely idealist orientation allows one to interpret factors of interiority and cognition, but not to treat the underlying material and organic factors which are foreign both to the historical subject under study and to social science theorists and their constructs. Equally, accounting only for material conditions underscores objective factors which obscure the activity of human subjects in the creation and actualization of social phenomena. In terms of systems theory, specific crises are perceived objectively as 'unresolved steering problems', which only allude to objective conditions associated with the integration of the system.

On the other hand, theory articulated from the perspective of lifeworld deals with social integration, that is, the social relations of speaking and acting subjects. Crisis is perceived in relation to the values and institutions which comprise the normative structures of society. From a negative perspective, systems theory neutralizes normative indicators, while theory developed from the perspective of the lifeworld precludes thematization of societal steering mechanisms, consequently denying form to the information at hand. So this materialist-idealist split in contemporary theory needs to be resolved by a resurrected methodology.

Habermas's attempt to resolve the dilemma between system and lifeworld led to the partial construction of a theory of social systems which, if anything, gives more latitude to theory associated with lifeworld than to systems theory. This admittedly partial solution embodies a continuation of a running debate with Niklas Luhmann over the role of systems theory in social analysis. Habermas acclaims three constituent components or 'universal properties' of social systems. They both reduplicate the dilemma of idealism and materialism and show Habermas's project to resolve that dilemma.

The first universal property, the exchange between social systems and their milieus, is contingent on a distinction between outer and inner nature. The former is related to production and the latter to socialization, a reduplication of the distinction between system and lifeworld, a duality of noetic modalities.

The second property deals with the phenomenon of change. Change in the goal values of the social system is a function of the state of the forces of production and the degree of system self-regulation (as outer nature), but the spectrum of goal values is circumscribed by a logic of development of world perspectives (as inner nature). Hence, from the point of view of systems theory, change makes possible paradox or even contradiction: A world view over which there is no theoretical control will develop in contradiction to a transformation evolving in the domain of the forces of production.

The third and most critical property is linked to the learning processes of a society, which in Habermas's estimation function in relationship to the possibility of social evaluation of these motivational and cognitive modalities between generations with different orientations and expectations. Here two distinctions are being rendered: one between theory and practice and the other between reflexive and non-reflexive questions. On the basis of these two distinctions, it is projected that one can in some sense quantify the level of potential and actual development within a society.

Examined from the point of view of the whole, Habermas's three universal properties of society comprise an argument against both systems theory and orthodox Marxism. Systems theory has focused exclusively on the steering component and the outer nature of society. But, in fact, if a projected social change occurs, the external mechanism of a society will be related intimately to the internal cognitive and subjective processes of society. The third of Habermas's universal properties is thus the pivotal one, for, in his synoptic scope, the 'institutionally permitted learning capacity' is related directly to the possibility of social transfiguration. The same argument is coined in a different currency against orthodox Marxism. This latter, exclusively concerned with the primacy of production as the generating force in history, falls short of perceiving the subjective role that must necessarily be played by cognitive processes.

In Habermas's perspective, a primitive social formation is organized around the institutional form of the kinship system, while more advanced traditional social formations function under the organizational principle of class domination with the sphere of production privatized. In both situations crisis or contradiction may arise. In the former case, external change simply overrides the steering system, undermining the kinship networks for lack of differentiation of the entailed segments, which are unable to make historical adaptations. In the latter, traditional society, internal contradiction tends to force the breakdown of the system. This contradiction emanates from the institutionalization of private property through a quasi-hereditary elite's ownership of the means of production, at first locally and usually in landed property, and from the predominance of a steering mechanism which derives its power from the privatization of the means of production in *real* history. For Habermas all this activity results in the empirically verifiable development of an unstable class structure which presumably threatens both social and system integration. We have moved from feudal-mercantile to classical capitalism.

In terms of the previously articulated framework regarding social systems, the political class rule which delineates social systems is transferred into what Habermas specifically classifies as unpolitical class rule in liberal capitalism, giving rise to the designation of the principle of organization, the distinction between wage labor and capital, as unpolitical. This depoliticization, according to the argument, results simultaneously in the system integrative economic structure taking over socially integrative tasks. To put it simply, from Habermas's perspective the class relationship in liberal capitalism is institutionalized in the labor market. Presumably the author intends to instruct us that under this form of organization class relations are no longer validated by tradition but rather determined by the economic structure itself. As a consequence, it is claimed, these relations are essentially unpolitical.

Crisis under liberal capitalism is then quintessentially system crisis. System crisis is Habermas's implicit version of a society riven by the principal alienatory feature of commodity fetishism. The class antagonism which has not become part of the steering mechanism of the social organization will evidence itself as a problem which is not accessible to reflection but indigenous to the economy itself. The upshot of the matter is that it is perceived as a problem associated with the continuous accumulation of capital without the proper level of consumption and strategic deployment of variable capital in order to augment surplus value. In sum, instability is charted at the crux of the system itself, since the capacity of the system to continue growing is contingent on its ability to continue to have high level consumption on the one hand and available labor power for ready exploitation on the other. Without investigating the nuances of Marx's predicted 'falling rate of profit', let it suffice to say that capital which is not consumed hinders the process of production, creates unemployment, and inaugurates a system crisis.

Late capitalism will be marked by the reappearance of a highly political state as a proponent of the economic system, impinging on fallow fields of civic endeavor to which it had been forbidden access in previous social formations because social evolution was paced by the market mechanism. Essentially, the circulation of commodities failed in classical capitalism because of overproduction (a systemic mismanagement of resources intrinsic to capitalism). Subjectivity had to be revived in the 'public household' in order rationally to stabilize conflicting roles/functions in the technical division of labor. The state is the best mechanism to adjudicate contradictory demands on the system.

> This improbable constellation has changed, and socially integrative functions of maintaining legitimacy can no longer be fulfilled through systems-integrative functions of the market and decrepit remains of pre-capitalist traditions. They must again pass over into the political system. Government activity now pursues the declared goal of steering the system so as to avoid crisis, and consequently the class relationship has lost its unpolitical form. (Habermas, 1975, p. 52)

The new role of the state under advanced capitalism will thus be that of legitimizing agent, attempting to buffer conflict and, most critically, to avert and/or manage crisis. Crisis will arise not only from the instability of the economic structure itself, as in liberal capitalism, but also from the ambivalent roles played by the different interest groups (labor and capital) which compose the state. The socio-cultural tradition which had once informed the rational ground of appeal in the functioning of the overall economic system will be weakened. The state compass of action will dictate the policies of the civil sectors to them, offering motivational inputs to shore up approved economic undertakings. Advanced capitalism, in this light, is a contradiction-ridden, institutionally overburdened conglomerate beset with potential or actual crises; its ground for rational appeal is to a complex of bourgeois values the very vitality of which is ever being sapped through the ill-conceived policies derived from an over-rationalized bureaucratic structure.

The main point underlying this picture is that governmental functions have taken over market functions, with the consequence that the class struggle is mediated administratively through the action of state organs. This means that the government constitutes the means of production; it facilitates the accumulation process through adaptation of the legal system; it performs market substitutable actions outside the range of what was observed under liberal capitalism as the normal ebb and flow of capital; it makes adjustments for the dysfunctional outcome of the accumulating process. From this nodal point of crisscrossing currents, the relations of production in late capitalism are essentially different from those in liberal capitalism. They are changed with respect to the production of surplus value; with respect to the wage structure, which is now quasi-political; and with respect to the heightened need for the legitimization of the political system related antagonistically to the emergence of better educated producer/consumers and a rising public awareness that somehow corporations are to be made responsible for their actions.

Theorems of rationality follow directly from theorems of economic crisis. The theorem of the rationality crisis is intended to meet the description of the nature of advanced capitalism. Inasmuch as under advanced capitalism the government budget is committed to the common costs of more and more socialized production, the so-called market strategy per se does not account for its rationality. Rather, according to this thesis, the issue has moved toward taxation. Government expenditures must be financed, with the consequent involvement of state organs in taxation. Consequently, under advanced capitalism, the government must rationalize the capitalist system anew. In its newly acquired role, rather idiosyncratic by the old standards of laissez faire capitalism, government through taxation must assume responsibility for the areas affected by crisis-plagued growth precisely to diffuse crisis into the tertiary sectors of society. Taxes must be raised selectively to continue to avoid problems caused by crisis-masked growth.

This is the point where the problem of legitimation arises. The state is mired in a dilemma. It is criticized publicly if current taxation fails to fulfill programmed needs. If it must raise taxes, it does so selectively and must account for its enterprise by evidencing resourcefulness and efficiency. This double dilemma is in congruence with J. Hirsch's 'modified anarchy thesis' (cited in Rasmussen, 1976a, p. 359). Presumably the point is that the state, given its commitment to rationality, must satisfy capitalistic growth indicators. Equally, it must tax in order to adjust to crises felt at the fringes which are not integral to the process of the accumulation of surplus value. Given the irrationality of the growth syndrome, current taxation does not necessarily lead to legitimacy. Government must therefore expand the modalities of taxation. Government must not only keep segments of the population at a minimal standard of living and subsidize segments which fail to meet criteria of productive capital through selective taxation, it must also seek legitimacy for that selection. Furthermore, government rules on the basis of modified anarchy, thereby perpetuating a continuous rationality crisis. The direct import of the economic and rationality crises produces a legitimation crisis which occurs as the result of government reaching a 'necessary limit' of available legitimations.

Habermas asserts that administrative systems per se are not generators of meanings. Rather, meaning is a latent force in the cultural tradition. Cultural traditions may be reinterpreted hermeneutically and reappropriated critically, yet when they are exploited for market purposes they dissipate their force and expose their vulnerability. Hence, conscious manipulation of cultural traditions, which proves to be necessary for administrative purposes, finds its limit in the lack of available meaning for legitimating its activity. Given the rationality crisis, which finds its fundamental expression in the domain of taxation and selective new taxation, official endeavors to override the legitimation crisis would be expressed most directly at the level of class structure. It would be necessary to exploit the productivity of labor by making new demands on it in order to augment the level of wealth and make feasible a tax base which would not require new forms of legitimation for extorting tax tributes.

The rationale of crisis leads to a motivational breakdown which engages, from Habermas's orientation, a basic critique of Max Weber's thesis that the underlying motivational principle which sustained the development of capitalism was derived from the ethic of Protestantism. In fine, according to the *Legitimation Crisis*, the Protestant ethic has been squandered in its regard to provide motivation. In general, Habermas claims that, since bourgeois society could never sustain itself on the basis of the new traditions it developed, it had to rely on pre-bourgeois residues, residues which supported civil and familial-vocational privatism. He wishes to show not only that these traditions have eroded but also that there are no functional equivalents left to uphold or replace them. To an equal extent, motivation is a psychological category. The tendency perceived in the analysis of the dysfunctionality between the privatistic ethic, based on a decadent cultural subsystem, and the motivational claims of bourgeois society, leads to a corresponding dysfunctionality within the personality system itself. Hence the capacity to believe in the value structure which supports late capitalism is increasingly difficult to maintain. Once the dysfunctionality becomes apparent at the level of personality, the disposition to abide by the standards of late capitalism dissolves. The penultimate crisis degenerates into a motivational one.

Habermas argues that systemic problems should be referred to the communicative community, which can achieve consensus through generalizable interests; for example, one interest could be to ascertain the root of inflation to reduce it to zero. But this type of problem would entail questioning the whole nature of the capitalist life-support system and the state which is its protector. In the hegemony of the modern state, generalizable interests are suppressed as assumptions based on the belief that more democracy entails less freedom and more suppression. Supposedly, the more individual rights are granted in an abstractly legalistic form, the fewer resources there will be for mobilizing to meet the rising demands, bringing, in turn, general downgrading of political activities with a concomitant upswing in 'ideologizing'. Witness, for example, the disintegration of the programs of the Great Society of Lyndon Johnson because of inflationary pressures brought on by the Vietnam War. In this instance compare also the limited aims of the civil rights movement to the realities: the incremental gains of the movement were tied very shrewdly with the rate of growth of the U.S. Gross National Product. The system in turn demanded support while engaging in a discourse between dissident groups, a discourse which should have been critical of the systemic suppression of the general interests of the common weal. But Habermas contends that it is conceivable to establish the relationship of motivation to truth - inversely. In fine, the solution to the problems raised by the crisis of legitimation, which is really, in the end, a crisis of motivation, results in a theory of communicative competence which will allow discourse between the various disenchanted groups of modern society in order to redeem normative validity claims. The eventual albeit hypothetical outcome is that it will be possible to constitute a tightly knit and non-antagonistic relationship between motivation and truth. People would be acting in an environment in which norms had been rationally conceived. The substance of such an agreement is a moot point for Habermas at this juncture in his theoretical exposition.

For Habermas, the prospect, failing his own solution, is that individual subjects, the guarantors of reason and truth, will be alienated from their own subjectivity and from the role of active advocates of their own history. This situation horrifies him.

> With the historical form of the bourgeois individual, there appeared those (still unfulfilled) claims to autonomous ego-organization within the framework of an independent - that is, rationally founded - practice. In those claims was laid out the logic of a general (if undeveloped, nevertheless continuously effective) socialization through individuation. If this form of reproduction were to be surrendered, together with the imperatives logically embedded in it, the social system could no longer establish its unity through formation of identities of socially related individuals. The constellations of general and particular would no longer be relevant for the aggregate state of society. (1975, p. 125)

Habermas must therefore conclude with recourse to the resurrection of the 'bourgeois individual', with potential for 'autonomous ego organization', to ward off the threat posed by 'systems theory' to 'reason' and 'practice'. By doing so he has posed the problem of late capitalism and the legitimation crisis accompanying it as a dichotomous dilemma, with systems theory in defense of positivistic science on the one hand and the 'bourgeois individual' with reason and practice on the other. 'Universal functionalism' or systems theory must assume that 'the end of the (possibility of the) individual' has been duly foreclosed. In this light Habermas must conclude in a curious manner with a plea, simultaneously a denial and an affirmation, for the partiality of reason. While denying both systems theory - which in his perspective dispenses with the individual - and his brand of Marxist heterodoxy, he affirms 'old European' thought, which presumably sustains both reason and practice.

With regard to Habermas, the problem is in part epistemological. The term must be used guardedly because of the difficulties associated with its use since the German Enlightenment. The problem with Habermas's approach is that he has been unable to resolve the dilemma presented by the hiatus between socially produced and individually appropriated knowledge. This dilemma coincides with that presented by the distinction between science and practical wisdom. Once this distinction is made, it is difficult to establish the nexus between the two spheres, particularly in modern thought. With considerable justification, Habermas has perceived this duality in the development of modern social science theory. Certainly he is within his rights in asserting that early modern social theorists, fascinated by the development of natural science, tried to use scientific methodology to interpret the modern *polis*. But in a curious way Habermas is left with a dilemma not unlike those of his chosen adversaries, namely, the dichotomy between the isolated subject of modern society and the productive mechanism of that very society, which estranges human beings from their historical roots and self-individuation. The mechanism, of course, is the highly overdeveloped division of labor which systematically suppresses affective and cognitive self-awareness.

That this societally structured bifurcation exists is made evident by the very selection of the problem with which the *Legitimation Crisis* opens. It is an undertaking to resolve the split between system and lifeworld in order to create a social scientific concept of crisis. That Habermas's project is to resolve that problem is manifested by his discussion of the universal properties of social systems, each of which embodies a resolution of so-called objective and social categories, for example, goal and world view, evolution and learning. Although each argument incarnates an attempted integration, the precept for integration remains unrevealed. Once more, in developing a tentative theory of evolution, a similar problem emerges. When, for instance, a distinction is made between primitive and traditional society, there is no generic rationale for the transition from the former to the latter. Instead, external change is cited for the decline of the original society. Without the ability to demonstrate the exact relationship between knowledge, internal change, and the productive mechanism, one can only deputize reasons sifted from a later period in the development of society for this basic transformation.

The section in *Legitimation Crisis* entitled 'The Crisis Tendencies of Advanced Capitalism' presents a similar instance of an objective idealism. The argument for an economic crisis which leads to a rationality crisis, a legitimation crisis, and finally a motivational crisis is indeed interesting, underlining a sub-claim that, whereas crisis under liberal capitalism was of the nature of a system crisis, crisis in the twentieth century is more germane to the lifeworld. However, arguing for this basic transition leaves open the question of the relationship of the system of production to motivation, a foundational issue. The issue of motivation in relation to the determining structures of capitalism is ambiguous because, at least from certain points of view, capitalism is less interested in generating motivation choices than it is in reducing alternatives. We can readily conceive of a scenario where the production lines break down if workers are not internally impelled to labor, and where wages are not a sufficient stimulus. If the issue begotten by late capitalism is one of motivation, we must still inquire how motivation is related to the economic system of production. The problem of a foundational social theory is among a certain number of generalizations to which Habermas has yet to give evidence.

The final section of *Legitimation Crisis* confronts the reader with the duality present at the outset of the work, and examines the question of motivation and truth. At first sight this problematic question appears to be appropriately raised, as it is, in the context of Weber's analysis of belief in modalities of authority. In terms of the two figures who inform the analysis, it can be argued that neither found such a correlation to exist even in liberal capitalism. Marx naturally thought of capitalism as a technique of social organization which manipulated society in order to dominate production. He did not assume that labor was motivated to support capital; the motivation was ensconced in the ideological acculturation process, but was not yet a culture industry in its own right. Rather, by his accounts, labor, when divorced from the means of production, found it necessary to support the capitalistic system of production for purposes of mere physical survival. This view has been borne out as one of the most crucial factors in fragmenting the labor movement into factions competing for a fixed allocation of resources from the state. This in turn imparts to the state tremendous leverage in procuring loyalty to the system by manipulating the tensions internal to the labor movement.

An option opposed to rationalized motivation was beyond the realm of possibility for labor to actualize. Weber, who wrote *The Protestant Ethic and the Spirit of Capitalism* in order to vindicate, against the materialist motive, the proposition that the triumph of capitalism could not have occurred without the support and motivational desire of formally free labor, professed the belief that the generation of wealth for capitalism is in itself a virtue. Its principal ideologues could then make a consistent theoretical defense for the mindless accumulation of capital for its own sake. Weber, in fact, adhered to the belief that the accumulation of capital reflected glory and status on the nation, even if it entailed supporting imperialism. The testimony of the principal advocates of so-called idealism and materialism therefore tends to undercut the assumption that there was, even under liberal capitalism, a claim to be made for the common 'destiny' of motivation and truth. One wonders why the relationship of motivation to truth is presumed to be the major question stemming from advanced capitalism, when Marx himself, whom Habermas has supposedly critiqued into a state of semi-oblivion, presumed it to be already an apocryphal issue under liberal capitalism.

The solution to the final proposal with respect to the crisis of late capitalism is to reconsider the question of the relationship of motivation to truth through the development of linguistic modalities of interpreting social reality. Essentially, this means the development of a theory of communication which will critique the 'suppression of general interests' and reportedly bring about the liberation of subjects who can attain a consensus through the articulation of generalizable interests. Individuals engaged in intersubjective communication can hypothetically reverse the basic trend of capitalistic suppression. It is exactly at this juncture that the reader, who might have been awaiting the final integration of system and lifeworld, must realize that the promise is not to be actualized. Even Habermas fully concedes this shortcoming on the basis of the primacy of individual subjects, whom he claims are light towers of rationality compared to what they are reduced to in systems theory. At the end of *Legitimation Crisis*, we are left with the same disruption of systems theory and lifeworld which was epistemologically posited at the beginning of the text. In the next section we will discuss at some length Fredric Jameson's theorems on 'textuality' in order to extend our theoretical perspectives.

The failure to integrate these two domains can be traced to Habermas's critique of Marx. Habermas interprets the history of modern social theory as a misapplication of the science of nature to the proto-science of society. Having spurned the classical qualification between science and practical wisdom, he argues, modern social philosophy took an approach to society based on a model of domination which had no recourse to the activity of individual subjects. The result was the misleading outcome of positivism. By associating Marx with this general (though apparently declining) tendency in modern social theory, Habermas can assert that Marx capitulated to the positivist trend of his day by undertaking to establish his analysis under the strict supervision of science. In this interpretation Marx is allied with the so-called orthodox modern-day apostles of his work and his analysis can be subsumed under positivism.

If, like Louis Althusser, one posits an epistemological divide in Marx, then only his 'mature' writings would be given theoretical standing and the positivist accusation would hold water. Critical theorists, on the contrary, redeem the outstanding accomplishments of Marx in perceiving the affinity between modalities of rationality and the productive mechanism of society: the fetish concept of commodity and power reverses relationships between individuation and a mechano-morphic process in a society operating on principles of false consciousness. Marx undertook to address the actuality of modern social theory on grounds critically different from those of his predecessors. His grounds presumed an actual unity between modalities of reason and productive enterprises, modalities which found their crystallization in the institutional form of capitalism, which was momentarily the progressive outcome over the ancien regime of Enlightenment values which were to sour.

Habermas, not having fully grasped Marx's synthesis of this epistemological rupture, feels compelled to deny its moment of truth. Having misconceived Marx's analysis, he undertook to resolve the epistemological dualism of subject and object on grounds which pre-dated Marx.

If this turns out to be the case in Habermas's future development, he will have seceded from the camp of Critical Theory. Paradoxically, he will then be making full use of the corporate structures of the university and associated research institutes which grind out surplus value for the very state whose legitimacy he is contesting. Apparently he is in a bind which he himself acknowledges. And the nature of his personal choice cannot help but be influenced by fresh currents of repression of dissidents in recent years by German authorities and their attendant policy of monitoring a newly won sense of civic responsibility among the youth. If he continues his silence, his stature as a 'critical' intellectual will come under even deadlier fire by those who partake of his vision of a pragmatic universal competency.

We now turn to the meaning of 'text' to concretize the preconditions of this idea.

The natural context of humanity: A 'textual' reaffirmation

The point of this section is to demonstrate how certain artifacts, art forms, and cultural manifestations in late capitalism can be debunked of their legitimacy and apparent truth-value with a critique modeled after the traditional hermeneutics associated with literary texts and their interpretation. The ideology behind these forms serves as an analogue by which to critique institutions and the associated rituals and behavioral styles employed to falsify reality. In this vein, Fredric Jameson's interesting approach to a hermeneutics of the 'text' (encoded routinized performances and production objectivizations of capitalism) fits with a critique of the society within which he is immersed and by which he feels victimized. His argument in *Marxism and Form* (1971) runs along lines similar to those in his 'Ideology of the Text':

> It will be our contention that this unavoidable slippage from what are essentially historical perceptions into the ideologizing of those perceptions is a function of an incomplete historical view and of the failure to make connections and on-going concrete modifications of the social order as a whole, the failure, - the unwillingness, to put all of these observations together and see them in terms of the long-range destiny of our particular socioeconomic system, or in other words, monopoly capitalism. (Jameson, 1976, pp. 204-5)

He adds:

> Even in the local regions enumerated above, however, this particular 'great transformation' grasped idealistically in terms of transformation in our modes of *thinking* rather than those of more concrete structures or situations - has rarely been the object of a systemic anatomy. Rather, the new conceptuality has been enthusiastically developed and applied, in the absence of a measured and diagnostic investigation of what Collingwood would have called its 'absolute presuppositions' or what more recent historians of ideas have called its basic paradigm (Kuhn) or its underlying *epistémè* (Foucault). (1976, p. 205)

'Textuality' may, in short, be received as a methodological hypothesis whereby the objects of study of the human sciences (not only the human ones: the genetic DNA 'code' has to be de-mystified to find the very textuality of life forming itself according to a hidden 'blueprint') are deemed to constitute so many texts which we decipher and interpret, as distinguished from the older views of those objects as realities or existents or substances which we in some manner feel driven to know simply at the level of sense perception. The advantages of such a scheme are visible in the non-literary fields, where it appears to afford a more adequate 'solution' than the provisory one of phenomenological bracketing to the impasses of positivism. The latter merely suspends the ontological problem and indefinitely delays the ultimate epistemological decisions of reconciling subject and object facticities.

Whatever foundational objections may be applied to the idea of textuality itself, as a strategy it has at least the advantage of excising cross-sections of epistemology and the subject/object antagonism in such a way as momentarily to neutralize both, and of centering the analyst's attention on his or her own mental operations and position as a reader. One finds oneself immediately obliged to render an account of the nature of the object of study qua text, and no longer tempted to perceive it as some kind of empirically existing reality in its own right.

These 'texts' in their ultimate decadent form are the prescribed norms of the division of labor which compel people to act against their collective 'good' in the name of sundry capitalist shibboleths. The fetish nature of state-sanctioned behavior must be broken down into its rudiments so that human beings in their true self-consciousness will understand the process which has perverted the quality of their lives to the point where even biological needs have been appropriated by the machine. Their sense of the sequences of temporality is distorted in that political activity 'disappears' along with the free space of a res publica. In disciplines like anthropology or sociology, in the reified aura of an older referential or 'realistic' positivism, the requirement to 'textualize' data serves to renew the concrete contexts in which the so-called data were collected, at the same time that it extends the interpretive situation to the totality of social life itself. It is in this spirit that the ethnomethodologist replaces the events of social life with people's own accounts and interpretations of those events. In the newer anthropology one finds the endeavor to dissolve the practices, habits, and rituals which were thought of as so many 'institutions' and to apprehend them as so many types of discourse a social group entertains about itself in reflection.

Meanwhile, in linguistics itself, the notion of the text offers the means of release from the factitious confinement to smaller and more abstract units of study like the sentence. It can evolve in the direction of pragmatism and grammars for the text which strive to re-assimilate the concrete context and originally intended positions of the participants, redeeming them from what is otherwise a hypostatization of language manifested by opaquely cloaked verbal phenomena.

> The central recommendation [of ethnomethodological study] is that the activities whereby members [of a given social group] produce and manage settings of organized everyday affairs are identical with members' procedures for making those settings 'account-able' ... I mean observable-and-reportable, i.e., available to members as situated practices of looking-and-telling. (Jameson, 1976, p. 206)

It is possible to perceive the new textual paradigm as a reflection of the changes wrought by the media, in our experience of society and of the world.

It is tempting to associate the illusions of a traditional Aristotelian realism (reality reposing 'out there', truth nothing but the adequate correspondence of the ideas in our heads with things themselves of which they are the pictorial representation) with a world in which the 'shimmering heat waves' of a host of signs and codes are not present to infringe on our gaze across the expanse which divides us from the *res extensa* (Jameson, 1976, p. 206). Certainly the sensitivity in recent times to problems of language, models, communication, and the like is tightly linked with the emergence of those phenomena as relatively autonomous and objects in their own right.

These problems appear to be understood in a manner analogous to the new distribution of control mechanisms of industrial capitalism. The text involves a *process of production* in which some *deep underlying genotext* is elicited (its operations ultimately rooted either in the structure of language itself or in that of the *epistémè*, the dominant thought form which propagates a surface dimension in the form of the individual work itself with its particular sentences). For the moment it suffices to stress the deep antagonism between the perception of the literary object as text, or as a perceptual production of sentences, and the more traditional perception guided by the formal Gestaltist completeness of the literary masterwork, in which everything contributes to some organic whole. For the crisis in modern criticism is certainly closely entwined with the more basic crisis in modern literature and art: the multiplication of styles and private languages. Adorno, for example, had argued that Stravinsky's composition of music about other music was a characteristic and virtually textbook illustration of one of the basic strategies of modern artists, faced with an overwhelming weightiness of inherited dead styles in a situation where it appears indefensible to invent still newer ones.

One of Roland Barthes's motifs is what he denounces as 'naturality'. He associates it with one of the bourgeois ways of rewriting the world to its own glory after its social and political crowning. Hjelmslev's connotative method is an agreeable medium for detecting the tendency everywhere in bourgeois society, from its advertisements to its works of art, to transfigure culture into nature. By this transfiguration he means the transmuting of historicity into eternity, which plays on the conditioned fear of aging and tries to deny the irreversibility of time by dwelling inwardly and morbidly on narcissistic themes. The ideological goal of this technique of naturalizing history and social phenomena is to naturalize meaning and thus to lend credence to the reality of the bourgeois story whose events are prefabricated to accommodate it comfortably to the status quo.

This naturalization is 'permissible' only because the significant data are conveyed by a purportedly 'natural' medium, language. Language, which in fact is the integral system of non-natural meaning, is employed to systematize the secondary meaning, to naturalize its production and to authenticate the narrative of the bourgeois society as archetype of socially acceptable behavior. We have already perceived how the naming system of language functions as such an illusion whereby social realities are inverted into 'natural' ones. Proper names, in this vein, are considered to be a 'natural' taxonomic system for the signified objects. Words become the referents which objectify the serialized levels of lived experience in reducing it to mere alienated form.

Where Barthes is innovative is in his account of the 'sentence' itself as the primary vehicle for just such a recondite ideological process of naturalization. There is a force in the sentence as a linguistic entity which pacifies the conventionality of the narrative, a meaning which supervenes on the meaning and is to be unraveled. We might call this diacritical, linguistic act constituent 'sentencing' (since it overhangs the articulation of the narrative units). That is, the sentence is an (estranged) nature whose task is to vindicate the culture-bearing of the narrative. Superimposed on the narrative structure, forming it, regulating its pace, imposing on its morphemes a purely grammatical logic, the sentence serves as evidence for the narrative. For language, by the way it is learned (especially by children), by its historical weight, by the apparent universality of its conventions, seems to have every right over a contingent anecdote characterized by a brevity of scope. The whole language coincides with the whole development of the species and is very revealing of the levels of community in which humanity has articulated its sense of the 'good'. In numerous ways this need to track down and deny the residues of 'naturality' in our culture is integral to the private thematics of Barthes himself ('the will to burden signification with all the justification of nature itself provokes a kind of nausea', Barthes tells us in *Mythologies* [1972, p. 9]). Indeed, it is merely the other side of the ideology of representation - the status of the subject - which has been plumbed widely in recent French theory - particularly in structural-functionalism and existential Marxism. The most incisive dramatization of the affinity between representation and the concept of the subject has been rendered by Michel Foucault in the first chapter of *The Order of Things* (1971).

The paradox to be faced is that the structuralist critics of representation are led to denounce the active and informing presence of the subject precisely in those texts in which this presence is repressed. On the one side, they rebuke its forgetfulness of itself; on the other, they call for its suppression. Hence Barthes's diagnosis assumes unexpected overtones in a situation in which, as we shall observe, schizophrenia has become a standard inspiring a whole ethical and political program.

We may say, that, in a sense, 'objective' discourse (as in positivist history) ... resembles schizophrenic discourse; in both cases there is a radical censorship of the utterance, in which negativity cannot be expressed (though it can be felt); and there is a massive reversion of discourse away from any form of sui-reference, or even (in the case of the historician) a reversion towards the level of pure referent - the utterance for which no one is responsible. (Barthes, 1972, p. 238)

One would be only too disposed to assert that one of the basic preconditions of some representational or 'realistic' narrative discourse is to be confirmed in the calculated effacement of the traces of producer and consumer, and that the surveying eye, faced with representational disquisition, has a vested interest in ignoring its own presence. Yet an unusual reversal occurs in the polemical appropriation of this insight by the realism/modernism contrariety; it is thenceforward exactly just such a subornation of the subject which is recommended to the reader. Barthes puts forward boldly what he believes to be exemplary about Flaubert:

> Flaubert, however ..., working with an irony impregnated with uncertainty, achieves a salutary discomfort in writing; he does not stop the play of codes (or stops it only partially), so that (and this is indubitably the manner of *proof* of his writing) *one never knows if he is responsible for what he writes* (if there is a subject *behind* his language); for the very being of writing (the meaning of the labor that constitutes it) is to keep the question *Who is speaking?* from ever being answered. (1972, p. 238)

The contradictions which arise from the structuralist strategy in ascertaining the locus of subjectivity appear closer to resolution if they are projected onto a more complex scheme of periodization and articulated in a more properly historical rather than ethical orientation. The problem is that the attack on the old bourgeois subject can take two forms. One is that of the undertaking to dissolve the subject altogether, and that is, as we shall observe in the case of Gilles Deleuze either an anarchist or a countercultural response - political doomsday or the ecstacy of drug-induced self-oblivion. The other would involve renovating the primacy of group and collective life over the bourgeois illusion of individual existence, and returning to a perspective in which the individual subject is a function of the collective structure, a condition of which, perhaps, the ethnographic portrayals of tribal existence impart to us the most vivid glimpse.

The same modification must be judged in the earlier leitmotif of 'naturality'; what is ahistorical about Barthes's critique of this particular facet of the bourgeois *Weltanschaunng* is the implication that the concept of nature is condemned to be reactionary. On the contrary, there have been moments - the sedition of the bourgeois revolution itself and the attack on the factitiousness of the feudal regime - in which the concept of nature has been a deeply critical and formidable weapon; and the only dialectical manner of evaluating such a theme is through analysis of its function in a given historical situation. Nothing is more idealistic than the idea that a given thought-form (the belief in the subject, for instance) is always and under all circumstances 'bourgeois' and ideological, for such a position is inclined precisely to isolate the form of thought (or its equivalent, the form of discourse) from the practical context in which alone its results can be empirically weighed. Ideologies can never be appraised apart from their function in a given historical formation; witness Alexander Koyré's clarifying the progressive character of Galileo's Platonism, as contrasted to the seemingly far more realistic and even materialistic Aristotelianism of his contemporaries and immediate predecessors.

A Marxist framework substitutes for the structuralist opposition between nature and culture the more dialectical and diachronic opposition between nature and history; yet even here the ideological character of 'nature' is by no means unequivocal, as may be inferred in the works of the very writer from whom Barthes himself first drew his suspicion of naturality and the literary instruments by which to denounce and combat it, Bertolt Brecht himself. For even in the Brechtian idiom there is a decided flexibility of orientations which makes visible the historical and constructed origins of seemingly natural attributes such as aggressiveness or avarice. One might also consider here the emphasis in *Mother Courage* on the unnatural character of the seemingly only too natural drive to turn over a profit. (This un-Brechtian reversal would then go a long way toward explaining the peculiar and ambiguous status of the latter play in the writer's repertoire.)

Indeed, there is a powerful tradition of a 'naturalist strategy' in Marxism itself, one dating to the *Economic and Philosophical Manuscripts of 1844*, which with their emphasis on a species-being, argue for, if not a fixed and eternal human nature in the conservative style, then for evaluations based on a notion of human potential. It is from such a notion that Marx seeks to demonstrate contemporary alienation. Moreover, there is a socialist-statist literature no less poignant than that of Brecht which draws its force from just such an interchange of the natural and the unnatural - an uncanniness of a humanity no longer of this world. Meanwhile, there are signs, particularly in the work of Herbert Marcuse, that in our own peculiarly anti-natural society the concept may once again recover some of its negative and critical thrust as an 'offensive' weapon and a utopian norm.

Realism and modernism must finally be perceived as specific and determinate historical elaborations related to the type of socioeconomic structure to which they respectively correspond, classical and consumer capitalism. Here we have a moment to give an accounting of the ideology of modernism. That consumer capitalism should secrete modernism as a byproduct is, when interpreted, a perfectly comprehensible phenomenon which can be analyzed in its own right. What demands remedy are the claims made by the apologists of modernism on behalf of their product. For modernism, radical in its denial of realistic discourse and of the bourgeois world to which it is contemptuously addressed, believes (falsely) that, if you tamper with the structure of artistic discourse in a decisive way, the realities to which it corresponds will find themselves analogously refashioned. If viewing the panorama of the world through the old 'bourgeois' categories is bad, then an adaptation in style will enable us to see the world in a fresh way and hence achieve a kind of cultural or countercultural revolution. Certainly, if consumer capitalism were a new qualitatively different and distinct socioeconomic form in its own right, as many now assert, something like this would presumably be thinkable. We would expect the new social form in due time to generate its own distinctive kinds of artistic discourse, leaving the realistic ones behind it like so many dead husks.

But what is peculiar about consumer capitalism is that it is merely a second degree construction on classical capitalism itself, the latter continuing in a paradoxical coexistence with it. The basic laws of classical capitalism (codified by Marx) are operative from a global perspective even though they are seemingly nullified and archaic if one looks at them within the bounds of the national experience of a single advanced country. Thus it happens that we dwell in the older world of everyday life of classical capitalism which we are simultaneously beguiled by the autistic aura of the media and the marvels of the supermarket-suburb complex.

The first of these realities is repressed as far as possible under the second into something which is not altogether unconscious. This is why our art, that of modernism, is not a new thing in itself, but rather something like a canceled realism, a realism denied and negated and *aufgehoben* in authentically Hegelian fashion. What we do with the works, showing the functioning of all those realities of capitalism (wage slavery, money, exploitation, the profit motive) which have not changed substantially since the times of the great naturalists, is to decree that they are boring and old-fashioned. Here boredom is the sign of what is to be repressed, and this reflexive and indeed visceral reaction to the older art forms belies the genesis of modernism itself in an aestheticizing compensation reaction against the quashed realities of a business civilization, about which we would prefer not even to have our art remind us. Hence the demise of the referent (the capitalist mode of production in all its anarchy and uprooting of human potentiality) has been greatly exaggerated. At best, awareness of its production of misery has only been driven underground.

In *Anti-Oedipus: Capitalism and Schizophrenia* Gilles Deleuze's and Felix Guattari's position (the romantic left of the present-day French Surrealist persuasion) may be perceived as the extreme working out of the Cartesian maxim from which all bourgeois subjectivism can be said to originate, as quoted by Barthes,

> always to seek to conquer myself rather than fortune, to change my desires rather than the established order, and generally to believe that nothing except our thoughts is wholly under control ... (Barthes, 1972, p. 245)

Here is a programmatic statement totally devoid of political content. The illusion of freedom and creativity enjoyed by the early modernists was a function of their transitional moment in which facets of the new consumer economy, the so-called second industrial revolution, had begun to transcend those of older classical capitalism. Today when modernism no longer represents this conquest of new material and situations but rather has assimilated itself into an economy functionally involved with its thought forms for its indispensable fashion changes and for the perpetual resupplying of a media culture (to fabricate legitimation of the reproduction of this late capitalist system), artists and writers who want to alter their styles radically may well once again come to the conclusion that they must first change the world. Otherwise, the special status of the intellectual will be forfeited in the manner Mannheim recommended.

We now have the tools to evaluate critically how certain trends in contemporary philosophy have been derailed, by 'idealist tendencies', from making their proper criticism of social problems. From the Marxian tradition, we will unmask philosophy's pretensions through a dialectic of 'negativities' which will give us the concrete loci of social anomie and contradiction.

5 Contemporary modalities of alienated consciousness

Negativities in the 'authenticity' of 'first principles' of philosophy today

We have traced the disruption of consciousness from its material context by contemporary hermeneutical and phenomenological methodology. The implications must first be examined rather abstractly before concrete inferences and recommendations can be advanced. Our discussion will proceed by examining Theodor Adorno's critical examination of these issues. In the process we will work toward a critical theory which is reconciled to action through the decanter of undistorted communication. So theory is really a second order moment in the making of truth, a field of reified signifiers.

As Adorno summarizes the dilemma in trying to impart a materialist substructure to phenomenology,

> consciousness, whose existence constitutes for Husserl the sole source of knowledge, is juxtaposed from the beginning to a transcendent world whose existence is not established by consciousness, although it derives its epistemological legitimacy only from its reference to consciousness. ... The assumption of a transcendent world, however, is in conflict with the premise of consciousness as a 'sphere of absolute origins'; it contradicts the basic principle of transcendental idealism. (*Philosophische Frühschriften*, quoted in Dallmayr, 1976, p. 370)

Exploring the background and ramifications of the contradiction, Adorno traced Husserl's dualism to his disregard of the submerged synthetic tasks of consciousness. In Husserl's estimation, all knowledge required vindication through direct experience. Since the structural or 'primary' qualities of objects were immune from such experience, recourse was taken to an extra-mental 'mana' of 'transcendent' origins (never actually substantiated or found to be heuristically defensible). According to Adorno, such recourse was apocryphal and unnecessary. The structural solidity of objects, Adorno speculated, was attributable not to a supposed transcendence but to their inherence in the a priori categories of mind, categories which were not accessible to direct experience. In a nutshell,

> Objects are not experiences but relationships between experiences - laws or rules for their occurrence; as such they are strictly and completely immanent in the framework of consciousness. (p. 370)

Once the status of objects or things was cleared away in this mode, Husserl's concept of 'noema' was placed precariously in his arguments. Differentiated from the 'unreduced' world of reality and simultaneously from the 'noetic' acts of consciousness, the noema (or 'intentional object') in Adorno's evaluation was a 'hybrid' of mental and naturalistic components: 'neither immanent nor transcendent, suspended so-to-speak in mid-air' (pp. 370-1). If the distinction between 'reduced' and 'unreduced' objects was shown to be artificial, the entire phenomenological method of reduction to *epoche* emerged as superfluous and unauthentic. Bracketing, Adorno enjoined, could not simply be employed casually as a heuristic method of inquiry, since any endeavor to talk sensibly about the world (including the world of the 'natural attitude') required reliance on the framework of consciousness. By manner of conclusion, his thesis (*Habilitationschrift*) of 1924 reviewed Husserl's enterprise to link transcendence and consciousness in a strategic manner, by submitting questions of 'reality' and 'unreality' to the 'jurisdiction of reason' (p. 371). In order to satisfy the postulate of immediate evidence, Husserl was forced to the conclusion that the 'idea' of a transcendent object was directly manifest to consciousness, although its substantive content remained the goal of an indefinite series of approximations. This outcome, the thesis reflected, was avoidable once the paradoxical idea of transcendence was replaced by the notion of the object as an 'ideal role' of appearances.

Countering allegations that the 'unconscious' denoted an extra-mental realm of nature or a transcendent 'thing-in-itself', Adorno stressed that all the qualities and features normally associated with the concept could be traced back to the framework or to the reservoir of a depthless consciousness. As presented in the study, the unconscious was an intricate domain comprising principally a quasi-experiential and an objective-categorical layer. While the former alluded to concrete experiences which had been forgotten or purged from memory, the second tier denoted a framework of lawful relationships or categorical rules which, though not accessible to direct experience, was the condition of the possibility of awareness.

The examination of the unconsciousness, Adorno affirmed, was imbued not only be theoretical or speculative motives. In denouncing vitalistic and organismic ontologies and their undertaking to convert depth psychology into a weapon against 'rationalism', the early writings of Adorno meant a challenge to the broad currents of the *Zeitgeist* which played a 'clearly specified and dangerous role' in the social situation of the time. In short, this role was to offer a *rationale* and ideological camouflage for predominant social and economic practices. Precisely because a developed industrial and capitalistic society was far distantiated from any 'natural' and 'organismic' order, the domain of the unconscious could serve as a viable counterpoise - a supplement granting individuals a temporary, although phantasmagorical, refuge from the grating features of economic competition. More critically, the conception of a hidden and unconstrained psyche indicated the malevolent underside of the capitalistic system. Its inclination toward domestic and foreign exploitation and its tendency periodically to be rent by economic crisis. In one of his early pieces, Adorno warns, 'not only limitless egotism but also the most sinister machinations of imperialism find their ideological justification in the natural eruptions of unconscious psychic impulses' (p. 373). At this nodal point, dogmatism and economic domination were in collaboration:

> In order to escape rational criticism once and for all, imperialistic trends - most directly the ideology of fascism - rely on ontological, extra-mental, transcendent and somehow sacred forces which present the destructive and self-destructive effects of the economy as divinely ordained and necessary. (p. 373)

Down to recent ontological conceptions, Adorno added, much of traditional philosophy had been predicated on the sovereign eminence of reason: more particularly on the premise that thinking was in some measure an adequate fit for reality and even for 'Being' itself (conceived as 'idea' or essence of the universe). However, 'the commensurability between thought and reality as a whole had disintegrated', with the outcome that 'the idea of 'Being' has become philosophically impotent' (p. 373). The disintegration was a sharp rebuff to idealism - a perspective correlated more than any other to the absorption of reality by consciousness: 'The crisis of idealism equals a crisis of the philosophical demand for total understanding' (p. 374). In general terms, phenomenology was delineated as a 'post-idealist' mutation of idealism, as 'an effort to reach objectively valid conclusions after the collapse of idealism but with the very instrument of idealism': autonomous reason or subjective consciousness.

In Husserl's case the endeavor to reach objective reality was manifest in his referral to 'primordial evidence' and in his development of a rigorous method of phenomenological description; nevertheless, every piece of evidence and every description were in the end subsistent on the unquestioned jurisdiction of reason and transcendental consciousness. What imbued Husserl's approach was its special aura and his intellectual good taste: his willingness to confine thought to the outline and intentional replication of the world, whose real structure and movement remained beyond consciousness and rational control. Words given theoretical status in sentences only exemplify a neurotic debasement in an involuted type of experience. According to Adorno, Schemer's writings were dedicated to the reconciliation of consciousness and objective or substantive reality, and hence to the elaboration of a 'material phenomenology'. However, after experimenting with a number of dogmatic world perspectives, he ultimately settled for a Manichean juxtaposition of material and ideal forces, of vitalism and rationalism. In Heidegger's case, the attempt to escape the bounds of consciousness took the paradoxical form of a direct appropriation of substantive features of subjectivity, producing a 'subjective ontology' in which concrete personal and historical experience acquired immediate ontological dignity. With this turn, phenomenology is inverted to its contrary: 'Ontology honors only those categories whose domain phenomenology sought to challenge: mere (mundane) subjectivity and historicity'. Overall, Adorno was most affected in his early academic years by Husserl. He located what he considered to be his fixed contradiction:

> On the one hand, Husserl demands the constitution of all things or objects through a return to immediate evidence; on the other hand objects are for him 'absolutely transcendent entities' which epistemologically may only be ascertainable through reference to consciousness, but whose existence is in principle independent of consciousness. (p. 401 n. 4)

Turning to the possible role of philosophical reflection in our time, Adorno credited science and scientific rationality for demystifying the excessive pretensions of speculative thought. However, he was by no stretch of the imagination prepared to accept an 'underlaborer' conception reducing reflection to the 'handmaiden' of science. Precisely when rigorously followed through in its inner logic, empirical science could not claim self-sufficiency, since the term 'empiricism' itself presupposed thought. Even in a scientific age, Adorno contended, science and philosophy were differentiated (though not segregated) by distinct tasks: the tasks respectively of empirical research and of interpretation, the former committed to relatively secure findings, the latter to permanent questioning. 'Interpretation' did not and could not lead to probing the intrinsic or underlying signification of reality, since reality was opaque to human purposes and subjective intentionality. The text philosophy had to unravel was not a coherent narration but 'incomplete, contradictory and fragile, in many passages perhaps the work of blind demons' (p. 375). Philosophical interpretation, confronted with a non-intentional world, could not delve into symbolism but had to resort to experimentation - arranging individual parts or elements into new patterns of structural designs - searching for the master key which would unlock the riddle of reality and thereby break its spell.

According to Adorno, interpretation in its reliance on experimentation was in close affinity to dialectical materialism, whose aim was to find the master key to a basically non-intentional and non-symbolic reality. In actuality, materialism's capacity to reach its goal was directly proportional to its success in 'cleansing its subject matter from any reference to "meaning"' (p. 375). The affinity between interpretation and materialism extended to the effect of the experimental method: the construction of a fitting design was not merely a theoretical exercise, but was meant to break the stranglehold of social constraints. From a materialist *Weltanschaunng*, this relationship between theory and practical change was called 'dialectics'. The juxtaposition of interpretation and a non-intentional reality conjured up (though in a new mystification) the Cartesian legacy of dualism Adorno had debunked previously in critiquing Husserl's writings. Besides, in stressing the experimental function of interpretation, Adorno in his early years seems to equate reflection with a purely 'instrumental' type of rationality, or, in any event, with building heuristic frameworks and paradigms familiar from positivistic methodology as programmatic statements for research. As he propounded his thesis, borrowing an insight from Walter Benjamin,

> The task of philosophy is not to search for manifest or latent intentions of reality, but rather to decipher nonintentional reality by means of the construction of designs and patterns of isolated elements which are able to dissolve questions whose precise (empirical) formulation is the province of science. (p. 410 n. 3)

In a 1932 paper entitled 'The Idea of Natural History', Adorno's point of departure was again the nexus between human design and an unintentional world. The two spheres were no longer presented as self-contained and epistemologically exclusive. The aim of the paper was to obliterate the customary antithesis of the two domains (now stated as 'nature' and 'history') and to exaggerate both to the point where the affinity and reciprocal impact behind their differences emerged. The term 'nature' in this context was meant to refer not to the object of natural science but to a realm of substantive, preordained, or necessary reality, in contrast to the dynamic, innovative feature of historical life. As Adorno understood, the phenomenological school, especially in its post-Husserlian phase, has endeavored to dissolve this antithesis. From the outset Husserl critiqued the characterization that phenomenology was adumbrated and suffused by the tension between nature and history. Efforts by his successors to attenuate the tension were undercut by the continued sway of idealism. Schemer's attempt at an ontological field of objective and timeless meaning was suborned by the capricious, subjective character of the chosen categories. The project was accelerated by Heidegger. Instead of pushing beyond appearances, he coalesced and collapsed ontology and concrete historical experiences to fashion a novel neo-Platonism, in a good and quasi-material way which nevertheless led to a reaction from Adorno.

Adorno faulted Heidegger for resorting to tautological formulae submerging contingent experience in abstract concepts, and also for emphasizing the ideas of 'tautology' and human 'project'.

In order to progress beyond the phenomenological boundary, Adorno contended, it was necessary not merely to process a conceptual synthesis but to adhere as closely as possible to concrete contingency and to the actual interdependence of domains. What was at stake was not only to vindicate a speculative correlation but show how history in its very historicity was infused by nature just as nature in its presumed autonomy emerged as a distinctive entity only through human events. The idea of 'natural history' pointed toward this path.

Two thinkers could file suit for copyright violation over this idea: Georg Lukács and Walter Benjamin. In his *Theory of the Novel*, Lukács had created the concept of 'second nature' to be applied to those layers of historical experience which had been deprived of all content, turned into 'frozen, alien' complexes, into a 'golgotha of decomposed internality' (Dallmayr, 1976, p. 376). The idea was developed more rigorously by Benjamin. While Lukács's 'second nature' was virtually severed from history and only recovered through an eschatological interception by that author, Benjamin presented history as an intrinsically 'natural' process, attributable to its largely unintentional, incipient, and dispersed characteristics. At the same time, nature, in that perspective, bore a deeply historical imprint referrable to the fact that it was fleeting and perishable not only in its elements but in its origin. The link between nature and history was offered in the aspect of finitude and mortality.

Against the foil of nature, the story of human and social evolution described itself as a story of human misery 'significant only at the points of decay'.

Under Benjamin's radical eye, Adorno criticized, 'reality is transformed into a panorama of ruins and fragments, into a golgotha of experience where the key to the nexus of history and nature is buried' (p. 378). The idea of 'natural history' was not intended to demarcate a ready-made synthesis. As Adorno stressed, the student of natural history had provisionally to accept the general discontinuity of fragmentation of elements, including the rupture between 'nature' (perceived as archaic-ontological substance) and 'history' (perceived as an innovative process). Instead of producing an indiscriminate amalgam or total overview, the task was to proceed from this rupture by exploring the 'historical' implications of archaic (quasi-natural) myths in the thick of the archaic strands of historical development (p. 401, n. 17).

Adorno directed his 'Thesis on the Language of Philosophers' against both nominalist/instrumentalist and idealist conceptions of language. Under the impact of modern subjectivism, he observed, words or linguistic symbols have steadily been transformed into vehicles of individual consciousness or intentionality. As a consequence, the tight fit of linguistic form and content has been rent, and replaced by a contingent relationship amenable to arbitrary maneuver. To resolve this negative outcome, idealism at times presented language as auxiliary to 'objective' mind, as a self-contained reserve of essential meanings. Far from being corrective, however, this modus operandi merely solidified the barrier between form and content. According to Adorno, a fundamental tenet of contemporary philosophy was to break down this obstacle and to rehabilitate language through avenues of openness to the world at large, hence engendering a renewed politics. The undertaking could not be accomplished by indulging in neologism or linguistic persiflage the way Adorno thought Heidegger abused philosophy in his more extreme moments. Instead of resorting to sleight of hand, philosophy had to take ordinary language fashioned not as an integrated fabric but as an ensemble of dispersed and partially disintegrated concepts.

The purpose of a 'configurative' approach was to associate words or symbols into recognizable modal patterns or counterpoint arrangements, which, bypassing subjective intentionality and conventional prudence, would allow actual historical experience to become manifest in language. Given the linkage of form and content in this light, words or linguistic symbols were no longer mere utilities, but acquired inherent value in the search for truth: 'The growing significance of a philosophical critique of language can be formulated as the beginning convergence of (literary) art and cognition' (p. 378). Given this way of freeing experience, we have subjectively here a moment in a possible enabling process of disalienation - a removal of mere facticity from the mind now engaged in historically orienting itself in its worldly objectivity.

The fundamental thrust of Adorno's thesis in the mid-1950s was sharply sketched in the opening remarks of the study *Zur Metakritique der Erkenntnistheorie*. Husserl's program, he explained, 'aims to uncover a "sphere of absolute origins", immune from that "organized spirit of contradiction" which was intrinsic to Hegel's dialectical procedure (quoted in Dallmayr, 1976, p. 382). In pursuit of this goal, Husserl was heir to a central and long honored tradition in Western thought: that of *prima philosophia*, of the search for 'first principles' or 'first beginnings'. As one of the last eminent examples of this legacy, his work also illustrated the contradictions in the attempt to sow ontology on the unfertile soil of subjectivity. The linkage of objective foundations and subjectivity had been the stamp of ontology from the outset of its enterprises. In every instance, ontology conceived as *prima philosophia* had tended to abort the critical, mediating role of reflection by claiming to grant access to a 'sphere of absolute origins' or realm of objective being 'in-itself':

> The first principles of philosophers involve a total claim: namely, that to be unmediated or immediate. In order to satisfy this claim, all mediations have to be removed as mere mental contraband, leaving behind the irreducible core of being-in-itself. (p. 382)

The reversion to first beginnings did not bear fruit. In Adorno's heated words,

> There is no level of immediacy in which philosophy can hope to escape the mediating function of reflection; no factual reality is accessible to philosophy except through thought. (p. 382)

In the last result, the Achilles' heel of *prima philosophia* consisted in the promiscuous fusion of opposites, in the self-deceit of laying the groundwork for the merger or identity of subject and object, consciousness and reality. The very process of awakening thought vitiates the pure identity of being. Transcendental phenomenology shared with traditional ontology, the infatuation with unmediated origins and ultimate identity. Adorno remarked,

> The identity of spirit with itself or the 'synthetic unity of apperception' is projected onto the 'things themselves' by means of a methodological ploy (such as *epoche*) and the thoroughness of the projection corresponds directly to the rigor of methodology. This is the original sin of *prima philosophia*. The philosophy of first beginnings which initially generated the idea of truth is in the very beginnings a falsehood (*pseudoe*). (p. 382)

In contemporary ontological conceptions, in the name of a (fading) rationality which is becoming dogmatic, there has been a widening rift between thought and reality only to provide countering steps in further attempts to resurrect first beginnings through intellectual edict. In short, subjectivism (in its idealistic apotheosis) fosters a truncated purposefulness with respect to its nature on reflected objectivity. As Adorno was the first to recognize, Husserl's thought was at variance from competing perspectives by dint of his stress on simple cognition and on existing standards for properly conceiving a status for phenomena. *Prima philosophia*, in this instance, took on the substance of a formidable epistemology. The endeavor to erect consciousness or subjective reflection into an armory for absolute knowledge was bound to fall short of its aims because of a fundamental lack built into consciousness. Too much substance was assumed, whereas the content of consciousness has to be accumulated through experience (a genetically unfolding historical patterning, so to speak).

> First beginnings cannot be identified with subjective reflection since subjectivity can never hope to absorb non-identical elements, and since reflection militates against the notion of immediately given beginnings. While *prima philosophia* aims at pure identity in an onanistic fashion, subjectivity - supposedly the source of secure knowledge - cannot be leveled into monistic experience. (p. 383)

As Adorno pointed out, the antinomial character of Husserl's thought was reflected also in the juxtaposition of 'apriorism' on the one hand and naturalistic empiricism on the other. Husserl's theory of knowledge, he noted, derived its authentication from transcendental subjectivity or the idea of the '*eidos ego*', while simultaneously claiming to grant access to an objective realm surpassing subjective limits. The term 'phenomenology' articulated the intrinsically antinomial design to apprehend 'trans-subjective' "things-in-themselves" as they appear to subjective consciousness' (p. 383). The very accent on transcendental reflection, in Adorno's estimation, had the result of transforming the world into external objects of consciousness while relegating subjectivity to the status of an a priori assumption bereft of concrete implications. In this manner phenomenology can be likened to photography:

> Just like the photographer of earlier days the phenomenologist covers himself with the black sheet of his 'épochè', entreats his objects not to move and finally snaps a family portrait in a passive manner without spontaneous involvement. ... The same correlation which exists in photography between *camera obscura* and external object prevails in

phenomenology with regard to immanent (or self-contained) consciousness and naïve realism. (p. 384)

So, in an alienated way, while the subjective constitution of the perceived objects is being stressed, the objects are actually being treated as remote and alien from the phenomenologist's own self, and they are considered congealed entities to the point of being delineated as 'second nature', inimical to human well being.

The epistemological dilemmas thus outlined, Adorno contended, were indicative of the social and political ramifications of Husserl's thought. Phenomenological 'reduction' and description were correlated intimately with the situation of late industrial society: The bourgeois individual, paying lip service to doctrines of freedom and contractual rights, was increasingly compelled to retreat from public life into complete privacy and to adopt the role of passive recipient of mass-produced standardized goods and services, irrespective of individual tastes. With the liberal individualism of a bygone era as an ideological yardstick, the contemporary consumer mentality was tied through the accent on the 'possessive' character of humanity or on individual penchants to treat the entire world (including cognitive insights) as personal property. Through its emphasis on absolute certainty and a priori evidence, Adorno wrote, Husserl's *prima philosophia* disclosed itself as a theory of property:

> Once the idealist notion of transcendental subjectivity is accepted as the central category, nothing remains that does not fall prey and in a strict sense belong to subjectivity. (p. 384)

In comparison with past versions, contemporary individualism was etched in a noncommittal mold. From this vantage point, Husserl's attempt to move beyond Descartes toward pure reflection carried a price: encroaching neutralization and privatization of personal affects and aspirations. At the dawn of modernity, individualism was implicated in public life as an agency changing hierarchical feudalism; in the succeeding era transcendental subjectivity was a synonym for passive consumption by an abstracted individual. In Adorno's words, Husserl's method was not so much an exercise of critical reason as an endeavor to pacify factual conditions whose hegemony and authority were no longer questioned, in order to intellectualize away real contradictions in society. With the advent of phenomenology, 'bourgeois thought in its final stages dissolves into isolated, fragmented categories and finds comfort in the mere reproduction of reality' (p. 384). The flaws of reason could be remedied only by pushing reflection to its limits and by divulging its mediating, dialectical chiaroscuro. To the degree that reason is equated with the totality of life and true beauty, we have at hand the measure of a reified *mathesis*. By revealing non-identity in the midst of sameness and renewal (of purposive behavior) at the crux of oldness or permanence, post-metaphysical thought was an exercise in 'natural historiography'. 'Attentive to the suffering sedimented in concepts, such thought waits only for the moment of their disintegration. ... What is needed today is not a first but a last philosophy'. The actualization of just such a last philosophy was originally posited in Marx's *Theses on Feuerbach*.

Heidegger's notion of *Dasein*, or existence, Adorno has said more than once, was only an abstract reified synonym for subjective experience, just as the term 'historicity' was an ontological mantle to cloak contingent historical events in a dubious respectability. On the whole, references to Heidegger in the *Metakritique* repeated and refurbished the critical theses of earlier papers. Heidegger's view entailed not so much a move beyond Husserl's antinomies as an attempt to mask and deny internal conflicts, particularly the conflict between 'timeless ontology' and 'history'. Husserl and Heidegger, the *Metakritique* noted, were used in the search for 'first principles'; in Heidegger's case, subjectivity gave way to a foundational structure supposedly above subjective reflection and imbued with object-ontological significance: human existence as rooted in Being. Because of the non-reflective trait of this foundation, *prima philosophia* in Heidegger's rendition exuded an aura of compactness and archaic simplicity unequaled in Husserl's work:

> Whatever is lasting and solid appears to philosophical speculation as basic and primordial. ... On the assumption that the basis (*hyperkeimenon*) is truer than the superstructure, truth and primitivism become synonymous. This is perhaps the most dangerous consequence of the doctrine of immediacy with its suppression of subjectivity and reflective mediations. (p. 386)

Adorno further charged that the dangerous undertaking of conceptualized immediacy falsified objectivity. As in the case of traditional metaphysics, the exposition of ontological origins was ultimately an excrescence of a subjective edict. Heidegger's emphasis on the non-reflective and non-volitional status of existential categories merely underlined vividly the incompatibility of *prima philosophia* and its apodictic premises and phenomenological reductions. He further contends that the political dangers of an objectivist ontology were manifest in fascism with its simultaneous stress on 'blood and soil' and the 'will to power'. Fascism tried to implement *prima philosophia*. The most archaic and most enduring was supposed to rule immediately and in a literal sense: myth and a perverted science merged. In this manner the linkage of first beginnings and usurpation was placed in stark relief (p. 403, n. 29).

In *The Jargon of Authenticity* Adorno reviled philosophical sophistry in the postwar years in Germany. He noted that the hierophants of jargon simulate 'the ascension of the word beyond the realm of the actual, conditioned, and contestable', 'as though a blessing from above were directly composed into that world'. As a consequence deceit 'becomes foundational and everyday language is spoken here and now as if it were the sacred one'. In Adorno's appraisal jargon was an articulation of withdrawal into privacy or subjective resentment on the part of a declining middle to lower middle class stratum incapable of mastering the historically given conditions. 'From its inability to cope practically or spiritually with social development, this class derives its claim to special, elect status: that of primordial authenticity' (Adorno, 1973a, pp. 10-2).

The entire gist of Heidegger's thought is actually in the effort not so much to overcome as to lay siege to traditional dichotomies, such as those between a priori and a posteriori, essence and fact, subject and object. 'As is well known', Adorno upbraids his audience, 'Heidegger supplants the traditional category of subjectivity with *Dasein* whose essence is said to be existence' (1973a, pp. 113-4). This revision let him take as his point of departure a concrete condition or givenness - an object of consciousness in terms of traditional epistemology - while at the same time treating this condition as 'more than mere fact', an 'absolute primordial premise' or 'pure condition of Being'. Conceptually outstripping Husserl, Heidegger preferred to interpret 'subjectivity as a concept of indifference: essence and fact in one'. According to *Being and Time*, the advantage of the ideal of *Dasein* was on two fronts. On the one hand, it condoned an association of an ontic domain-existence with a concrete individual experience; on the other, it indicated an ontological structure:

> In this manner radically contradictory connotations are directly ascribed to subjectivity: it is treated as fact or reality and simultaneously - in line with traditional philosophy - it is viewed as consciousness and thus as a basic facticity as its pure concept, its essence, and ultimately as Husserl's *'eidos ego'*. (pp. 116-8)

Against this recriminatory backdrop, Adorno further castigated Heidegger's notion of *Dasein* insofar as it emerged as a synonym for a subjectivity rent of subject, much in the vein of Fichte's absolute ego.

As in the case of *Dasein*, Heidegger's subjective objectivism was manifest also in the concept of 'authenticity'. For example, his use of the concept was indebted to Husserl's quest for objective reality or the sphere of 'things-in-themselves', a quest which indicated that the essence or core of things was 'not something arbitrarily fabricated by subjective thought, nor a distilled synthesis of characteristics'. As Adorno reflected, Heidegger's approach remained a descendant of Husserl's to the degree that it treated authenticity 'directly as an aspect of things and thus as a special domain of reality'; from his heritage stemmed 'the substantialization of authenticity; its elevation to an existential category and to a status of givenness' disassociated from subjective reflection and amenable to a 'purely descriptive account' (p. 124). Perceived this way, Heidegger's use of the concept gave rise to its reification and even to naturalistic determinism; hence authenticity entails a type of jargon in philosophy that Adorno finds abhorrent because he aims for non-identity, believing that in non-identity truth dwells. Adorno says,

> Introduced initially as a descriptive category in response to the relatively innocuous question regarding the essential core of things, authenticity develops into a mythically imposed destiny; despite the antinaturalistic thrust of an ontology erected on transcendental foundations, the category operates as a naturalistic constraint. (pp. 126-7)

By Adorno's measure, Heidegger's prejudicial premises were manifest in the treatment of authenticity as a personal (albeit purely internalized) property: as an ultimate divining rod for the acquisition or loss of individual identity and selfhood. Once the concept was cleansed of external or empirical connotations, reification dissipated into random choice: 'Devoid of any objective content, authenticity falls prey to the arbitrary decisions of the individual determining his authentic selfhood' (pp. 120-1). In the context of existential analysis,

> mediation (a moment in dereifying false consciousness) is transformed into an immediate identity of mediating reflection and mediated world; although neither element can subsist without the other, the two are by no means the same - as Heidegger's basic thesis alleges. (p. 121)

The 'overthrow' of mediation sustained in the Heideggerian vernacular involved the muting of negativity and the suppression of dialectics.

'The appearance of negativity is an integral aspect of pure thought. To think means to identify: self-contained and self-contented, the conceptual framework obstructs access to the subject matter of thought' (Adorno, 1973b, p. 5). Idealism in particular was committed to the canon 'that the non-ego, the other and everything resembling nature is inferior - a ready prey to the voracity of synthesizing and self-perpetuating thought' (p. 10). Despite the emphasis on objectification, even Hegel's philosophy was in essence narcissistic, 'since spirit extracts from objects only their spiritual or mental parameters' (p. 12) The danger of narcissism could not be remedied by the retreat of reflection in favor of naive realism or a sham immediacy of experience. Only by pursuing its inherent antinomies to their limits could thought hope to escape from its constraints and attain its goals. 'The utopia of cognition would be the ability to unlock the conceptual domain with conceptual means - without reducing the one to the other' and the strategy for dissolving the bonds of reflection was 'dialectics - but a dialectics which, instead of adhering to a mental synthesis, pursued its aim in a strictly negative manner' (pp. 22-3), by realizing the insufficiency and incongruence of its conceptual repertoire:

> To change the thrust of conceptualization in the direction of non-identity is the emblem of negative dialectics. Insight into the constitutive character of the nonconceptual domain would dissolve the constraint of identity which, in the absence of critical scrutiny, characterizes conceptual frameworks. The seeming autarchy of concepts as self-contained units of meaning is overcome by reflection on the purpose of knowledge. (p. 27)

In addition,

> Dialectics is the consistent awareness of non-identity; it does not adopt an apriori standpoint. Thought is driven toward dialectics by virtue of its inevitable insufficiency, by its guilt toward its subject matter. (p. 27)

As Adorno amended this insight, negative dialectics entailed not so much the construction of a new philosophical system as the arrangement of conceptual configurations or 'constellations' attuned to the nonsystemic and idiosyncratic nature of reality. It is to appreciate the multiplicity of things and the plurality of experiences in a coherent phenomenology residing in the *Mitwelt* (to take a term from Heidegger):

> The inadequacy of every concept necessitates the reliance on other concepts; thus arise those constellations which alone preserve some of the virtues of some individual names. The language of philosophy approximates names through their negation. (p. 53)

This type of negation brings about communion of fellow philosopher-practitioners to the extent that reality is demystified and people can define a common domain to explore communicable experience or even a *vision du monde*.

Given its objectivist impulse, existentialist analysis also is a pacemaker for alienation and reification. To an extent, ontological speculation could be deemed the 'metaphysics of reification', since the assumption of an immediately given facticity deforms reality into a composite of reified dates. The idea of '*Seinshörigkeit*' (yielding to and genuflection before the splendor of Being) by Adorno's imagination was clear evidence of the alienating pull in Heidegger's thought: its disposition to offer surety to existing forms of social and political repression. 'Although claiming attachment to the universe,' he cited that 'ontological submissiveness supports without further ado every type of particularism or parochial arrangement which is able to demonstrate forcefully enough the subject's weakness' (pp. 84, 105). In the course taken by Heidegger, ontology tends to be grasped as the disposition to abide in a heteronomous social order detached from the need of rational legitimation. Whatever the exact meaning of existence, the insistence on the internal character of authenticity deprived *Dasein* of objective yardsticks and opened the door to capricious dealings:

> Removed from otherness and objectification (authentic) existence - viewed as a yardstick of thought - implements its decrees in the same autocratic manner as in politics the dictator implements the ruling world view. The reduction of reflection to the thinking subject brings to a halt the genesis and maturation of thought which alone would give sustenance to subjectivity. (pp. 127-8)

Given the paradoxes of Being viewed as conceptualization of ultimate reality, the only legitimate philosophy in Adorno's mind was a philosophy of incongruence. This notion took seriously the insufficiency of thought in pursuing its goal of absorbing reality: 'What is proclaimed by ontology as manifestation of a positive entity, has its truth and legitimacy in negativity' (pp. 82-3). As Adorno was quick to stress, the critique of Heidegger's thought was not meant to herald a new ontology replacing Being by facticity and non-identity; such attempts would be in vain and in internal contradiction by 'conceptualizing the non-conceptual' (p. 136). Negation and negativity designated not retreat but rather a ceaseless struggle waged between thought and reality. Locked into the quest for reality, bypassing reification or ideological deceit, negative thinking was in Adorno's terms equivalent to dialectical materialism, provided the latter was not put into an epistemological form. Countering the Leninist theses of the Third International, Adorno insisted that cognition could neither be pared to object nor molded into a pool of mental 'images'. The idea of images in particular was an idealist 'surplus value':

> The materialist aspiration to grasp reality aims at the opposite - only in the absence of images could objects be known. Such absence concurs with the theological ban on images. Materialism secularized this ban, preventing the positive portrayal of utopia: This is the core of its negativity. ... Its chief longing would be the resurrection of the flesh - a notion completely alien to idealism and the realm of absolute spirit. (p. 207)

Regarding the comparison between Heidegger and Marx, Adorno stated:

> Despite some affinity, the term 'Being' means something entirely different to Marx and to Heidegger: the ontological doctrine of the primacy (or transcendence) of Being over thought contains a distant echo of materialism. The doctrine of Being turns into ideology when it spiritualizes the materialist element by transposing it to a level of pure essence beyond ontic reality - thus discarding the critique of false consciousness inherent in the materialist notion of Being. The notion which was meant to mobilize truth against ideology degenerates into complete falsehood: the demise of idealism into the proclamation of an ideal sphere. (p. 200)

By any standard, *Negative Dialectics* is the acme of critical theory, a damning accusation of the injustices that infest capitalism in terms of Adorno's intellectual development, this tour de force fulfilled a lifelong endeavor to come to terms with the prevailing academic fashions of our time, particularly with the foremost proponents of the phenomenological movement. Concerning social and political implications, his writings highlighted the bourgeois affinities of transcendental phenomenology - by pointing to the connections between the notion of *eidos ego* and the heritage of 'possessive individualism' and, now definitely, to the association between phenomenological description and the consumerism which defines the fetish-like personae of late capitalism, applicable even to the industrial bureaucratism of our time. While repudiating the inadequacy and counterproductive qualities of phenomenological methodology, Adorno hailed Husserl's ambition to overcome the limitations inherent in the traditional dualisms and antinomies, including the split between idealism and objectivism. In pursuing this goal, and in formulating his phenomenological design, Husserl remained in at least one way an inspiration for Adorno: his steadfast commitment to critical/rational inquiry and his refusal to forsake reflection in favor of experiential immediacy or ontological intuition. From the fulcrum of critical theory, the antinomial structure of traditional philosophy could not be superseded by intuitive short cuts or by a leap into made-to-order syntheses. As Adorno never ceased emphasizing, the atonement for past dualisms did not lie in the indiscriminate merger or monistic identification of opposites, since identity was merely a synonym for idealist usurpation.

There is a convergence between Heidegger and Adorno on certain points. Adorno's caveats against individualism and the philosophy of consciousness coincide somewhat with Heidegger's critique of 'subjectivism' and the tradition of Western metaphysics with its emphasis on subjective reflection. Similarly, Adorno's comments on the ambivalence of Enlightenment thought and modern rationalism find a parallel in the existential ambivalence toward logical calculation and the conception of human beings as 'rational animals'. In particular, the thesis that the domination of 'instrumental' rationality ultimately reflects the human 'will to power' - the desire to subjugate and alter nature - recalls Heidegger's treatment of modern technology. A further linkage, particularly telling in the thrust of the 'critical' program, can be elucidated in the common stress of the two thinkers on historical exegesis and on the importance of 'pre-understanding' or tradition for human cognition. The effulgent defense of the hermeneutical technique in the introductory chapter of *Negative Dialectics* offered a correction not only to instrumental rationalism but also to the affectations of a purely critical stance. The Enlightenment attack on prejudice and repressive authority, Adorno observes, was by no means misguided initially, provided the critique does not entail the wholesale repudiation of our common past:

> One easily forgets that tradition dwells at the heart of knowledge as the mediating element of the subject matter under scrutiny. ... Even where form and content of cognition are segregated, knowledge takes part in tradition as a reservoir of unconscious recollections: no question can be articulated without somehow preserving and focusing the legacy of the past. (p. 54)

Of more crucial significance, the relationship between the two protagonists can be focused on their respective attitudes toward hermeneutics. Despite his appreciation of the role of tradition, Adorno has his eye trained on wider ambits of reality, transcending the artifacts of culture and their historical exegesis. Human experience through the ages, in his perspective, does not simply mirror an intentional design or a continuous sedimentation of meaning which could be clarified through a dialogue between participants and interpreters. While not bereft of meaningful patterns, history can also be studied as an outcome of unintelligible events or a configuration of 'decomposed' clues and symbols: as 'natural history'. Approach to this facet of historical experience is offered not through cultural exegesis but in complex decoding mechanisms, particularly the linguistic 'configurations' designed to unlock the conundrum of reality.

Adorno, at this juncture, departs from cultural or 'philosophical' hermeneutics in favor of an orientation which appears closely akin to structural analysis. Structural investigation in this context is not merely a doctrine or strategy according to which symbols and actions are ultimately grounded in cognitive matrixes or substantive endowments of the mind. In comparison to this cognitive or 'positivist' kind of structuralism, Hayden White at one point demarcated what he called an 'eschatological' brand, championed principally by Lacan and Foucault. The positivist genre, in this respect similar to hermeneutics, mainly pursues the goal 'to render the strange familiar', while eschatological structuralism 'is imbued with the spirit to "defamiliarize", divulging the strangeness in presumably intelligible happenings':

> The eschatological structuralists ... deal in epiphanies - not the epiphany of the Word made Flesh which is the supreme insight of their Christian counterparts from St. John the Evangelist to Karl Barth, but rather that of the 'Flesh made Word'. (in Dallmayr, 1976, p. 397)

To some degree, the relationship between hermeneutics and 'configurative' analysis in Adorno's thought may be compared to Paul Ricoeur's distinction between a 'restorative' and a 'defamiliarizing' hermeneutics.

The accent on 'natural history', opens a major divide between Adorno and Heidegger, provided the latter is placed in the camp of philosophical hermeneutics. This interpretation may fall short in that it may be too close to Heidegger's early 'anthropocentric' phase with its concentration on 'hermeneutical phenomenology'. His later writings disclose a progressive dissatisfaction with intentionality and a growing concern with the embeddedness of thought and action in a broader network of human relationships.

If Being and world are indeed related in the intimate manner of Heidegger's later writings (the postwar period), then Being cannot be discussed abstractly, conceptually, or merely speculatively. Instead of vindicating a purely contemplative asceticism, the 'Being of reality' would seem to engender worldly and even political involvements (without sliding into a near-sighted empiricism). In fine, the ideas of ontological 'difference' and 'mutual belonging' appear to be against the grain of the socio-political 'neutrality' adopted by Heidegger in later decades. In his own terms, ontology does not provide a 'cover' from the world, so it is difficult to fathom how he remained removed from worldly troubles, including the socio-political debates which overlap with his more philosophical concerns about 'man-in-the-world'. Adorno sharply reminded the Heideggerians that ontology in our time cannot simply signify the retreat into an esoteric position of wisdom or the return to a pretended innocence. Seen in this light, Adorno's criticism offers not only an external commentary but an internal critique of existentialist thought, or rather a stage enabling the reader at crucial crossroads 'to think with Heidegger against Heidegger' (p. 397).

Some passages in Heidegger's oeuvre, picked out with perspicacity by Adorno, seem to hark back to an idyllic setting proper for humanity if we are to be at home in our universe. Against this background, existential ontology emerges as a pacemaker of a rustic primitivism opposed to the complexities and cosmopolitan tendencies of modern life. Even when approached in a sympathetic and non-ideological way, Heidegger's works overall convey an anti-urban, anti-political spirit. Robert Sokolowski in his *Husserlian Meditations* adjudged that Heidegger's thoughts 'are most appropriate for the village, not the city' (quoted in Dallmayr, 1976, p. 400). In stark contrast, Adorno's orientation is out-and-out suffused by urbanity and hence qualifies as a 'philosophy of the city'. One may wonder, especially after *Negative Dialectics*, enjoining against images or projected visions of the 'good life', whether the focus of his preoccupations is a city without hope. In his last queries he wondered whether the bases for a 'new autochthony' might be illumined 'even in the atomic age', and put forth as a lodestar the mode of 'serenity', entailing simplicity and a kind of resignation in the midst of the roil and toil of technological revolutions which are uprooting the world. Adorno, in a last sour (if not bitter) rejoinder to Heidegger's pastoral images, has this portrayal to make:

> ... negative dialectics implies concretely that, in order to be true (at least for today), thought must also be ready to think against itself. Unless willing to measure itself against those extreme situations which elude conceptual formulation, thought assumes from the outset the character of a mere musical accompaniment - similar to the background music with which SS officers liked to drown out the screams of their victims. (1973b, p. 365)

Thought thinks against itself to prevent reification of the lifeworld itself, giving us a flexibility of concepts in a historically defined permanence of a materialist phenomenology.

In the next section, we shall discuss more concretely a phenomenological hermeneutics of the social world and how we methodologically proceed to objectify such a world by rather unconventional techniques.

Affirmations: The *Aufhebung* of unintentional truths

In ferreting out negativities, arguing against the ontological categories of 'Being', 'thrownness', and 'historicity', Adorno insisted on the historical specificity of people's (not humanity's) condition. But even when fighting with Heidegger he recognized that both owed much to Husserl. Both agreed that subject and object were necessarily entwined (Husserl had posited that thought was always thought-of-something, and Adorno abided by this postulate, while Heidegger spoke in terms of humanity's Being (*Dasein*) as always being-in-the-world). Heidegger simply postulated this relation as immediately given in experience; Adorno demonstrated their mediated matrix through the prescription of argumentation. Both wanted to establish a concrete, 'materialist' analysis of phenomena, a phenomenological hermeneutics of the sacral world. To Heidegger this meant unveiling a general, 'essential' truth out of the particulars of lived experience; Adorno wanted to expose within the particular the general structure of a historically developed society. 'Materialist' to Heidegger entailed relating particulars to the ontological categories of Being; to Adorno it meant connecting them to Marxian categories of analysis. Heidegger internalized the Hegelian dialectic of Being and non-Being, conceiving it in terms of the relationship between subject and object.

Both were critics of mass culture and positivism. Heidegger saw the *Angst* people suffered as an existential, eternally fixed ontological category and demanded that people change themselves; Adorno insisted on the transformation of society. Adorno took from Walter Benjamin the insight: 'The goal of the revolution is the elimination of anxiety'. (The invocation of the cant of revolution has become so ritualized that it now has a deleterious role to play in Critical Theory; the concept of possible revolution is the Frankfurt School's weakest point. The mood of the school is very much analogous to the Left Hegelians of the *Zeitgeist* of the 1840s.)

Language for Adorno formed the crux of later dilemmas of philosophy. The (idealist) premise of identity between subject and object, understood by bourgeois idealism to be the requisite for knowledge of a truth which, it postulated, was necessarily both absolute and total, dissolved. 'The adequacy of thought and being as totality has decomposed'; furthermore, the thesis of autonomous reason out of which reality developed simply collapses with the critical analysis for lack of material objectifications.

Max Horkheimer, a collaborator of Adorno's, used the less metaphorical language of *Ideologiekritik* to sketch the demise of the identity principle on which bourgeois metaphysics had been found in terms of a change in the social relations of production:

> The idea of an unbroken harmony between reality and reason belongs to the liberalist phase. It corresponds to a social economy marked by a plurality of individual entrepreneurs. ('Materiality and Metaphysics', Horkheimer, 1972, p. 12)

Since the 1960s, the slogan 'Back to Kant' has spelled out the disillusionment among philosophers with all metaphysics. Yet neo-Kantianism, the product of new historical conditions, never really did go 'back'. Whereas Kant's critique of metaphysics had been radical in its social implications, these new Kantians turned critical reason into an ideology of resignation, a technocratism which was really a default to the public status quo, the passive acceptance of the world in its givenness. According to Adorno, concurrent with the waxing 'crisis of idealism', the 'given' world of the bourgeois social order became more and more difficult to justify. As reason and reality lost contact with each other outside philosophy, they became disassociated within philosophy as well, and the relationship of subject and object became the most pressing technical problem facing modern philosophy, in fact menacing its very existence.

Protesting abstract formalism, Husserl maintained that knowledge was always knowledge of something, yet simultaneously he removed himself from empirical existence because, as fleeting and transient and very much dependent, it could not afford a base for the absolute knowledge he so much wanted. He strove to distinguish between the material, 'natural' object and its presence within thought, hoping to establish a transcendental sphere of thought-objects which would be analyzed by pure logic untainted by empirical heterogeneity. He employed this example. When I think of the apple tree in my garden, the object of my thought, while particular, is not the same as the actual, 'material' tree. The latter can be 'bracketed out' in phenomenological technique because, even if it burns up, the 'meaning' of the tree remains as the 'intention' of my thinking act. Adorno had already protested against this distinction in his first *Habilitationschrift* for Cornelius in 1925, arguing against the empiricist position - 'particular things can burn up'. The meaning of the tree, the truth that it could change, resided in just that heterogeneity which Husserl had tried to expunge.

It is critical to realize that what was being debated as a philosophical problem was more than a mere scholastic concern. At stake was the very possibility of rational understanding. For if reality could not be brought into identity with universal rational concepts, as idealists since Kant had claimed, then it threatened to fragment into a multiplicity of particulars which confronted men and women as opaque and inexplicable. These intractable, inexorable 'things', which Hegel, from the macroscopic perspective of a rational totality, had been able to dismiss as 'lazy existence', suddenly lost their easy familiarity and swelled up on the horizon as threatening; they became the source of overwhelming anxiety.

Sartre, along the lines described above, argued that the impossibility of subsuming particular phenomena under general, abstract categories was proof that existence was absurd. To Adorno, it proved only the futility of the whole taxonomic process and the equation of such pigeon-holing with knowledge. This philosophical warning was in congruence with Sartre's experiential observation. But where Adorno felt existentialism (as well as phenomenology and *Lebensphilosophie*) made its error was in accepting 'natural' phenomena as 'given' immediately in experience. Hegel had already demonstrated the illusory nature of such endeavors as 'concreteness' in the opening of *The Phenomenology of Mind*, contending that the immediately given 'this', 'here' was in fact the most abstract. Adorno explored Hegel's argument (using the language of Benjamin) in his critique of the founder of modern existentialism, Søren Kierkegaard:

> It may be said that abstraction is the seal of mythical thinking. The ambiguity of the guilty connection with nature, whereby everything communicates with everything without differentiation, knows no true concretion (only facile and abstract mediations). Here the names of the created things are confused, and in their place remains the blind matter or the empty sign. The wide-spread custom of ascribing to mythic-archaic-thought the highest degree of concreteness, due to the conceptually immediate perception of the 'this-here', leads to error. (quoted in Buck-Morss, 1977, p. 82)

For Adorno, 'concreteness' prompted grounding the particular in its dialectical, mediated relationship to the totality. The object was hence more than itself and knowledge of it was more than the tautological $A = A$; by the mediation of conceptual reflection, one must prepare a critical theory of practice to reappropriate alienated processes which have been sedimented into institutions.

The 'totality' Adorno had in mind was not that of Hegel's closed metaphysical system but the Marxian meaning of the total socioeconomic structure of relations which depicted the bourgeois order. Detached from this whole, looked at as an isolated, 'natural' entity, the object 'congeals ... into a fetish which merely encloses itself all the more deeply within its existence' (p. 83).

The fallacy of existentialism (and Husserl's phenomenology) was that, by stopping with the immediately given object, they did not see through the opaque and fetish-like medium, whose reified form Lukács had analyzed as 'second-nature'. Heidegger's phenomenological approach was simply to ignore the fetish character of objects as commodities. He spoke of things as if their use-value was still intact, rather than, as Marx and Adorno stressed, having been superseded by the abstract exchange value characteristic of bourgeois commodities. Both Sartre's and Husserl's obliviousness to the social nature of objects was evident from the start in their very choice of a tree, a 'first nature' object, to illumine the essence of the cognitive problematic. But, as might be expected (with Adorno's inclination for enclosing opposite tendencies in dialecticized tensions), another dimension emerged. If the existentialist perception needed the remedy of dialectical mediation, then dialectics in turn, in forsaking closed metaphysical systems, needed to confront the particular phenomena of everyday life.

What distinguished Adorno's approach was not only his assertion of the dialectical relations between the particular and the general, but also the direction in which his thought moved in the process of dialectical cognition. Instead of proceeding outward from the particular to the totality (as had Hegel), Adorno moved inward, and indeed, within the 'atypical', the insignificant, and the uncanny entities. At the intersection of two apparently contradictory positions, insisting on the dialectical relationship of the phenomenon to the totality and simultaneously on the necessity for microcosmic analysis, Adorno explicated his concept of the 'concrete particular'. This was something akin to what Hegel had formulated in *The Phenomenology of Mind*: his 'deductions' of 'objective mind' (or *Logos*) in nature.

When Lukács analyzed the structure of bourgeois theory and plumbed within it the commodity structure of the social totality, he provided the paradigm for Adorno's own efforts to find the general within the particular. But the difference lay precisely here, in Lukács's preference for the totalistic picture over details to give us the material for explanation:

> The greater the distance from pure immediacy, the larger the net encompassing the 'relations', and the more complete the integration of the 'objects' within the system of relations, the sooner change will cease to be impenetrable and catastrophic, the sooner it will become comprehensible. (Lukács, 1971, p. 154)

Unfortunately, this genre of dialectical materialism is so sweeping in its orbit that state policies made in its image can readily succumb to the siren call of a totalitarian solution. Lukács in fact 'sold out' to Stalin.

Walter Benjamin's 'microscopic gaze', as Adorno often called it, through which the most common objects appeared remarkable, was a uniquely personal characteristic, but it was more. As an 'instrument' for philosophical cognition, it provided a means for making the very particularity of the object exude a significance which dissolved its reified appearance and revealed it to be more than a tautology, more than simply identical with itself. At the same time, the knowledge it freed remained bound to the particular, rather than sacrificing material specificity by moving to a plane of abstract, ahistorical generalization. This caring attitude toward all things in being is compatible in politics with a dialectical humanism which is actually more characteristic of the utopian than of the scientific socialists.

Subsequent chapters will examine the transition to this socialist humanism in Habermas's recommendations for soliciting a consensually derived truth in a voluntary community of like-minded, 'political' souls. He is deeply steeped in the existentialist tradition, including Heidegger. He fertilizes his ideas generously from other arts and humanities, so that his 'Marxism' centers critically on a subjectivity which fully knows the powers of its own agency. So his maverick brand of 'socialism' is as much immanent as transcendent. By the mid-1990s, his politics had become an idealized intersubjective dialogue where democracy as space collapsed into a time of a future past.

Microscopic analysis was a method of textual analysis, with Marxist categories as the underpinning, such that Benjamin's approach appeared to Adorno as a potentially productive means for dissolving idealism. A microscopic analysis, which could identify the general (the bourgeois social structure) within the particular (the details of bourgeois philosophical texts), could indicate more than the social function of ideas (*Ideologiekritik*). It promised to make possible statements of objective truth, although historically specific. Rather than simply exposing the ideological implications of philosophical schools by highlighting the manner in which the general positions (positivism, irrationalism, and the like) acted as supports of the status quo, this method took Adorno deep into the particulars of the philosophical texts so that the very words and their configurations, and the seemingly trivial details, became meaningful, divulging a significance not even intended by the author.

Precisely 'unintentional truth' was the object of Adorno's critical inquiry. Before studying this idea (which was Benjamin's originally), it may be an illuminating summary to make manifest the facets of 'non-identity' embraced within the notion of the 'concrete particular'. The whole idea of unintentional truth runs against the grain of building great systems which had characterized much of philosophy, particularly in the classical era of capitalism.

The particular was not a case of the general; it could not be identified by placing it within a general category, for its significance lay in it contingency, not its universality. In addition, the particular was not identical to itself. It went beyond tautology because it was concretely mediated in society. Like Leibniz's monads, each particular was unique, yet each carried a picture of the whole, an 'image of the world', which within a Marxist categorical analysis meant an image of the bourgeois social structure. Against Leibniz, it was itself 'sedimented history' and not ontologically and eternally valid, because the general social reality was not absolute but a particular moment within the social totality. So 'what dissolved the fetish' (i.e., the "given object") is the insight that things are not simply so and not otherwise, that they have come to be under certain conditions' (Adorno, 1973b, p. 52). That the particular could not even adequately be comprehended as an instance of the concept but leaves a remnant is expressed by Adorno repeatedly:

> It is *not* up to philosophy to exhaust things according to scientific usage, to reduce the phenomena to a minimum of propositions. ... Instead, in philosophy we literally seek to immerse ourselves in things that are heterogeneous ... without placing those things in prefabricated categories. (1973b, p. 13)

For instance, a natural object is not only natural but historical; a historical phenomenon is not merely history but material nature; and so on ad infinitum.

There was also a utopian thrust to non-identity as it related to the concrete particular. The ephemeral quality of particulars was the promise of a new future, while their very small size, their evasion of categorization, indicated a defiance of the very social structure they reflected. Reading the non-identity of the particular as a promise of utopia was an idea Adorno solicited from Ernst Bloch. Adorno applauded the efforts of Bloch:

> While he pursued the historico-philosophical character of utopia materialistically in the illusionless struggle for the fundamental necessities of life, he searched for the 'traces' of utopia, of finite redemption shining into [the present] in the smallest features of ... reality. (in Buck-Morss, 1977, p. 90 n. 55)

Insisting on recognition of the 'not-yet-existing [*Nochnicht-seinde*]', Bloch premised hope for the future in those non-identical traces (*Spuren*) of utopia already experienced within the present. In his inaugural lecture at the University of Frankfurt, Adorno made the point that 'only in traces [*Spuren*] and ruins' was there 'hope of ever coming across genuine and just reality' (in Buck-Morss, 1977, p. 90). Thus the genesis of utopian hope was in the small things, in details which slipped out of the conceptual matrix. Adorno had already articulated this ideal in his philosophy of music, for example on the music of Schubert: 'But change succeeds only in the smallest thing. Where the scale is large, death dominates' (p. 90); it remained important in his aesthetic theory. Within this utopian impulse or hope, there loomed an anti-totalitarian premise in that the sanctity of each profane object rendered it immune from politicization and technical domination.

Crucial to *negative dialectics* was not only the object's non-identity with itself but its non-identity with the knowing subject, the mind and its logical processes. In Adorno's inaugural lecture, this level of non-identity found expression in the term 'unintentional truth'. This choice of words was not without import. At the time Horkheimer and his collaborators at the Institute were also emphasizing that subject and object were not identical: certainly not inverted, for that would be reificatory or schizophrenogenic. The idea of 'the unintentional' said more. If the Institute's *Ideologiekritik* essays divulged the untruth of identity (i.e., of the Hegelian claim that the real was rational), Adorno was stating the converse as well: non-identity was the locus of truth and dialecticity. Hegel, of course, spoke of the identity of identity and non-identity which was to alienate alienation in a return to Absolute Knowledge, a rationalist vision certainly in accord even with Freudian precepts. Benjamin in his *Trauerspiel* gives a dialectical materialist account of the following meaning:

> Truth never enters into a relation, and particularly not an intellectual one. The object of knowledge as something determined within conceptual intention is not truth. Truth, built out of ideas (rather than appearing with them), is unintentional Being. The procedure which adequately conforms to it is therefore not an intending within the knowing process but an entering into [truth] and disappearing. Truth is the death of intention. (Benjamin, quoted in Buck-Morss, 1977, p. 91).

The subject needed to go to the object, to plumb its depths; to stop at the threshold of the 'thought objects' was to uncover nothing more than the subject's own reflection as 'intention'. Benjamin was merely assertive in his exposition. Later, Adorno, in his *Metakritik*, an attack on Husserl, would demonstrate how the latter's method led the latter inescapably back into the closed ambit of idealism which he had tried to leap over transcendentally. In turn, Benjamin employed his criticism to validate his own materialist premise of unintentionality.

It should be observed that this idea was 'materialist' not so much in the

Marxian sense as in the simpler one of pre-Kantian empiricism. It was greatly exaggerated, however. Adorno stressed that philosophy must recognize as 'matter' not only natural objects but *geistige* phenomena as well (including Husserl's 'thought objects'). The 'material' of ideas, theories, concepts, novels, and musical pieces, like physical matter, lived, aged, and disintegrated. Not even the products of thought, then, were mere subjectivity, and this factor entailed that they, too, were the locus of 'unintentional truth'. To dismiss these *geistige* phenomena would be to engage in subrealist discourse where overgeneralization would lead us to lose the concrete totality and the processes inherent to it. Even thinking itself is an environing and practical activity which makes a sharp separation between subject and object inconceivable since they mutually interpenetrate in a well worked out synchrony of social structures and diachrony of political actions.

Describing phenomena as if they had a life of their own, as if they elaborated a truth their human creator was not cognizant of, was a sui generis fact of Benjamin's writings. It was a kind of anthropomorphism, a modern indication of the archaic, which surfaced in Adorno's works as well. Rather than robbing nature of its otherness by identifying it 'deterministically' with the subject, this anthropomorphism had the inverse effect of augmenting the non-identity, the uncanniness of the object. Benjamin called this estranged affect 'aura'. In the 1944 *Dialectic of Enlightenment*, Adorno wrote that the archaic fount of 'aura' was the 'mana' of natural objects whereby primitive people acknowledged the object's otherness. Mana was the fount of both fear and holiness:

> When the tree is no longer approached merely as tree, but as evidence for an Other, as the location of *mana*, language expresses the contradiction that something is itself and at the same time other than itself, identical and not identical. (Horkheimer and Adorno, 1972, p. 154)

Herein lies a phenomenology of fetish commodities which is a critique of false consciousness, exhibiting subjective and objective elements in a combinatorial fashion which can be called material spirit.

Objects have always borne the mark of a specific social period. Cultural 'objects' - texts, documents, artworks, and the like - demanded interpretation, and, according to Wilhelm Dilthey, this interpretive hermeneutic approach was what characterized the method of *Geisteswissenschaften* from that of the natural sciences. Adorno renders a similar qualification between science and philosophy in his inaugural address: philosophy purports to be interpretation, science to be research. Despite the fact that Adorno's negative dialectics was clearly a hermeneutic procedure, it varied radically from Dilthey's hermeneutics, and the idea of 'unintentionality' provides the key to the difference.

Dilthey treated *geistige* phenomena as psychological expressions; his aim in interpreting them was to restore the original meaning, the original intention behind the written word or other culture object. Adorno wanted to know what the cultural objects were saying by the standards of the *Zeitgeist*, despite their creator's intent, so that its ideology could be debunked. The problematic could be imputed to the basic assumptions of philosophical interpretation in constructing small, unintentional elements within *geistige* phenomena. Adorno was interested not only in the creator but in the distinctive totalizing quality embracing the artwork within the configuration of the socioeconomic complex.

Dilthey's stress on intentional meaning led his theory to an impasse. An end of interpreting historical texts was reliving them through empathetic understanding of the psychological experiences of past eras, implied the tenet of an ahistorical similarity of subjects, a universal essence of human nature which blanked out the very historical particularity which had been the raison d'être of a *geisteswissenschaftliche* method in the first place. The Diltheyan interpreter re-experienced him- or herself. One could understand only one's own likeness and hence knowledge could divulge nothing new. As Rolf Tiedemann has written,

> thus the Diltheyan historian acknowledges in history only what extends into the present, which is an 'expression' of his own 'life', and thereby accessible to his 'understanding'. (quoted in Buck-Morss, 1977, p. 94 n. 75)

Dilthey was ensnared in a circle of psychological subjectivism, while historical relativism undermined all evaluations concerning reality external to the subject. He was thus cast adrift without an authentic methodology to orient him in his socio-historical reality, a reality he alienated by his univocal, unchangeable standard. When the non-identity between written word and subjective intent was grasped, and when the former rather than the latter became the focus of interpretation, historical phenomena were shown to have no eternal meaning but instead a life and death of their own because we find ourselves immersed in a historical materialist approach. Then the whole Diltheyan paradox could be resolved.

Benjamin contended that the truth of the novel depended neither on the interpreter's ability empathetically to identify with the mood in the novel nor with the author's intent; it lay within the novel itself. This truth was not impenetrable to historical techniques, and perception of it was in fact magnified by the temporal distance dividing the interpreter from the object. For Benjamin, the truth content of an artwork was not identical to its substantive embodiment:

> For, in separating within the work, they [*Wahrheitsgehalt* and *Sachgehalt*] decide the question of its immortality. In this sense, the history of the works prepares their critique, the power of which is thus increased by historical distance. (in Buck-Morss, 1977, p. 95 n. 79)

But not until Benjamin and Adorno expatiated on this problematic within the framework of a Marxist theory of society did they name the *fons et origo* of the 'unintentional' constituents: the socioeconomic structure mediated all *geistige* production and hence articulated itself within cultural artifacts alongside (and often in contradiction with) the subjective intention of their creators. *Geistige* phenomena were hence not spent by an analysis of subjective psychology. They were also not reducible to the substructure, as the 'copy theory' of orthodox Marxism maintained. Against both psychological and economic reductionism, Benjamin contended:

> The question is namely: if the substructure determines the superstructure to a certain degree, its thought and experience material, how is it then - totally apart from the question of its causal origins - to be characterized? As its expression [*Ausdruck*]. The superstructure is the expression of the substructure. The economic conditions under which society exists come to expression in the superstructure. (p. 95)

Unlike most orthodox Marxists, Adorno could maintain that bourgeois art, and also bourgeois philosophy, was not simply ideology, and that it could be interpreted as more than false consciousness. Ideology was exposed by demonstrating the historical character of premises which were accepted as 'second nature', morbid rationalist condensations of duration which were anti-dialectical insofar as there pertained to the situation only the identity of the identity. Such a reificatory event negated any notion of the totality in which experience could be humanized and reconciled with the richness of its depth. The sense of Self in relation to its object-world would have the proper spatio-temporal dimensions for human possibilities to be reasonably embodied in praxis - the process of becoming is important insofar as change is perceived as essential to differentiating one's self from any permanent identification with the fetish-objects of a pre-constituted lifeworld. To cite Lukács, he meant that this 'second nature' is whatever philosophy does not find problematic, and this gives us a problem of false consciousness and the psychopathology of everyday life.

The truth content of bourgeois thought lay in the opposite direction, in the 'breaks' in its logic, the paraphrasis in its systematic unity. Because truth disclosed itself in the non-identity between psychological intent and its concrete objectification, the bourgeois thinker was most prone to expound truth when feeling most distantiated from the object of concern. Paradoxically, then, the thinker's truth gained in value in proportion to its concession of failure, for this failure bore testimony to a reality whose real contradiction could not be resolved on the plane of thought alone. The bourgeois thinker's truth was elaborated unconsciously, or, rather, truth broke through like a Freudian slip of the tongue in the inconsistencies of theory, now, more than ever, because of philosophy's 'disintegration' (Adorno, quoted in Buck-Morss, 1977, p. 96).

Logical breaks involved 'giveaways' which disclose the truth of the matter insofar as it surfaces and reveals itself wholly to the naked eye of the mind. Adorno described his early development and how he backed into a dialectical materialist position by default of its opponents:

> If later, in regard to the traditional philosophic texts, I not so much let myself be impressed by their unity and systematic coherence as I concerned myself with the play of opposing and conflicting forces which goes on under the surface of every self-contained theoretical position, and which codified philosophy sometimes accounts for as force-fields, then it was certainly [Siegfried] Kracauer who gave me the idea. He made the *Critique of Pure Reason* present to me not simply as a system of transcendental idealism. Much more, he showed me ... how the eloquent parts of the work are the wounds which the conflict in the theory leaves behind. (p. 97)

Late in life, in *Negative Dialectics*, Adorno was to perceive:

> In sharp contrast to the usual ideal of science, the objectivity of dialectical cognition needs not less subjectivity but more. Philosophical experience withers otherwise. But our positivistic *Zeitgeist* is allergic to this need. (1973b, p. 40)

Here the focus changes from consideration of the concrete particular as the generation of unintentional truth to the role of the subject in interpreting that truth. It is a critical adaptation, for, like Husserl, when confronted by the merely 'given' world, Adorno returned to the subject as the source of knowledge, but not at the cost of giving up the non-identity between subject and object. This very non-identity is the medium in which historical agents employ a distinctive praxis addressed to the nature of the divide of *this* particular subject/object alienation. In a theoretical innovation, he perceived them as necessary co-determinants: neither mind nor matter could dominate the other as a philosophical first precept. Truth dwelled in the object, but it did not lie ready at hand; the material object needed the rational subject in order to unleash the truth which has been sealed in the cave by reified modes of theory-formation in its interconnection with estranged conditions of life institutionalized by 'legitimated' authorities. The greater part of reality falls under the shadow of a false and readily falsifiable consciousness.

The next chapter explores false consciousness in order to see how damaging the socio-politically deformed irrationality of a *Zeitgeist* can be for the interaction of subject and object and individual and collectivity. The very profundity of false consciousness leads us to the kinds of contradictions from which the truth often 'unintentionally' 'stands out' in stark contrast. At this juncture we need fresh concepts to show that the Unhappy Consciousness may also be a mad one.

6 False consciousness: Ideology and mental pathology

Joseph Gabel, a leading authority on existential Marxism, looks at the psychopathology of everyday bourgeois life and attempts to show its interrelationships objectively in alienated social structures. The reified mind bonded to an alienated life experience gives us in an existential sense the general phenomenon of false consciousness. The particular reaction of the individual, then, is a self-reflective feeling of inauthenticity focused on a lost freedom. But Gabel imparts high significance to subjectivity, the ability of individuals to situate themselves in the historical mainstream and weather its cross currents. This realignment of forces in the dialectic has made for Gabel a major philosophical contribution to anthropology and its input into social science theory. He has penetrated behind institutionalized roles to give us the quintessential nature of the process of the defunctionalization of active subjectivity in the division of labor.

Gabel has studied intensively the relationship between ideology and psychopathology in the 1940s and 1950s in a genre which recalls the work of the Frankfurt School in the comparable period. His major category is 'false consciousness' in its most pathological manifestations, but subjected to a dialectical materialist approach. His 1975 magnum opus, *False Consciousness: An Essay in Reification*, claims to create an anti-fanatical hermeneutic critique of the totalitarian mentality in which the false consciousness of the individual and the apologetic ideologies of collectivities are bound together inextricably by a 'mad' *Dasein* subverted by capitalist rationality. This same kind of rationality undermined socialist goals in Eastern Europe. *False Consciousness* is a work of political psychology, somewhat akin to the study by Adorno and his associates, *The Authoritarian Personality*. Gabel, however, believes that the destruction of reason cuts much deeper.

Gabel's point of departure is the processes of alienation and de-alienation. The ideal is to live truth and truthfully, not just to reason about various philosophical propositions. In the tradition of the Hungarian Marxism to which he adheres, his analysis scores the popular fashion of the historicist and humanist Marxism which slights the material-objectivist determinants to the exclusive advantage of the 'dialectical humanist' ones. In the steps of Lukács, that is, with alienation centered around the concept of reification, he examines the anti-dialectical, spatialized, and schizophrenic characteristics of reified consciousness and existence in itself. Reification means not just the experience of 'thingification' of self or others (which is a form of 'objectification' and, to a point, natural), but also a mode of existence which is spatialized uni-dimensionally (rendered a-historical). Both false consciousness and ideology are characterized by this second quality in addition to the first.

Although these facets of a cancellation of praxis are conceded as functions of the development of technology, and although it is also accepted that reification is intensified in capitalism's time of crisis, the treatment of alienation as false consciousness and ideology is not analyzed merely in terms of its economic determinants. Gabel departs from Lukács not only in partially factoring out the economic context and class relationships, but also in proposing a 'total' rather than 'partial' concept of alienation, so it becomes a universally applicable category for the human condition under capitalist auspices. This permits him to include in his compass such significant phenomena as schizophrenia and utopian consciousness. The nature of the relationship between base and superstructure is then muted, an issue to which the author had little inclination to address himself; he leaves any metatheoretical considerations to his numerous critics.

Gabel begins by presupposing a parallel between collective and individual manifestations of false consciousness (i.e., ideology and schizophrenia). Reification is the underlying principle. He seeks to justify this assumption by showing that there is a common structure to disorders of political reason and psychopathology, appealing to sociological and clinical data. His claim is that reification is Janus-faced. It poses itself at the center of false consciousness in the collective life, and potentiates itself in the further development of ideologies which are expressions of, and systems of justification for, the reified consciousness. The same reification fashions the anti-dialectical consciousness of schizophrenia as he understands it; it is responsible for its 'morbid rationalism' and for the deranged perceptions of a creature who, consumed by the embeddedness of historical processes, is left with an ego which is 'contentless' in adapting on a day-to-day basis to the novel social permutations and even the simpler demands in late capitalism.

The concept of 'morbid rationalism' is central to Gabel's thesis: he sees it as essential to the general theory of alienation. Part of its significance is that it binds Gabel's thinking to the phenomenological psychiatry of E. Minkowski and Ludwig Binswanger and incorporates the *Daseinsanalyse* of both. This technique was first employed by Minkowski to diagnose and treat the de-dialecticized characteristics of schizophrenia. In Gabel's reinterpretation it is extended to characterize the collective form of false consciousness as a kind of rationality sui generis, with its own reified and reificational epistemology, rather than as an epiphenomenon of 'class interests', 'techniques of persuasion', or 'crowd psychology'. Morbid rationalism in both its facets can ultimately be analyzed in terms of the particular spatio-temporal structure of consciousness. The reification and loss of praxis which compose the morbidity are in effect an egocentric loss of 'temporalization'.

Therein lies the anti-dialectical evanescence of concrete historicity from existence, which results in an alienated experience of a homogeneous, 'spatialized' world lacking the fourth dimension (and to the degree that it is time-related even the third dimension of 'depth'). Spatialization, consequently, is a nullification of the flux and irreversibility of time. In the socio-political sphere, 'utopian thought' provides an example of the reifying spatialization of the future. To take another example, the anti-Semitic implication of an innate schizoid disposition in Jews is itself spatializing in the sense that it falsely identifies a consequence of long historical repression with a destined and exceptionless biological outcome. Similar but equally virulent stereotypes have held for African Americans and their 'intelligence'. This one critical factor, however, can give rise to stereotyped political animosities, destabilizing the general social order. In general, it is the breakdown, then, of the capacity to perceive, especially in the subject/object interplay to which we must be alerted.

Deterioration of the subject/object dialectic in reification is invariably depicted not only by spatialization but also by a dissociation of concrete totalities. This factor engenders the configuration of illegitimate abstractions, such as the 'privileged system' central to ethnocentrism or the reified symbols severed from their meaning if placed in the proper context. The *pars pro toto* fallacy is integral to the logic of dissociating thought: splitting symbols off from their historical genesis so that they have a hallucinatory autonomy of their own, not grounded realistically in any stabilized span of time or space. A major consequence of this de-totalized activity is devaluation, particularly of any sense of selfhood in relation to others. Gabel invokes Lukács's 'axiological-dialectical parallelism' to highlight the neo-Marxist category of Totality. Rather than deriving axiological concepts from the economic base alone, or from some other 'extrinsic' source, he considers values to be the intrinsic subjective experience of the dialectical structure of the whole, of the Gestalt arriving at 'goodness of form'. Good forms are those which have 'consistency' (a degree of self-regulation and self-comprehension of the whole to the intertwining parts) and 'precariousness' (the suppression of a part reverberates throughout the whole, destructuring all its internal and external interrelationships, thus vitiating its integrity). For example, in racist false consciousness, traits of the victim are isolated and made into fixed biological essences, much like fetish commodities.

This de-totalizing reification devalues its object through both dissociation and objectivization. Thus loss of value (axiological alienation) portrays all ideologization. In an analogous way, we could allude to Sartre's picture of a flattening of the world, a loss of differentiating valuation, in depressive states. This homogenizing loss of depth is also a spatialization, since when parts of a totality are dissociated capriciously they lose their place in the irreversible historical sequence along with their precarious value. We, then, suffer under reified conditions of existence.

For Gabel, false consciousness is a necessary but not sufficient condition for ideology; the latter is an expression of the former. The qualitative difference is that it is principally the fragmenting of totalities which portrays the loss of dialectic in false consciousness, while it is the more spatializing dissociation of the present from the past and future which comprises the loss of dialectic in ideology. While false consciousness is a diffused mental state, ideology can pose a theoretical condensation legitimating it. Ideologies are 'delirious' systems which disseminate an illusory dialectic to justify false consciousness by building a pseudo-history to serve as a substratum for alienated human activity. So even much of historiography is written in the vein of a 'false consciousness' whereby the authoritativeness of empirical studies is undercut by faulty epistemological foundations. Freud once warned against treating a client for neurosis only to bring forth a full-fledged psychosis. Many scholars have deceived themselves into accepting the illusion of a matter for fear that a more thoroughgoing study would plunge them into the abyss. This fear begets a nihilistic epistemology like Paul Feyerabend's, which has both debits and credits (Gabel's reference is to Feyerabend's *Against Method*, 1975).

A touchstone for the identificatory process of ideology is that in its false portrayal of the matter at hand it obfuscates the real socio-historical conditions and their origins and how they are subsequently reproduced on a larger scale. But prejudice can exist as false consciousness before it receives an ideological articulation. Various types of anti-intellectualism, which nourishes false consciousness because it reifies, depersonalizes, and devalues the 'intellectual' in cruel caricatures, have a sociocentric quality evincing the egocentrism of a collectivity which dichotomizes the world in an 'us-them' antagonism with no empirically warranted justification. But this anti-intellectualism does not compose a full-blown ideology since the requisite degree of rationalization and institutionalization are lacking.

Much of Gabel's project is the hermeneutic re-reading of 'ideology', distinguishing this critically from the orthodox meanings it has acquired in its bourgeois forms. One departure from common usage which is clearly apprehended in *False Consciousness* is that deliberate ideological misrepresentations are not mere epiphenomena. Often the idea of the superstructural depiction of ideology has carried a pejorative connotation. Even so, in a return to the dialectic, Engels in his 'Letter to Conrad Schmidt' (1890) established that the sundry components of ideology have objective reference and a causal power in themselves, so they 'react back as an influence upon the whole development of society, even on its economic development'[1] We might observe that this reaction is part of a prior action of the infrastructural economic factors in determining the ideologization in the first place.

A second, more important departure from common use follows on Mannheim's segregation of the 'total' from the partial concept of ideology. The latter is much closer to ideology-without-false-consciousness. Gabel faults this dissociation in the final analysis. To use his exposition in ideology-critique, the partial concept (a) upbraids the opponent on the basis of a part of that opponent's position instead of interpreting the standpoint as a whole, quashing the possibilities of a vindicable countercritique; (b) renders 'ideology' an extremely generalized notion ranging over all situationally conditioned conceptual frameworks; (c) 'reads' at the psychological level of an opposing ideology rather than at the theoretical level, leaving the impression that ideology is an act of decision more or less amenable to the will; and (d) aligns itself with a non-dialectical, utopian consciousness, thereby exempting itself from the constraints of its own historicity. Within this partial perspective, the tendency is to stigmatize the opponent as politically prejudiced, as a manipulator of the facts, and as a factotum for a specific political movement and an instrument of state indoctrination.

All this entails a very selective choice of the 'facts'. Not accounting for false consciousness reduces ideology to a set of values with the implication that these are purely subjective and idiosyncratic in character. This is tantamount to irrationalism, which fails to acknowledge any degree of rationality intrinsic to ideology. The resulting underestimation of the power and coherence of ideology in an ideology-critique tends to exclude the realization of the dialectical tension between conflicting perspectives both molded by the history of social life. Such an orientation also lacks critical self-consciousness. The 'partial' diversity of ideology-critiques would itself be susceptible to designation as false consciousness.

Alienation, explains Gabel, is popularly equated with 'estrangement' or even 'deviance', which is an anti-dialectical conception since it presupposes the status quo of a privileged system for delineating the 'normal' or unalienated with respect to the 'social'. 'Popular' sociology of knowledge has taken on the forms of pure reductionism, construing the social as, first, an 'external' factor, and second, a totally relativizing influence. This is equivalent to reducing all 'text' to its 'context', an ultimately self-contradictory action, which (in Ricoeur's terms) fails to balance a 'hermeneutics of restoration'. Such a tack corresponds to the reduction of all science to ideology through reference to its situational subservience or to the 'psychology of interest'. This is what Gabel calls 'surface sociologism' when he is criticizing Pavlovism, which threatens to utter no more than the empty and incontestable banality that mental illness is essentially a part of society. This misconception is society seen as an afterthought rather than as constituting the person in the individual/social dialectic.

Furthermore, to uphold any specificity of concepts, alienation and ideology demand more than the existence of 'social conditioning'. There must be in play an anti-dialectical variance in just one presentation of reification. Hence false consciousness is not just in error, it is insane or schizophrenic. In effect, social conditions play a constitutive as well as a selective role in engendering an ideology. Society does not simply come in *post festum* to effect a natural selection from alternatives which are already operative; it is integral to the process by which those very alternatives are generated.

We might also note the problem that even the word 'dialectical' can suffer an analogous debasement to the level of generality. Herein resides a constant threat to critical disciplines like American 'dialectical psychology'. Thus 'dialogical' may be understood partially as 'dialogical' (or interactional), as 'changing over time', as 'contradictory', or even as 'paradoxical' or 'ambiguous' At the boundary of its misuse, 'dialectical' is taken to refer to a liberal idealist's 'flexibility of consciousness' or to a relativity of all knowledge and truth, including even a static relativism such as Thomas Kuhn's which inquires after the inter-translatability of paradigms. This perspective is self-contradictory in that it uses rationality itself to undercut all rationality, reducing it to a rhetoric of rationalization.

Such a perspective on the dialectic subverts its own bases. It also abets conservatism and political laissez faire. Such a 'dialectic' lacks the interpenetration of opposites, the implication of the whole in each part, and the potential for active self-transcendence of dialectic in the Hegelian/Marxist sense. It amplifies 'dialectic' in a movement toward concretion in all directions and dimensions', so that the particular significance of the dialectical relation as a subject/object reaction is not lost. Several crucial distinctions are preserved, such as those between existence and consciousness and between change and development.

To return to Gabel, not only can the dialectic be confounded by 'popularized' versions, dialectical exposition is further confounded with 'valid theory'. Susan Buck-Morss's Lukácsian critique of Jean Piaget opens itself to this confounding. The very concept of 'objectivity' is historically situated and must be considered in that context. The anti-dialectical consequences of misapplications of Piaget's theory are held to compromise its objectivity. Furthermore, at a higher level of abstraction the concrete historical consequences of a particular concept of objectivity can lead to the invalidation of the concept itself (again the danger of epistemological nihilism). Buck-Morss contends that Piaget's abstract theoretical formulism merely reflects the commodity structure of the socio-historical relativity of individual abstract thought. As Gabel notes, however,

> there are great discoveries which contribute nothing to Marxism and have nothing to do with the dialectic, as for example, the discovery of the syphillitic origin of general paralysis. (1975, p. 140 n. 1)

The theory that general paralysis is a variety of hysteria attributable to social conditions would be dialectical in character, but false. Lukács himself distinguishes false consciousness from objective error or false evaluation. This distinction means that science retains its potential for objectivity even in the context of a reificational structure. Gabel illustrates this point with an anecdote: Marx contended that Darwinian theory reflected the historical contingencies of British society of that day, yet he esteemed it so much for its scientific contribution that he wanted to dedicate *Capital* to Darwin in gratitude. Conversely, a dialectical theory may well turn out to be false when examined experimentally. There are no grounds for sectarian identification of dialectic and truth. Any form of knowledge can plummet into false consciousness, especially when applied to fields far removed in structure.

Here is why Gabel is compelled to appraise his speculative dialectical assumption of socio-psychological parallelism against the findings of psychologists. Manifestly, the anti-dialectical assumptions of Piaget's theory do not immediately confer a judgment on its objectivity; the validity of the theory is a practical question to be appraised by the weight of the evidence. The relativity of the theorist as situated in certain socio-political and historical conditions needs to be distinguished from the relativity of the theoretical objects to which the theory can be applied (for Piaget, the 'stages' of cognitive development).

Although ideology is a form of rationality, criticism of it not attended by a de-reifying reworking of the socio-historical sources of alienation will be limited in its range for measuring conflicting interests. As Merleau-Ponty often said, it is not the human critical faculty but the structure of human space that safeguards us from derangement. The relation between ideological self-deception and classical defense mechanisms has yet to be investigated in depth. This gap is partly attributable to the suppression in humanistic, neo-Freudian ego-psychology of the dialectic of sacred and profane, at the expense of the profane. As Foucault reflects on the matter, however, the activity of defenses exhibits an essentially iterative structure, which already shows a nexus with spatialized ideological thought. In terms of these classical factors, the transition from socio-political to clinical alienation is first made by considering how useful it is to characterize ideological thought as schizophrenic, that is, to suggest in an anti-conformist spirit that the 'social fact' of reified living conditions may be unacceptable as such, without a gnoseo-pathogenic excursus, since the 'social fact' has become deranged.

Gabel's intention here is not to point to a facsimile but to identify the logic of ideology with morbid rationalism, and to show this state of affairs scientifically rather than by analogy. The task is to execute this tour de force persuasively, without succumbing in the process either to a false consciousness which exploits the parallel for the purposes of stigmatizing ideology or society at large as 'insane' (and claiming a privileged, non-ideological status for one's own perspectives) or to the conceptual anarchism of castigating all forms of classification as degrading 'labeling'. The task also calls for sensitivity because 'schizophrenia' is widely disputed as a diagnostic unity. Gabel is therefore hard-pressed to authenticate 'schizophrenia' when characterizing ideological thought as 'schizophrenic'. The attempt involves a major gamble and a possible high theoretical payoff. To show that alienation in the form of schizophrenic consciousness is determined by a reificational mode of existence and not just by a capitalist economic reification, and, moreover, to establish the schizophrenic nature of ideological thought, makes credible the proposition that political alienation is also not the direct product of economic reification but something to be examined as a mode of existence in its own right.

In the psychopathological domain, Gabel gives further indications of engaging a hermeneutic style in his recruitment of the phenomenological psychiatry of Minkowski, who shares with the Budapest School an indebtedness to Bergsonian ideas, and hence elliptically to the heritage of the Eleatic paradoxes of motion. When set over ideological scientism, Henri Bergson's views on time and space still constitute an effective de-reifiying critique, despite his own ahistorical reifications such as the élan vital. In summoning attention to the unconscious determinants of scientific thought, Bergson can be compared favorably to the '*Lebenswelt*' movement in the critique of positivist science, a critique which is only beginning to have an impact on the field where one might expect it to be most accepted, psychology.

What in Bergson's case amounted to a philosophical criticism serving as 'ideology critique' here assumes (by dint of the assumed parallelism) the shape of 'psychopathology critique'. Minkowski characterizes schizophrenia as geometric in its mechanistic, measurement-oriented perception of space (which thereby forsakes its 'lived' quality as habitat), and as morbidly rationalistic in its loss of a dynamic sense of duration (which amounts to a 'loss of praxis', meaning a personality impervious to experience and prone to self-encapsulation, detachment, and defensive over-abstractness). Gabel interprets morbid rationalism as an excess of identification. An example of this would be the essentializing 'I've always been this way' experience in mental illness, in which the person 'chooses to forget' the origins of the disorder in his or her own concrete history.

This conceptualization is intended to be comparable to Meyerson's approach, which sees the principal goal of scientific thought as the spatializing elimination of non-identities. Thus the law of causality is at its crux the concept of identity applied to the existence of objects over time, the synthetic equivalent of the analytic identity operation in logic. Objectivity resists over-identification in thought much as it does in science. The identity of cause and effect in mechanics implies reversibility, and so denies the irreversible temporal differentiation of nature. The principle of mechanics culminates in the elimination of time, moving toward reliance on laws of conservation (interchangeability of matter and energy; devitalization of life energy of personality); on substances (X means Y; over-identification); and on constants ('force'; magic); all of which imply that nothing happens (there are no discrete events) except vacuous displacements in space.

Gabel claims that Meyerson's work is an 'epistemology', but it rather seems to fall under the rubric of philosophy of science. As Dewey, Habermas, and others have reminded us, the province of knowledge is far from exhausted by the systematic and conscious rationality of science. Meyerson tries to portray conclusions with a broader vista by suggesting that scientific thought may be the preparatory study for all forms of consciousness. This heuristic but assuredly contestable concept would, for instance, restore the notion of perception as unconscious inference which was dismissed by critics like Merleau-Ponty. The point to be made is that scientism, ideology, and schizophrenia are homologously related in the sense of sharing a distorted spatio-temporal structuring.

In the morbid 'epistemology' of schizophrenia, the reification of consciousness is portrayed in an egocentric, anti-dialectical logic which forms illusory identifications on the basis of predicate identity. Such a restructuring of experience is inspired by purely subjective factors and by singular events in the personal history of the schizophrenic, which now erupt onto the cognitive plane. Symbolic objects now undergo a corresponding distortion in perception. After expanding our understanding of ideology through an account of its 'schizophrenic' structure, Gabel reverses the situation to indicate how a Marxist theory of alienation could deepen interpretation in psychopathology through the development of a general theory of mental illness pivoting on the concept of alienation. De-alienation could be construed as the reversal of this 'loss of praxis', the so-called 'dark space', the key critico-practical indicator if we are to redeem our alienated objectifications voluntarily and wholly.

From the Marxist perspective, no one in the twentieth century had a greater hold on the quintessence of the problem than Lukács. Here is his luxurious and penetrating comment on the nature of deranged experiences in the historically determined time of the 1920s.

> For the proletariat, however, this ability to go beyond the immediate in search of the 'remoter' factors means the *transformation of the objective nature of the objects of action*. At first sight, it appears that the more immediate objects are no less subject to this transformation than the remote ones. It soon becomes apparent, however, that in their case the transformation is even more visible and striking. For the change lies on the one hand in the practical interaction of the awakening consciousness and the objects from which it is born and of which it is the consciousness. And on the other hand, the change means that the objects that are viewed here as aspects of the development of society, i.e. of the dialectical totality become fluid: they become parts of a process. And as the innermost kernel of the movement is praxis, its point of departure is of necessity that of action; it holds the immediate objects of action firmly and decisively in its grip so as to bring about their total, structural transformation and thus movement of the whole gets underway. ...
>
> The category of totality begins to have an effect long before the whole multiplicity of objects can be illuminated by it. It operates by ensuring that actions which seem to confine themselves in particular objects, in both content and consciousness, yet preserve an aspiration towards the totality, that is to say: action is directed objectively towards a transformation of totality. We pointed out earlier in the context of a purely methodological discussion, that the various aspects and elements of the dialectical method contain the structure of the whole; we see the same thing here in a more concrete form, a form

more closely orientated towards action. As history is essentially dialectical, this view of the way reality changes can be confirmed at every decisive moment of transition. Long before man became conscious of the decline of a particular economic system and the social and juridical forms associated with it, its contradictions are fully revealed in the objects of its day-to-day actions. (Lukács, 1971, p. 175; emphasis in original)

The elegant idea is to look for the dynamic behind apparently catastrophic events, which is simply a deranged perception of a well-patterned sequence of actions which seems to the untrained eye to be a *camera obscura* view of reality. For example, the attempted elimination of the Jews during the Second World War is seen as 'catastrophic' - like some event in nature - beyond human capacity to grapple with historically. In a reflexive reaction, Holocaust Studies has arisen to treat this era of history like some pre-determined Greek tragedy, where all the actors, living and dead, are playing before the present audience to win our sympathies. The effort may be emotionally gratifying and even release tension, but cannot bring intelligibility to the network of events which led to this debacle. Purpose, agency, and responsibility, personal and collective, must be sought out. Lukács, Gabel, and Habermas, who complement each other theoretically, have given us constructs of reality to sift out the meaningful from the dross of that era.

To complete our discussion of these issues, we must go beyond false consciousness and ideology to the utopia where human hopes and rationalizations are projected. Utopia is the link to the future which makes for commitment to humanity on the part of intellectuals. We can thus ground the hope to transcend all reificatory phenomena and institutions which lead us into the pathogenic forms of bad faith and levels of alienation which deny and suppress the wellsprings of theory for *poiesis*. The concept of utopia is ambiguous, spoken of as having both positive and negative roles, references which convey unnerving Manichean currents and indicate two types of psychopathological damage. This distinction has interesting sociological bearings for the study of utopian consciousness. The *surrealist* concept of utopia (delineated by an overly dialectical and therefore insufficiently reified perception of reality) sees it essentially as a factor in socio-historical change, as a revolutionary instrument which 'shatters' being. The *subrealist* concept (diametrically opposite in structure) alludes to unrealizable projects which are carried out by marginal people and have no relation to historical reality. Far from having a 'historical-generative' quality, the subrealist version can be a pretext for escaping from history and its ardent demands.

As an example of the ambiguity of the concept of utopia, we must consider

Thomas More, who, as the creator of the term, is generally considered the model utopian. Marx, on the other hand, is taken as a 'futurologist' before the fact; that is, his thrust is labeled 'anti-utopian' in the sense to be defined below. But when one considers that More projected a kind of colonialism, the deployment of fifth columns, and the exploitation of slave labor, while Engels predicted the withering away of the state, one can wonder which is the utopian and which the futurologist. With good reason, true utopians have been upbraided for being unable to recognize the coherence of the historical situation, that is, for denying the historical validity of the dialectical principle of totality. But More's sense of this coherence is astounding. He understood fully that the 'socialist' organization of society has as a permanent and necessary corollary the existence of a strong state, which by its very nature will find itself, at least initially, surrounded by 'enemies' - something Engels did not take into account in his historical formulations. Paradoxically, the creator of the word 'utopia' must not be classified among the 'traditional' utopians. In fact, More unknowingly discovered one of the great historical laws of founding collectivist systems. The process has nothing to do with the 'withering away of the state' or the jump from the 'realm of necessity' to that of 'freedom' as expounded by those 'utopians' Marx and Engels.

The swirl of controversy around Zionism and its meaning, particularly its condemnation as 'racism' by the United Nations, can also be instructive. The Zionist idea may have condensed a political error in the imperial manner of its founding by Great Britain, the United States, and the Soviet Union, and its birth may have given rise to injustices, but one would have difficulty calling its system of ideas reificatory or a case of false consciousness. False consciousness is a corollary of alienation and reification. Racism is an 'alienating ideology' not because it identifies ethnic differences but because it reifies them by biologizing them, and then authenticates this reification with terms drawn from the natural sciences. By contrast, Zionism is a socio-historical functionalization or relativization of such disparities. It is by no means certain that the 'Zionist' represents a higher human value than the pre-Zionist Jew. Progress in dignity and 'civic' virtue may have overcompensated for a regression in intellectual percipience and sense of a universal message. In a Nietzschean way, we might say that no Jew was more Jewish than Jesus of Nazareth.

From another perspective, it nevertheless seems true that the prodigious human mutation provoked in such a short time by Zionism is an ultimate refutation of racism. In that meaning, Zionism is a disalienating ethos. Indeed, the optimal in 'socialist solidarity' is probably attained in the kibbutzim. The Zionist experiment has more or less attenuated the stereotype of the masochistic, cowardly Jew. It is impossible to overthrow a stereotype without needing to smash all other idolatrous stereotypes, such as 'lazy Negro' or 'inefficient Arab', without shattering stereotypical thinking as a general phenomenon. Hence Zionism offers a 'principle of hope' not only for Jews but for all oppressed and undervalued minorities in the world. The time may arise when historians will explain what the contemporary Arab renaissance owed to fascination with the Zionist pattern; there was certainly a phenomenon of 'identifying with the aggressor', to use Anna Freud's terminology.

The Zionist model proves that Ernst Bloch's surrealist utopia is not necessarily a corollary of alienation or false consciousness. To prime this interpretation, we must note three facts. (1) According to Bloch, utopia evinces a 'principle of hope' (in fact the Zionist anthem is called 'Hope'). (2) The temporalization of the surrealist variant of utopia, in the vein of Bergsonian 'duration', is a living temporality, dialectical and value-fashioning, rather than, like subrealist utopia, corrupt, spatialized, non-eventful. One of Theodore Herzl's works, '*Altneuland*' (the old-new country), perspicuously relates us to the unity of opposites. (3) Herzl's work carries as a subheading 'If you will it, it is not a fable' (Gabel, 1976, p. 183 n. 8).

Gabel understands the 'subrealist' conception of utopia as the

> Mathematical, logical and rigorous construction of a perfect city subject to the imperatives of an *absolute plan* which had foreseen everything and tolerates neither the least fault not the least questioning: a *synonym for totalitarianism*. The ethno-psychiatric diagnosis which can be applied to utopia is that of a devitalizing nationalism, a morbid inclination for stereotypes and abstraction, and political schizophrenia. (Gabel, 1976, p. 184)

The judgment is harsh but not at all unfair. Only the assimilation of utopia to totalitarianism gives way to reservations. The term 'political schizophrenia' unambiguously poses the problem of utopian false consciousness. Gabel's main reference to this question will be Raymond Ruyer's classic *Utopie et les utopies*, which he describes as outlining the most crucial facets of this utopian consciousness:

> a) fixation on a time and space that can not be spanned from the 'Me-Here-Now'; utopia is anti-historical, or according to Döblin, it offers 'a human plan to interrupt history, to jump out of history and reach a stable perfection'; b) the mood of omnipotence, recurrent in the type of schizophrenic psychosis defined by Geza Roheim as a 'magic psychosis'; c) the intellectualism of utopian constructions that are modeled down to the last detail for all eternity; individuals appear to

totally lack an unconscious, as well as human warmth (which recalls Minkowski's conceptualization of 'morbid rationalism' or Binswanger's analysis of the temporality of love; d) its caricaturized dimension which is essentially the consequence of dissociation; e) its antidialectical immobilism of general life processes; hence quantity can thus never be transferred over to quality. (Gabel, 1976, p. 184)

As a consequence, the dialectical category of totality is foreign to that utopian mentality which proceeds willingly by the mechanical juxtaposition of conflicting givens whose sole common denominator is their positivist valuation. An unexpected analogy emerges between the structure of the utopian universe and that political demagoguery which also juxtaposes things helter-skelter, without due consideration for compatibility or coherence and generally with a rather negative appraisal. It is in this sense that Marx was not a utopian but a futurologist. His historical projection proves in fact to be very totalizing. He makes rational choices between wholes, subdividing them to perceive empirically the flaws in any political plan.

George Orwell was another master of the literary genre of anti-utopianism. His novel *1984* is surely one of the most edifying works of its kind. Based on an incisive extrapolation of the lessons of the Moscow Trials, it depicts a totalitarian society which has successfully exploited scientific progress to concretize total control over private life. The dominant configurations of this world are (1) suppression of history by constant reappraisal of the past grounded on the exigencies of the present; (2) dissociation of thought ('doublethink'), an outcome of extreme heteronomy; (3) repression of sexuality and concern with puritanical standards unlikely to be met in real life; (4) anti-humanism and generalized depersonalization; and, finally, (5) development of an artificial language ('newspeak') designed to create intellectual standardization.

The contradiction between an egalitarian ideal and a hierarchic order recurs in recent consciousness, either as structural assimilation (Louis Althusser) or by an ideological-utopian (surrealist) declaration, that is, without relation to the concrete historical possibilities of the egalitarian ideal (the black nationalist Louis Farrakhan movement). At this juncture a simple but ineluctable conclusion is conferred on us. The human sciences would accelerate their departure from their interminable prehistory if some consensus coalesced on their main research concepts. It would be particularly satisfying to find the appropriate vocabulary for the notion of utopia; the revelation of this pressing need is perhaps the main result of our examination of the relations between utopian and false consciousness. The need for utopia stems in part from the illusion imparted by the sense of completeness designed to compensate for the feelings of inadequacy which humanity can attribute to the idiosyncracies of biological evolution and the civilization accompanying it.

The human organism is highly sensitive to its vulnerability to annihilation by a plethora of real and imagined forces which put the ego on the defensive. This sense of inadequacy provides a challenge to which history, dialectics, and the universe of values (i.e., culture) respond. Utopia can be a pretext to escape from freedom once again by invoking its name in vain. The rather surprising conclusion is that the anthropological significance of utopianism in its 'subrealist' forms is not far removed from racism. The universes of racism and of subrealist utopia are two forms of ahistoricism and two variations of the illusion of completion.

Human beings have a nearly compulsive fascination for identity which greatly transcends the epistemological sphere. It manifests itself in phenomena as varied as sexual fetishism, morbid rationalism, a penchant for the uniform (in both dress and thought), and a general manner which can be called 'heterophobia': hatred of differences. The intellects of most people are simply not trained to assimilate a wide variety of rich experiences. One can even conjecture whether the death instinct of psychoanalytic literature is tied up with reificatory phenomena in a more than metaphorical way. Clearly the 'subrealist' utopia springs primarily from this tendency.

> What is remarkable in all these constructions which ruthlessly exorcise the collective memory of the group is the deliberate will to reduce the exuberance, the richness and *diversity*, of a village or city worthy of the name - i.e., infused with a mythical density only realized slowly, generation after generation - to the monolithic coherence of identity. (G. Lapassade, quoted in Gabel, 1976, p. 186)

Note

1. It must be added that both Marx and Engels were very wary that intellectuals often produce reified theories which run counterfactually to actually lived working class experiences and their conditions. On numerous occasions Engels sharply attacked intellectuals:

> What these gentlemen all lack is dialectic. They never see anything but here cause and there effect. That this is a hollow abstraction, that such metaphysical polar opposites only exist in the real world during crises, while the whole vast process proceeds in the form of interaction (though of very unequal forces, the economic movement being by far the strongest, most elemental and most decisive) and that here every-

thing is relative and nothing is absolute - this they never begin to see. Hegel never existed for them. (letter to Conrad Schmidt, October 27, 1890, 1942a, p. 484)

Engels had a clear conception of dialectics, not something boiled down to a pure economics, but

> According to the materialist conception of history, the determining element in history is *ultimately* the production and reproduction in real life. More than this neither Marx nor I have ever asserted. If therefore somebody twists this into the statement that the economic element is the *only* determining one, he transforms it into a meaningless, abstract and absurd phrase. The economic situation is the basis, but the various elements of the superstructure - political forms of the class struggle and its consequences, constitutions established by the victorious class after a successful battle, etc. - forms of law - and then even the reflexes of all these actual struggles in the brains of the combatants: political, legal, philosophical theories, religious ideas and their further development into systems of dogma - also exercise their influence upon the course of the historical struggles and in many cases preponderate in determining their *form*. There is an interaction of all these elements, in which, amid all the endless *host* of accidents (*i.e.*, of things and events whose inner connection is so remote or so impossible to prove that we regard it as absent and can neglect it), the economic movement finally asserts itself as necessary. (letter to J. Bloch, September 21, 1890, 1942b, p. 692)

7 Materialist phenomenology of language

We now move from the domain of false and pathological consciousness to semiotics. This discipline affords us a method of elucidating the rational connection of desire and action mediated by *Logos*, which assumes a praxis which moves beyond the merely symbolic and beyond the naive and pathogenic consciousness in successive stages toward a true *Bildung* of socialist humanity. We must also examine the type of objectifications which constitute a de-reified dialectics. Within theory, words mediate the moments between objects. To see how the mind treats these objects requires a semiotic construct which cuts through the alienated appearances of reality to capture the truthful essence ontologically, which is of course the business of language and the theory of language.

Semiotics must then get rid of the strictures put on it by the problematic of the sign and construct a theory of discourse. For that perspective to claim its legitimate place in the theory of discourse, it must undergo an essential change. Written language and literature are more than the reification of the fluid rhythm of the spoken word and the consequent alienation of language from its own spontaneity. The written word is not merely the copy or representation of the spoken word, for it has touched from within the experience of discourse, the core of language. Speaking is a modality of language within a discourse which has, once language is introduced, two essential possibilities, two essential transmutations of the sign. Meaning is transposed from the written to the spoken word.

Simultaneously, a boundedness in style, syntax, and effect makes it clear that a transposition has occurred. The sign consequently serves as a medium from level to level, from place to place, and from system to system. This passage brings about a metamorphosis which delineates in a preliminary way the experience of meaning within discourse. The passage from spoken to written word indicates the sensible existence of meaning which can undergo the essential permutation in the movement from sound to visible mark without establishing its independence from either. The metamorphosis brought about in discourse is a lateral movement from one dimension of sensibility to another. The evidence of its existence spotlights the fact that culture at the plane of symbolic structures does not originate in an impression. Linguistic sense is a constituent of sensibility; it is heard, spoken, and seen. Nevertheless it is not a sensible *qualia* as that term has been understood since Locke's *Essay on Human Understanding*. In express terms, then, there is no experience of linguistic meaning, in the sense of an act bearing on an identifiable object whose traits on the impersonal plane would be identity, unity, and presence. Linguistic sense is a passage between different levels. The experience of linguistic sense is hence an experience without an object. The equation 'object = meaning' (either as denoted thing or as concept) does not capture the nature of the experience of meaning in discourse.

Analogous observations would have to be made about the structure of meaning latent in the naive or pristine relationships of the spoken word with the gestures of the body. The naturalness felt there, the facility with which the spoken word issues into pantomime and dance, is in fact the same encounter of level with level as that between writing and spoken language. The transposition of the sign is present in those mutations of meaning; gestures also signify laterally as refractions of another system. Hence writing clearly intercedes within the spoken word, not as a superimposed layer of factitious forms (an assemblage of representations reserved for cultist purposes), but as a testimony to the difference between levels to which it owed its being and from which it gets sanction to speak and be listened to.

The phenomenology of language, the parricidal naming of language, thus cannot be the quest for an object - for an identity within a stream of profiles and perspectives (that would be a form of autism *deranging* the subject/object dialecticity). There is a certain ingenuousness to be found in such a presumption which nonetheless forms an integral part of the latent structure of Western thinking. The confrontation of the spoken word with writing reveals a more basic problematic: Marxist in its intentions, since that term alludes to a definite conception of theory in practice; bound to a perspective of history and of signifying relations as the instituting of meaning across levels and registers; and prefigured in the distinctions between superstructure and infrastructure in the materialistic theory of history.

The transposition of the sign from the spoken to the written word exposes to appraisal what Ferdinand de Saussure termed the value of the linguistic sign. The movement of meaning from signifying level to signifying level constitutes a reassembly of the sign. The sign signifies in terms of other signs and its relations with them. The power of the sign to signify emanates from its locus in the system. The character of the sign is diacritical; it signifies in and through its differences from other signs and the experiences of its meaning; and semantic weight is accrued in and through the systematic relations between signs.

If the essence of language cannot be grasped in a naive naming - the search for an object possessed with identity, the reason is that the language sign is not an object but a juncture, an interval and a difference. Language is experienced in the metamorphosis effected in the passage of the sign from writing to speaking and from speaking to writing. Furthermore, in a way just as important and in a sense more basic, it is to be met at the crossroads of word and gesticulation, of articulation and hearing, the crossroads of the languages of the world, the Babel of tongues as the historical confrontation of varied cultures, whose structures are nevertheless shown to be isomorphic by semiology.

The lateral relation of sign to sign is not founded on the physical relations of things, the yet unspoken laws of physical objects, but on what is already spoken once the task of language is taken up: the matrix of social relations, the pattern of meaning which communication exposes as the web people spin around their lives as they fashion their social institutions. The fact that the significance and meaning of the sign is divulged in its diacritical nature signifies that the nature of the sign is insinuated not in the strictures of formal logic but in a material logic which in being a real relationship of sign to sign is a social logic. Roman Jakobson has indicated this basis in communication for the analysis of any verbal code: 'Any verbal code is convertible and necessarily comprises a set of distinct subcodes or, in other words, functional varieties of languages' (quoted in Gillan, 1976, p. 411).

A verbal code is a code stemming from the convertibility of distinct discourses into each other, which hence institute a communication grid. Language or a verbal code is not a simple unity but a procedure for the convertibility of the messages of distinct discourses and so is underlined by an experience of communication or a social logic.

On the basis of the above analysis, the theory of language, while not isomorphic to discourse, is nonetheless a discourse of sorts. Its nature stems from semiotic perspectives: rather than a mirror of language, it is the extension of language. Theory is the constitution of a divergent signifying level, the constitution of a differentiation within the experience of language. That level arises through the differentiation of the written text. As metalanguage, theory is a discourse which relies on the possibilities for language opened up by the written text. It encompasses a genre of reflection which would be impossible without the progressive acquisition of concepts which the writings of a culture make conceivable and practicable in actuality. It is simultaneously a break with the spoken word. If there is a social practice of life in every discourse, then theory is a break with that social practice in order to extend the horizons of that practice. It is, in that specific sense, critical, for it is not a recapitulation but a critique of the first plane of discourse. Its critical sense rests on the fact that language as a verbal code is convertible into functional discourses which portray specific relationships to social contexts and assimilate those contexts. Language itself ties theory (in this case, language on language) to the world of social praxis.

Language itself gives witness to the shape and nature of its possibilities and in that way attests to the possibility of rationality. Just as there is a science of politics, there is a politics of science. Language stands at the crux of that confrontation, for in that confrontation resides the possibility of a theoretical language equal to the task language imparts to it to divulge the manner in which language signifies the world, not as the mirror of the world but as the semiotic, convertible code of systems which renders to the world the locus of the sign. The cultural and the linguistic sign bear the responsibility for the meaning of social justice. To uncover their structures entails the critique of the ideological integument overlying theoretical discourse in the contemporary world. That disclosure engenders critique as an essential moment of the phenomenological *epoche* which prunes language to its essentials.

At this moment in history, the critical theory of language intervenes in the political and theoretical struggles of Western culture. This intervention is specifically as theory of practice or practice of theory, but its critical force is the result of a practice not bounded as if for a theory in the wings, so to speak, but defined by the tasks and structures of theory itself. It is true, as Althusser has acclaimed of Lenin, that critical philosophy is the practice of philosophy as an intervention in theoretical questions for the sake of political and scientific elucidation (Althusser and Balibar, 1970). Grounding theory in a critical theory of language demands two tasks, which are in principle the same once their common implications have been made evident: semiotic critique of language (the description of meaning in the sign) and development of that problematic within the dialectic of mystification and basic de-fetishization.

Within the critical theory of language, these two tasks, though of different historical origins, are inherent moments of the same problematic. The task of the critical theory of language is to demonstrate that the problematic of description, basic to phenomenology's self-understanding (historically and in principle), is not in radical opposition to the problematic of demystification essential to the development of a critical interpretation of the nature of language and the essential facets of culture. In light of Althusser's analysis of the development of the young Marx's and Marcuse's critique of phenomenology, it is clear that a critical theory of society and social meaning is in contradiction to a *prima philosophia* of phenomenology's aspirations which limits its scope to the structures of an idealist consciousness and an empirical, transcendental description of the operative intentionality constituting the activities of the lifeworld. The development of Marx's problematic beyond the *Economic and Philosophical Manuscripts* evokes the same problems phenomenology must meet if its course is not to be restricted in this way (Husserl, *Cartesian Meditations*, quoted in Gillan, 1976, p. 417).

The critical significance in the metamorphosis undergone by semiotics is that the theory of the sign must be a dialectical materialist theory, that is, a critique of the material practice of language in light of the actual material possibilities. The structure of the sign is a structure which exists, for linguistic communication is an actuality. There remains the question, in what sense communication exists. That question poses the other half of the problematic of a material semiology, revealing what is confabulated in communication under present social conditions. That this distortion is a distortion in light of language is not yet indicated by its distorted reality in its bourgeois forms. That distortion, its institutionalized actuality, requires us to interpret language through its lack of identity with itself to break its reificatory shell. In short, language as a means of communication between ego and 'Other' (alienation) is the objectivized outcome of hypostatized human relationships where the private ownership of the means of production stands in contradiction to the fact that the whole ensemble of production is a societal act. The de-dialectization of the whole into antagonistic parts gives rise to private languages embodying these antagonisms. The modalities of communication, then, are separated from everyday life and commodified to serve the ideological (and subrealist) apparatus of those who rule. In terms of its possibilities, the context of communication produces the experience that language in its practice-discourse can establish another, more liberated context.

The focus on difference, rupture, contingency, and non-identity does not validate an abstract critique. Rather, since these terms apply only to the historical experience of the world, critique must necessarily be an interpretation of the material meaning behind the appearance of things. If the formal nature of the sign is hollow and if communication processes can obscure the messages in communication, that is because language does not have a formal definition, only one which is material and thereby valued dialectically.

The critical theory of language is the description of that mediation of linguistic sense through desire. The phenomenology of language becomes critical at the juncture where it focuses on what Adorno called the 'addendum':

> the impulse, intramental and somatic [which] to philosophical reflections ... appears as downright otherness because the will that has been reduced to pure practical reason is an abstraction: without it, there would be no real will at all. (1973a, p. 229)

Certainly, access to the desire which speaks in language cannot be obtained through pure eidetic concepts. That desire as the concept of an experience is only accessible in terms of the distance it is necessary to travel from the idea of the rational will and from the idea of consciousness to what these terms deny or neglect. It is accessible in the practice of language, a system of signs, but also through specific texts, in a configuration of statements which together establish their context.

The unity of the problematic of critical semiotics and phenomenology lies in the character of the linguistic sign as juncture. Hence the revelation of the significance of that description of the sign will be accompanied by a parallel revelation of the dimensions and roots of critical theory. Critical theory, unveiling historical myths which run counter to social reality, is not just the product of a particular historical epoch, the nineteenth century, but is coextensive with language as it turns its back on itself to speak of its relationship with the world. A review of Platonic dialectics shows not only this fact but also that dialectical language is spurred by an *eros*, a desire which accounts for the radical turn entailed in critique. The roots of critical theory can be exposed only by subverting the epistemological tradition which has concentrated on logical meaning as the form into which every other element of discourse must be reduced, and by exploring the current of desire which runs through the structure of the sign. The result would be a repetitive subtemporalization, a reificatory retreat from an onrushing world, the fear of mundanization. There is a desire to speak which accounts not only for the perversions of language but more basically for the breaking of silence, the rupture which fashions a world. Desire does not obscure the original logical purity of the sign and language; rather, it sponsors the passage of the sign, the way in which the sign confronts the world of perception and, within culture, the way it confronts other signifying levels.

The desire which energizes the sign is a dialectical desire beyond the compass of the satiety which comes with the satisfaction of impulses. The passages in the *Phenomenology of the Mind* which acclaim the fortunes of that desire for the recognition of the Other at the same time chart the fortunes of language. To desire to speak is to desire not satiety but the discourse of the

Other, to desire the desire moving that alien discourse and to want to be immersed in the recognition which comes from being spoken to and from experiencing the desire of the Other in the word spoken. That desire explains why language mulls over itself, why it ruminates over the mysteries of the earth in myths, and why to speak begets a universe of meaning sufficient unto itself. The universe of language is a world of constant repetition, of familiar phrases, of greetings and of echoes of greetings, of clichés which can divulge as much as they conceal. The desire to speak is the current which pulses through generality and anonymity, the feeling of being uprooted in a dense world, of the spoken world. Language ever changes in its density and boundaries; people talk incessantly when to all appearances they have little in substance to relate. In spite of this fact, people do engage in discourse, for it is a way of sensing the dialecticity of one's self in a non-egocentric and sociable way. This universe of signs and counter-signs ensures their authentic humanity and their right to be called *free* people.

Habermas has appreciated what critical theory does to advance freedom in a post-Enlightenment era where formerly 'eternal' values are being overthrown:

> The new ideology consequently violates an interest grounded in one of the two fundamental conditions of our cultural existence: in language, or more precisely, in the form of socialization and individuation determined by communication in ordinary language. This interest extends to the maintenance of inter-subjectivity of mutual understanding as well as to the creation of communication without domination. Technocratic consciousness makes this practical interest disappear behind the interest in the expansion of our power of technical control. Thus the reflection that the new ideology calls for must penetrate beyond the level of particular historical class interest to disclose the fundamental interests of mankind as such engaged in the process of self-constitution. (Habermas, 1970, p. 113)

Critical theory feeds off the distance between language and the world, but also off a desire to be human, a desire to speak and be spoken to which underlies the original articulation of the structure of language. The question of the natures of the sign and of language is not a question of the first utterance or the first word, but one of the way the structures of sign and language are articulated within the dimensions of the signifying. To respond to that question is not to construct a theory in the sense of accounting for a living experience in terms of formal relations, of explaining one level of experience by manipulating signs at another level, but to describe the experience of signifying within discourse as a universal meaning which is perpetually elsewhere and for whose interpretation new expressions always arise.

The shape reality assumes is the shape given to it through desire and the workings of desire in and through the structure of symbolic language. To live the symbol is to live human reality, to take possession of the word in the breadth of its signifying relations. At the end of that symbolic journey, as Lacan points out, lies the freedom of the open world.

The plenitude of symbolic language is acquired across the eros of the flesh and within the symbolic discourse in which desire speaks its latent significations and thoughts. In the symbol, the flesh speaks, and it speaks of things. Yet the flesh speaks through the fundamental mediation wrought by desire, by the quest for the lost object, and by the natural libidinal impulse for the recognition to be found in the desire of the Other. The desire of the flesh in its articulation across the dimensions of the body (the zones in which the erotic sensibility of the flesh is centered) articulates the structure of the symbolic. The symbolic is not the natural relationship between signifying and signified, as Saussure thought, but the sign in its signifying, transformed by desire and articulated into a metaphoric dissemination of meaning by the signifying intentions of eros. In its signifying structure (distinct from the structure of its signifying, the paradigmatic facets of language which are true for every discourse) the symbol is mediated by desire. And eros is as much the speaking of eros as it is the eros of speaking. Hence discourse is itself that eros: passion which speaks and synthesizes for human *Bildung* in a dialectical and de-alienating manner. Language does not speak for desire and in its stead, but as its movement and its eruption between people. Words and actions stand in constant need of interpretation. They are not self-sufficient, for they are oriented to one another for consecration, words to gestures and gestures to words, consummating the totality of becoming. Each is invoked to stand surety for the truth of the Other, but without rest or repose. Words never totally speak for themselves, and gestures can always belie the intentions they appear to elaborate. The possibility of reciprocal confirmation and interpretation lies in the fact that desire moves through both words and gestures.

The symbol speaks the affective meaning running through the relationships which bind people together for other-centered tasks in a common social world. Simultaneously it speaks of the reality latent within those relationships and of the transparency of a world where desire can speak in manifest symbols and not through a facade. In this context, the project of the critical theory of the symbol, the sign transvalued by the mediation of desire, is to form a descriptive interpretation of the sign which divulges the involutions within the structure of the sign which assure the autonomy of the symbolic order and the concomitant praxiology. Unchained from the fetishisms of a limited imagination, the symbolic order or disquisition directly speaks the relation to the Other. The language of freedom is composed in symbolic discourse whose signifying supports are to be constituted in social relations.

By the very fact of accepting the challenge of occupying that space between ideology and undisturbed discourse, semiology creates an open space within discourse where the significance of history and politics can be spoken. There are other spaces where such questions have no relevance: those fashioned by technological language and the formal analysis of language. Hence the creation of an open space where the sign can become manifest in its social and political structure is the prolegomenon to the clarification of social life through political experience. The space within which people speak is also the space in which they act. Only a theory sensitive to the dimensions of the political word suspended between the poles of ideology and elucidation can reveal the structure of the discourse of politics, not as rhetoric but as freedom signifying itself within the structure of symbolic discourse. Consequently the necessity for the critical theory of meaning stems from the dominance of the symbolic, the priority of the word within the relations between people.

If, as Sartre has amply shown in *Being and Nothingness*, it is impossible for human beings to coincide with their being, then the symbolic occupies the place of that absence or non-coincidence. The ontological locus of language within social relations is the negative space open to praxis prepared by the difference between discourse and things and between human beings and their being (Gillan, 1976, p. 423). The word and the caress, that is, how one structures the values of one's spatio-temporal world, are carried by language and contingent on the historicity and possibilities of the symbolic. To attain freedom, it is necessary to be able to interpolate meaning-structures for life within the totality of symbolic discourse. If this perspective on language is borne out, then freedom - the release of meaning through action and the work of language - is to be found in the practice of symbolic exposition. The interpretation of symbolic discourse is, therefore, political *logos* and the commitments that follow therefrom. It is the fashioning of the open space within language where political practice can speak and indicate its intentions, and in that manner assimilate into its institutional base the social nature of human freedom.

Habermas provides fresh insights into how theoretical inquiry can break new ground through a critical theory where action takes root in a radicalized understanding of a remarkable human nature. He realizes fully that the Other must be reformed into an alter ego if alienated communication is to be overcome. In his two-volume magnum opus, *The Theory of Communicative Action*, Habermas reaches the acme of his career illumination the history of the Enlightenment decline when he shows how the history of reason has lost its foundations. To this day, he is trying to find himself again in a negative dialectics housed in language. But is it a house built on shifting sands? Is the end product nihilism?

Language, then, where properly structured semiotically, is a liberatory vehicle for truth. For Habermas, truth is relative to the extent that it relates tangibly to the level of the material development of a society. It is absolute in that mind knows itself only through the authenticity of *Logos*. In the next chapter we will examine how Habermas defines a disalienated existence spatially and temporally.

8 Work and communicative competence

To understand human existence, Habermas has situated human interests of a cognitive/epistemological order in his initial theory. We must elucidate these interests, which are constitutive of a historical materialism, through the act of linguistic analysis. A social theory of knowledge will emerge to enable us to mediate conceptually cultural practices with political activities in the *telos* of discursively overcoming the static and bourgeois categories which separate subject and object in the search for totalization. Critical theory attempts to dissolve gnoseologically the hypostatizations which prevent that dynamic from surfacing.

This transitional chapter moves to more concrete problems of society. It uses the conceptual repertoire of earlier chapters to locate contradictions in the actual operation of late capitalism. A model for practical group interaction will be developed to ground the transcendental impulse toward liberation in a real life situation with universal implications. So critical theory undertakes to understand not only its object but also its own role as a moment in the dialectical movement and transcendence of that object. Marx observed that the communists 'do not anticipate the world dogmatically, but rather wish to find the new world through criticism of the old (letter to Ruge, September, 1843, in Marx, 1967a, p. 212).[1] This evocation rings through a statement by Habermas, although to a more select group:

> Historical materialism aims at achieving an explanation of social evolution which is so comprehensive that it embraces the inter-relationships of the theory's own origins and application. The theory

specifies the conditions under which reflection on the history of our species by members of the species themselves has become objectively possible; and at the same time it names those to whom this theory is addressed, who then with its aid can gain enlightenment about their emancipatory role in the process of history. (Habermas, 1973, pp. 1-2)

'Late capitalism' has features Marx anticipated but could not have exactly predicted. Science and technique, developed and implemented through the labor of 'reflective workers' (engineers, industrial scientists, teachers, etc.), become the leading dominative and productive force. They render labor more productive, cheapen the fixed factors of capital, and inflate the rate of growth of surplus value. The 'scientization' or disenchantment of social relations accompanies this accumulation process. Late capitalism is inclined to develop a 'sensate mentality' about which Pitrim Sorokin wrote - technical, absorptive of facts, and mechanically materialistic. Within academia, this scientization process envelops philosophy and the socio-historical sciences.

For Habermas, this outcome is a blatantly regressive development. With the Anglo-Saxon establishment either unknowing or at least oblivious to its consequences, science and its rationale have assimilated philosophy to serve their purposes in ultimately accumulating capital. In the social sciences, the triumph of neo-positivism demands rigor, predictive certainty, and adherence to the standard of 'scientism', science's unquestioning belief in itself. Positivism is an inverted and alienated reason which renounces inquiry into the knowing subject's constitution of its object. The positivistic disciplines suppress critical rigor in that they make little or no attempt to distinguish between the evaluation of truth and the grounds of that evaluation. The social sciences thereby lay the bases for massive social engineering and more of the present technical rationality.

In late capitalism, the political process takes on a technocratic guise. Its objects are immersed in a culture of public science and private orientation toward career, leisure, and consumption - the 'goods' life. This situation appears fated because priorities formed according to economic injunctions cannot be opened and reviewed by public discussion. President Jimmy Carter's first 'open' television 'talkathon' was a symbolic and well calculated public relations performance staged for largely political purposes. There is no sense in which this act involved the people in a real dialogue where truthful propositions about the state of the nation could be worked through. The contempt of a Richard Nixon for public opinion is more in line with the 'imperial', or at least very imposing, character of the U.S. presidency. Power cannot be deconcentrated by symbolic gestures. Politics has largely degenerated into an administration of things, from the top. Bill Clinton, on the contrary, follows public opinion polls like a whipped puppy.

Conceptions of democracy must be refocused to coincide with the touted administrative injunctions; hence an important legacy of early liberal bourgeois society, the 'public sphere', is weakened by late capitalism itself. Ensconced originally in the distinction between public and private in ancient Greece, the public sphere was resurrected by the European bourgeoisie in its dismemberment of feudal structures. Intended as overseer of the state apparatus, it coincided with such claims as the right to representation, freedom of speech and assembly, and an informed public opinion. Late capitalism upholds the form of this public domain as the state takes on the task of instituting ideological projects largely to substitute for and indefinitely postpone substantive reforms. The public realm includes 'spectacles' and unwarranted accolades to public officials together with a 'democratic' display of 'self-disclosure' and constant calls for a renewed faith in America. Behind these 'texts', we see how unevenly power and wealth are in fact distributed. Amid the anarchy of civil privatism, public vitality and political commitment recede to the background.

The whole drift of events, according to Habermas, is counterpoised by an inclination toward cultural crisis, an ominous expression of the dialectic of domination and liberation in late capitalism. It is a prominent development in which critical social theory must participate by comprehending and nurturing the concrete possibilities of liberation from our ignorance of wider currents of events beyond our own personal interests and sense of powerlessness. Ironically, one element of this tendency culminates in the state apparatus attempting to stave off economic crisis. As politics becomes administration, public attachment to that process depends on successful governmental action to deal with a permanent fiscal crisis. Government is compelled to intervene in areas beyond the market and even in 'sick' industries which are no longer competitive but whose employment of large numbers of workers is essential to political stability. When the state fails to perform according to standardized expectations, the people's sanction is the withdrawal of legitimation (which they have no real way to articulate beyond individual discontent) and there is little or no administrative production of meaning from which people can take their cues. In the latter instance the society can be brought to the brink of an anaesthetizing national malaise (much like that in the United States during the early 1970s, when the Vietnam War and 'Watergate' coincided). Today, we have Whitewater. Too, devastatingly, the global marketplace has shifted toward Japan and other East Asian countries.

Furthermore, as spheres of everyday life are progressively 'statized', the bourgeois ideology of civil privatism and possessive individualism is shown to be fraudulent. This disillusionment leads to a motivational crisis and disturbs the 'life cycle' (in Erik Erikson's sense). Habermas's preference for the expression 'late' capitalism highlights his crucial thesis that, in the reproduction of this capitalist society, resources of legitimation and motivation help reproduce the system. In the end, substantial losses of capital may be needed to keep the allegiance of the society, mostly through social welfare programs and 'spectacles', propped up by security and surveillance under innocuous code names so as not to alarm the national constituency. Habermas's conclusion is somewhat airy:

> ... a legitimation crisis can be avoided in the long run only if the latent class structures of late capitalism are transformed or if the pressure for legitimation under which the administrative system stands can be removed. (Habermas, 1975, p. 30)

This vision does little to excite the imagination, let alone induce anyone to take a course of action, to make a *commitment*.

Habermas's critical theory tries to revolutionize this late capitalist society by anticipating the need for intercession on its own behalf. The relationship between theory and practice is understood at the epistemological level by proceeding from the meta-assumptions that 'the achievements of the transcendental (self-reflective, self-transforming) subject have their basis in the natural history of the human species' (Habermas, 1971, p. 312), and that such self-conscious activity is human in that it transcends mere adaptation to fortuitous circumstances: 'Knowledge equally serves as an instrument and transcends mere self-preservation' (1971, p. 313). Knowledge, through reflection, can become aware of its own constitutive conditions, but cannot expunge or uproot the grounds Habermas calls 'interests' which 'transcendentally' orient people in the flux of changing times. These interests indicate our ties with external nature and the manner humans have historically raised themselves beyond their nature through social organization.

Hence, Habermas's conception of the transcendental activity of human subjects is qualitatively different from the pure Kantian form, in which transcendentals are to be comprehended neither psychologically nor naturalistically but as deep-rooted domains of vital human activity. They are, in fact, a subtle adaptation of the Marxian notion of social labor; that is, they are 'invariant' in that all self-producing social organizations are conditioned on their fulfillment. As 'generalized motives for systems of action', they are indelible, dynamic fountainheads of all human knowledge. They are, therefore, not impediments to the objectivity of knowledge (as positivists would have it in their naive belief in 'pure theory') but the very condition of objective knowledge. They embody a

> system of primitive terms (of the 'transcendental framework' within which we organize our experience *a priori* and prior to all science, and to do in such a manner that ... the formation of the scientific object domain is also prejudged by this. (1973, pp. 7-8)

As furnishing categories of both cognition and action, it follows that epistemology is only conceivable in the form of social theory. It is through the two 'basic' interests of work and symbolic interaction or communication that human subjects consciously objectify their world in the double sense that it is simultaneously constituted and disclosed to them. (The 'emancipatory' interest is the third.) Through work and interaction, history is an evolutionary process by which external nature is humanized and human nature is transmuted. The distinction is so fine that we must elucidate the matter.

> In the functional sphere of instrumental action we encounter objects of the type of human bodies; here we experience persons, utterances, and conditions which are, in principle, capable of being manipulated. In interactions (or at the level of possible inter-subjective communication) we encounter objects of the type of speaking and acting subjects; here we experience persons, utterances, and conditions which in principle are structured and to be understood symbolically. (Frankel, 1974, p. 43)

Habermas stresses that this qualification is only analytic, and that the two interests are always empirically interwoven. Whether he understands them as dialectically bound is a problem that arises later. At least he does not intend to make the distinction objectivistically (i.e., according to a contemplative consideration of the character of the object to which theory alludes); work and interaction are analytically separate areas in which self-conscious human subjects act, thereby changing themselves and the world.

Work, or purposive-rational action, is that moment of human activity portrayed by its orientation toward external nature. It strives to expand and extend the productive forces and the power of technical control over nature. Purposive-rational action is not a distinctively human activity, but it is an essential moment of the ontogenetic process by which first hominids and then humans change both nature and themselves. To the extent that the goal of this activity (subduing nature) is an a priori dictate, it is, according to Habermas, a technical, instrumental process. Informed by empirically derived technical and strategic rules and information (that is, pure and applied science), it is the means by which, to use Kant's expression, we 'compel nature to respond to our question'. (Habermas alludes to the technical cognitive interest.)

Interaction or communicative action, the other moment of conscious human activity, encompasses that domain of social institutions (family, mass media, and so forth) which is mediated by language and governed by social rules. It is the socio-cultural lifeworld. Work is the development of both technical skills and productive forces, and hence the pre-condition for human emancipation from material wants. But symbolic interactions equip human beings with internalized norms or personality structures and thus the potential for the constitution of consensus within unconstrained social harmony. Habermas alludes to the moral-practical cognitive interest, for the truth of social rules depends not on testable laboratory processes but on the advancement of mutual comprehension of obligations and expectations. Inquiry in this domain must be occupied not with behavior and interpretation of that behavior but with the concern with how we can make the social world meaningful and intelligible to its interacting constituents. Surely, in the context provided by late capitalism, it cannot be assumed that such consensus has already been established. The potential for its actualization is to be sketched theoretically in two interlocking steps. First, via the understanding tendered by the historical and cultural sciences, we must strive to demonstrate the historical continuity and contingency of the present. Second, through its insights and liberatory potential, critical social science theory undertakes to demonstrate the potential for freeing human understandings and actions from dependence on apparently natural, hypostatizing structures of power and domination in the domains of work and interaction.

Habermas himself acknowledges Hegel's early use of these categories differentiating theory from practice, particularly in his Jena period. There Hegel echoes Kant's abstract 'I' and comprehends (idealistically) the dialectically related categories of family, language, and tools as the media of the self-transformative process of *Geist*. Paraphrasing Marx's *Critique of Hegel's Dialectic and Philosophy in General*, Habermas radicalizes Hegel's subject/object mediation:

> ... it is not the spirit in the absolute movement of reflecting on itself which manifests itself in, among other things, language, labor, and moral relationships, but rather it is the dialectical interconnections between linguistic symbolization, labor, and interaction which determine the concept of spirit. (Habermas, 1973, p. 143)

Habermas imparts a fresh conceptualization to this old distinction in order to come to terms with certain key theoretical and practical problems in the context of late capitalism.

His most forceful claim is that science has become ideological in two senses.

The first involves Roger Bacon's notion that science, by 'subduing' and 'vexing' nature, would be an integral moment in the overcoming of 'the inconveniences of man's estate' (quoted in Keane, 1975, pp. 89-90). In the form of John Galbraith's technostructure or Daniel Bell's post-industrial society, this thesis about the social benefits of 'shaping nature as an anvil' through science and technology persists unmitigated to the present. By distinguishing the technical-cognitive from the moral-practical interests, Habermas shows that science per se cannot attain this futuristic goal. The mastery of external nature provides a social project for the 'global village'. That is, the development and application of science and technology in the realm of work is always a project within, not abstracted from, the domain of interaction and relations of power. This claim is but a refutation of the common distinction between 'pure' and 'applied' science, and a reaffirmation of Marx's view in *Capital* that

> Technology discloses man's mode of dealing with Nature, the process of production by which he sustains his life, and thereby also lays bare the mode of formation of his social relations, and the mental conceptions that flow from them. (1967b, Vol. 1, p. 372 n. 2)

In the period of late capitalism, the scientization of the accumulation process merely serves to prolong and repeat the irrational exploitation of external nature and the domination of the many by the few. At present, the domination of internal human nature coincides with that of external nature. This is one aspect of the maturing recognition of a crisis in the natural sciences brought about by their 'industrialization'.

The second way science is ideological has to do with the Enlightenment perspective of the immanent tie between scientific knowledge qua knowledge and morality and happiness (in Voltaire, for example). Habermas insists that science has no necessary moral-practical significance. Modern post-Aristotelian science as depicted by Nietzsche and Scheler is a priori fitted to technical use because of its internal conceptual apparatus. The actual thinking of this science is steered toward the goal of establishing supremacy over the external environment. The dissemination of natural scientific modes of thought into the domain of interaction, and their self-misunderstanding as a type of universalized ultimate knowledge, tends to infuse those social relations (through scientific management, intelligence testing, the scientization of the medical industry, and so forth), auguring the advent of the realization of Nietzsche's aphoristic repudiations of that moral-practical ignorance embedded in Western civilization. In distinguishing interaction from work, Habermas's strategy is analogous to that of the Heidelberg neo-Kantians Heinrich Rickert and Wilhelm Windelband, who used the Kantian qualification between pure and practical reason to establish the domain of social life to which they referred. Habermas realizes that domination in social relationships is being screened by technical rationality. So, in this sense, technology has taken on legitimacy through the ideology of positivism: more and more of the same materialistic hedonism is fixated in a petrified Present.

The reduction of the category of communicative reflection to that of social labor - only too consistent with the proliferation of positivism in the twentieth century - also reappeared in the 'economism' of vast segments of the modern socialist movement. Habermas's reworking of the category of communicative interaction (through which reflection on fragmented and occluded communication proceeds) is hence an endeavor to evolve beyond Marx's (reductionist) ambiguity and the Marxist orthodoxy of the now defunct Soviet Union, where the forces of production were apotheosized and hypostatized such that 'new classes' arose from the infrastructure if judged by Five Year Plans. The spheres of work (which substitutes for the idea of the substructure of society) and communication are hence complementary for transcending the present via orientation to the past and future. In reinstating the category of interaction, Habermas refigures the major political priority for Marxists in the context of the refractive communication of late capitalism: a cultural offensive spearheading widespread involvement in the simultaneous process of demystification and the reconstruction of a popular will.

But this is not a program conceived in voluntaristic terms for cultural politics. Analogous to the manner in which Marx's theory of the possibility of proletarian action within the crisis tendency in nineteenth-century market relations resorts to a subtle mixture of deterministic and volitional elements, Habermas shows that cultural political action is conceivable in the context of a proclivity toward cultural crisis, itself an articulation of the partial breaching of the defenses of late capitalist ideology by contradictory processes intrinsic to the society. Today, in the mid-1990s, the opposition between the grand potential of the productive forces and their more circumscribed social deployment has no necessary outlet in forcing a system crisis, as it did during the nineteenth century. Certainly, in late capitalism, capital accumulation is for capital rather than vice versa, and continuing cycles of booms and recessions bespeak the irrationality of private relations of production. But now the crisis of realization on the market has been shifted from the metropolises to the peripheral underdeveloped world, where there are crises of accumulation. If anything, the relations of production in late capitalism are irrational in their self-perpetuating capacity to develop the productive forces and motivate the requisite but insensate patterns of mass consumption. Habermas's working class circles extend from traditional blue collar to white collar workers, to which we may now add reflective thinkers, women,'queers', and people of color.

Marcuse's mode of measuring alienation theoretically evades the problem of generating public reflection on patterns of distorted communication. This is not to say that, in spurning Marcuse's stress on the instinctual, sensuous moment of human activity, Habermas reopens mind/body dualism by conceptually removing sensuality from human activity. Habermas merely wants to refocus the issue that liberation of the trammeled senses can be most concretely conceptualized through the medium of verbal communication. Language always spells out exactly the conditions of life.

Habermas understands the real importance of Freud's psychoanalytic paradigm as being its stress on interpersonal dialogue and methodological reflection on the wellsprings of structural repression ('unrecognized dependencies'). This self-reflection or 'working through' is the very element blocked by positivist methodology. The Leninist and Lukácsian model of party organization is hence rejected as being only too conformist with the model of the technocratic, unreflective character of late capitalism. In recommending the psychoanalytic model at the social level, Habermas is thereby preoccupied with the theory of ordinary language communication. In his essay 'Vorbereitende Bemerkung zu einer Theorie der kommunikativen Kompetenz', he condemns as 'the paradoxical achievements of ideologies' the fact that 'impediments to communication which make a fiction of the reciprocal imputation of accountability simultaneously support the belief in legitimacy which sustains the fiction and prevents its being exposed' (Habermas and Luhmann, 1971, quoted in Keane, 1975, p. 94).

Habermas discusses at length the problem that the very structure and context of language and dialogue contains the *telos* of an 'ideal speech situation' or 'an organization of social relations according to the principle that the validity of every norm of political consequence can be made dependent on a consensus arrived at in communication free from domination' (1971, p. 312). Furthermore,

> We name a speaking-situation where the communication is not only not hindered by external, contingent influences, but also not hindered by forces which result from the structure of the communication itself. Only then does the peculiarly unforced compulsion of a better argument dominate. (1970, p. 131)

Dialogue in late capitalist society is premised on openly articulated but counterfactually derived truths of what the theorist is undertaking to convey unambiguously, and that dialogue should be readily understood by others once the institutional blinders are dissolved, that is, de-reified. 'Through its structure, autonomy and responsibility are posited for us. Our first sentence expresses unequivocally the intention of universal and unconstrained consensus' (1971, p. 314).

Covariant with the very structures of distorted symbolic interaction in late capitalism is the promise of liberation from that distorted communication via widespread dialogue, practice, and critical reflection on universal truth claims and 'facts'. This exposé of intentionality structures through dialogue is to be comprehended by a process of anamnesis whereby individuals arrive at self-consciousness. Dialogue becomes enlightenment. Paradoxically articulated, the universality of truth assumes an a priori form and yet is also dependent on individual subjects in their struggle for recognition for their constitution and actualization in a *condensation of reciprocating praxes*. Communication structures portray the epistemological caesura between essential and apparent reality. Emancipation is posited for us by the contradiction between ideological domination and the potential for communicative practice and reflection. Mediation in actuality, rather than in some counterfactual anticipation requires at least a partial breakdown of the system in its performative roles and norms. This breakdown is needed to initiate the ideal type of moral/practical dialogue Habermas envisions not only in classrooms but in homes and streets. A whole counterculture in embryo must be prepared to take over and radically restructure society; it must be willing to summon resources to quash any violence which would deny the holistic expression of the people as defined by the people and not by some sectarian group. In this very loose sense, the alienating offshoots of power could be pruned. The situation really warrants a constitutional convention at the very least, to measure the national temperament, determine new policy norms, and develop structures to carry them out through organs of the people.

We may now offer criticism of Habermas's argument. It must be asked whether the equation of work and instrumental activity is not a problematical deviation from the 'standard' Marx. In the footsteps of Marcuse and from the Aristotelian perspective that workers qua workers can never liberate themselves, Habermas's understanding of work as instrumentalism, problem solving, and the learning of skills leads to a surprisingly uncritical respect for the alienated work process in late capitalism. What is in contention here is not the analytical separation of work from interaction but the failure at this juncture to apprehend them as dialectically intertwined. To equate work with technical activity is either to ontologize that activity or to pigeonhole it as an a prior category. Historical processes can then never qualitatively change that interest; they can merely change the 'combination' of the two interests by a 'diminution' of work and an 'expansion' of communication. While without some form of work human activity is unthinkable, it also rises above the mere necessity of blind nature. Embedded in the sphere of interaction, it can become a moment of human life itself. A society freed from distorted communication implies radical improvements in the conditions under which humans produce, for example, the shortening of the working day through automation and the cancellation of unnecessary forms of production; the development of qualitatively new productive techniques (for late capitalism's interaction patterns have entered the very structure of its productive forces); and the common ownership of the means of production and the eventual self-rule of the producers. Work, like interaction, offers social activity in which humans can consciously create and individuate themselves. Workers' control has again come to the forefront of a renewed humanist Marxism and is central to the movement's self-definition.

Habermas does not fully appreciate how work and interaction are dialectically attached at both the categorical and historical planes. He argues the need to interpolate the concept of reflection into these broad dicta of natural science research by pointing to the relevance of C. S. Peirce's model of a reflexive, instrumental logic of discovery. Repudiating both the objectivism of positivist science and rationalist endeavors to unravel the ultimate phases of nature, Habermas understands scientific reasoning as a reflexive system of purposive/rational action. This system works as a regulative precept for the accumulation of fresh information, itself to be revised when failures in the projected results manifest themselves. The pivotal meaning of any scientific statement is that it is a conditional prediction which relies on and prefigures successful human manipulation of natural objects.

We suspect that the impending ecological destruction hidden in instrumentalized reason presupposes the idea of a natural science which, in its very conceptual structure, seeks a non-repressive mastery of external nature. Surely, Habermas must believe that the sciences must communicate with an enlightened public about its ecosystem. His schematic design certainly is not averse to other nonscientific (e.g., aesthetic) modes of human interaction with external nature outside the domain of work. To understand science as inevitably technical in its conceptual structure (and thereby in its practical consequences) is to hypostatize it, to perceive it (unrealistically) as virginal, pure, and immune from the capriciousness of socio-historical life. This technical-instrumentalist science is ideological in that it simultaneously hides and uncovers the technical, monological essence of late capitalist society's understanding of external nature as a thing - an anthropomorphized one at that - to be cruelly and selfishly exploited to the limit. We must remember as a social body that nature is our inorganic body.

Habermas's uncritical evaluation of the analytic character of modern science must be countered by the development of at least one holistically conceived system (ecology) which can apprehend the dialectical operation of this humanized ecosystem. Our interaction with nature through the sphere of work indicates the *telos* of a nonrepressive preserving, fostering, and releasing of external nature's 'potentialities' for human benefit. As human beings, we are to advance the 'completion' of nature by improving ourselves in scientific, technological, and aesthetic interaction with that nature through the domain of work. This approach requires a heightened awareness of the destructive impact of some human techniques and, conversely, cooperation between human beings and nature. The liberation of nature would begin to overlap with the liberation of human beings. What is assured is that Habermas's comprehension of the dialectic of distorted and non-distorted communication is seductively formalistic and poorly grounded. This dialectic hovers over its potential subjects, offering no real insights into practical struggle and organizational problems and priorities where capricious or well-planned police oppression of an overt sort is impending.

Habermas's response to this criticism is to distinguish between communication and dialogue, which remain directly subject to the constraints of actions, and discourse, which transcends such barriers. In splitting the moment of theoretical discourse and argumentation from that of the organization and implementation of the enlightenment process to make good on promises to be found in any consensus, Habermas thereby appears to collapse partially into a supine position before potential converts. This is the case despite his favoring radical reform in the new Germany. Hence the notion of an 'ideal speech situation' is foggy and not well supported, and empty of suggestions as to which institutional forms might actualize that undistorted communication. His prescriptions revert to truisms. In the end, he will be left without either the rationale or the means of revolutionizing late capitalist society.

Through a combination of a critically grounded hermeneutics with a mode of dialectical exposition, we can see certain intrinsic limits to Habermas's method. In particular, we must be wary of idealizing material circumstances of long standing. Our utopian visions must be positively rooted in the past before we can even begin to project any modicum of radical change.

Note

1. Marx here evidences a really strident tone. In his hands philosophy is a weapon of criticism to trumpet down the walls of Jericho. He continues,

> Philosophy has become secularized, and the most striking proof for this

is the fact that the philosophical consciousness itself is drawn into the torment of struggle, not only outwardly but inwardly as well. Even though the construction of the future and its completion for all times is not our task, what we have to accomplish at this time is all the more clear: *relentless criticism of all existing conditions*, relentless in the sense that the criticism is not afraid of its findings and just as little afraid of the conflict with the powers that be. (1967a, p. 212)

On these grounds, American universities and the tenured faculties have suffered a failure of nerve because by a natural selective process profits are the criterion of survival in their world governed by financial struggle. The siren songs of praise for capitalism have replaced critical thinking at an institutional level. Hence, in their conservative world views, the elite schools have become part of the problem, mainly attaining redistributive justice with social equality without sacrificing their basic functions and tasks for authoritarian regimes. Americans have an authoritarian socio-political regime without equality or justice, but nonetheless maintaining ideological power of traditional abstract freedoms with little meaning.

9 Whither critical theory and its exponents

Theory grounding: Dialectics and hermeneutics

In trying to define the lifeworld of human activities, Habermas has developed a mode of interpretation which can be called the best variety of critical theory to date. To understand Habermas, we must observe how he comes to terms with his rival Hans-Georg Gadamer. Gadamer's *Truth and Method* challenges the very premises of the Enlightenment and its legacy of fragmentary presentations of artificial systems of rationality. In a rather urbane manner, Habermas calls Gadamer conservative because the latter rehabilitates authority and tradition while claiming that authentic authority does not have to impose itself in an authoritarian way. Gadamer describes the recognition of authority as an invariant element of historical understanding, and one which is compatible with freedom. For the recognition of authority is essential to any understanding which, not certain of itself in a solipsistic way, is dependent on the tradition of language. Tradition poses a voluntary language which is attributable to the finite nature of understanding. It occurs in politically naive forms and whenever we claim that a text of the historical past says something to us which we could not have learned in our contemporary environment or found on our own initiative. It happens as well whenever we find that we cannot conceive of ourselves without reference to a given order of social life (such as the state or the family), in spite of all its shortcomings. This is so because the recognition of such an order is usually linked to tradition and to the obeisance to those wielding authority.

As interesting as Habermas finds Gadamer's theme of a rehabilitation of authority and tradition, he does not provide a full-fledged critico-practicoresponse, possibly from fear of being 'ideological'. This new brand of conservatism must be confusing even to Habermas when he elucidates the crises wracking late capitalism. For Habermas himself has fallen into the mode of being 'value free', and at this juncture is engaged only theoretically, although this discourse is a low grade of praxis. To his everlasting credit, Habermas has fully defended the uniqueness of the Holocaust and collective German responsibility. In this light, Habermas is a giant in his stand against revisionism of history and its meaning. He also understands that Gadamer's perspectives are connected to a formidable analysis of the process of *Verstehen*.

In this vein, Gadamer's work embodies the paradigm of the critique of progress, to which critical theory must address itself. Habermas therefore implicitly credits Gadamer with insights which sharpen the focus of critical theory, and he views himself to be in a position to assimilate those elements of the critique of progress which hermeneutics brings to the fore. Habermas himself must somewhat share Gadamer's conviction that our reconciliation with the historical past which is shared and made by us cannot be delineated as solely the linear and cumulatively preceding accumulation of knowledge. For any endeavor to understand a subject matter is an element of interpretive understanding. Nor can communicative interaction and the attainment of understanding in it be defined in such a manner. Both Gadamer and Habermas indicate that the 'text' has an 'authority' which must be reckoned with. Not all things, institutions, texts, or persons in the world can lay an equal claim to our attention, and there is no class of items in the world, be they institutions or not, which we can single out in advance as having of necessity the 'right' to expect the surrender of understanding and of reflection. The surrender rather transpires in the process of understanding, but will be regained later in dialectical reason.

In giving an account of hermeneutical reflection, Gadamer assimilates the theory of action to that of communicative interaction. The latter perspective impels his gifted critique of instrumental reason and provides a methodological basis for the redemption of authority and tradition.

If critical theory is no longer assured of its conceptual means to handle the logic of history, and if it cannot resign itself to merely expressing the experience of the irrationality of its course, an elucidation and review of its logical and epistemological status becomes imperative. Critical theory, interpreted by Habermas as a philosophy of history with political intentions, is the theory of historical understanding which (1) is diacritical from a theory of historical explanation as it unfolds in history as a science and (2) adumbrates the task of interpretive understanding in social practice. The relevance of Gadamer's discussion of hermeneutics is that hermeneutics expounds on both these matters, because it takes historical understanding to be a practice of life and describes the practice of life as the practice of speech, which fleshes out our historical existence in terms of communicative interaction. But critical theory takes itself as the reflective component of social practice. It finds useful a theory which sees itself as adhering to a practice as well. Hermeneutics is the reflective determinant of the continuous appropriation of tradition which affects our mores and motives while incorporating us as historically existing beings. But the limitation of hermeneutics as such is that one can command a praxis only obliquely from its sources.

Critical theory has become a critique of instrumental reason. If technology and science have become a supportive ideology for contemporary conditions, then the critique of political economy is to be overcome by a critique of those standard Marxian modes of collective interpretation of our social situation. Critique presumes a structural situation of domination and an affective one of alienation. But hermeneutics also works on the dynamic differential of *praxis* and *technē*. It strives to describe interpretive understanding as distinct from the objectifying methods of the sciences. The upshot for hermeneutics is that it can help critical theory clarify the difference between solving practical problems like those encountered in communicative interaction (for instance, all those entailing social norms), and those to be solved with the aid of scientifically geared techniques of instrumental control. What is demanded, then, is a theory of 'ordinary language communication' which can cogently outline the boundaries of communicative experience over against scientifically objectifiable data of experience, whose rules wall off the human mind from the finished product (of its project) when in fact phenomenologically the overall outcome has a historical *telos* which makes it a *pars pro toto* of human culture.

Because of this new grasp of the importance of discourse, critical theory has become increasingly critical of the objectivist elements in Marx's philosophy of history. Marx could not advance the idea of a critique of ideologies of 'objective' illusions, so the criticism runs, because he equated critique with natural science and so tended to distort reflection naturalistically. The argument, then, is that we must critique Marx himself because his 'lower' form of 'critique' falls under the rubric of a natural science with a positivistic tendency toward reificatory communication. In a sense, then, we are attempting to restore willed intentionality by fully formed human agents within the historicity of universal events.

But even though Marx acted within these constraints, it would not be the case that he suffered from a false consciousness. Marx also presumed communicative interaction to be subsumed under the category of socially organized labor. Hermeneutics intimates the sketch of a theory of communicative interaction, apprehending the ties between the critique of illusion and a theory of interaction, with the two not to be confounded. Its focus on dialogue with the foremost philosophical and poetical texts of the historical past reconciles and recovers our past history in an enlivened interaction directed to the concerns of the present day. But if critical theory is to be true to its genesis in Marx and Hegel, it will have to address both a materialist and a language interpretive theory of history, not merely take one side or the other.

Gadamer seeks out experience of truth surpassing the controlling domain of scientific method. In these experiences we understand ourselves in a unique manner in coming to question our own being: the nature of our *Geworfenheit*. In facing our historical legacy, we learn to confront conceptions of how we are to be which may question what we really already are and the possibilities therein. The speech we deploy to articulate such self-understanding are the words in which we express the orienting effect which experiences have. Consequently they are not denuded of historical content, nor organized by a theory. These pristine experiences do not have the form of propositions asserting facts. They are not like scientific terminology, which so objectifies experience that no historical component remains. We may learn to venture our pre-understandings and appraisals in obtaining an openness for new experience. The methodical exercise of scientific research may turn out to be a quest for an illusory insulation from the *Lebenswelt*, if the truth unraveled in science is the only one to which we are committed in the end. But we all remain somehow ensnared in the historical logic of instrumental reason, in which we become as alien to ourselves as to our historical origins. In this vein, hermeneutics poses a critique of instrumental reason.

Critical political sociology also has an interest in vindicating the claim to truth which may stem from communicative experience in a community and the norms of its organization. Communicative experience is difficult to subject to scientific discourse. It is better imagined as a participatory relationship between the understanding subject and the confronting alter ego. Here reshaping the milieu requires divesting oneself of a part of one's subjectivity. In so doing, through lived corporeality, the subject comes to know and recognize the other when and where they are engaged on common concerns. The dialectic of recognition does not coincide with the logic of objectifying statements and controlled experimental conditions. In particular types of participatory understanding, for instance the therapeutic dialogue, one may even actualize a particular truth claim in living it authentically. Here the surrender and banishment of self-deceptions is clearly not only an outcome to be attained by scientific method, or the consequence of a technique instrumentally applied. Somehow one comes to hold one's very existence in awe, in order later to redeem oneself as a more authentic personality as opposed to the persona one self-consciously partakes of in capitalism.

For the critical theorist, this problem of instrumental reason can also be found in the empirical social sciences. For there, on the whole, the methods do not allow for a participatory understanding of data with access to it via the understanding of meaning. Therefore a critique of the empirical social sciences is necessary to amplify the themes the hermeneutical critique will touch on in other domains. It must assure communicative access to the data of social science and explain the validity of comprehending society in the array of its historical forms.

But critical theory is not hermeneutics in the first place, for it purports to be a critique of our industrial society and the history of its modes of production of capital goods and relations. Therefore, unlike hermeneutics, it is oriented toward emancipation from our historical past, to the extent that this history can be viewed as one of domination and repression. We must understand collectively the nature of the needs for ritual behavior as totems no longer useful for assuring leadership and group coherence. These 'residues' are superstitions which trammel the forces of production and their further reasoned development.

Here, therefore, critical theory links up with science to critique hermeneutics. Science is to obtain for us a new means of control over our natural condition. Critical theory must assimilate science conceptually if it is to be also a critique of the values inherent in tradition. But the vantage point for this critique cannot be adduced from the rationality of science and the discourse of its particular social form. The idea of emancipation, in the name of which critical theory turns against tradition, implies a shared form of life experience, one of mutual consensus which no longer needs to be revoked when challenged by particularistic interest groups acting in the self-anointed role of defender of the general weal. But it is with regard to the possibility of fashioning such a construct of an ideal form of life that hermeneutics takes its stance counter to critical theory. Precisely in order to supersede the hermeneutical hypostatization of past human experiences, which congeals and obstructs the progressive and refluxive flow between the temporalities, critical theory must pose an alternative plan of social justice. This plan must allow members to be communicatively competent in their speech acts and realize that the redemption of humanity entails communicatively competent practices and a politics of confrontation toward those who persist in being dominative. Idealized speech acts border on being ideal types which inadvertently are coopted by the establishment as it buys time in bad faith and hopes that the contradictions somehow will be suppressed without too much discharge of critical resources.

We must now examine more carefully how the hermeneutic project draws Habermas into its fold and what factors he leaves aside. We recall that critical theory and hermeneutics both identify a critique of instrumental reason as the major task under present historical conditions where the legitimacy of late capitalism has come into question. The two schools approach the task in different terms. This fact can be illustrated well by observing features in Gadamer's hermeneutics which do not easily fit into the space designed for hermeneutics in Habermas's metatheoretical odyssey. Habermas proposed to use Gadamer's judgments on interpretive procedures in the social sciences as supplementary explanatory methods. By opening access to meaning generated in communicative interaction as the fundamental datum of social science, hermeneutics can help rectify the instrumentalist distortion rampant there: the exaggerated technical division of labor. Hermeneutics can ameliorate the morbid, rationalistic preoccupation with objectifiable and technically instrumental knowledge through an interest in a knowledge controlling experience which is schematically accessible and respectable. Yet hermeneutics is germane to the project of a critical social science and its philosophy in an even more profound way. It offers a mode of reflection which makes it possible to diagnose the state of the social sciences as suffering from the same instrumentalist delusion which is supposed to be ruling over nature and human nature and the very institutions binding them. In doing so, it also gives the will free play in the practical context of life; this aspect is still typical of critical theory, even in its most sublimated form.

What makes it possible to conceive of hermeneutics as a critique of instrumental reason? In *Truth and Method*, Gadamer takes as his point of departure the *Geisteswissenschaften* and methodological reflection on them. He stands against Dilthey's perspective that what is called 'method' in contemporary science has universal validity: 'What makes the human sciences into sciences can be understood more easily from the tradition of the concept of *Bildung* than from the concept of method in modern science' (Gadamer, 1975, p. 18). Dilthey advocates a reconstruction of what we think is general to the understanding of one's cultural heritage in literature, history, and the arts, and what is typical of the appreciation of art and of fidelity to customs and tradition.

At least since Kant, philosophers have instructed us that such understandings cannot be called knowledge unless they are supported by some kind of scientific method or theory. The consequence could be that we can no longer account for the manner in which the reading of literature, the experience of art, or historical tradition are 'humanizing' and conducive to the self-transformative understandings which prevent us from falling into barbarism. Suppressed in their legitimacy, they lose their dignified status as items and modes of 'knowledge', with the result that this genre of experience is relegated to an unimportant role in our positivist scheme of things. They hence become constituents and artifacts of a practically sterilized subculture for 'professors'. For Gadamer, therefore, all those facets of our historical experience where strict methods do not yet play a predominant role are to be rehabilitated as a kind of knowledge. Only then can we hope to recover their moral and practical relevance and infuse them with a new purpose and orientation . We require this kind of thinking for a critique of instrumental reason. Hermeneutics cannot merely be a 'doctrine of method', not even for the *Geisteswissenschaften*. Moreover, if there are experiences of truth transcending the sphere of control by scientific method, interpretation is to be perceived as a constituent of much of pre-scientific experience, and the phenomenon of *Verstehen* and of adequate interpretation is not just a special problem for a doctrine of method in the 'spiritual sciences' - the human studies. The hermeneutical phenomenon is fundamentally not a problem of method at all, but at its core one of empathy.

Gadamer builds on Heidegger's existential analytic. Interpretive technique designates the primary movement of human existence, which comprises its finitude and historicity and thereby encompasses the whole of its experience of the world. The movement of understanding is encompassing and universal. Therein is what we take to be the 'ontological' posture of hermeneutics, as opposed to the ideal of interpretive understanding as a set of procedures fixated on the humanities. They, on the contrary, 'are joined with modes of experience which lie outside science: with the experience of philosophy, of art, and of history itself' (Gadamer, 1975, p. xii). The authentic staking out of territory for hermeneutics is a philosophical one: what is problematic 'is not what we do or what we ought to do, but what happens to us, over and above our wanting and doing' (1975, p. xvi). The considerations of hermeneutics are distinct from epistemological or methodological ones. They are definitively ontological. The process of understanding ontologically is coextensive with experience of our world and history, in which preconceptually we are not the master of either. Therein lies the meaning which experience mostly conveys to us. Becoming experienced, then, does not have the sense of acquiring a skill and successfully exercising it. It means that one has learned how to live, possibly without being able fully to conceptualize these moments which leave no material determinants in their wake.

Knowing how to live is a form of *phronesis* and does not always and necessarily imply mastery of the conditions of life. It may convey recognition not only of what one cannot change but even more of what one ought to attempt to change. Meaning can emerge without conscious manipulation:

> I maintain that the hermeneutical problem is universal and basic for all interhuman experience, both of history and of the present moment, precisely because of the fact that meaning can be experienced, even where it is not actually intended. (Gadamer, quoted in Misgeld, 1976, pp. 173-4)

Gadamer takes interpretive understanding to be an element of all activities of human life. As such, hermeneutical reflection on the interpretive component of practices of life is not constrained to the analysis of phenomena of reflective appropriation of meaning. Not only what we can perceive as our motives for action in everyday life counts as a hermeneutical phenomenon. Subjective meaning-intentions, which we can explicitly ascertain as our own and objectify, are only a small part of the meanings in which we participate. What we partake of, be it a form of life, an intention, a social role, or a tradition, we know about somehow, but we cannot give an objective account of it which would not require or even forbid the use of personal pronouns. We may not be able to express it in any form of conceptually articulated knowledge. In a most basic way, what we participate in is language, and we can never account for language by allusion to principles of a reasoning activity conceived from the beginning as outside or beyond language.

Language, then, is the primary infrastructure for any kind of communicative experience. Otherwise, the experience is solipsistic, a dream world of detemporalized space, and to that extent may fall in the realm of the psychopathology of everyday life where one is driven by real forces beyond one's control or even knowledge and to which one attributes mystificatory and cthonic powers which systematically deny one's individuality.

We participate in language, Gadamer informs us, by 'belonging' to it. We can say that in speaking we appropriate meanings of words without being able to account for them solely in terms of our own meaning intentions. History, as mediated by language, gains supremacy over our individual consciousness, expectations, and practical intentions. Hence we speak of the tradition context of language as that to which we belong, in which we are at home in a sense; we try to convey the idea of being domiciled in the interstices of the 'black holes' of the universe. This is so, not because language (in the sense of our capacity to speak) is a generic trait of human beings or a substantive crystallization of our historical experience, but because in our use of language tradition speaks or our collectively inherited culture makes it purposefully present to us. Language is our heritage, but it speaks as the historical past to which we still belong. Gadamer delineates our belonging to the tradition context of language cum speech as analogous to the manner in which we are conscious of participating in a game:

> We have seen that a game has its being, not in the consciousness or actions of the players, but, on the contrary, it draws these into its own realm and fills them with its spirit. The player experiences the game as for him an overpowering reality. (1975, p. 98)

This overpowering reality is attributable to a morbid rationalism which condenses human individuality into a spatio-temporal domain which does not further differentiate but takes on an alienated essentiality destructive of the one characteristic which invigorates humanity's spiritual corporeality. That is praxis, a generic, self-transformative energy which involves humanity in critico-practical activities around the theme of collectively realizing freedom as a new phylogenetic urgency. We say urgency rather than necessity because people act according to rational projections within a narrow range of optimally calculable possibilities, and any number of configurations of errors can overthrow this hope.

So hermeneutics finds that our having a world is dependent on the availability of language and the experience of the world in language is absolute. It reaches as far as our practices of speaking, while universally conceiving interpretive processes and activities, and is as broad as our modes of experiencing whatever happens in human events. Language remains quintessentially the language of dialogue. It obtains its reality only in the flux of communicating and reaching a determinative understanding. Since we simply cannot concretely objectify or transcend the tradition-bound context of language toward the material conditions of factual history, as if we could look at language as a tradition-laden content from outside, language is always ahead of our understanding it, as is history in its making.

Hermeneutics is in the mode of gathering critical momentum over against the technological enmity to history-making. Practical motives emerge from this preoccupation with historical tradition and the interpretive procedures of everyday life communication, in which drawing on a heritage of one's own becomes a part of contemporary forms of life. Technology, scientific method, and even the rationalism of the tradition of critique in philosophy from Kant to Hegel, Marx, Husserl, and the Frankfurt School have something in common, in Gadamer's perspective. They aim either at knowledge without presuppositions and ignore the historical embeddedness of those modes of knowing which transmit effective self-understanding, or at knowledge with the practical impact of making societal and historical actors totally rational. Both lend themselves to a predestined combination of technological and political utopianism, since both are directed at replacing historically evolved institutions and mores by more rationally organized ones. Usually political utopianism and the idea of emancipation from 'natural' or historically grounded circumstances seek support by using scientifically objective methods to elicit factors in social life which stand 'behind' the actors and are not part of their self-understanding but are the really 'determining' ones.

What Gadamer calls *wirkunsgeschichtliches Bewusstsein* is a 'consciousness of the effectivity of history within understanding itself' (1975, p. 267). History is even at work in our consciousness of our situation, so much so that we can never place it in front of ourselves. Habermas's suggestion to bind 'tradition' to other structures of the social lifeworld as 'labor' and 'domination' has a constructivist ring from this view, giving it the appearance of an idealist delusion. Herein lies the reason Gadamer says that *wirkungsgeschichtliches Bewusstsein* is more being than consciousness that being, whose essence issues in a universalized determinably bounded nature, is never fully manifest in encompassing the fundamental order of our being which is not susceptible to volitional interference and cannot be 'produced'. Rather, it has to be venerated. Therefore, in Gadamer's hermeneutical tradition, the emancipatory thrust is blunted. There are 'fundamental' realities which individuals had better learn to adjust to and, as for science, 'Whatever science is able to achieve, it will not be able to transcend a limit, which perhaps no one knows and which, however, is placed before everything' (Misgeld, 1977, p. 177). Nowhere do his statements illustrate real historical concreteness, and one cannot infer that particular systems of government, values, the major religions, the monogamous family, or even philosophy comprise such boundary requirements for historical change.

Biological and physiological factors like birth and death, and also moral ones like freedom and responsibility are not to be taken as anthropological invariants, defining human nature without any reference to historical interpretations of them. They are rather boundary lines for a commonality of understanding which is constantly built up and maintained throughout history. What they 'mean', one might say, depends on interpretations provided by the members of society themselves, acting and interacting historically by reference to them. We cannot actually define them. They can be delineated only in terms of the interpretive procedures actors and understanding individuals apply to them.

Hermeneutics remains phenomenology in the sense of engaging the method of 'intentional analysis'. But it also avows that meaning can be experienced even where it is not actually what one had intended. The more basic the order of reality referred to, the less experiential meanings can apparently be intended and the more they assert themselves of their own accord, with a power of persuasion which supposedly cannot be broken by reflection. Hence there are recurrent dilemmas humanity faces irrespective of the social order we build, because there are certain built-in, existential constraints which absolutely prohibit any remedial practice.

Human morality, of course, is just such a recurrent dilemma. It is not simply the *logos* of a common language that Gadamer entertains in his mind. And these problematic areas of 'existentiality' are in no way imposed on humanity as an externality. There are sociologically and historically more concrete conditions of our self-understanding as well, which we cannot simply dismiss in understanding and which exert a normative force. Gadamer concurs with Hegel when he deems humanity to have issued forth historically. Understanding ourselves as belonging to such a history becomes a norm of interpretive understanding, merely because this is the norm in terms of which we have historically learned to comprehend what comprises humanity.

There are no ahistorical social norms. Long before we came to understand ourselves through the process of self-examination, we have understood ourselves in a self-evident way in the family, society, and state in which we live. Metaphorically portrayed, 'The self-awareness of the individual is only a flickering in the closed circuits of historical life' (Gadamer, 1975, p. 245). Family and state would seem to be supra-individual entities of historical life to which individuals find themselves subjugated in any event. Even the historically more variable and contingent configuration of factors we may encounter in family or state evince much more mutual consistency, continuity, and adaptability to change than we are usually willing to impute to them. We are victims of a perspectival illusion if we fancy ourselves able to achieve emancipation from tradition and history, which, from the scientific rationale, may appear as malfunctioning experimental designs to be corrected by the human engineers. The prevalent attitude toward authority provides the prime example, for instance, in our national leaders, religious figures, parents, and so forth. Not only have we always recognized these 'authorities', that recognition is unavoidable because of the very vulnerability of the human maturational process from birth through death. It is inconceivable that we could ever make sense of a process of education, even if outlined in terms of a process of self-transformation as in the schematic put forward by Habermas, without imputing some legitimate role to such 'authorities'.

Herein lies the critical insight Gadamer consistently brings against Habermas's counter-critique of tradition, authority, and pre-judgment. When we construe the relation between reason and authority as one of absolute incompatibility, we do not allow for the possibility of all those actually occurring events where authority is recognized, not on the grounds of blind obedience but from an insight into its justification: for 'givenness' has a certain level of imperative moral content simply as a reference point for being in the world. Authority and tradition can embrace a rational modus operandi. The burden of disproof, therefore, lies on the critics and revolutionaries. There is, then, authority which is freely recognized and perceived as 'natural' and useful to the utmost. It also provides humanity a spatio-temporal history and 'home' in the universe. It does not have to present itself in an authoritarian way but can be unassuming, as in the case of an expert who restricts him- or herself to a tightly defined domain and realized limitations. Gadamer's hermeneutical reflection on methods in the humanities makes him conclude that the interpretation of texts and other works cannot simply be divorced from historical experience and the manner in which we comport ourselves toward the past in life. The genuine concern is not distantiation and freedom from what is inherited. 'Rather, we always stand within traditions - and this is no objectifying process, i.e., we do not conceive of what tradition says as something other, something alien. It is always part of us' (1975, p. 250).

Gadamer consequently claims to overcome the abstract opposition between a most natural, inadvertent appropriation and preservation of tradition and historical research of the latter. Such research comes to be perceived as merely a more deliberate execution of a reflective appropriation of tradition with which our pre-theoretical preservation of it is already entwined. Hermeneutics does not propose suspending all claims to our attention emerging from the ongoing process of assimilation and transfiguration. It does not pursue the illusion of 'value-free' science. We must speak of an objectivity which is proper to language over against the speakers and their naturally acquired communicative competence. The issue of the universality of hermeneutics sees itself as that of the extent to which knowledge depends on the tradition-context of language. Gadamer does not articulate a theory of interpretive understanding in order to remedy the course of the social sciences and their positivism. Nor does he propose that the interpretive understanding be fused with explanatory procedures in the social sciences to flavor the social sciences with a *geistig* quality.

If hermeneutical understanding is out-and-out inadequate to give a historical and material accounting for its own phenomenological claims, then no real understanding but only a kind of viscous, emotive affectivity is being expressed. But hermeneutical understanding is at least as reflective as critical theory has proved to be, particularly if judged by the works of Habermas. Communicative access to the data of social science implies recognition that theorizing depends on the modes of understanding embedded in social practice, where they are always at work. Critical theory will have to begin with them and return to their environs to be capable of forming a theoretical objectification. Every theoretically or methodologically construed insight abstracted from communicative experience is to be retranslated into this context, where there are no privileged powers with transcendental stature beyond criticism.

But for Habermas the relation of such societal processes to language as a 'meta-institution' is to be conceived in analogy to the role of 'unconscious motives' in our understanding of our own action. The processes and (as we should add) structures are 'labor' (mode of production and the productive forces issuing forth) and 'domination' (in the sense of institutions controlling or legitimizing means of coercion and power). 'Labor' and 'domination', we must assume, consist of sets of infra-linguistic conditions which 'determine' the constitution of social action in communicative interaction by providing it objective conditions. Under these conditions, the fetters of reality reveal themselves as external nature, to be rendered controllable and reflected in the procedures of scientifically instructed technical control, and with the coercive and compelling nature of drives mirrored in societally condoned modes of repression.

Here we must grasp social action in terms of an objective contest evidenced through language, labor, and domination. For critical theory, while reaching agreement in the discursive examination of reciprocal and competing truth claims, is offering a normative challenge to the capitalist work ethos. A frame of reference is to be elucidated which allows us to transcend the context of tradition as such.

Habermas anticipates the possible hermeneutical objection, 'How shall such a frame of reference be legitimated if not itself by the appropriation of tradition?' (quoted in Misgeld, 1976, p. 181). Critical theory has complicated matters by extending the grounds for appropriating territories belonging to other disciplines. If it is to adhere to the perspective that in a process of enlightenment there cannot be any privileged knowers, how can it wish to transcend the context of tradition as such? For in doing so, assuming it can be done, must not new privileges accrue to the one developing the 'frame of reference' which facilitates the projection of a freedom from tradition? Must the theoretician not rely on a conceptual repertoire not available to ordinary communicative competence? There is the danger that one might have to translate back into the context of communicative experience a theory grounded on the basis of abstracting from this experience.

Habermas's problems arise because he claims to have an all-inclusive theory of the contemporary age. He also wants to retain a linkage with praxis, which he himself grasps as not capable of being fully guided by a theory. For praxis has its own grounds of intelligibility, independent from a theory making it the object of comprehensive reflection. The theory of communicative competence and the project of a universal pragmatics is to establish the basis for a communications theory of society, in which the data base of social science is anchored in a stable and expectable manner such that the social scientist inserts subjective attitudes and inclinations into the making of his or her own data, in effect constituting them as a modality of a natural language. It is claimed, then, that it becomes possible to elucidate how historically specific modes of communication emerge, and also how their distortions are systematically recomposed. The competence to decipher them as distorted cannot issue from mere dependence on the historical reconstruction of the events or on a reconstructionist theory of the pragmatic universals of speech. It requires the perception of one's own pre-understanding as an act of practical discourse, and an initial engagement in a communicative action denying, in its very attainment, its own communal basis.

Such a rupture, opening a cleavage in communally shared understandings, cannot be assured of its own groundedness no matter how elaborate the theories informing it. It remains a practical, situated activity. In this vein, critical theory may still be viewed as somewhat dependent on hermeneutical determinants. For it is impossible to secure intersubjective understanding before we have entered into a situated discourse with others about the specific matters at hand in that very situation. It cannot maintain itself on the plane of tradition transcended.

The very confrontation between a hypothetical anticipation of possibilities beyond all known traditions (and societies) and the reality of tradition will transpire initially - as a moment - without a tradition-restricted culture. Generational changes in critical theory formation to date have been inadequate. The third generation of this school's disciples is now at hand as we enter the twenty-first century. Reflection transcending tradition will either have to learn to evaluate itself as implicated in the formation of tradition or forsake the possibility of becoming practical and not utopian. It is not altogether clear whether Habermas is willing to recognize the antecedence of everyday 'sense' as outlined here.

So we see the severe methodological limitations to critical theory as expounded by Habermas. In the next section, we shall take up an equally serious epistemological question.

Habermas: Teleological subjectivity and objective free will

In this section, we shall pursue specifically the epistemological limits in the critical theory developed by Habermas. We shall come to see once more the Unhappy Consciousness as subject and object are not ultimately resolved. We must explore the question whether alienation, then, is not the ontological human condition witnessed by the circumscribed modes of our temporal mediations in a shrinking public space. For only through a false faith in a positivist science could humanity aspire to transcend the realm of cruel necessity dominative of human nature.

To elucidate the meaning of our traditional foundation of 'teleological subjectivity' (coming to self-consciousness), we must illuminate the historical horizon within which Schelling had first conceived of the categories of freedom and necessity in this way for German classical philosophy. This quest will lead us back to the Frankfurt School and the advanced theoretical work of Habermas - the 'retrograde' elements of which will be studied, if not necessarily transcended. The previous section and earlier chapters show from contemporary hermeneutics that we understand the notions which determine our thoughts only after we have successfully traced their genealogy. For present purposes, the historical configuration of the meaning of 'freedom' and 'necessity' is intended to demonstrate that the contradiction between them is immanent to the traditional foundation of 'teleological subjectivity'. Anyone who develops a 'theory of history' on the basis of teleological subjectivity is thus urged to take issue with this contradiction.

Ever since the time of the Greeks, some of the ideas underlying our understanding of the 'necessity' steering a process have been that of *telos*. Schelling's concept of history is premised on this purposive ideal. The 'realizing' of one idea is a movement proceeding from the beginning toward a highest goal which directly determines all stages of the development from the beginning and compels them all to be 'fleshed out' and completed at this absolute polarized point. Since 'progress' also delineates Schelling's notion of history, the movement is not really self-sealing and circular but rather irreversible and unrepeatable. It is a purposeful movement toward the future.

Under the influence of the Jewish messianic hope and the Christian hope in an apocalyptic judgment and the return of Christ, the inspiring thought of *telos* developed into that of *eschaton*. It would be more valuable to depict the 'process of history' for Schelling and others as eschatological rather than teleological. In any event, the impelling force dominating the movement of *telos* and *eschaton* has the markings of an event which takes place independently of and often in opposition to conscious human freedom. This trait is entailed in the category of 'necessity' in Schelling's philosophy of history.

In Greek philosophy, the idea of *telos* has been formed in conjunction with those of *nous* and *logos*. The pre-Socratics understood *nous*, or *spirit*, as the power which lights up all that is and makes it translucid. They also understood *logos* as that which stringently establishes its order. In conjunction with *nous*, that stringency epistemologically entails that everything is organized in a consistent way. This trait of *logos* also entered into the sense of necessity.

Of course, Schelling and Hegel, in the diversity of their accomplishments, were assimilated by Marx in a materialist dialectic. Habermas feels he stands to Marx as the latter did to his own predecessors, which would make Habermas not a Marxist. The question is whether Habermas has overcome the traditional guiding thought of *logos* - logical subjectivity - in his conception of history. A negative response is already suggested by the fact that he has employed so many basic determinations emanating from *logos* philosophy. A critical reader becomes most suspicious after reading his recent *Postmetaphysical Thinking*. He evidences such a sympathy with all his interlocutors that his insights reinforce the status quo and privilege, however unintentionally. He presents the Marxist positions as if Marx himself had thought of them as 'epistemological' and 'transcendental'. He even portrays the economic mechanism of the historical-generic development as adhering to a 'history of transcendental consciousness' (Habermas, 1971, pp. 58, 65). Besides, he claims that Marx's characterization of 'man as an objective essence' is not anthropological but epistemological: it was forged by Marx, says Habermas, as a 'transcendental task' because it correlated with the structure of a world in which reality comes under the conditions for the objectivity of possible objects. To cite another example, labor and class conflict are subsumed by Habermas under the rubric of a 'synthesis'; this concept is among the most critical outcomes of transcendental logic. Knowing and doing rest on a 'natural basis'. Thus he holds, for example, that the 'synthesis' of the labor process is 'both [the] empirical and transcendental effect of a generic subject historically engendered' (1971, p. 43). It does not produce an 'absolute identity of spirit and nature'; rather unity is 'imposed from the subject on nature, as it were' (43).

In contrast to Marx, Habermas uses the category of reflection to understand the process of self-generation of the human species, a process of oppression and liberation of the self and of social formations. He proposes that 'Not new technologies, but stages of reflection characterize the way of the process of social formation' (76). By that account, the concept of 'synthesis' he conceptualizes delineates not only self-generation through labor but also formation through social praxis, which for him signifies reflection or self-reflection. The determination 'reflection' has its genesis in the philosophy of *logos*, which in its modern development has taken form as the precept of self-consciousness or logical subjectivity. The reflective turning back of the self on itself - the *cogito me cogitare* of Descartes - allowed the essence of the I as self, the *res cogitans*, to emerge. In the subsequent history of thought this was elevated to the status of precept.

For Kant, reflection became the 'method' to fathom the transcendental subject as this principle. Kant's transcendental investigation indicated the subject as the fount of knowledge - the condition for the possibility for theoretical knowing - and as the rational good will which has autonomous and free legislative force as the origin for all ethical action. For Fichte, reflection was no longer merely method. It constituted the essence of subjectivity, conceived as the principle of freedom. This was so also for Schelling and Hegel insofar as subjectivity encompassed and constituted objectivity. For Habermas, too, self-reflection marks the human capacity for rational autonomy, for freedom from repressive forces, both subjectively, in regard to the ego and its search for identity, and objectively, in regard to rationalizing the powers of nature and human institutions. Since Kant, this capacity has been recognized as 'practical reason'.

For Habermas the exercise of self-reflection explicitly embodies the realization of practical reason. Just as Hegel extended individual practical reason to universal or social practical reason, so for Habermas reflection consummates itself as 'social praxis'. There can be little doubt that Habermas's idea of self-reflection issues from traditional subjectivity. But why can it be maintained that Habermas's 'theory of history' presupposes teleological subjectivity? In the inverted reality of capitalism, this teleological subjectivity presents an epistemological problem of the first order. Habermas may be over-identifying two dimensions of social ontology which have no real, material basis. He has used abstract general categories not mediated by the vital processes of *Homo faber* for the analysis of legitimating crises fostered by the tensions between production and social relations in the context of both their reproduction and the production of subrealist thought. The effect is that no explanatory power inheres in his studies despite incisive interpretive remarks. In effect, he has somewhat de-realized the effect of the dialectic, to the neglect of the causes involved in the dynamic of human suffering. Real class antagonisms are absorbed categorically, that is, epistemologically banished, by the pragmatic universal competency he seeks, which, though suggestive, is spatio-temporally dissociated in some remote utopian distance. Thus the very material of politics is purified, but for just intellectuals, the privileged?

We can now express in terms of traditional philosophy of history what Habermas's 'theory of history' shares with his 'antediluvian' predecessor Schelling, the idea that history is a process of self-constitution and the realization of one ideal by the human species. Habermas's ideal is the 'single one [idea] ... of which we are master in the sense of philosophic tradition', and it is for him 'maturity' or pure responsibility. It is 'realized', he notes, 'through the human species in the manner of an "advance" to an emancipated society'; this signifies that 'communication is a non-repressive dialogue of all with all'. An emancipated society which has realized the non-repressive discourse of all its constituents is the *eschaton* of 'successful living' that a particular society 'fantasizes'. there is no word on 'struggle'. These statements tell us that Habermas's theory of history is 'teleological'. Does this dimension not imply that he must assume a necessity governing the very methods to this *telos* in its growth to maturity? Also, we must wonder whether Habermas does not confabulate epistemology with his normativism to create fallacious arguments in his 'rationality' paradigm.

It seems that Habermas's orientation toward Marx should, at the outset, preclude partaking of Hegel's assumption of a conceptual nature of universal self-consciousness. But we emphasize once again that in *Knowledge and Human Interests* Habermas builds his theory of history as a deliberate parallel to the *Phenomenology*. Just as Hegel distinguishes the reflection of the philosopher, the 'we', and the reflection of the consciousness the philosopher has thematized, and just as he shows that the former relates itself to the latter, so Habermas distinguishes the reflection of the theoretician of society and the 'process of reflection in general' carried out through acculturation by the human species itself. Hence for Habermas the issue is the demonstration of the process of self-formation, a 'history of education'. We must keep in mind that for Habermas this 'history of 'education' is to be a history of the conflict of 'class consciousness' which after traversing a 'highway of despair' is to reach its goal in the *telos* of an 'emancipated society', not that of absolute knowledge. 'Class consciousness', furthermore, is precisely not an 'idealistically' conceived shape of 'phenomenal knowing', but a 'materialistic' embodiment (1971, p. 83), an accidental and historical one. It is in every way contingent; even Habermas concedes this one-sided aspect of class consciousness. Why does he, nevertheless, proceed to call the historically verifiable the accidental and demote 'natural consciousness' to epiphenomenon, and treat consciousness as such in terms of the basic difference in the *Phenomenology* between merely contingent natural consciousness and phenomenal consciousness which realizes consciousness qua concept?

In addition, the reflection of 'phenomenal knowing' in the *Phenomenology* directs itself 'skeptically' against all this self-liberation until it wends its way to its true essence, its conceptual nature, and becomes 'in and for itself'. But if it were not already 'in itself' a concept, then it would not be induced to enter this movement of teleological reflection. How can a contingent, materialistically conceived class consciousness come to reflection at all? Habermas asserts that the reflection of the class consciousness is initiated by means of 'the growing potential for disposal over the processes of nature objectified in labor' (1971, p. 83). He does not show in what way such movement from a materialist basis to reflection is returned to an actually determined consciousness. Also, according to the method of Hegel's *Phenomenology*, the *primum movens* of 'phenomenal knowing' transpires in that the consciousness which measures its changing shapes against its own standard rests in its conceptual nature.

In the end, Habermas's approach is something of a 'monadology' where omniscient and omnipresent consciousness works from an assumed universal abstract inwardly thrusting movement to mediate particular moments which are 'deduced' by the 'Logic'. It tests whether each particular knowing is a veritable one and whether each particular content corresponds to it as a true one. By means of this movement of testing, consciousness moves by itself from an old object of experience to another one. Class consciousness, which does not have its impetus in the conceptual nature of self-consciousness, is not capable of such a self-appraisal and self-correction.

The 'authentic' Marxist could not take such a view seriously. This is so despite Habermas's assertion that the 'phenomenological class-consciousness' apprehends each 'existing untruth' in the 'incongruity between that repression which is demanded institutionally and that which is objectively necessary', and that it has the critical faculty which 'shows up the abstraction of an existing form of life and thereby revolutionizes it' (1971, pp. 83-84). Not in the sense of a materialist *Umstülpung*! Such a capacity clearly prefigures the notion that universal self-consciousness has the proto-essence of a concept, a presupposition which, as we have already shown, could have been inspired by Hegel.

Perhaps Habermas does not want so much to delineate the reflection of the 'human species' in its primordial determinants as to fathom the reflection of the critical theoretician of history in such a manner that this reflection has the power to attain the *telos* of the human species. It is out-and-out inconceivable that the theoretician of history acts in the same way as the phenomenologist in the *Phenomenology*. The latter is capable of recognizing a 'chain' behind the back of 'phenomenological knowing', a chain which gives to the teleological process exactly that 'necessity' with which it develops up to the last form of the 'history of education'. Again, this chain is formed only through the Bacchanalian movement of 'phenomenological knowing' an object which it once assumed to be true; hence it passes on to another object and another developmental phase, discontinuously so in logic and history.

This methodology as well is constructed on shaky pillars. Only the 'self-chosen elect' philosophers, the phenomenologists, grasp that this new object contains the experience obtained on the basis of the old one, so that there is a unity of concept ('Absolute Knowledge') in the diversity of forms. Habermas knows that what to phenomenal knowing appeared to be just nothing is a nothing 'determined and filled' with that experience. It is 'ein bestimmtes Nichts' - a 'nothing' which contains the necessity of a dialectical movement from the antitheses of the contradictory experiences of 'phenomenal knowing' to the synthesis, an apparently transitory one, which this 'new object' embodies.

The theoretician of history in Habermas's theory of history will never encounter such a 'nothing' determined and filled with the experience of the preceding one. That theoretician will never be able to apprehend such a chain simply because class consciousness, which lacks a historicist conceptual nature, is not able to follow through on a movement of testing and self-regulation. This factor rules out a dialectical movement, which signifies that there is no material necessity instructing the process. Habermas's attempt to assimilate the role of the critical theoretician of history to that of the phenomenologist falls through if that turns out to be his ultimate intention.

The decisive factor for the failure of these endeavors at assimilation is to be seen in the fact that for Hegel both 'phenomenal knowing' and the reflections of the philosopher are ultimately guided by categories (although in the *Phenomenology* categories only appear as 'moments', as the standards for the self-evaluation of phenomenal knowledge). All categories adhere to the *one* concept which, if developed, forms the 'System of Pure Reason', which, as Hegel says in the Introduction to his 'Science of Logic', 'shows forth God as he is in historical essence before the creation of nature and of the finite spirit' (Johnston and Struthers, 1929, 1: 60). Habermas has no such 'ghost in the machine' to bail him out, and historical reason has no real mediations in an immanent sense.

With Freud, Habermas undertakes to determine 'social reflection' according to the 'modern' paradigm of reflection of the neurotic patient as the guide from the unconscious to ultimate 'normalcy'. Habermas still upholds the idea of 'stages of reflection' emanating from Hegel's history of education and the Marxist history of class conflict. He transfers the interaction between therapist and patient, driven by the wish to be healed, to the strategic oppositions of class conflict. He argues that this *social self-reflection* through class struggle can render manifest everything in the real political and institutionally ordered world, which determines us but which has remained hidden until now because the global strategy against capitalism has fallen short of the promise. By means of this type of illumination, he holds, we can encourage political intelligibility after the real political relations have already gelled. In recent years, Habermas has been rapidly retreating from a historical materialist position to a more eclectic panlogism of a universal intersubjective discourse as an ideal type in Weber's sense.

Habermas's attempt to plumb social self-reflection on the model of the work of reflection 'worked through' by the neurotic patient points to a tremendous expansion of the power of reflection in comparison to those traditional conceptions. He himself stands at the threshold of reified theory. The paradox is that we can have a 'sick' society in which so-called adjusted individuals are the norm. For instance, an imperialist power can be well integrated socially through a powerful state mechanism and an ideology internally coherent but externally precarious, in that empirically it is living off a legitimacy borrowed from its citizenry while its collateral in national goods and services falls short. At any point in time, there can be a situation where there are many rootless and marginal people, in the sense that their self-esteem is destroyed by the lack of any manifest productivity on their part, yet where the system 'bails them out' in order to keep up the facade of strength and projecting power. This is a very paranoid theme in American history. Eric Hofstadter, William Appleman Williams, and Michael Lind have been especially sensitive to this problem area.

Even in light of these revelations, Habermas believes his scheme can be applied to large groups in such a manner that enlightenment of social consciousness not only negates 'false consciousness' but also actually resolves the objectifications of this consciousness, objectifications which for him consist in repressive compulsions and ideology. But he does not fathom that it is a matter not of individual guilt but of collective and social malformations supported by a division of labor built on the production and consumption of fetish commodities. The omnipresence of fetish images inverts the perception of social reality. This 'adoption' of Freud does not really enlarge the power of reflection, that is, of freedom, so that it could conceivably serve as the motor for Habermas's teleological construction of History. In fact, he appropriates the limitation of the power of reflection which Freud himself indicates in his theory of culture. In the chapter on Freud in *Knowledge and Human Interests*, Habermas speaks of the logic of the movement of reflection directed against domination and ideology. He identifies it merely as a 'logic of trial and error' such that the actions of enlightenment can only be understood as an enterprise to 'test the limit of the realizability of utopian content of the cultural tradition in given circumstances' (1971, p. 283).

When social consciousness is defined so cautiously and with so many reserve clauses, one can hardly claim that it can assure a teleological trajectory, as this entire project of a teleologically conceived theory of history would demand. Because of his secularized *ratio* of a final goal of history posited for the human species, he builds his theory of history with a teleological dynamo, that is, one where *necessity* should play a role. From his belief in the power of the Enlightenment and social praxis, he tries simultaneously to rescue reflection and that which attendantly signifies practical reason, freedom. He is moving toward the traditional formulation of the contradiction between freedom and necessity, a contradiction we claimed as inherent in the traditional basis of teleological subjectivity.

Habermas never directly addresses himself to this criticism. Instead of augmenting the power within human freedom (reflection mediated through praxis) which, for a theory of history without an allusion to fate, chance, or God, would seem to have to be the sole guarantor for the consummation of the *telos*. Habermas, under the influence of Freud, eventually defines reflection so tentatively that its critical power is lost in the overall 'grand' design. His theory of praxis needs to be more concretely developed and objectified. He makes praxis conditional on reflection.

Referring to John Searl's speech acts, Habermas constructs an ideal speech situation in which an ideal distribution of performatory roles for the speakers is similarly predetermined. For him this construction is no mere deus ex machina but rather a 'counterfactual' anticipation which every speaker and hearer must act out if understanding is to be possible at all. This construction can be quasi-analytically inferred from the 'metacommunication' engendered in every dialogue. But, in the given 'context', one must ask, 'And with what texts?' Anything resembling a litany can prefigure as organization, the 'Party'.

Habermas in his two-volume tour de force *Theory of Communicative Action* has undertaken to define anew some basic determinations of his theoretical outline. The theme here is language theory. But this undertaking does not signify any advance over the difficulties we have been pointing out at length in his philosophy of history. His so-called universal pragmatism treats only the 'logic' of speech, with achievements which emerge from the universality of 'latent' good intentions or from the ties of performatory to propositional sentences. It deals with the competence of the speakers, determined without any allusion to lifeworlds of a historical nature. The 'rules' of the communicative processes are completely non-historical, and they in no manner embrace a *primum movens* for emancipatory progress.

His theory of 'counterfactual anticipation' is also of little solace. Although this anticipation should have constitutive significance for the communication actually transpiring, it only has significance as an injunction for the future development of the human species. One could conclude that Habermas possibly has turned away from teleological thinking. But there is still the fact that his philosophy of history remains oriented toward Hegel and Marx. As his work of the past decade shows, progress and necessity are still crucial categories in his interpretation of history. In the earlier *Legitimation Crisis*, he sketches the project, still bolder and transcending the economic realm, of a 'logic of moral systems', that is, of 'world views'. If for Habermas there is still a 'logic' immanently at work in historical development, then our question remains. What is the 'prime mover' for this development in concrete terms for the future, and with what kind of necessity does it advance? Hence, even in more recent publications (and in spite of the interesting idea of counterfactual anticipation, which he concedes needs clarification), Habermas has not been able to resolve the dilemma in his philosophy of history brought about by the implicitly teleological thinking he himself is inclined to look askance at but cannot overcome. In the last instance, does not teleological thinking succumb to the very fantasizing he dislikes? He comes close to this abyss. Fantasies, like dreams, are not materially well constituted in reality. Even when they may be so, they are constituted in a distorted form of highly unstructured elements. This possibility bodes poorly for a pragmatic universal competence unless Habermas overcomes his own ambiguities. Perhaps he should reread the caveats and strictures of his old teacher, Theodor Adorno, and take heed. Otherwise, a whole tradition is endangered through inadequate representation of its original premises and goals.

We will now turn to the issue of student consciousness to see whether critical theory has a possible mass base in the universities. By and large, the student movement was issue-oriented, over issues eventually resolved by the state to maintain its legitimacy. The base dissolved, leaving neither a core of cadres nor any distinct body of central writings. The historical descendants of the Frankfurt School can now be said to be institutionalized and very much establishmentarian. The dynamic of this historical reification may now be examined.

10 Hermeneutics and political visions for the universities

The *Geistlos* pedagogy demystified

There is a certain preparatory dimension to the 'gilded' lifeworld of students at the universities. Education to date has pivoted on certain 'sacred' texts for 'indoctrination' into the total experience of the corporate world. By a critico-hermeneutic method we can at least debunk certain tendentious beliefs in order to give bourgeois students the political space to enrich the experiential freedom constitutionally heralded. We now proceed to this problem.

The term 'transcendental' should be taken to signify not merely the perceptive ground which outlines the investigation of phenomena according to positivist truth systems (verification procedures, definitions of meaning, falsifiability, etc.) but also the political grounds which legitimate the procedures of knowledge production and just why they are sustained generation after generation, defying history's 'judgments'. In short, what we are considering is the ontological domain which mediates the relationships between people in their practical lifeworld. The lifeworld alludes to the primordial significations and social relationships which build up and are encoded into the specialized languages of work. In addition, praxis, in the first moment, refers to the symbolic interaction in the context of everyday existence. The critical theorist investigates the way the mediation of these orders mirrors how human needs are delineated and how such definitions affect the stability of the political system. Clearly, the transcendental framework of any theory of knowledge counts as something in the world to the extent that it is made concrete in practice.

Educational activity in conjunction with this 'transcendental' practice is simultaneously the introduction of a transcendental plane toward which that practice moves. Educational theory, in consequence, far from being without presuppositions, is normative in two interlocking steps. (a) It lays down paradigmatic techniques for addressing the pedagogical tasks set by corporate capitalism to serve its needs, while ideologically saying that such 'education' for 'moral' responsibility (i.e, reflexive adherence to the Protestant work ethic) is in the national interest. (b) As an attendant function, it sets down a societal raison d'être for an abstract freedom which is collectively to serve the general interest while actually working for particularized individual interests.

Habermas has shown the workings of this combination of logical/methodological rules tied to constitutive interests by exposing what he considers the three 'transcendental' categories of all inquiry. First are the analytical/empirical sciences, with a technical/cognitive interest. Second are the historical hermeneutical fields, with a practical/cognitive interest in self-understanding. Third are the critical sciences, with an interest in the emancipatory public disclosure of repressed political understanding. Supposedly, when we are liberated from deep, unconscious inhibitions we can better explore real possibilities.

Richard Bernstein seriously challenges this line of argument, the only American thinker of the late twentieth century to do so persuasively and systematically. Political theory is not politics! Theory is always retrospective and makes value judgments about particular political contexts. Political theory is the crystallized experience of humanity suppressed by epochal changes in human history in the past; at present it is the search for tools to return our collectively alienated memories to us. Politics, on a more mundane and even instinctual plane, is the series of practical events forming behavior through reified public institutions to govern by what appear to be 'naturalized' universal norms. These rules have invariably taken on a life of their own in the service of the 'privileged' who do not have the universal competence to protect the commonweal. Here is the crux of alienation in all its multi-tiered, petrified facticity. Public welfare is at the mercy of private individuals who have a corporate image of civil society which can be quite at variance with any responsible interpretation of what is sensible and holistically 'political'.

Within the terms above, teaching is an event delineated in a lifeworld of dialogical relations between equal subjects; the supposed motivation is self-understanding through dialogue. Discourse, then, is the essence of educational praxis. James Palermo quotes John Hellenes as claiming that 'by speaking I claim and confirm myself as subject and the 'other' as an autonomous co-subject' (Palermo, 1975, p. 130). A fortiori, we can speak of foundational studies (for bourgeois character formation) as at once praxis and theory in their convergent and divergent manners of recognizing the processes of individual and social self-formation. Because of this structure, the ground of these foundations is ontological and the conceptual lens applied for interpretive purposes must be critical. This ground of foundational studies stems from its description of educational praxis. This factor can be studied from a Marxist/phenomenological perspective. Educational praxis, like all praxis, gives a definition of the 'human essence'. To quote from Marx's *German Ideology*, this 'essence' is to be elucidated in 'interlocking relationships of men who together with other men produce and create the world' (Marx, 1967a, p. 409).

Marx examined people's actions in changing the physical world and the concomitant change in their understanding of the world and themselves as it issues forth from these social-material nexuses. Because of the biological disruption between the generations, praxis, especially as it signifies the creation of cultural institutions, is a ceaseless, never completed project in a totalizing spiral of differentially derived activities. To repeat this point is to underline the phenomenological tenet that humanity is first of all temporal.

In Heidegger's terms the ontological medium of the 'human essence' is *Dasein*: being there-in-the-world. This is the world which through authentic interpretation is seen as factually the place into which I am thrown and the situation in which my own possibilities are generated. Specifically, this critique is penultimately directed toward unraveling the repressive, exploitative modes of authority which reify these human possibilities by the authoritarian management of specific praxis lifeworlds to absorb them in an all-encompassing, technical rationalization through human engineering.

The term hermeneutics comes from the Greek *hermeneuein*, signifying to make clear or interpret. To do so entails apprehending a meaning and its specifiable communication to others. The interpreter is the mediator who recovers the language of the text from its obscured meaning and conveys it, no longer cryptically to those to whom the message is addressed. Through the interpreter's activities of saying and translating the textual meaning, which had been alienated from witnesses' experience, it now becomes lucid, intelligible, and meaningful in an amplification of de-reified reality which can be directly appropriated by the subject. In its contemporary manifestations the hermeneutical science 're-presents' the dialectical fusion of the other modalities of interpretation which preceded it and made for an adaptable tradition.

Characteristic of each mode is the attainment of self-comprehension. Nevertheless achieving this goal must necessarily allow for historicity. This would demand what Ricoeur calls the interiorization of norms which sanctions institutional social roles. This strengthens the capacity of present historical agents to take up the significations of the past in a novel interpretation adjusted to changed circumstances and hence to advance communication.

It has already been indicated that hermeneutics has metamorphosed through six modes. It was originally the work of biblical exegesis. Next it was sacralized as the methods of biblical exegesis were appropriated by a general system of philological rules. Then, in Schleiermacher, it expanded into a quest for the requisite grounds for understanding in all dialogue. In Dilthey, its text was expanded to include human historical objectifications in art, politics, writing, and behavior patterns supported by societal institutions, particularly as they related to performance in a status hierarchy. The fifth articulation led to Heidegger's hermeneutical dialogue with Plato, Kant, and Nietzsche, recovering the 'beingness' in humanity in the temporality of hypostatized human existence (*zu Sein*). Most recently, with Ricoeur, hermeneutics becomes an 'interpretation of a particular text or collection of signs susceptible of being considered a text' (Ricoeur, 1970, p. 18). Ricoeur excavates from the text's overt structure its latent deep structure with its universal findings of certain indisputable signs and meaning-structures to give us the key to the human generic essence. In this hermeneutical demystification, the symbol is bared as the source and embodiment of a false consciousness.

Habermas summarized the hermeneutic sciences in the following profile:

> [T]he meaning of the validity of the propositions is not constituted in the frame of reference of technical control. [That is], theories are not constructed with regard to the success of questions. ...
>
> Hermeneutic knowledge is always mediated through [the interpreter's] pre-understanding, which is derived from [his] initial situation. The world of traditional meaning discloses itself to the interpreter only to the extent that his own world becomes clarified at the same time. ... He comprehends the substantive content of tradition by applying tradition to himself and his situation. Lastly, ... hermeneutic inquiry discloses reality subject to a constitutive interest in the preservation and expansion of the intersubjectivity of possible action orienting mutual understanding. (Habermas, 1971, pp. 309-10)

The practical/cognitive interest of hermeneutics is directed by its very structure toward the achievement of agreement among historical agents in the operational field of a self-understanding derived from tradition. Here is an area of possible disagreement. Habermas perceives the hermeneutical appropriation of tradition as the subjection of self-understanding to dereifying action patterns and functionless typification of rules and attitudes which together erect law-like necessities in the social organization of culture. These factors obstruct critical self-comprehension and preserve the latter's ideological language.

The counterthesis is that the hermeneutical sciences and critical self-understanding can be dialectically reconciled. A 'transcendental' framework realized in labor provides a definition of the 'human essence'. Practical and emancipatory interests with their categorial reservations could then be dissolved into each other's modus operandi. Critical self-understanding enlightens us if we first analyze those words and symbolic behaviors encoded into labor relationships as the paleological backbone of institutional structures. In fine, we must return to the lived-world pre-understanding as the map for all cognitive interests.

The experience of meaning resolved itself not in the context of 'now' instants which ever evanesce like a river into an ocean, but in a past and future implied in every present experience. In Merleau-Ponty's terms,

> the fact is that I should be incapable of perceiving any point in time without a before and later, and that in order to be aware of the relationship between the three terms, I must not be absorbed in any one of them. (quoted in Palermo, 1975, p. 141)

Simultaneously, we must underline that the 'human essence' as totalizing movement is basically not consummated; the human being is

> a being oriented in direction of what he is not, and thus we are always brought back to the conception of the subject as *ek-stase*, and to a relation of active transcendence between the subject and the world. (Palermo, 1975, p. 141)

Phenomenology begins with events which are now non-thematically lived out. These events are mediated by interpretation, and one returns to praxis with a critical understanding of the kaleidoscope of possibilities previously submerged in that praxis-world. The activity and its import are not reducible to scientific precepts, instrumental causes, or facts, but always remain an event. Indeed, 'in becoming a fact, the experience of consciousness becomes degraded and loses its reference to an "I" which lives in its experience' (Palermo, 1975, p. 141). Facts are the ultimate precipitants of technical interests and the alienating reduction of the subject into an anonymous empirical object.

Alienation is thus basically a distortion of humanity's being in irreversible time; the three temporalities are disorganized and we become estranged from our lifeworld and its supporting circumstances. This is the outcome of rending to pieces the temporal horizon within which all instrumental acts accrue meaning. When actions are defined as role functions, the concrete whole is absorbed in the abstract part. Lived experience is rendered atemporal and the subject becomes reified in a status ascribed by largely accidentally derived factors spun off by legitimate institutions. Past and future are disassociated and not germane to one another. The circular explanation of hermeneutics is an interpretive assemblage of parts intertwined with the whole; the past is, in a discrete manner, immersed in chronological time bound to a present context; and both temporalities are attuned to the critical evaluation of the subject's praxis-project of becoming.

In fine, a specific context-event of already taken-for-granted meanings comes to confront the listener as the text applied to the praxis-world which is divulged to that listener. It is a conflict of interpretations which must be adjudicated. The *telos* of this process is 'perpetual motion' involving a prototypical situation where there is a projection of possibilities within the materio-productive relations of the praxis-world. In Heidegger's words,

> to the extent that *Dasein* as an entity with the possibility of existence, has ontological priority over every other entity, 'hermeneutic' as an interpretation of *Dasein*'s being has the ... specific sense of an analytic of the existentiality of existence. (Heidegger, 1962, p. 62)

Merleau-Ponty raises the incisive point that

> what we understand by the concept of institution are those events in experience which endow it with durable dimensions, in relation to which a whole series or a history - or again those events which sediment in me a meaning not just as survivals or residues, but as the invitation to a sequel, the necessity of a future. (quoted in Palermo, 1975, p. 142)

Because all these events of the institutions take on certain characteristics with meaning, official documentation of these facticities is needed; this comes to define the nature of the culture and civilization one lives in. To the extent that events are built on antecedent events which define the durability of the culture and civilization operant through its institutions, a historicity is recorded. From the data left in this chronicle, we have the information for reconstructing the present status of this textuality. A society can only survive by teaching its progeny the meaning and assimilation of standardized forms of regulated behavior. Hence the socialization process is most systematically inculcated at the school level.

To understand dialectically the relations of the school to the corporate goals of the society, we must look into the fact that 'in man the past is able only to orient the future or to furnish the frame of reference for the problems of the adult person but beyond that to give rise to a search' (Palermo, 1975, p. 142).

Belying this 'search', given his fetish worship of operant conditioning, B. F. Skinner defines education as 'the most important branch of scientific technology' (Palermo, 1975, p. 142). This hypostatization of theory carries over to educational *praxis*. The subject/subject relationship of educational dialogue is changed into the subject/object relationships of educational technique which prompts a misguided definition of self-comprehension. This reified relationship disguises the educator's domination over the students. The education falsifies the situation whereby we must recognize that the individual student belongs to the same order as the themes under investigation. In debasing the status of the relation to the pupil to an authoritarian one of mere technical manipulation, the teacher, in also forsaking his or her own individuality, undermines the cultivation of a possible rational university or pragmatic competency in communication where 'islands of liberation' could thrive in the schools. Of course, the educator is often not a policy maker and must submit to rigidly defined norms of a higher authority in a bureaucratized hierarchy. The situation potentially is at hand where only processes rule and all subjects are bracketed out, leaving us with an object/object abstraction in a society without a goal. With no recognition of the Other, a Master/Slave opposition becomes a general condition of schooling. Eventually this irrationality evidences itself at the ontological level as the conjunction of praxis and *Dasein* (the 'human essence' 'presentified') in the socio-historical lived-world of the school institution. But there is a surrender of subjectivity to the sedimented praxically inert field of this binarily determined situation.

From this context people interiorize norms which are intrinsically alienating. The surface definition of educational control obscures the deep structure of social domination even as it legitimates that domination, because such a dialogue, in its one-sidedness, vitiates that event in the specialized character of the institution by the imposition of scientistic fact experiences on the participants. People appear to be fashioning the world and transcending the past, but they actually are miming social relationships which are past and dead. The teacher who applies Skinnerian operant conditioning (when it is the 'fashion', a type of textuality to be examined) and who comes to control others by manipulating artificially induced contingencies becomes, as Sartre put it in his *Critique de la raison dialectique*, the source of the reciprocity of interiorized reification. That is, 'each individual [realizes himself] ... as being objectively characterized by the inertia of what surrounds [him]' (quoted in Cumming, 1965, p. 444).

The object-human which instrumentalized technique evokes mirrors the workings of the entire institution. The learning process merely recapitulates conditions set up by the experimenter. The learner's praxis no longer presents itself as an event; it is not the realization of a real future but the quasi-human practice of pacified action. The pacified practice of molding behavior is now perceived as the characteristic of the ultimate pedagogy itself. The role projects of teachers and students become facts and not in-depth events because they are passive in their falling into an inert future within which we strive to determine our own future. But the future has been resorbed into an objectified past which has impacted the human mind to see its possibilities reversely in time! These reified roles substitute for real learning situations, and the compass of a world shrinks to a mere point.

That 'point' is the very essence of a totally debilitated state of unfreedom. Our task then becomes critico-hermeneutic: to disentangle fiction from fact and then transform the analysis into a praxis. That is, politics must suffuse the whole educational experience if we are to have anything like a *paideia* to invigorate the graduates who will shortly by cooption assume responsibility in society. We do not want conditioned creatures populating our lifeworld and making policy in the *res publica* for us strictly on pragmatic/technical criteria, because we would then lose the capacity for democratic self-government.

The problematic aspect of these contentions could be used to reexamine what is in fact the 'American dream'. Is it a lost text? The problem to be explored is how to create an educational praxis in a corporate world which has developed a parasitic relationship to the universities to make knowledge into 'exchange value' and cultivate from the host a legitimating ideology.

Embedded student consciousness and the corporate-capitalist imago

Universities, some of whose essential purposes have just been outlined, are being absorbed into the division of labor. Dissenting intellectuals consequently are losing the right and the political space to criticize social policy as they slip to the margins of our society. Critical theory is put even more on the defensive, if not at the brink of dissolution.

An anti-historical notion of 'sedimentation' fails to measure its depths for perspectives essential to establish institutional sets of meaning and power. It is inclined to overlook the ordinary ground from which new forms of communication and action may emerge. In radical centers of activity, it can be seen in an unwillingness or incapacity to meet head on the 'internal crisis' of Marxism: the problem of the subject or, better, the role of 'intersubjective constitution', including intersubjective consciousness, in the temporal dialectic of the totality. This problem has been central to this study in defetishizing language, which in its obscuring materiality has cast a shadow over social reality. Much of our reasoning has borne out Marx's point that the call for humanity to abandon illusions about the human condition is a call to abandon a condition which requires illusion. Reality is likely to be misapprehended grossly if the conceptual dyad of illusion and actual conditions is interpreted in current dualistic terms of 'subjective' and 'objective' rather than the dialectical logic of critical phenomenology.

Paul Ricoeur may have most energetically enlightened us about the contemporary issues for critical political theory by addressing the problem of the 'dialectic of work and the word' which runs against the grain of behaviorist and other epiphenomenalist explanations of the so-called cultural superstructures of society. Indeed, Ricoeur argues forcefully that the challenge also applied, from a different slant, to the 'hermeneutical philosophy' itself, warning that 'forgetfulness of the trilogy work-power-languages can always lead to a disastrous retreat into a philosophy of language which would lose its anthropological breadth' (Ricoeur, 1963, p. 162).

The Frankfurt School's attack on the Myth of the Proletariat and the quixotic romanticism encumbering Labor remains timely, for there is an inclination for some academic centers to 'split off' the category of 'work' conceptually from the stated trilogy and impart to it an 'autonomous', self-determining status in the climb of the 'hominoids' to species-being. Reified images of 'power' (the 'System') proliferate on all fronts, including groups which operate on the assumption that the self remains as an oasis in the institutional 'wasteland'. Linguistic games are abundant and provide a major concern for those who think they have found a political haven and professional status in taking the purist stand of academicism. But critique of all such forms of self-consciousness relies on a dialectical vision which they either reject or fall short of, resulting in distorted forms of communication at the levels of existence where work, power, and discourse are calibrated. At that juncture the major problems of critical theory can be given the form of a project.

The theoretical reappropriation of subjectivity in the critique of the sciences must be realized or recognized as a project of conceptualization and 'historical production'. Max Horkheimer and modern-day critical theorists have undertaken to show why critique of the limits of theoretical knowledge and of practical choice cannot be disengaged from each other. Trent Schroyer's dictum on the historical development of the dialectical bases for a critical theory of society warrants the utmost interest:

> Hegel had demonstrated that we can ground knowledge adequately only on a phenomenological radicalization of critical philosophy that reflects not just on the process of science but on the general self-formation of consciousness. We must recognize that in establishing the limits of possible knowledge reflective critique will, at the same time, reveal the constraints of cultural norms that block the development of

consciousness. Critique of the limits of theoretical knowledge and of practiced choice cannot, therefore, be separated. We cannot comprehend the possibility of objective knowledge without at the same time reconstructing the cultural constraints that block the pursuit of truth and or 'path of the soul'. (Schroyer, 1973, p. 129)

Hence, a critical project by its own definition launches a project for political re-education in the present-day United States and attempts to incorporate reflectively in the critique the evolving currents of liberal and technological ideology in relation to the institutional development of the corporate-capitalist political economy. In conjunction, these ideologies furnish a hegemonic cultural perspective for this economy. The difficulties of critical, political education at least in its segmentation may be measured by the extent to which public consciousness is infused by a deterministic sense of its own development. However, political domination cannot be confronted solely as a problem of 'cultural hegemony where the 'cultural' is reified and narrowly conceived in terms of a mind/body dualism. Antonio Gramsci avoided this 'fault', thinking of hegemony instead as an equilibrium of *'direzione'* and *'dominazione'* (Gramsci, 1971, pp. 55-7 n. 5). Rather, as dialectical dimensions of the concrete totality of socio-historical relations, we meet cultural direction and institutional domination as the conscious, embodied, and empowered beings we are and purport to be.

It is this problem of the embeddedness of student identity in a falsifying cultural/institutional context which will open a major area to reflection: Exactly where would one most likely suspect 'real thinking' to be taking place? Instead of leading us to think of educational dialogue as an encounter of 'free given lifeworlds', this orientation helps anticipate its own obstruction by the 'unarticulated authority relations in the particular education situation in its totality' (Rasmussen, 1973, quoted in Reid and Ihara, 1976, p. 225). The learning situation is geared toward thematizing, historicizing, and critically analyzing these obstructive relations in terms of the political rather than technological responses required by the emancipatory *telos* constitutive of the human sciences. These relations are concentrated particularly in the modes of institutionalized identity, which, when investigated, uncover both the power structure's variable predefinition of the self and its general penetration of the educational institution, molding it to the dictates and imperatives of the corporate-capitalist *Weltgeist*. The typical patterns of American identity embody the general passage or time through the medium of culture, inclined to block any substantial basis for political action except as the illusory ideal of an elapsed time frame which must be given a new interpretation.

The educational project of critical political theory is to facilitate discovery of and reflection on the institutions mediating these patterns and the cultural infrastructure sustaining them. This entails, among other matters, plumbing the 'commonsensical' stereotypes through which institutions, identities, and their deep structures are mystified in 'obliviousness'. Nevertheless the human foundation for education as a critical discipline must not be obscured in the goal of ideological critique. For, as Ricoeur warns,

> A simple critique of distortions is just the reverse side and the other half of an effort to regenerate communicative action in its full capacity. If we had no experience whatsoever of an effective communication - even if this comes from the narrow sphere of interpersonal relations - the regulative idea of communication without frontiers and without constraint would remain a kind of wishful thinking, if not an outburst of schizophrenic demands in modern society. (1973, p. 172)

One way of showing the significance of this remark is in the realization of the dialectical sociality of critical evaluation; the grounding of temporality and the recovery of totality are reciprocally engendered. Ricoeur may be quite correct in counseling that we consider the 'recovery of totality' as a totalization in a process which is heedful of the radical temporality of human and world. The ethical command of this blight of reified existence exhorts us to bring to life what envelops us, all that is caught up in the exploitive structure of daily life and tends to mechanically reflect to us an overwhelming 'real World', exactly insofar as we are unable to resist the fragmentation and control of our temporal existence, the fetishization of our (depersonalized) identities, and the attenuation of our faculties and sensibilities for practical action.

In the classroom, the structure of sociality must be perceived in light of the actual historical situation from which it began. All the participants likewise must work through to a critical awareness and examination of the actuality of identity which has been institutionalized, which lies at the base of the socialization process of which this structure is partially a result. In fine, there must be a self-consciously shared questioning of the institutions mediating historical traditions and social identity patterns. At least, critical theory in the classroom must conceptualize and maintain interpersonal sensitivity to the actuality of the social situation in which the social identity structure unfolds as problematic. We are truly without a national ideology. Perspective must be maintained if we are not to succumb to a mechanistic, elitist theory of revolution, or a nihilistic despair which substitutes terrorism for political action in the cultivation of virtues for a counterculture.

The American political tradition is not unitary and its meaning should not be allowed to be monopolized in mainstream ideological versions. The monopolization of the cultural process has been an essential domination of societal development by American business elites and their spokesmen. (Reid, 1974, quoted in Reid and Ihara, 1974, p. 289)

A related theme is given a great deal of examination by C. B. MacPherson in *The Political Theory of Possessive Individualism*, concerning the possessive quality of individualism in the United States, insofar as the individual is the

> conception of the individual as essentially the proprietor of his own person or capacities, owing nothing to society for them. The individual [is] seen not only as a moral whole, but as an owner of himself. ... The individual ... is free inasmuch as he is the proprietor of his person and capacities. The human essence is freedom from dependence on the will of others and freedom is a function of possession. (MacPherson, 1964, quoted in Reid and Ihara, 1973, p. 3)

The context of American values and how they are generated can only lead to the conclusion that the development has long been arrested. Disdaining the constitutional theory of our first professional political scientists, Sheldon Wolin has astutely taken a reading of the American political culture for the present day:

> The aim of political organization was not to educate men, but to deploy them; not to alter their moral character, but to arrange institutions in such a manner that human drives would cancel each other, or, without conscious intent, be deflected towards the common good. (Wolin, 1960, pp. 60)

This dissolves into the reified states of altered perceptions which depersonalizes individuals embedded by institutions. Life takes on a thick, viscous, inertial, existential surrealism, with outbreaks of localized violence (the 'sixties' was such a serialized era) to search for roots. Instead, many of our youth of today's generation look for solace in the subrealism of an eternally recurring hedonism. There is no critical idea of the general will, and no authentic notion of a polity and political responsibility which is well developed at the personal level.

In the classroom and in politics, the internalized norms of possessive individualism advance an attitude which takes goals and institutional settings as stage props. Attention is on the means of attaining ends within a given institutional chassis. In the classroom, this disposition tends to reinforce the centralization of authority in the university. In politics, this attitude nurtures a 'realism' which tends to delegitimate all efforts to overcome the established universe of discourse by dismissing them as 'fantastic' or 'utopian'. There follows the degeneration of political rationality to instrumental rationality and a gradual spontaneous increase in the authoritarianism in our political life.

American political culture, according to the critical theorists who oppose tearing down the existing establishment, has been progressively reified as a 'second nature'. In perspective, inevitability has become the central guideline of practical and political discourse and permeates all strata of society. Not only do most individual citizens assume a resigned attitude toward their powerlessness, for which they have been educationally well prepared, but these same individuals are willing to portray and exonerate even those in top positions not as actors in their own right but as powers moved by superior forces. There is a widespread assumption that the elite are a fair sampling of people from all walks of life, and that they are simply overwhelmed by events and selflessly doing their utmost in a difficult situation for the public good with no personal gain as the motive force: the American myth par excellence.

Almost a half-century ago Siegfried Kracauer, in a most lucid statement, wrote that American society is

> historically conditioned to neglect the emotional for the rational, to cultivate utilitarian ends more intensely than emotional aspirations ... our civilization or culture has developed no communication lines that offer really satisfactory outlets to any part of our potentialities (so we compensate through a cult of sex and violence experienced vicariously, much in the mode of paranoid delusional fearing and staring at strangers in the midst of a hellish world where we do not even know our own bodies, let alone minds) ... as technological reasoning and the acquisitive instinct attempt to reduce our civilization to pure calculation and exclude any kind of activity that has only its own pleasure as end, the private jungle of our still-born passions; ... the result is that we find it very difficult to commune with each other, since all personal elements are kept hidden away in many different private jungles. (Kracauer, 1948, quoted in Reid and Ihara, 1976, p. 230)

More recently John O'Neill, summarizing the analysis of MacPherson, Arendt, and Marcuse, says unkindly that

> Political imagination is shackled by the corporate organization of modern society. ... Modern society is increasingly consensual and apolitical; it generates a comfortable reality which tempts us to identify the rationality of its industrial metabolism with the whole of rationality

and thus disengage ourselves from the critical tasks of reason. The tendency to identify technological rationality with social rationality is the major threat to the survival of the political imagination. It underlies the liberal abdication of politics in favor of the market economy. (O'Neill, 1972, quoted in Reid and Ihara, 1976, p. 20)

The lack of moral freedom of public with respect to private space in the modern world weakens critical reason in its relative strength before instrumental/ technological rationality which then assumes an ideological hegemony so that the boundaries between the properly political and technical orders are blurred. Think, for example, of the idea of separation of powers intended by the authors of the *Federalist Papers*. The 'bureaucratic epistemology' of daily work life and the contemporary university scene evolve into the 'given' mode of 'really knowing', with no limits or norms put on this kind of growth.

Parallel to the above context of corporate domination, as Edgar Litt points out, is an ascendant civic education tailored to fit the expectations of the larger society; in this sense

> the representative citizen ... is the person with the analytic, technical skills, highly trained to perform an intellectualistic, specialized task. In such civic learning, participatory and allegiant norms are fused with highly concentrated instructions focusing on narrowly defined career tasks, including those of political management. The language of the liberal ethos (rights, duties, civic obligation), and the discourse of the period of nationalization (adjustment, consensus, equilibrium) are increasingly replaced by a techno-rationalistic syntax (systems, tooling up, stabilizing mechanisms) reflecting the dominance of bureaucratic and scientific political elites. In the process, the moralistic and the analytic or 'realistic' forms of political instruction are replaced by more abstract and impersonal conceptual units. (Litt, 1969, quoted in Reid and Ihara, 1976, p. 299)

Litt has explored at length the permanent imprint the 'bureaucratic epistemology' made on the curriculum of the public vocational university. The result underscores tendencies in the curriculum which further repress spontaneous demonstrations of emotion and more complex reactions to others. This kind of formal rationality entails the effective isolation of students from their efforts to understand social reality and its relationship to them. By depending on a necessarily bureaucratic type of training, a taboo in the name of science and administration practically circumscribes student efforts to become autonomous and substantive thinkers (in Reid and Ihara, 1976, p. 232).

Vocational training directs people to learn their social beliefs by reference to the authority of an alien apparatus, the Behemoth of the assembly line or office desk, and it is in line with one maintained by the bureaucratized reason of our time. The industrialization of academic life, in particular the dissolution of problems of social inquiry, cannot result in a liberating education role of initiates, nor can it sustain such a role for involved social scientists. Thus the vocational university's anti-developmental curriculum creates a fragmented milieu in contradistinction both to the performance of liberal education and the political task of the social sciences and the humanities and to their intellectual premise, which is to enable students to overcome such fragmented and abstracted milieux and become aware of historical structures and the place of the individual within them.

The anti-development theme in the contemporary bureaucraticized university is both an outcome of and supportive of the industrialization and functionalization of culture. There is a tendency to shore up possessive individualist norms, for instance, in the pursuit of a career. The career, preparation for which engenders professional or pre-professional training, is equated with freedom, or the right to acquire and dispose of private property (and the lives of others) at will. As a consequence, the classroom becomes a privatized space where individual career goals are pursued. Privatization in the university is but one dimension of a lifestyle in the larger society. Consumerism, the privatistic pursuit of the 'goods' life, is a manifestation of the shrinkage of individual awareness dictated by a corporate capitalist society. The outcome is a definite loss of any consistent *Weltanschauung* to orient the individual critically and substantively in political context for any type of meaningful political action, let alone that taken in conjunction with others.

One critico-practical activity of the teacher is to assist the student in the endeavor to supersede the familiar American anti-intellectualism stigmatizing 'book knowledge'. This involves the advancement of the appreciation for ways in which the references of the text 'open up the world'. Once again, Paul Ricoeur's work helps to illuminate the problem, which is to 'understand a text' in such a way as to 'light up our situation' by reference to the 'possible modes of being' of another 'world'. For instance, he notes,

> We speak about the 'world' of Greece, not to designate anymore what were the situations for those who lived them, but to designate the non-situational references which outlive the effacement of the first and which henceforth are offered as possible modes of being as symbolic dimensions of our being-in-the-world. (Ricoeur, 1971, p. 536)

The 'commodity self' (one is the simple sum of one's possessions and marketable personality) is the immediate 'buyer's context' presupposed (and nurtured) by the repressive communication. Student comprehension of the history of this concept or construct in the development of the corporate capitalism advertising industry provides an essential stage toward the critique of ideology. Beyond this point, the 'commodity self' and the 'technological ego', condensed in what the whole automobile 'civilization' symbolizes in the power, the wealth, the whole objectivated mode of having, which undermines all sympathetic human qualities for a civic culture of democratic measures. This self and this ego must be fathomed as the complementary goals of corporate programming of the population.

Underlying both perspectives is the subjectivization of the human bases of needs and utility and their dissociation from the public arena, which is rationalized in terms like 'consumer freedom'. The rehabilitation of the cultural forms of these needs and values in student consciousness becomes one more expression of the instability of the institutional totality, as inauthentic modes of that totality are being destabilized in their value-generating capacities to react in novel ways to change. These educational structures and their possibilities are being de-dialecticized through 'incorporation' in the very crux of the division of labor. The recovery of the sense of the totality and its thematization basically entails a process of temporalization which opens up the once democratic meanings of the American political tradition in order to venture beyond the monopolized versions of mainstream politics and the 'culture industry'.

Max Horkheimer in *Critical Theory* has made an incisive remark about alienated Western humanity which would be a good warning to American students to be wary of how to define their basic life choices:

> The scholarly specialist 'as' scientist regards social reality and its products as extrinsic to him, and 'as' citizen exercises his interest in them and through political articles, membership in political parties or social services, organizations, and participation in elections. But he does not unify these two activities, and his other activities as well, except, at best, by psychological interpretation. *Critical thinking*, on the contrary, is *motivated* today by the effort really to *transcend* the *tension* and to *abolish* the *opposition between the individual's purposefulness*, spontaneity, and rationality, and those *work-relationships* on which society is built. *Critical thought* has a *concept* of *man* as *in conflict with himself until this opposition is removed*. (Horkheimer, 1972, pp. 209-10; emphasis added)[1]

Since most people move through the universities nowadays as part of a *life stage*, the available facilities there would be superior grounds for re-creating a public consciousness which can put technical rationality back into perspective while reappropriating the public space for political purposes.

Note

1. Horkheimer in no uncertain terms identifies his principal thesis:

> Society is in a new phase. The upper stratum is typically represented no longer by competing entrepreneurs but by managements, combines, committees. The material situation of the dependent classes gives rise to political and psychological tendencies which are different from those of the earlier proletariat. ... Despite its dangerous potential, despite all the injustice that marks its course both at home and abroad, the free world is at the moment still an island in space and time, and its destruction in the ocean of rule of violence would also mean the destruction of culture of which the critical theory is a part. (1972, p. ix)

In particular, Horkheimer was aware of the threat implicit in the breakdown of the rule of law and its consequences for the larger society on which it impinged. He quotes Otto Kircheimer on the outcome of logical positivism in the sphere of law:

> The system of technological rationality as the foundation of law and legal practice has superseded any system for preservation of individual rights and thus has definitely made law and legal practice an instrument of ruthless domination and oppression in the interest of those who control the main economic and political levers of social power. Never has the process of alienation between law and morality gone so far as in the society which allegedly has perfected the integration of those very conceptions. (1972, p. x)

As I write these words, in September, 1995, the Philadelphia police force has been under investigation for abuses of power which would rival the first stage in Hitler's consolidation of 'legitimacy' by turning over the security apparatus to Herman Goering. To refresh the reader's historical memory, Herr Goering set up the Gestapo and the concentration camps with the extra-legal use of 'enabling decrees'. Today the words 'African Americans' can be substituted for 'German Jews'.

11 Toward a post-Auschwitz ethics

Introduction

Enlightenment reason has lost its emancipatory thrust. No longer are its interests coincidental with that of human well-being. By fusing practical knowledge and experimental science, Western intellectuals have instrumentalized reason as a material end in itself, rather than as a means toward forging a hierarchy of values to ground the pursuit of normative will formation and the penultimate values of the good life that lie on the horizon of social life forms. Reason has taken on an ideological veneer to justify not only the status quo and a philosophy of materialism, but a gross ignorance of historical processes. Humanity, in consequence, forfeits its freedom.

C. West Churchman illuminates my main point by his ideological extremism, which epitomizes the axioms of the Behavioral Revolution since the 1950s. His *Theory of Experimental Inference* embodies this spirit of hyper-rationalism, which has alienated its capacity for self-reflection by fixating on facts as if they were divorced from the foundational source of moral reasoning generated in social processes, in power struggles, and ultimately in the consensus of the scientific community on facts, hypotheses, and theories. At its core, we can call this process normative ethical discourse. There are acceptable procedures to arrive at certain tentatively defined truths. Sciences are not inherently moral. How paradigms are made hegemonic in their respective fields is all too human and quite political; that is, for a paradigm to be workable is contingent on the good faith of the members of the field. Is it ethical? Does it contribute to the good life? No! - but a weak no. Science in its applied permutations in the world dominant system of the capitalist mode of production has been gradually, but irresistibly and irreversibly, destroying the resources of the globe, including the capacity of Homo sapiens for self-consciousness in terms of placing moral constraints on the limits of knowledge as it disrupts traditional values and ways of life.

Could science be used for purposes that would ennoble the human race? I answer tentatively yes, if and only if it is under a socialized communal institution with global power. This socialist government would underpin truly democratic principles where the consent of the governed in the people would be radically reconstituted. Then public and private interests would coincide to the extent that any contradictions will be non-antagonistic because ownership of the means of production would be socialized. The development of human capital would be paramount. Masters and slaves will be no more. Most pertinent, education and its main buttresses in science and technology will unfold in the open spaces that have been liberated from colonial domination in the ideological and political life of free peoples.

Thus, with hegemonic public policy agendas abolished, there can be untrammeled development of the democratic personality. System requisites of institutional life will no longer need to infringe on human solidarity and dignity. Jürgen Habermas in *Between Facts and Norms* illustrates my point:

> Marx and Engels, satisfied with allusions to the Paris commune, more or less put aside questions of democratization. ... Specifically, one could argue that they read Rousseau and Hegel too much through the eyes of Aristotle; that they failed to appreciate the normative substance of Kantian universalism and the Enlightenment; and that their idea of a liberated society was too concrete. They conceived socialism as a historically privileged form of concrete ethical life [*Sittlichkeit*] and not as the set of necessary conditions for emancipated forms of life about which participants themselves would have to reach an understanding. (1996, p. 478)

I take issue with his lack of concreteness in his theory-mongering habits. And what of the *Paris Manuscripts*? It is this concreteness that allows for the primacy of politics in praxis which in turn leads, by gradualism or leaps and bounds according to historical circumstances, to the consummation of Enlightenment reason in socialism. Otherwise that reason dissipates itself into the mists of German idealism. And what mischief that has created in the twentieth century! By setting the scientific method as the only standard for examining life, Western liberal thinkers of the positivist persuasion have unthinkingly alienated reason as a utopian cutting edge in communicative action. To engineer a utopia with a substantive nature, this blinded reason has given too many anonymous men cause to use reason imperiously as a political weapon to implement totalitarian visions. Though this attitude does not describe West Churchman and his intentions, we must nonetheless deal with the realities of the social context of science, not idealize this social force as something transcendental to human conflict. Instrumental reason and totality in aberrant political praxis gives us a colonized social lifeworld.

In a nuclear age, we find the survival of the species to be the central question, one involving an existential choice whether reason's imputed limitless powers are to be restricted to a more circumspect critical stance, committed within particularized interests through political discursive will formation. So when scientism is merged into an ideology under the control of people addicted to power, we as citizens find democracy threatened. In the end, I use Churchman as an archetype of the liberalism of the welfare state era, one who intends the good of all while unintentionally fostering an ideological mode of 'reducing' the complexity of the world to omniscient science. Intolerance and social conflict ensue when other perspectives of knowledge are put forth. A true theory of communicative action with a practical intent to transform late capitalism into social democracy is the only logically compelling answer. Unfortunately, we humans also make aesthetic and affective value judgments that are not logical but rather compelling in reaching decisions in the collective with a mutual orientation toward group self-understanding as the procedural preparation for the deed.

Theory and action, however well reasoned, can nonetheless fall afoul of radical historical contingencies that often lurk in the background of *Dasein* to frustrate the greatest of human projects. If science gives us predictions, politics gives us accidents. That accounts for the 'take no prisoners' attitude of our cultural wars. Habermas has tried to build a bridge with his two-volume *The Theory of Communicative Action* and *Between Facts and Norms*. These two works can be considered by their brutal will to power in defining the very limits of social theory formation as inevitably destined to be part of the Western canon. However, their elitist tone and subject matter exclude all but specialists from partaking of their cultural treasures and benefits.

The argument

In *The Theory of Experimental Inference*, Churchman is a strong, if not unparalleled, advocate of the scientific/experimental method, with its emphasis on physically observable and numerically measurable cause and effect as a tool for philosophers of all persuasions in their rendering of valid and verifiable statements. He undertook to update the world view that a philosophy of ethics is ontologically continuous with a philosophy of nature. He suspends all critical judgments on the nature of mind and consciousness. Operational principles for the study of ethical conduct are not to be differentiated epistemically from principles for the study of natural phenomena. A theory from experimental inference can be applied to both domains in which laws can be ascertained. In orthodox scientific methodology, when examining hypotheses we try to nullify them by seeking counterfactual observations under 'controlled' laboratory conditions. Churchman claims there can also be a science of ethics in which operational means can be used deliberatively to determine calculably good, desirable, and rational ends or purposes. His overall model endeavors to create a rationally organized society where human conflicts are engineered to enhance the public weal while individuals pursue their enlightened interests without inadvertently or willfully injuring others. There appears to be a hidden agenda for a socialist society. In fact, a welfare state liberal might say that the terminology of the text anticipates John Rawls's *A Theory of Justice*.

To achieve the ends of a rational society by controlling class interests (subsuming any racial or pseudo-racial categories, in the given case of the Jews) requires a highly centralized state, provided we assume the provisional continuation of a capitalist mode of production. In order to monitor the totality of society, such a state in turn engenders a bureaucracy where state and society overlap to a large degree. Such a coincidence may not result in a happy marriage because it undercuts the power of the people at the local level, where democracy originates in the consent of the governed, and where they have the right to revolution when the trusteeship between governors and governed is broken.

There is also the problem of the people alienating their will in public affairs to experts who possess the exclusive technology and vision of the just society to make 'responsible' and authoritative decisions in the name of the people to whom they say they pay allegiance. There is no mechanism to make the scientific institutions amenable to popular demand and sovereignty because contradictions are accentuated by the monetarization and bureaucratization of the lifeworld. The actual ties of science have been to the military/industrial/Ivy League Academy complex and more generally to the capitalist mode of production, with the state as an executive committee steering society toward the goals determined by the capitalist ethos.

Churchman instrumentalizes reason by equating knowledge with science. Scientific method is given paramount status because its techniques are deemed the way to validate the knowledge which is subsequently to be applied to public affairs. Churchman apparently believes this public good is knowable by measuring discrete utilities of pleasure and satisfaction. His presupposition is that science elicits deterministic outcomes offering itself to a felicific calculus of a Benthamite stripe. Ironically, this scientism is compatible with both the liberal and the conservative world views. Scientism engenders a naturalistic attitude to pervade the human lifeworld in such a way as to reify the very people who are supposed to be reaping the benefits of inexorable progress. In the end, this attitude also reifies the historical process, taking it away from the human decision making, where a host of unknown variables deviously subvert human intentions. At best, we can infer why human catastrophes have happened in the past and try to ameliorate future situations by understanding the dynamics of policy making, though never infallibly.

In short, the American republic is in a crisis because a multinational corporate society has materialized with the public 'unconscious' of a source of power no longer amenable to control by the central government. I have explored this post-democratic phase of our history in this book. Americans in almost every walk of life have forgotten their sense of history because of insufficient information about and indifference to the sheer massiveness and inertia of the institutions of the powers-that-be which do not respond to public inquiry and demands. Notably, in the past generation, there has been a reduced role for the public intellectual outside the compromised Academy with its ties to big business and the military. In its stead have emerged the lobbyist and the professional bureaucrat, who manipulate representatives of the people and mass opinions and tastes.

One orthodoxy of the scientific method is that a counter-factual instance of a phenomenon construed to be a contradiction to a law poses a threat to the validity of the model or paradigm underlying the theory involved. In the interplay of facts and theory we find too often an attitude of hyper-factualism and a slighting of the corresponding theory. This abstracted naturalism consequently obscures human vision, especially in the social domain. The status quo is inadvertently reinforced when we allow facts per se to organize reality. Social behavior, in a mass sense, can only demonstrate probabilistic regularities that are arbitrarily configured according to the political agenda of the researchers. At what level of significance should the null hypothesis hold? Probably, given human frailty, at a very low level. That judgment ultimately depends on the examination of a certain problematic historical context, and we must construct procedures for consensus building before constructing theories of reality. Both are then ever subject to revision, so that we are always looking retrospectively at the human condition. In essence, we still have a Babel of tongues, none of which can speak authoritatively. We cannot really accept the infallibility of the scientific method, for that method is no better than the community of scholars acting in concert simply to negotiate the boundary problems of whatever situation is of interest at that historical moment. So we are limited by the relativism of the changing perspectives of competing groups of social scientists, humanists, and even poets.

We can speculate to some extent from several possible histories that one finding that contradicts a projected story does not necessarily invalidate a theory, if that theory derives from interpretation and understanding of conflicting human intentions and motivations, and if it uses forms of discursive reasoning in contradistinction to any explanatory power posited as deduced from a mathematically precise and elegant formulation of a hypothetico-deductive chain of iron laws of necessity. Human beings have the elusive quality of 'free will', whereby they can correct behavior in the middle of executing a supposedly pre-set course of action. The negative and discontinuous feedback can be just as much or more aesthetic or affective as scientific/cognitive in inspiration. Furthermore, what one recognizes as a 'fact' in the human condition at a particular moment will - rightly - be denied by one's alter ego.

Ego psychology can generate endless studies to demonstrate the separability of the indeterminate ego from the determined personality system as a whole, which is dominated by unconscious forces of desire and aggression, the latter often death-driven. Spontaneity and novelty characterize unique breaks in the history of social forms by which humans opt to live. Churchman believes in the inevitability of progress and the continuity of history toward an imaginary perfectly rational end state of happiness and 'manufacturing'. His positivist reading of linear history excludes revolutionary breaks or regressive collapses into barbarism, ironically so given the date of publication of his impressive opus, 1948. This oversight corroborates the claim about the absence of a sense of history among Americans. The philosophy of gradualism tempers his analysis of how the human condition is inevitably progressing. In the end state of this social evolution, planned societies will use only value-free and efficient means to the predetermined end of a just order of things, a scenario close to Engels's communist administration of things depicted in his *Dialectics of Nature*. This positivism introduces necessity into history. In the hands of a Stalin, the state was used as an instrument to impose a total plan on an unsuspecting and intimidated citizenry in which the existential, humanist dimensions of Marxism were purified for reasons of state through unconstrained terror. Stalin, in the final analysis, was the state, which tried to create a communist man in the image of its charismatic-terrorist leader.

In America we had the heavy-handed view of a Lyndon Baines Johnson, formulating the Great Society: an ideological vision without historical perspective. In Russia, a liberal thesis about the emancipatory thrust of Enlightenment reason, epitomized in Marx, degenerated into totalitarianism, largely because the Leninist party with its experts on dialectical materialism devolved into a conspiratorial cabal of terrorists at odds with the democratic soviets and Constituent Assembly, whose leaders they first duped and then physically liquidated. The historical conditions did not conform to Marx's analysis of how not to make leaps into emancipation.

Correspondingly, in Churchman, for all his humanism, there lies at least the seed of totalitarianism in handing over scientific policy making to experts who aspire to reduce error in performing 'good' deeds without actively consulting the people, who are not given participatory powers to countervail wartime presidential authority when it runs amok. Robert S. McNamara's *In Retrospect* tragically illustrates how foreign policy in Vietnam went awry when the axioms of system theory were blindly applied to a different culture. Certainly, the 'domino effect' and its assumptions were wrongly conceived; they led to the destruction of that generation of American youth and to a division in American society to this day, in that we have not effected closure over who was responsible for the debacle. Basically, liberal and conservative intellectuals sold out the people and exploited the ideology of anti-communism, whether from conviction or Machiavellianism. In turn, the left-wing ideologues sold out their graduate students and the working poor by allowing themselves eventually to be coopted in the name of 'marching through the institutions' to seize power narcissistically for themselves.

With the wisdom of hindsight, my conclusion is that the greater number of both groups were never serious and were guilty of extortion. We have neither recovered from the psychological wounds nor paid off the trillion-dollar debt incurred. In effect, the unholy alliance among Harvard-trained policy makers and West Point-brainwashed Pentagon generals and commissioned officers helped destroy the very backbone of our democratic civic culture. These people were never brought to justice for war crimes under the Nuremberg precedent. There is no statute of limitations for bringing these perpetrators to justice. Suspected war criminals who graduated from West Point in the years 1960-70 should by the very fact of their membership in an unindicted criminal organization be banned for life from public office or professional responsibility until they individually give a full account of their conduct to make sure it was above reproach. If complicitous either by passively issuing illegal orders or training others to kill innocent civilians or by actively engaging and executing in the field those horrific crimes against humanity, then, with their removal from public life and incarceration for life, we can achieve cathartic closure as a nation. Commanders and their political superiors, too, are liable. We must expose the whole chain of responsible agents.

At that juncture, we can work through our economic problems by transformation of the system by the people, who will be self-reflective as to their true consciousness. The agency could well be a revived union movement in conjunction with working intellectuals whose world view transcends mere careerism. Given the present malaise in the United States, many thinking individuals are at the threshold of a conversion experience in which there will be a transvaluation of all values. Such a de-sublimation of our basic organic repressions in the political psyche could bring about a collective body electric where ordinary men and women take control of their lives and dictate policies to a new breed of politicians: Renaissance men and women who turn against the moral bankruptcy of the material world with its corruptions of republican virtues centered on a species self-consciousness. Today's false prophets in the Christian Coalition, headed by people like Pat Robertson and Ralph Reed, with their claims that Jews have no souls and hence are morally unfit citizens, disrupt the values of the new American multi-cultural family. If the shameless pursuit of a moneychanger relationship with millions of gullible believers through the Christian Broadcasting Network is any indication of well-deserved damnation, then the Jews and Muslims are in no imminent danger of forfeiting their souls.

The members of the quasi-hereditary, quasi-feudal military/industrial/Ivy League intelligentsia complex are treasonous in their creeds of logical positivism that equate their self-serving interests with that of the national and international good. The outdated two-party oligarchy system can no longer offer the people real choices. The lobbyists buy influence that is institutionalized in Political Action Committees (PACs), which represent the crux of an administration that has failed to honor the trustee role derived from the sovereign people. All these selfish and mutant political forms have a life of their own, evolving independently from the informed consent of the people. They will be rejected and deracinated from a system in need of a revolutionary overhaul because they are so overspecialized that their benefits are outweighed by inordinate and inefficient costs. These costs have buried democracy itself and therefore cannot adapt in any conceivable way to the new challenges in the world environment in the third millennium, where we will not be the dominant power or the center of the political universe.

In fact, much as the Germans of Hitler's time did with the Jews, American scholars in the pay of 'think tanks' and their corporate sponsors rewrote the script of history to glorify the sacrifices of U.S. soldiers in the Vietnam war. The foot soldiers, who were ghetto blacks, blue collar youths, and 'white trash' from the South, were sold a falsified bill of goods. The war criminals in the White House and the Pentagon, the administrators and officer corps running the military academies with instructions from the U.S. State Department, should be held to account, so that we may forgive but never forget. My Lai is just as much a part of the American heritage as Gettysburg. David Harris in *Our War* concludes that

> Leaders eager to talk the talk did their best to send us to the far side of the Pacific when it came time to walk the walk, and there things turned a lot uglier and a lot more even than we ever imagined. Our America

debased itself out in that tall grass ten thousand miles from home, sowing pain over all hell and gone for no good reason, no good reason at all. ... It was wrong, and nothing has been quite right for us since. (1996, p. 191)

American troops also committed an atrocity that went unpunished at Kent State University, where four students were shot to death in the most cowardly domestic incident of that war. Unfortunately, the job of the military academies is to graduate such mindless robots who kill on command. Granted, National Guard reserve troops did the actual shooting, but responsibility must be located in the chain of command, and falls on the military academies and their government sponsors. Behind the government, in turn, are the corporate interests and the intellectuals who generate the policies to be 'cleaned up' for public consumption.

We war on our own children. That is what is so unconscionable and unacceptable. Basically, the oligarchs and their executioners are in the employ of the military/industrial/Ivy League complex, not that of the citizenry. The military murders genocidally. Corporations make super-profits by permanently 'downsizing' the very workers who in good faith made them their money, assuming that there was an implicit social contract guaranteeing lifetime employment. And the new breed of professor/administrator/fund raisers have defiled their historical mission by turning from the intrinsic nature of their high calling: to form the ethical character of the youth. And for what? Too often, they transmute knowledge into the gold of power with no pang of conscience. Capitalism is an impersonal and revolutionary force not only in science but in the ideological superstructure where morality is relative to the opportunities at one's command. Adulthood in America is crassly measured by income. If you teach for the sake of teaching, society condemns you for your naive idealism and unwillingness to 'grow up' and make a 'real' (nine-to-five) living. The temptations to sell out are built into the environmental press of capitalism.

Mr. McNamara, General William Westmoreland, and Dr. Henry Kissinger personify this paranoid style of politics. All three represent their groups effectively, creating artificial enemies to convince the American public of the legitimacy of their Realpolitik. The cynicism of these groups makes for a statecraft inspired by nuclear weapons, one surpassing the best of Machiavelli's prescriptions, but it does injustice to national security and totally misrepresents the national interest by creating budget deficits that cannot be eliminated. Their oath is not to the nation but to their special interests: plutocratic business and academy on the one hand and adventuresome military on the other.

In the 1960s and '70s at my alma mater, the University of Pennsylvania, there was in practice a kind of schizophrenia, as undergraduate students demonstrated for civil rights and against the Vietnam war while the board of trustees made profits from government contracts. The faculty, to assure tenure, at best played a double game. Eventually big business interests prevailed over the mythological ideal of creating a sane human being who could be a citizen of the world. The pseudo-cultural wars of the 1980s and '90s only serve to disguise the political, economic, and social hegemony of an overclass that, as has been true since the beginning of the American republic, is basically white, Anglo-Saxon, and male. Late capitalism cannot reform itself because it is not about politics or individuals but about a system of interlocking institutions with no mechanisms to correct the pathologies it generates. The only corrective is its revolutionary transformation.

This complex of interests makes the world unsafe for democracy because the United State is the last superpower that can arbitrarily impose its will at any time and place. The national hubris suffered, and rightly so, in Vietnam. It takes more courage to say 'no' than dastardly to follow a manifestly unlawful and insane command to 'open fire'. Such is the respect for human life taught at American military schools. But if you cannot respect yourself because you submit yourself blindly to sadistic discipline, why would you have any empathy with the Other? In fact, killing and maiming others will be a source of professional pride. There is a deep, dark joy in hurting others who cannot retaliate. That is my definition of a coward and a criminal. Multiply what happened in Vietnam by the two million martyred freedom fighters and innocent women and children massacred in cold blood, and you reach an assessment of American national character: perverse, perfidious, and paranoid.

The dysfunctional veterans of that war, who exercised command responsibility, are then put into positions of authority in civil society and wreak havoc on innocent civilians in every possible field of social interaction, blindly and compulsively acting out their frustrations and aggressions. Yes, they are our lawyers, corporate leaders, educators, and even the medical establishment, which has become a power responsible only unto itself. For example, the American Medical Association with its lobbyists and lawyers has become big business and maintains a cozy relationship with the legal profession to handle the proliferation of malpractice suits. It is almost impossible to purge a bad doctor from the profession.

Lawyers litigate the middle class out of existence because average people cannot afford to pay fees of $200 to $400 per hour. In civil cases in particular, the individual does not enjoy due process. The very concept of the rule of law undergirds democracy. The American Ideology, the ruling mythology on this issue, states that everyone should have his or her day in court with proper representation, to tell one's story on an equal footing with one's adversary. Again, this win/lose format of the juridical profession reflects the profound class differences in U.S. culture, where justice is a transaction in which judgments are bought and sold as commodities. The lawyer is looking not for just causes but for billable hours; that is how to achieve a partnership in a corporation. For lawyers there is nothing comparable to the physician's Hippocratic oath. Doctors do not necessarily adhere to that standard, but they can be called hypocrites or sued if in their practice they do not honor it. But a rogue lawyer can only be tried as an enemy of the people. In particular, lying, called the Socratic method, is considered an acceptable stratagem in being a competent advocate for your (preferably rich) client. The legal profession has prostituted the English language so that words no longer serve the public interest and democracy.

Predatory lawyers commit crimes against humanity because their Big Lies solely feed into fostering an American Ideology of might makes right. Words are instruments of death that not only ruin the lives of good people but involve us ultimately in genocidal wars. When the revolution comes, these lawyers will be purged from the body politic and, in cases where a troika of good citizens issue the proper death warrant, hanged as objective enemies of the people. Then we can live in the millennium of the rule of socialist law. Once citizens understand that their rights cannot be guaranteed by 'proper representation', then the legitimacy and authority of any regime is undermined. In totalitarian states, the leaders break your body. In the plutocratic United States, Big Brother allows you to live in economic ruin as an object, a reminder to others to toe the line. But if people see the law as arbitrary then fear and loathing set in. American democracy is a sickness unto death where many have psychologically seceded from the electorate because they see the illusions and fraud rampant at the elite levels of interlocking governmental domains. The common denominator is the absence of responsibility among the elite to any authority higher than their own peers. The very maintenance of a *Rechtsstaat* has become a high bourgeois illusion believed in by the masses because credit cards let them misconstrue their existence as one of middle class upward mobility. Rules have been blatantly replaced by administrative decrees to manage conflict. The class struggle now is in the very American ideology itself. It is a life and death struggle for people's minds. But with language denatured, thinking can only be distorted.

The work of freedom fighters, who think of themselves as citizens of a world republic, is to educate people to these institutionalized deceptions to prepare them for the critico-practical activity of praxis, where by any means necessary we take back the public spaces that have been divided into 'iron cages'. The handful of lawyers who do pro bono work are in a distinct minority and usually reserve their energies for capital cases and landmark civil rights suits. Too, there are distinguished lawyers who are great teachers because they model exemplary conduct for youth. Lani Guinier of the University of Pennsylvania is such a soul force. Her kind are engaged in critical legal theory designed to empower the poor. Similarly, tenure protects the irresponsible teacher.

The lesson to be learned is that corporate property rights have now largely displaced individual rights and reasonable expectations of happiness. There is no longer an ethical quality to the lifestyle of the average American. Children are given second rate medical attention because the medical establishment is another guild industry that can be subsumed under the rubrics of Big Business. By triaging who receives health care, medical practitioners are practicing de facto euthanasia on the working poor, and in particular on African Americans in the ghettoes. After a poor public school education, young people are put at risk in pointless wars. When they return they receive the reward of mediocre jobs with no security.

The war crimes of the military/industrial/Ivy League professorial and legal complex were never punished because they are their own judges. Many of the war criminals from the Vietnam era are enemies of humanity who should be put on trial at the Hague. Alternatively, it would be in the public interest to pension them so as to remove their influence from the body politic. But our terminal narcissism prevents us from looking at ourselves honestly and being held accountable by the standards we piously and hypocritically apply to other states. The net result has been a drug-addicted and divided society where multiple sets of normative rights are ideologically interpreted, debated, and disputed to the point where there is a constitutional crisis about the very legitimacy of what laws should be applied uniformly and with authority on a national basis.

The originating principles of the First Republic are now defunct. Fundamentally, we are in need of the birthing of a new nation in a Second Republic, where there is a Great Awakening to the need for socialist 'founding fathers' acting in concert with other progressive forces in American society, so that democracy can arise, Phoenix-like, from the ashes of a decadent plutocratic overclass. We must, too, prepare for the day when there will be a confederation of states and political entities in a world republic. It is in this light that Habermas must update his theory of jurisprudence. He assumes that the hard-won 'inalienable rights' of the Enlightenment are our legacy forever. But no. History can regress, and terribly so. He has an excellent historical memory for the German nation and its crimes, but he does not see that there are latent recessive traits in capitalism whereby the model of bourgeois democracy no longer holds true for the United States. We have become our own worst enemy, and consequently that of the world since we are the last superpower.

To return to Churchman, true democrats everywhere may well deny this meta-objective of rendering history error-free. This final end of a socially efficient history free of class bias coincides with a doctrinaire world view that hypostatizes efficiency in reaching this goal. An individual in general sympathy with such a goal could issue two critical reservations: that its details are ambiguous and categorically empty, and that the commitment to the use of experts and the inevitable national bureaucracy to implement the plan preempt, however unintentionally, participatory democracy. Authoritarian rulings and administrative laws then replace democratic discourse where the unforced force of the best argument can prevail over violent or ideologically inspired solutions to political problems. Pure efficiency is biased toward a totalitarian outcome. In a pluralistic society of contending interests, on the other hand, conflict resolution often entails inefficiency and the outcome is less than the maximum originally demanded by the contestants. Viable democracies tend to promote procedural due process and prolonged negotiations between competing claims over mere substantive satisfaction of material wants by a ruling class enjoying a privileged position in policy making. Because bureaucracy spells hierarchy, domination, and stagnation in the private and micro-environments of society, lack of informed public consent can lead to a crisis of legitimation and motivation.

There is also the parallel problem of economic democracy. Churchman incompletely develops a quasi-Marxist argument. Society, he frankly concedes, is plagued by a basic class conflict, in that social cooperation results in the capitalist mode of production, but in the social relations of production the capitalists appropriate a disproportionate bulk of the wealth and consequent political power for their private, egoistic interests. He seems to infer that the sheer quantity of a mass production society will compensate for the qualitative differences in access into the hierarchy of the American status and class (and caste) system. Unfortunately, the forces of production within capitalism are so destructive as to disallow an equitable distribution of goods and services. Tens of millions of Americans live below the poverty line. The so-called middle class has become proletarianized. The emphasis on 'family values' is nonsense because there is no longer a normative image of the American family. 'June Cleaver' is a narcoleptic and illusory fiction for the naive, and even most children do not recognize her as 'Mom'. Churchman hints at an antidote in putting the wealth into a state welfare bureaucracy in trust for the people. He falls short of the Marxist dictum of expropriating the expropriators. In fact, he sounds more like John Dewey, particularly in the vain hope that we will produce such a cornucopia of goods that everyone in the end will benefit from the political and economic 'trickle-down' phenomenon in laissez-faire capitalism. As the erstwhile Soviet experiment in state socialism indicates, a new bureaucratic/intellectual class seized power by literally collapsing society into state organs with repressive differentiation between mass and elite.

Here we have a quintessential example of how power corrupts its authority wherever it derives from intellectuals and their utopian schemes rather than from the wellsprings of common sense of the people. In the United States since Churchman's time, Ronald Reagan dismantled much of the welfare state bureaucracy with its entitlement programs, thus further marginalizing the already poor, namely the African Americans, and also reducing the middle class to a proletarian status and creating a deepening chasm between those who have and those who have not. The ultimate effect will be to radicalize a large army of overeducated people who will eventually turn on the system that failed them. The domestic policies of Presidents from Jimmy Carter through Reagan, George Bush, and Bill Clinton, with their hidden agenda for the wealthy, have increased the misery of the majority of the people, compensating the injured parties with digressive military foreign policies (e.g., the Gulf War) and voodoo (supply-side) economics. Republicans and Democrats have fused into a bipartisan coalition resembling the politics of Mexico more than those of other democracies in the First World. The relationship of beneficiary to trustee in the dismantled welfare state has destroyed a central principle of our democracy: the *informed* consent of the people. John Locke's revolutionary principles in *The Second Treatise of Government* are but a dim memory. What chance has Marx, then, to be influential?

The momentum of Churchman's argument seems to have pointed toward the socialization of the means of production. But during the Cold War the ideological connotations of making a radical ideal explicit may have deterred him from calling for the overhaul of the political system itself. A science of ethics, if such a discipline is possible, would be linked instrumentally to political science so as to limit choices to one best, most feasible answer. This determinist attitude that there is such an answer is a social problem that ultimately rests on an article of faith rather than being discursively justifiable. In the end, Churchman postulates a unity of sciences, natural and hermeneutic, to make all knowledge the product of 'good' experimental research designs. Churchman predicates this organon for humanity partly because he is interested in the connection between the just individual and the just society, but he judiciously declines to explicate the connection between the probabilistic laws of historical causation and the laws of nature with their predictability. Are the qualities of a human being qua human being the same as those of one's membership in a group or society? Does the human race have emergent properties as we transcend levels of analysis from the molecular to the molar? Natural science can answer such generic questions both theoretically and technically. The social sciences cannot - to date. Indeed, their record is so poor that we cannot even extrapolate better empirical possibilities for the near future.

We are left, then, solely with hope. Churchman affirms that the context of discovery is the same for both the social and natural sciences, and we need only time and some definable amount of research to realize the expectation of the eventual unity of all knowledge and practice. But there is too much 'noise' in the picture of human behavior at the individual, family, societal, state, and international level to make even probabilistic predictions practical for policy making. In a mini-experiment with my own thoughts, I note that even as I write I change as thoughts, emotions, and associations surge forth from the subconsciousness. This self-analysis can even tap the demiurges of eros and thanatos from the unconscious as they desublimate onto the page in a fury beyond my rational control. I edit what I say, arbitrarily at times, to make a preconceived point that alters as I continue the discourse with myself. Other personalities, some real and some imaginary, have evolved from the dialectic of the reality and pleasure principles to provide a way to deal with the random events in the universe that constantly derail me from reaching what seem to be palpable and realistic goals. Interaction with these figures produces a fusion of horizons with them, resulting in a never-ending dialogue with no conclusion and no resolution of the tension with the demons that plague my own existence.

Being human, every individual wants the respect and mutual recognition we think of as a matter of entitlement. Hannah Arendt calls this the principle of natality. Our personal validation is *birthed* by sincere if conditional recognition by the generalized Other. The ego reciprocates. At an emergent level, that natality principle should be applied to birth an international polity. When it is denied at the collective level, political revolution can ensue. The American Revolution was not just about taxation without representation. More profoundly, it was about England's dismissal of the colonials' incipient feelings that an American identity was being formed in the face of common challenges. England made itself the enemy with its high-handed imperial attitude. The Revolution was a mind game, which we won because we were righteous people. We can no longer say that today, when every idea, however fresh, is negotiable in the nature of things. There will never be closure except with the release of death. Perhaps that is why the twentieth century has been one of unresolvable *Angst*.

Again, the Vietnam example comes to mind. A never-ending process of defining the number of troops needed provided the pretext for that evasive final victory. We were decisively defeated because considerations about how the Vietnamese would and could fight to the finish were not given proper weight. In the final analysis the fight was not about communism or the national interest, but about our attitude of non-recognition of Vietnam as a nation in formation. The Vietnamese were an *it*, not a subject. That attitude hurt them badly enough that they returned the pain by honorably taking the battle for the mind to the field of combat. They were the righteous ones. And we still hate them for their exercise of their right to national self-determination. They fought in the name of our own principles.

Perhaps we can learn from the Vietnamese a point about political ethics. We should beg for their forgiveness. For the prejudiced individual on the front lines, the war at the 'gut' level was at its crux about losing to a yellow race. That notion was taboo. Our national psyche is presently suffering post-traumatic stress disorder. Even after a generation we cannot comprehend the incomprehensible in the eternal recurrence of our repressed memories. History has been rewritten to forgive the unforgivable by building memorials for ourselves when we were clearly in the wrong rather than face our own demons. A peasant society thoroughly defeated the superpower of the century by dint of sheer will. That will emanated from the power of right. The memorials we build to our dead are in the end our epitaphs, for we have repressed our political culpabilities and collective memories in an attempt to rewrite history to enhance once again the phantasmagoria of national interest and national security. Will we ever learn? If we destroy the data bank of our archives, then we are doomed to continue to act out our deepest fears, which really emanate from our most violent inclinations. For Americans, the use of violence has been the recipe for cutting the Gordian knot of societal and international problems.

Churchman defines problem-solving as falling under the authoritative purview of science. For example, not untypically, he states with certainty (not intuitively, but by positing an epistemological terminus ad quem beyond rational dispute) that

> the techniques of answering any question in science, whether they be questions of mechanism, or teleology, or sociology, require presuppositions of *efficiency*: we must have criteria of the most efficient methods of solving problems before we can give responses to any questions. Now the extent to which we go in the hierarchy of explanations will depend upon where we take the true measure of efficiency to lie. If we take efficiency to be a term that is relative to the individual in a specific question, then his techniques of problem-solving will be the measure of efficiency. (1948, p. 48, author's emphasis)

Here Churchman implausibly shifts his argument to the level of analysis of social groups and their properties to bring individual choice under the discipline of social laws. But the larger the numbers the less dependable is any forecast of collective behavior. Given the open-endedness of information that goes into the millions of calculations necessary in processing the bits of information that conceive an action, predictability is simply not feasible, even in the age of super-computers. We are not infallible, disinterested, or intelligent enough to do so. It is human judgment and intelligence that births the concept of any bit of information. In fact, our very diversity assures so much disagreement, so many disturbing biases and capricious and random decisions, as to compromise severely the possibility of making a hard science of human behavior. The human condition is irrevocably one of virtual chaos and perpetual uncertainty.

Churchman concedes the danger of his own relativism in that there is no universal or even general consensus as to his assumptions. Basically, he presents an idealized model of how he would like the multifaceted world to be, so as to reduce it to natural laws. He intends to leave no natural or human phenomenon outside the bailiwick of scientific knowledge and explanation. The positivistic bias of his proto-scientific language about the realm of human affairs boils down to the way a social investigator of the human condition chooses his or her scientific presuppositions. Paradoxically, he takes a position transcendental to the problem he is involved in while carrying out his investigations. But one simply cannot stand outside one's own history. What is humorous about Churchman is that fifty years later social scientists are operating under the same mistaken premises as we head toward the third millennium and what looks to be the conclusion of the human project if we cannot find a way to sublimate war under institutional control. I would rather read Churchman, however, because he writes clearly and unambiguously. He does not try to dazzle the reader with statistical tours de force but rather sincerely engages the reader in debate.

Certain unique paradoxes suffered by human beings are not scientific problems in the vein understood by Churchman. For instance, nothing in the scientific method can instruct the individual on the attitude to take toward one's own death, something no one else can experience for that individual. An ego can only intuit that this finite, affectively recognizable temporal horizon compels me to live my own life more fully in the here and now. In an estranged time frame in which themes of death and freedom are dominant, such an 'I' might be better facilitated in reaching this goal of the good life by reading Jean-Paul Sartre, Martin Heidegger, Hannah Arendt, and Karl Jaspers on the ontological structure of existence. With their help in seeing the horizon, I might choose my pathway. They cannot tell me what is right or wrong; rather, they can assist me in recalling the species memory of our history and its life and death struggles in both competition and cooperation. All is not red in tooth and fang. But this kind of idiosyncratically experienced truth is trivial or even non-existent by the standards of Churchman and the liberal/conservative tradition of which he is a leading example. A computer printout cannot record these feelings beyond mere physiological responses. No laws of probability can tell us how to live toward death in an ethical framework. Science can render no ontological insights on how to alleviate existential anxiety; rather, the determinism of the scientific method might well heighten anxiety by focusing on death's natural inevitability and rendering this anticipation meaningless in terms of existential experience.

Erich Fromm in *Escape from Freedom* does not 'explain' but illuminates and interprets our penchant for totalitarianism by saying that the irrational and infantile fear of death induces people to alienate their free-choice-making capacity to 'mean little men' who promise that their sacrifices will achieve greatness and immortality in a thousand-year Reich. Instead, they use them solely as means for the end of state power epitomized in the charismatic leader. Fromm's *The Anatomy of Human Destruction* documents how the collective unconscious of the German people served the purpose of the necrophilia of Hitler, whose 'death instinct' found repressive desublimation in political form. This interpreted death instinct is a creative construct knowable in the hermeneutic dialectic of students of the Holocaust. The scientific method, however, does not provide either teleological or mechanical explanations *why* Hitler of all the political choices available 'best' embodied German fantasies and hopes for an effective historical consciousness at the moment of its greatest crisis of the modern era.

It would seem that German political culture is not ethically redeemable simply by its democratic content. But this statement would be 'nonsense' according to Churchman's methodological dicta, because an intuitive grasp of German history shows its predictably unpredictable predisposition to discharge social tensions by waging total wars on out-groups. The essentially untestable hypothesis is that the sum of the individual Germans' death fears emerged into a collective disposition to wage war because their societal and political institutions were too immature to attenuate tensions internally. They must therefore be projected outward by liquidating scapegoats. The defense mechanism of denial and projection is entailed here. What one hates about oneself and cannot authentically face is repressed, and then thrust in condensed form on a helpless 'other'. The victim is so helpless and hopeless as to kiss the very hand that strikes his or her face and turn the other cheek in expectation of more abuse. With a feeling of no control, the victim is willing to internalize the enemy's values in order to assimilate the enemy's strengths. Paradoxically, then, enhancing one's self-esteem requires first a recognition of the feeling that one's 'unworthiness' is grounded in the overall moral scheme of things as dictated by the tormentors.

Hitler and his gang called their Jewish brothers and sisters 'useless eaters'. But you reap what you sow, and often in an ironic way. In the end, after the war, American Jewish philanthropists fed the starving Germans without expecting any reward. For confirmed and murderous anti-Semites, this reversal of fate must have created cognitive dissonance that they carried to their graves. The slaves liberated their masters, as Hegel had outlined in his *Phenomenology of Mind.*

We understand this phenomenon of internalizing the negative images generated by a merciless enemy who obsessively-compulsively and hysterically portrayed talented Jews as biologically filthy and undeserving of life itself. You must burn them whole in order to cleanse your own unconscious guilt and latent anxieties about your very masculinity, something about which Germans have always been very ambiguous. In the end, in a most tragi-comic turn of fate, the Germans and their beautiful cities suffered the same fate they had visited on their prey. Hitler in his *Political Testament* called the Germans biologically unfit to rule and berated them for failing him. He still held to the delusion that the Jews had started and won the war, though he made them pay a deep price by exterminating their culture and population centers in Eastern Europe. The delusion continues with his praise for the Russians as the new superior race who were to dominate the Eurasian land mass. Paranoia closes all boundaries to receiving new information that might generate hypotheses other than those of race and geopolitics, a most limiting type of reductionism common to logical positivism. So Hitler lamented that the Germans were unworthy of his great leadership after seven million died for *der Führer*.

On the contrary, Hitler and the Germans deserved each other because they matched each other's needs and affects in a psychologically perfect complementarity of world views. Daniel Goldhagen, in *Hitler's Willing Executioners*, irrefutably documents the ugly truths about the German psyche and its murderous inclinations during World War II. Have the Germans changed? They are quiescent now because they are well fed and lulled by a welfare state with entitlements covering every contingency of social security, something about which Americans can only dream. But Germans are ethnocentric. Their homogeneity as a population is being threatened by immigration. There have been thousands of acts of ethnic intimidation by right-wing paramilitary groups whose activities are connived at by the police, either actively or passively. The actions can be traced to official policies in the Kohl regime itself. He is of the old school. The neo-Nazis talk of a right-wing revolution to restore traditional values (family values too, I would imagine). The Holocaust is a Zionist fiction. At Bitburg Helmut Kohl and Ronald Reagan honored the German soldiers who were Hitler's willing executioners. The not so subtle message was that we are happy that Germany is *Judenrein* and 'Deutschland ist für immer über alles'. Germany is making its moves now with a massive economic and military presence in the Balkans. The Deutschmark is the currency of Europe. Today Germany, tomorrow the world. Indeed, character is fate, individually and tribally. And if there is an infantile collectivity then democracy is only in form, particularly in the laws that are the ideological dressing for the new Junker class in the corporate world.

If Germany wages war in the future, a good positivist like Churchman would argue that social scientists must look for causes in analytically observable stressors, such as political reality constrained by geography, which dictate foreign policy. Unfortunately, Karl Haushofer's geopolitical 'laws' about the necessity for controlling the heartland of Eurasia led Hitler to some falsely conceived adventures in eastward expansion. He mistakenly thought that Russia was the same entity as in World War I. He also mistakenly thought that his 'Aryan' nation would triumph over a sub-human race. But statesmanship is more a matter of sound historical judgment. 'Facts' must be disciplined by hermeneutic inquiry and an ethically built consensus in the *demos*: national priorities and goals must be put in tune with collective historical memory of what plans have been operationally effective. The paranoia imputed to Germany would have to be qualified because the judgement is impressionistic, based on a 'reading' of that nation's tragic history and the even more tragic history of peoples blighted by its aggressions. Such a reading of German behavior since the Thirty Years War could be devalued as pre-scientific. But at this writing a Berlin-Teheran axis is threatening to exploit the situation in Bosnia for reasons of state and economic gain. Germany already dominates Austria, Slovenia, and Croatia economically. Croatians have historically been sympathetic toward Germans and rivaled their mentors in atrocities in World War II.

Perhaps the perennial problems of the human condition can never be analyzed as somehow reducible to mere prudential objectivization. Mature world actors, advised by scholars and foreign policy experts, can best be helped by a sound collective common sense when decisions are openly arrived at via the ethos of an informed citizenry. No more Tonkin Gulf Resolutions. The anti-nuclear movement today is an example of a world interest group at odds with the armament plans of the National Security Council, which even after the demise of the Soviet Union continues to plan winnable atomic wars, no matter how improbable, against imaginary enemies at all points of the compass. The Strategic Defense Initiative (SDI, 'Star Wars') is still being funded under Bill Clinton. But there is no way for the general public to determine who is irrefutably in the know. So the average citizen, with a vital interest at stake, is virtually in the dark about matters that concern the life and death of the human race. Ironically, certain policies about nuclear strategy might end humanity in the new millennium. Do we err, then, toward the safety of the human race or toward paranoid abstractions sanctified by the name 'national security'? What is bothersome is that these defense programs gravely implicate the military/industrial/Ivy League intelligentsia complex. It is ethically compromised by the fact that its key personnel have a vested interest in the lucrative contracts that lead to large-scale production of weapons of mass destruction. Elite American universities have deeply betrayed the public trust -

the disinterested pursuit of truth - by exchanging knowledge for power. This pact with the devil prevents the formation of a public intelligentsia who are not for sale.

Phenomenological hermeneuticians argue that we must comprehensively understand and 'sense' historical events and bring their truths to light in rational dialogue, where the unconstrained moral force of the best argument prevails. Before undertaking to explain the hidden agendas underlying current world historical events, too often with the intent of controlling 'undesirable' political behavior, good citizens must realize such a goal harbors a potential for unparalleled violence. In a nuclear age, an exercise of state power with the potential to unleash Armageddon would be irresponsible. In the name of a scientifically conceived historical dialectical materialism, the former Soviet Union intended world domination. Fortunately it never had the physical capabilities to do so. Americans have exaggerated its strength, more out of fear fed by anti-communist rhetoric than out of malice, though there was a sufficient degree of the latter. And our foreign policy objectives have always been suspect since we emerged as a superpower at the end of World War II. False pride cometh before the fall from grace. Our power outran moral and ethical modesty in the exercise of our responsibilities. We have been blatantly mistaken in believing that American democracy must be exported, even to countries with political cultures hostile to our form of government. If that form of government is presently hostile to the General Will, then the sovereign people can change that government to suit their needs. That is an axiom of politics

In the name of a scientifically conceived genetics, the Nazis liquidated an entire people. In the name of a scientifically conceived good life of consumerism, the United States imposes its will on Third World nations to establish 'friendly *democracies*' with their attendant Most Favored Nation trade conventions. From the historical record we can tentatively conclude that the interests of a rational politics and the scientific community, tied into hegemonic economic interests, do not necessarily coincide. Likewise, there may be forms of socially lived knowledge not conceived by the scientific method, even if the latter's modus operandi hedges its claims on redeeming the cultural world in terms of more temperate laws of probability because the purposive behavior of human beings often does not fit the template of determinism characteristic of the natural world. The objectives of human will and intention are frustrated by the cumulative aggregate of the collective Other, and sheer facticity and capricious contrariness actively frustrate the more 'rational' designs of other major players who are seen as competitors for the same valued goods. Thus hidden and competing agendas for strategic actions cancel each other out. Too, human intuition cannot be programmed. Witness Kasparov versus Deep Blue in the chess competition. Even though Kasparov lost, he demonstrated his intellectual virtuosity by being highly competitive against a super-computer that made 230 million calculations a second. They represented the aggregate of the whole history of all the chess moves ever made. Kasparov's thinking processes approached the speed of light. Hence human beings in their collectivities can even less likely be precisely factored for predictability and technical domination. Intimidation, yes; ultimate political control, no.

Churchman confounds methodological rigor and its tortuous statistical jargon with knowledge and presumed wisdom:

> If weighted legitimacy scores can be obtained, then it should be possible to formulate measures of loss and risk, and to construct a science adequate to answer the basic problem of decision which statistical theory leaves unanswered. This is the appeal of this essay: that the sciences, and society in general, collaborate in setting up a controlled science of ethics. (1948, p. 263)

In the end, method may dictate post hoc right and wrong if hooked uncritically into the status quo. But the ideology of methodism need not spell the final demise of the self-constructed human of Enlightenment reason.

The culture of death in the University of Pennsylvania Political Science Department: The shot heard round the world

In this section I use the names Thanatos, Cerberus, Afrikaner, and Anonymous for four professors. They are composites and do not correspond to particular actual individuals, but the section is a true account of actual events which I witnessed as a graduate student in 1965-78 and which motivate this writing. It is rather belated, but I have felt an obligation by not naming the perpetrators to protect their innocent victims who are still alive from further pain, and also to render honor to the dead who were sacrificed to the shibboleths of the Behavioral Revolution of the 1960s and '70s. The latter produced no significant scholarship to justify the human misery they caused. The modified prescriptions of the Behavioral Revolution were applied in U.S. foreign policy on the Vietnam war; logical positivism dictated that we bomb the Vietnamese back to the Stone Age.

These events, which can be independently validated and verified, also provide an argument for the abolition of tenure. There is no other comparable profession except the church where individuals are given an exalted status and professional carte blanche for life after one period of review by one's own cronies. Power corrupts. Absolute power corrupts absolutely. Knowledge is transfigured into bureaucratic influence. Privileges can be quasi-hereditary, as one's children are offered an inside track to full tuition regardless of merit. Such practices are elitist and anti-democratic. A teacher should be 'purer than Caesar's wife' because he or she serves as a model of what students be expected to emulate. Instead, we offer students a corrupted world view and a Machiavellian creed that bullying, manipulation, and perversity will transcend the disinterested pursuit of truth and the self-examination conducive to ethical conduct. Teachers of *aretē*, who can teach, do research, and obtain grants, will always be in demand and can work on long-term contracts, if they so wish, until the day of their death. The others should be weeded out of their sinecures with due prejudice. I am talking about institutional practices in higher education and professorial malfeasance in the performance of assigned duties, particularly in teaching introductory undergraduate courses. And I am not simply dealing in 'sour grapes'. There are universal principles to be learned here from the concrete individual. Who is a better witness to the curriculum vitae of Ronald Jeremiah Schindler than 'I' myself? The truthfulness of what I report can be ascertained further both by examining one's own experiences and by referring to primary documents and their interpretation by independent experts.

A bureaucratically powerful scholar at the University of Pennsylvania Department of Political Science (now called Political Studies) had a hypothesis (H1) which he revealed to me in front of two witnesses when I was his graduate student in 1966: 'Hitler's killing of the Jews improved their genetic pool'. The null hypothesis (H0), according to the scientific method, would be 'Killing the Jews did not improve their genetic pool'. The minor premise was that the 'smart' Jews emigrated and the 'dumb' ones stayed behind. The conclusion would follow that the Jews were responsible for their own fate and should stop blaming the Germans for misreading the situation. After all, Germany should be for the Germans. Right?

As we constantly revise history to suit *Realpolitik*, truth may suffer if we do not refresh our memories as to what happened and at least achieve agreement among civilized people who have common sense. Of course there are no controls in the reconstruction of such a tragic history. In this logic, a type II error entails rejecting a true null hypothesis, with the consequent legitimation of the destruction of Europe's Jews. But the pernicious logic goes farther, toward a form of Holocaust denial now in vogue in academia. If the Jews shared responsibility, then the Germans cannot be held responsible, since they were willingly complicitous in these 'co-determined' extermination policies, lending their killers a kind of surrealistic authority.

As a Jew of Holocaust parents, I was deeply offended. The professor was actually trying to flatter me by saying that I must be 'intelligent' because my parents had the 'discernment' to leave Germany under death threats. Ironically, in Germany they lived across the street from Gestapo headquarters, and at three a.m. they regularly heard the sound of goose-stepping SS blackguards singing the *Wesselhorst*. The message was loud and clear. Needless to say, such conditions, under such great duress, do not leave real choice. Their escape was purely accidental, controlled by and large by circumstances having nothing to do with their foreseeing the future. This Teutonic scholar's implicit conclusion is that the Holocaust was the fault of the 'dumb' Jews who did not leave Europe. He said this with a gleeful tone of *Schadenfreude* in his voice that was chilling. I wrote him a letter later that semester saying that he was 'obtusely insensitive', and he has conducted a thirty-year vendetta against me. He could not believe that I had the chutzpah to defy the godhead. My letter of complaint disappeared from the department dossier on me; his 'truth', in a letter of indictment, is to this day in that file. In my own dossier, I am voiceless. Hence, because there is such an asymmetry of power between teacher and student, he can literally re-write the history of this relatively trivial event into a major transgression that ruined my career. He is in the tradition of Yezhov, Yagoda, and Beria. I am now at the threshold of the fourth decade of seeking justification.

That is why I find Jürgen Habermas so upsetting when he cannot see that the narcissistic power drives of the status-quo sated intellectual class are far more pertinent to university life in the United States than his fascination with the disinterested pursuit of the truth by his colleagues in the American academy. Habermas has unimpeachable credentials in both his research record and his personal integrity. But he does not realize that he is part and parcel of the university lifeworld of the late twentieth century. I suspect that he generalizes his search for truth impartially, innocent of the fact that American scholars have corporate interests that compromise their research designs because funding is contingent on pleasing institutions outside the academy. These outside groups are not known for their tolerance of research results that deviate significantly from their norms, especially if such results challenge the profitability of their enterprises. There is an element of misanthropism as well, since politics and economics operate from different originating principles, one noble and egalitarian, the other base and elitist.

Habermas's 1996 tour de force *Between Facts and Norms* again develops a theoretical structure for the deliberative processes that shape the values of our laws and Constitution. If he had actually examined the American case, he would have noted the ways in which it is exceptional. But in an instance of the fallacy of misplaced concreteness he mistakes his ethereal and beautifully beguiling abstractions for the dirty politics practiced in our nation. Justice is brought about by monied men. Similarly, tenure is played as a game at the major institutions where bluebloods and rich-boy swells run the show from behind the scenes. Political life has become a matter of image-mongering to reduce complex problems to pabulum. Economics is a matter of the bottom line. The military corrupts young men by socializing them into a blood brotherhood with homosexual overtones, with the subtext of death as the threshold for entrance into an elect group. The ongoing scandals at the Citadel military college relentlessly expose the sea change of values in America toward corporate, quasi-feudal fascism. Their heroes are not from our revolutionary heritage but Hitler and his Nazi confederates. The cadets are the reincarnation of the Third Reich. These young men will die for an abstraction called a democratic America that has not existed since 1776 (and possibly 1787), when democracy was direct and could literally be conducted in town meetings.

All these apparently loosely formed groups are tied to the entrepreneurial Christian Coalition, sanitizing their ideological drive for domination in the name of 'family values'. Ethics is the strategic manipulation of others by power and money to buy into the 'good life', where addicted consumers indulge their wildest fantasies by worshiping commodities with fetish status. These very practical enterprises are screened and conditioned by the elite academic institutions that produce our political oligarchy. Where else in the First World can one find candidates for the presidency of the low caliber of Clinton, Dole, or Perot? The best theme of the 1996 presidential campaign was Dole's Laffer curve. The historically repressed returns to haunt the body politic. Put simply, bourgeois capitalist democracies produce vastly differential access to the sources of power in multinational corporations. We are a nation politically equal before the law but, because of caste and class divisions, socially and economically permanently unequal before the Fortune 500 corporations that shape our collective behavior. Though re-elected, Clinton has no mandate from the citizenry. Rather, he is now paying off his debts to his corporate sponsors. The greater part of his time is spend fund-raising to pay legal fees for his libidinal indiscretions of earlier days. In the meantime, our ship of state has no captain.

Habermas undeniably realizes this distinction, but he does not realize how fundamental the fault line has been since our July 4, 1776 founding. So I find his 1996 volume quaintly erudite but inadequate in explaining or understanding the collapse of democracy in the United States. We need a sociopolitical and economic revolution to create a Second Republic equal to the task of forging a General Will with the help of Habermas's ethical style of discursive will formation. His problem is that he sees the United States through the lens of the rational administrative laws of the state civil service of the *Bundesrepublik*. That professional civil service is far more advanced than ours, which seems to be more subject to outside political pressures and lobbying interests.

I call the tactics I experienced at the University of Pennsylvania academic racketeering. Dr. Thanatos remains to this day, wandering about the campus, sniffing the air, probably tracking down enemies he has not yet disposed of. He has the paranoid look of a man fearing anal penetration. He has built a network of allies who cover his ass, so to speak. Thanatos and his department-based cabal of Cerberus (retired), Afrikaner, and Anonymous still work informally to place their right-thinking graduate students in responsible, nationally prestigious teaching positions. No upstart left-wing Jew (at the time I actually had no political convictions; they were imputed to me by mere religious association) was going to show them up! I have always believed that these provincial bumpkins were anti-Semitic in a highly nuanced and treacherous way. It was not what they wrote but rather what they said that was punishing. Of course, with no witnesses who would come forth with testimony and documentation, they could always deny anything potentially publicly embarrassing. I felt a deep shame at having to validate my personal self by defending and constantly obsessing on my Jewish origins. This permanent feeling of hopelessness and powerlessness in the face of rogue authority figures has depressed me to this day. The anachronism of tenure gives them lifetime immunity in the name of the right to free speech, even if that speech is slanderous and libelous.

As for Dr. Cerberus, an initial supporter of General Auguste Pinochet, I had no doubt about his thoughts of Jews as 'dastardly'. He simply did not show the mutual respect and recognition toward other groups necessary for our multicultural society to flourish in a democratic culture. Dr. Afrikaner, an erstwhile counselor to General Mohammad Ayub Khan, was openly contemptuous of graduate students. He labeled me with the sobriquet 'Flak', which I did not find amusing. What goes around comes around: I always thought of him as 'Fat Boy' because he reminded me physically of the atomic bomb dropped on Hiroshima and had the bellicose temperament to match.

These Four Horsemen of the Apocalypse sabotaged my grades. Such grades, if they had been valid, should have terminated the contract between student and department. I took my 1967 work to a visiting professor from the University of Notre Dame, who asserted that my grades were not being given objectively, and that I was clearly an A student. It is no less than theft deliberately to downgrade me as an individual by subtracting grade points I had earned. Furthermore, it is a civil crime to manipulate life and career opportunities away from me and toward their sycophantic doctoral students. The rules of fair play in this department have long been in abeyance. Jobs are not competitively advertised but are "fixed" though a patronage system. The implied fiduciary relationship between student and teacher never applied to me.

By luck and perseverance in the job search, I have achieved the status of Visiting Professor in the Intellectual Heritage Program at Temple University in Philadelphia. I was the top-ranked teacher in the student evaluations for the spring 1997 semester. In these evaluations, the recurring positive evaluation of me is 'fairness' in grading. In the end, those professors' denial of my existence steeled my character to be a better person than I might have been otherwise. At least, I had negative role models to avoid emulating.

It is ironic that these four gentlemen have no respectable publications to their names. Thanatos in particular was originally given tenure by the grace of charitable senior faculty on a promissory note that he would soon be the new genius of geniuses in the logical positivist movement of the 1960s and '70s. Both he and the movement 'fizzled out', although it still has numerous adherents who conduct a rearguard action that dominates controversies in American social science, where specialized theories talk past each other in the name of interdisciplinary solidarity.

Who then oversees the judges who do not live up to their own standards, standards which are applied rigidly to others, even though the latter have more significant publications and stronger teaching recommendations from students? To this day I suffer from the actions driven by their unconscious conflicts. Unfortunately, their self-definition comes about by means of the stereotypes they entertain about people they dislike by prejudice. I did have friends, mostly among Marxist intellectuals, Jewish professors, and some Christian gentlemen/scholars who could separate prejudice from their moral obligation to render an objective grade.

I am a deeply reserved individual who is hard to like at first encounter. People misread my attitude and mistake that inherited social shyness for arrogance. Furthermore, some used malicious gossip to poison the minds of other teachers into seeing me as an 'agitator'. Numbers of my less than heroic fellow graduate students feared that befriending me would hurt their careers, so they kept a wide berth. I was isolated by a departmentally sanctioned ostracism, so silent but so effective. The Hitlerites my parents escaped from in the Germany of the 1930s could not have more effectively dispatched me with a bullet. I am number six million and one.

My future was compromised at the same time. The four gentlemen did indeed read Machiavelli and still practice his science of politics, with greater finesse because their decisions may influence world politics as they grind out 'doctored' reports to suit their governmental and corporate patrons. After all, there is Henry Kissinger for an inspiration. My peers once bragged that once they had their degrees in hand they would 'tell those bastards off'. Once they had jobs, they forgot, and so they did not even have to forgive the reign of terror they claim they had endured. Most real decisions at the department are made in conversations that are never recorded and so never happened. Department members never answered my letters asking for help in seeking work. The one response from Dr. Anonymous came two years ago, after I had pledged a small amount of money for impoverished graduate students, designated for students of working class origins in the traditional sense. He accepted the money. I wrote further letters declaring my terms and intents. These letters went unanswered. Thanatos, I surmise, determined that my existence should forever be denied, and Anonymous will not contradict the organizer and orchestrator of the network of power. Too, Anonymous has no mind of his own, witness that he loathed me and ignored me without ever talking to me, let alone sharing my presence in a course. His attitude has always been that I am persona non grata to him. Yet his whole construct of me is based on gossip of malicious origin. Of the four, he is the most contemptible because he has the capacity to think and judge critically.

In these men's bureaucratic minds it is better for impoverished graduate students to suffer than to have to reassess the evaluation of an inconsequential, marginalized individual. Their weak egos would never admit that terrible wrongs have been committed for three decades, both to hundreds of students and to their own colleagues whom they purged. During the period of my studies, 1965-78, these bigoted, redneck yahoos, who were the ruling political class at the time, reduced the department's national ranking from among the top twenty by thirty notches. Outstanding talent left voluntarily in this atmosphere of verbal violence and mutual acrimony.

In spring 1997 I had a four-hour interview with a leading Russian Studies scholar at his home in New York. He knows the Political Studies department at Penn well. I asked him directly in the course of the conversation whether in a generation's time there had been any corrections made with respect to changes in personnel and policy. He said, 'Thanatos does not know what he is talking about ... with respect to Eastern Europe. ... The department has no ranking; at the university it is 'nothing''. He asked to remain nameless because he has regular dealings with faculty members in other areas of specialty on the Penn campus.

At fifty-four I am still a wandering Jew looking for a home in the universe. Justice delayed is justice denied. That department provided my Gethsemane.

Jean-Paul Sartre in his *No Exit* knew well that hell is other people. Yet what I suffered other graduate students also suffered to a greater or lesser degree. The events in that department were not just a personal tragedy. Three of my fellow graduate students are known to have committed suicide in a two-year period around 1970. A Vietnamese student, a good friend of mine, blew his brains out when Dr. Thanatos destroyed him in his final dissertation defense, an institutional event that is normally merely formal. He killed himself with one pistol shot within hours of being betrayed by Thanatos and losing face at an organized public humiliation. The eternally recurring question is why someone will kiss the hand that slaps him across the face and look up at the master in adulation. The paradoxical and ironic answer, in part, is that the day may come when slaves who have internalized the enemies' values may reverse the field of power because paranoia prevents the enemies from testing reality. There does come a day when the wretched of the earth see for themselves that the emperors have no clothes. The political psychodynamics of the implosive collapse of the Soviet Union proves that there are ultimate limits beyond which people spontaneously demand freedom and revolt to seize it, even if they do not have the historical experience to benefit immediately from changed power relations.

There is a destructive cultural narcissism that does not allow Americans to perceive others as they perceive us. This racial hubris accounts for much of the debacle of Vietnam. These times were at the height of the Cold War and the Vietnam war, and the department was compromised to the hilt, committed to American world domination. Anyone who was 'different' was the enemy, and the front was everywhere. Even the College green harbored 'suspects'. Playing Frisbee was a Communist plot to subvert the Protestant work ethic. Writing intelligence reports to be used by the Foreign Policy Research Institute on campus was a 'patriotic duty'. But there is a phenomenon I call the 'reverse domino effect'. By the end of the 1970s the department was clearly out of control in its massive abuses of power. After one of the most comprehensive investigations ever undertaken by the University of Pennsylvania into the internal affairs of a department, the Dean of the College of Arts and Sciences put it into receivership under a distinguished professor in the Economics Department. I wrote one letter to him. Showing his bad will, he never deigned to reply. Why?

But the more things change, the more they stay the same, and absolute power protects relative power in a positive feedback loop. There is an attitude of 'Aryan' supremacy and brotherhood among males of Anglo-Saxon, Germanic, and Irish Catholic backgrounds, and, needless to say, the trustees and Dr. Thanatos are part of the Teutonic overclass that rules the University of Pennsylvania. Dr. Thanatos today is the foremost expert in the department on human rights abuses. He makes suggestions for international conflict resolution, organizes conferences, and 'trains' business heads to be cognizant of these sensitive themes. The department has been running low on graduate students in the intervening twenty years, and to justify a salary equal to that of a corporate executive requires diversifying one's consumer base. Thanatos is not a simple aberration. The fact that he is held in high esteem as a 'good old boy' in Penn's faculty shows that there is a character type that prevails in Ivy League institutions. The man charms as he disarms. He is an ultimate gamesman who builds coalitions for his own survival among the modern Princes of the Reich academy.

Even Jewish scholars, out of necessity, find him 'pleasant'. They, too, sell their souls for filthy lucre, power, social status, and an unprecedented life of privilege and freedom from an overseer. Too, two thousand years of persecution have made many of my religious colleagues stereotypically self-hating! They imitate their tormentors. At the level of the grotesque and obscene, we have that archetype of schmoozing in Philadelphia Mayor Ed Rendell's political groveling before Louis Farrakhan, the arch-anti-Semite. In short, Rendell is willing to negotiate away his natural right to exist in order to appease a demagogue. We see University of Pennsylvania President Judith Rodin tolerate the hate literature of the Nation of Islam's book display in front of the University Museum in April 1996, despite protests. Rodin, in a misguided interpretation of the First Amendment, forces every Jew to be in the position of having to justify and validate his or her birthright without any expectation of reciprocity. But *no-one* should ever have to be in that compromising position. There is no longer any moral compassion in this Age of Political Correctness, because we have virtually all become careerists and hence opportunists. We all have 'dirty hands' and need the holy water of revolution to cleanse ourselves. Better annihilation than *schmutzig* capitalism.

In the struggle for existence, the conformist *nomenklatura* survive in this highly specialized environment. The potential innovators and reformers with their well-intended major modifications of the dominant cultural belief/value constellations lose the war for 'territory' in the academy because they are isolated. They cannot 'reproduce their kind' to transform the system to address higher needs befitting a conception of a nobler human nature. However they might be judged by an ultimate God in the heaven above the heavens, in the lifeworld of the academy the functional requisites of the system dictate the administrative ethics. The sheer inertia and self-protective design of administrative interests maintain patterns that constrain universities and their faculties from doing anything unique, and most new ideas disappear by necessity into a 'black hole'. Such an ethics is Metternichian and social Darwinist in its idea of a state of nature with a war of each against all. In the academy no one really likes anyone else, for the other is a potential rival for the limited spoils. Success is rather like winning the Irish Sweepstakes, where capitalism holds sway and blind forces generate the 'winners'.

Succeeding presidents of the University of Pennsylvania have more and more become figureheads, acting as agents of the Board of Trustees, whose power comes from Wall Street. Individuals like myself are only gadflies that the system knows how to ostracize. I know I am a dead man walking. Thanatos signed my death warrant in 1966. Only my epitaph remains to be written. I will that outcome to be done by myself. Time buries all their crimes against humanity. It is the general will of the tenured faculty members that prevails, not the wills of the transients called students. The University of Pennsylvania is the flagship for capitalism, and is particularly aggressive in recruiting willing tools by making plays for black male doctorates as commodities for higher education, Big Business, and the executive committee of the high bourgeoisie, that is, the state. Play the game at the elite institutions and under the atavistic custom of tenure you, too, will have immunity for life from the rule of law. These affirmative action programs, however, though they may place minority members in the money, will make them only trophies, not the social equals of their white patrons. Some minority members have moved from the fields to the Big House, while a good third of their brothers and sisters have been socialized into accepting a hereditary Third World status.

Colin Powell is a tragic instance of an individual who has 'sold out' his people to give legitimacy to the racist Republican Party. He appears to be acting in good faith, thinking that by his example he will change the heart of the Republican leadership. But he would do better checking out the Republican Party agenda under Bob Dole, Jack Kemp, and William F. Buckley, Jr., with their plans for further tax cuts to redistribute more wealth from the poor to the top 1 percent who govern the country. The benighted Powell might then see not only that they do not recognize the suffering of his people as a caste, but that the Republican Party's management of him as an 'exceptional Negro' demonstrates that they do not really respect him as an African American man. Rather, he is an 'exhibit' to lull blacks into thinking they can break into the inner circle of those who rule and participate fully in the power brokering system.

The same story is writ large in the Ivy League institutions. There is an intimation of full validation of the humanity of the black race when in fact affirmative action only accepts a token number who are socially and psychologically screened for compatibility. The Golem that whites create will one day turn on them in the full fury of revolution, to destroy the mode of production of capitalism. Capitalism cannot reform itself because it needs the *lumpen* masses of minority group members to be unemployed in order to discipline the labor force and have in reserve cheap labor who will work below minimum wage.

Cooption works at different levels of interaction. Undergraduates, already by and large ideologically converted, are further socialized, subtly, into accepting the powers that be with their promises of degrees, money, status in the political ruling class, honor, buildings, and schools named after them. No matter that they barely passed their courses. The University of Pennsylvania, vulgar, perverse, and corruptive, debases the youth with its false values, which at the core are elitist and anti-democratic. The university betrays these undergraduates by not teaching them critical thinking. Nor does it show them that there is a wider world outside the society that affords them the privilege of its extremely lucrative reward system, a society to which they have responsibilities. There is a personal and professional satisfaction involved in earning a diploma, of course. But Penn is a Potemkin village. At first sight the buildings are magnificent and the grounds beautifully maintained. But once one becomes acquainted with its population, from top administration to hourly staff worker and first year student, a revulsion sets in. I have observed Penn for thirty-six years. The self-centeredness, greed for power and money, and sheer unbounded narcissism and arrogance of its members in general makes one ashamed to be an alumnus, an American, even a member of the species called *Homo sapiens*. Few survive the system psychologically intact. And the problem is not just a matter of disturbed communication patterns among sick individuals; it is that the whole world view of elite institutions like Penn is pathological and unable to correct its own defects by critical self-examination. We have then the clinical manifestation of the notorious 'Penn type'.

The University of Pennsylvania today is conspicuous among Ivy League schools because only Penn so exclusively emphasizes the production of an overclass for Big Business. Even the liberal arts are touted merely as an alternative to making money. Knowledge for knowledge's sake is not the school's philosophy. It may be so among a handful of enlightened professors, but I never heard the expression used, even though when I matriculated I imagined it would be the byword of the whole curriculum. The Wharton School of Business and Commerce, through the Board of Trustees headquartered on Wall Street, sets the ideological tone even for undergraduate liberal arts majors. A prime example is the ongoing scandal in the Hospital of the University of Pennsylvania, which was fined $30,000,000 for submitting false bills to insurance companies. No one was dismissed. That money is a cost that will simply be passed regressively onto the working poor who patronize the hospital. It is not unusual to find medical doctors with MBAs or JDs. These combinations of degrees enhance the bottom line - profits, profits, and more profits! Penn truly models the master paradigm of the redistribution of income to the top quintile from the other four. Consequently in our post-democratic society there is a class difference between haves and have-nots that is irreconcilable and cannot be meliorated under a capitalist mode of production with its logic of a perverse and ceaseless quest for profits on ever larger scales.

Yet high school students by the tens of thousands seek admission to the University of Pennsylvania and the other more esteemed Ivy League schools, indicating how deeply the norms of the applicants are oriented toward capitalism. Basically, they come to Penn with an attitude of entitlement, an attitude that 'I am for sale. How much will you pay for me?' These children of the governing class are not happy people. They are so highly competitive because they have been socialized into the belief that they are the elect, chosen to rule when their time comes. They are 'nervous' because they are incapable of any type of friendly interaction on the campus. They come seeking *Gemeinschaft*, or community, but in its stead they find that they are part of a *Gesellschaft*, or corporate Leviathan, where no one really recognizes - or even cares - who they are as individuals. One can pass through the institution over four years as a socially invisible persona. Coincidentally, I came to Penn searching for a family to replace the one I had lost in World War II. My dreams in time became screams. Penn is a continuation of Auschwitz at the ideological level: you are only a number to be administered.

In fact, Kafka's *The Castle* should be required reading because it prophetically describes this generic multi-layered alienation in our modern age. Unfortunately, to date no one has come up with a way to humanize the ecology of the mega-university. Perversely, the university continues to expand its real estate holdings in West Philadelphia. Commerce and profit displace resources to engage and develop sound educational praxis. A false consciousness prevails that this organization of the lifeworld is an eternal given.

But there are choices that could be made if we are willing to make revolutionary sacrifices. The fundamental first choice would be to replace dollar values and a quasi-hereditary sense of entitlement with human values. An undergraduate can spend four years at Penn without a tenured faculty member supervising his or her curriculum. Slowly the undergraduate realizes that he or she is a mere commodity who is dispensable at will. A generalized anxiety and hostility emerges in the face of the process of the survival of the fittest in the hierarchical system. Almost 100 percent of the entering students at Penn are in the top fifth of their high school class, but in the University grading system 80 percent of them lose that prestigious rank by sheer numerical necessity. The result is frustration and consequent aggression, usually internalized as depression. There are dead souls walking the campus. On Locust Walk, the main thoroughfare for undergraduates, students avert their eyes from others, that is, from the Other who is the enemy to be defeated in the competition for the finite rewards of life. They walk like people old and cynical beyond their tender years, with hysterically conditioned stiff gaits, stereotypical body postures, and tics that reveal deep emotional scars and unresolved conflicts (with parental figures in family and school). In their paranoid lifestyle, they cannot accept an unsolicited 'hello' from a stranger because they have forgotten the simpler virtues of kindness. Their world is one where the vices triumph, and to be kind and friendly is to be weak and effeminate, not characteristics desired for running a corporation.

A cowardly breed of 'mad' bicyclists has emerged to 'assault' pedestrians on Locust Walk, prompting rules that are obeyed not by these cyclists but by those who are already civil in their behavior toward pedestrians. In the summer of 1994 I picked up a bruised child of two who had been run down by an undergraduate. I told off the student in no uncertain terms. I was roundly booed by a crowd of onlookers on the grassy knoll near Van Pelt Library. As I turned back to speak to the biker, she spat in my face and took off. The crowd cheered. There are group psychoses at Penn. The worst incident occurred on October 18, 1993, when black teamsters - again in front of Van Pelt Library - tried to run me down with a truck. The year before, on July 4 weekend, we had exchanged words when I objected to their describing my religious brothers and sisters as 'fucking Jews'. Irresponsibly, I did not report this hate crime of ethnic intimidation to the proper authorities. I rationalized to myself that no harm was done, except that in the end I lost my self-respect. Nonetheless, I forgive them. They are too ignorant to know their true friends.

In short, the bases of multicultural diversity have to be rethought by university policy makers. I do not see unity in difference. I perceive age-old ethnic hatreds driven by real and irreconcilable class warfare simply recapitulated: writ small at Penn, so, consequently, more intense, ideological, fanatical, and potentially lethal.

In the summer of 1996 I so shocked an undergraduate by simply greeting him that he burst into tears, so shamed was he by his socialized inability to recognize an other who is friendly and human. I had shattered his Manichean but frail philosophy of life. For me, the moment redeemed my faith in human nature: if youth are taught by involved individuals who value their education, then we can practically change the world. Those tears redeemed him, baptizing him at his rebirth from a boy-man into a human being. But I felt guilty because I had inadvertently compelled him to reconsider his values against his will. I asked myself what gave me the right to make him free against his will. It was unbearable for him to have to reciprocate, to reply to a greeting, from behind his Great Wall of defense mechanisms.

There are lighter moments, however. That same summer, an undergraduate left his laptop computer on a counter in Houston Hall as he mailed a letter. I ran after him and returned it. Sullenly and wordlessly, he reappropriated *his property* as if I were an offender. In role reversal, I thanked him for making my day, for allowing me to do a good deed. I told him how good he made me feel morally. We were then in the coffee shop, so I bought his beverage and doughnut. His mouth was agape and his face a fiery scarlet. It was a sweet-and-sour moment for me. Though I did what was 'right' and enjoyed a chuckle, I sadly realized at the same time that I had encountered real age prejudice. In his mind, he did not understand why I was in *his territory*. The 'Penn type' is communicatively incompetent because he or she does not know the norms of civility.

What kind of society have we become? In the corporate world of the University of Pennsylvania, there is little room for ethical considerations to play a formative role in educating students, that is, shaping a human being who is functional as a citizen of the world. Rather, the system makes a one-sided professional who is an expert in career matters but underdeveloped with respect to skills with people, a cog in the machinery of capitalism without a true friend in the world. Penn, the only Ivy League school with an undergraduate business curriculum, has a world view dominated by the Wharton School. The result, in the final analysis, is the monetarization of the liberal arts program. Instead of becoming generalists, students are subverted to opt prematurely for the cash nexus of capitalist society. Relationships with things replace relationships among naturally sociable people. So the graduates walk the treadmill at work throughout life until they literally drop dead. In higher education today there is a betrayal of trust because administrators and teachers do not properly mentor their students but instead kill their dreams and souls. The Huns have stormed Rome because the constitutive values of the elite schools are those of a venal overclass that cannot correct its own flaws. To do so would result in self-negation, and institutional self-preservation is an axiomatic political principle of higher education.

With the rule of the plutocrats the United States has passed into its post-democratic stage. This transfiguration happened by popular acclaim. Too, there was once a man called Hitler who ascended to power by legal means and then destroyed the Weimar Republic. Who will be our 'great man'?

As for Dr. Thanatos, he dispassionately disclaims statistical error or personal prejudice in his social scientific observations. However, were he to admit the error of his historical gedanken-experiment about why Jews survived Hitler, he would probably attribute this catastrophe of humankind not to evil but to 'good faith' scientific error on the part of the Germans, that is, their failure to set up a control group that would have led them to abort their program once they had seen the error of their extermination operations. The logic is clear, though non-linear. Thanatos is literally blaming the victims for their 'stupidity' in not avoiding genocide, a reductio ad absurdum of social Darwinism. This unthinkingness, so typical in academia, is the evil Hannah Arendt talked about in her *Eichmann in Jerusalem*. To prove an obtuse point that does incredible violence to the listener, this scholar uses his theory of eugenics to concretize fashionable prejudices about reified ethnic and, more especially, religious groups, to the point where he does not empathize with their suffering since emotions must be subordinated to the instrumental reason of one-sided theory formation. He vehemently claims to be 'value free' and 'objective'.

The road leads from Heidegger to Dr. Thanatos, from the universities to the power centers that ultimately wage war in the name of abstract ideologies.

Habermas has demonstrated in his several scholarly tomes that the very nature of the discovery process in both social and natural science research is politically driven and hence loaded with biases that must be brought to the fore to be understood. There are vastly different modes of justification to be applied; there are no hard and fast rules, much less final judgments. It is necessary to read Habermas's *The Theory of Communicative Action* and *Between Facts and Norms* thoroughly and very critically to see in systematic form what have been the major issues behind the twentieth-century research designs of a man who still believes in the force of Enlightenment reason. Belief in the Enlightenment itself is in the end an article of religious faith. It has unprovable, though quite appealing premises. But has the chronicle of human conduct at the collective level been any indication that those premises are valid?

Thanatos knowingly and personally insulted me as a son of Holocaust parents, and I had no means to make him apologize or retract what he said. In all likelihood, this incredibly insensitive individual still entertains these views in his obsessive/compulsive Germanic mind and indulges in hysterical outbursts when people attempt to engage him in reality testing. The generic form of this ad hominem reasoning ultimately takes the form of 'reasons of state', and accounts for the mindset that led to the debacle of Vietnam. This professor's schizoid and phobic world view brackets out the very humanity of Jews as a group. In fact, he validates Hitler's policies by his bizarre thought experiments in the name of scientific inquiry. But science cannot be divorced from moral and ethical considerations, especially when people's personal lives are intruded on in the name of vulgar abstractions that do not contribute at all to human knowledge. Thanatos's work is in fact a net loss to the process of inquiry. Other more judicious and mature scholars have to repair the damage he does to both scholarship and students, whom he betrays in his institutional capacity as representing not only the university but higher education itself. For it supposedly embodies the best moral schemes, scientific theories, and practical inventions of the cultures of the world, along with the hopes of humankind for a new dawn of liberation of everyday people from the forces of economic repression and administrative colonization. This Enlightenment religion could well be a mass delusion that not only has devastated the twentieth century but may destroy us in the third millennium.

The prejudiced person is so invariably, across the board. As a case in point, I do not feel that my genes are better or worse than any other person's; in fact, the very terms of such an argument make an academic pseudo-problem since they cannot be the basis for an intelligible discussion. The meager possessions I have are the result of diligent work. Yet I have met others like Thanatos well placed throughout the university system. They seem to reproduce their own hard breed and cannibalize their own children. They are in education, medicine, the military, law, religion, government, and business, wherever there are bureaucracies in which individuals must abide by a code of behavior determined by the 'iron cages' Max Weber explores. I believe the more severe pathological types in the academy can be screened out of the system before they are given their initial posts. Good mental health must be part of the accreditation process.

At the national level, there has been a tendency for American policy makers to colonize Third World peoples through asymmetrical trade agreements in the course of 'scientifically' (forcefully and ideologically) implementing the national interest. America's racism and use of the sciences to reify people of color, now applied to political problems, threaten the survival of the species. Yet we are still talking nonsensically about winnable nuclear conflict because policy makers play and win simulation games in surrealistic Star War scenarios. But when the day comes, and it will, all these simulations will be vaporized in the 'burning whole' of the human project. Where is there room for error in these calculations of instrumentalized reason, from Churchman to present-day positivists like Thanatos? Are the Jansenists correct? Did God create a 'botched' universe and flee on seeing what people do in the name of God? We have seen how the politics of science can degenerate into theological questions and ad hominem attacks. That is not necessarily a desideratum when we consider that the very survival of the species is at stake.

Conclusion

Churchman presents another point typical of his optimistic world view:

> We who are led to the next step beyond relativism, to the search for a unifying purpose of all science, thus find the solution to the problem of importance in this very purpose: *One question (of fact or law) is said to be more important than another if a response leads to a greater degree of progress*, where the degrees of progress may be measured by the general reduction of the errors of estimates of empirical quantities (1948, p. 269; author's emphasis)

Quantifiable progress, which he projects as the goal of all rational people, is the desired end state. The Frankfurt School of social theory has critiqued this theme as indicative of false pride in an instrumental reason gone berserk. Habermas hammers at this point:

> When one does science ... one has only to do with truth claims in the narrower sense. ... On the one hand, the assumptions of empathic

theory are tailored to 'truths' from which the moral and aesthetic-expressive aspects have not yet been split off. On the other hand, a critical social theory must also proceed scientifically: it can only make pronouncements with a claim to propositional truth. ... [One] must then see how it is possible, within the social sciences and, first and foremost, in the formation of philosophical theory, to bring into play the experiential domains of both the aesthetic-expressive and moral-practical without empiricist redefinitions, and without endangering the requirements of theoretical descriptions. That is the problem of *non-positivist approaches to theory in the social sciences*. (1986, p. 101; author's emphasis)

In relentlessly dominating nature (something explicitly advocated by Churchman), we have not been made aware of the fact that the possibility for the reproduction of the whole species may have been undermined in this thoughtless process. An empirical question arises, too, insofar as the resources of the world are finite. There may be a limit to the usefulness of progress, and this limit may have already been reached. Furthermore, Churchman has concretely (and ecstatically) identified this ultimate value of progress with the manufacture of capital goods in the industrial sector, something whose possibilities enthrall his imagination. Perhaps we should take a good look at this point in the incredible destruction of the physical and human ecologies in the hearts of the largest one hundred metropolises in the United States.

To be fair, Churchman did tie his ideal of development to the material redistribution of wealth to achieve justice. If he had followed this line of criticism more systematically, he could have contributed substantively to the depiction of human progress toward more realizable short-term progress. But he shows his *état*-ist philosophy when he concludes:

> ... and hence personality becomes in general a measure of inefficiency. If the analogy can be carried one step further, we might call the characteristics of the state an aspect of 'personality' of the community. The ideal here is a production and distribution process which will have maximum efficiency, and hence the ideal is really the perfection of the community personality. (1948, p. 243)

This buzz word, 'community personality', carries overtones of the state under corporate/fascist administration, where the grossest human appetites are used as the basis of debased moral standards of judgment and the democratic individual is assimilated to them. Leo Strauss was firmly convinced that there is a causal relationship between Enlightenment reason and the destruction of reason itself under Hitler because the rationalization of reason lowered its status to that of value-freeness. The next step is a radical ethical relativism, where the powerful impose their will according to the capricious whims of the totalitarian tyrant. Without a moral compass, this eviscerated reason can be tied to state policies, including genocide, making such policies lawful if not ethical or moral in terms of the transcendent interests of a *Gattungswesen*. The unfortunate alternative in the United States is that the neoconservatives detest the *lumpenproletariat* scum. A detached elitist attitude toward politics can also lead to programs of euthanasia of the unfit. Simply recall the controversy around Richard Herrnstein and Charles Murray's *The Bell Curve*.

This brings us full circle with Churchman. The bias toward the measurable and observable derives from his idealization of scientist and a consumerist ideology:

> So here we demand of a progressive society that it not only provide a technique for evaluating and making consistent *consumer desires*, but that it also become better and better in its role of satisfying those desires, and that it be able to measure the degree of progress in this direction, just as science can measure the degree of her progress toward absolute precision. (1948, p. 276; my emphasis)

A social philosopher may well question whether consummating consumer desires ever more perfectly has the same moral persuasive force as the march of science toward absolute precision. Is pushpin as good as poetry? In short, Churchman's final sentence tells all, in his approval of Edgar Singer's dictum that 'The measure of man's cooperation with man in the *conquest of nature* measures progress' (1936, quoted in Churchman, 1948, p. 287).

The lessons of history point out that the social forces dominating nature converge to dominate human beings too. Such a predisposition of nature is not subject to a 'best statistical test' but to a critical reason that has re-apprehended its historical sensibility. My own testimony is part of the historical record for all to judge. In late fall 1996 I called my intellectual model, Dr. Habermas, in his retreat at Starnberg. The following speech acts are reconstructed from memory.

Schindler: 'Dr. Habermas, good evening. This is Ron Schindler calling from Philadelphia. How are you?'
Habermas (deeply agitated): 'Mr. Schindler, I have work to do! ...' (Silence)
Schindler (chastised): 'I am sorry to have disturbed you. Good night'.

I had called to ask for a letter of recommendation. Obviously, I am not deemed by him to be one of *his chosen* people, worthy of communication and fraternity. And are those norms not the ethical germ of the university ideal itself? Yes, but in myth only. In that brutally short exchange I finally saw the light. My last illusions about university professors came to closure. They love humanity in the abstract; concretely, they are misanthropes. One honest manual worker is worth the whole of academia. That is my conclusion. My own educational pedagogy for my students at Temple University is to be a hero (male or female) yourself. You do not need a Habermas or a Schindler to validate your own existence. You validate yourself simply by existing - ecstatically. Please, no apologies!

12 Conclusions

The tradition of critical theory finds its meaning clustered around the idea of 'critique' and its many ramifications in a matrix of humanistically inspired disciplines. In a widely respected programmatic essay, Max Horkheimer deferentially cited Marx's *Critique of Political Economy* as the model for a critical theory of society, but the pre-history of Marx's concept of critique remains of central and crucial importance for the tradition. The choice of the epithet 'critical' distributes the epistemological imprimatur between divided allegiances. The idea of critique is a direct product of the Enlightenment. The term is even more venerable and formidable today in that it has global implications when properly deployed. It was first engaged by the humanists and reformers to outline the art of informed judgment appropriate to the study of ancient texts, whether the classics or the Bible.

The process of critique claimed to subject to its judgments all domains of life which were accessible to reason, but it renounced any endeavor to dwell on the polity. Yet the peaceful coexistence of competencies began to disintegrate. Theory did not correspond to new realities. Apparently confined to the République des Lettres, the activity of critique became first indirectly, and then directly, political. In salons, clubs, lodges, and coffeehouses, a new moral authority, the *public*, found its earliest institutions. Critique became one of its legends and an endless proliferation of books and essays included the word 'critique' or 'critical' in their headings. Kant accurately claimed, in the 1781 Preface to his *Critique of Pure Reason* that his era was the true age of critique and that neither religion nor the legislature was exempt from its measure. The process of critique had acquired public force.

The continuing allegiance of critical theory to the Enlightenment ideals, which give rise to a nostalgia manifest in works as divergent as Horkheimer's

Eclipse of Reason and Habermas's *Strukturwandel der Öffentlichkeit*, indicates a commitment to this strategy of critique, that is, critique as oppositional thinking, as an activity of unveiling or debunking the shibboleths of the prevailing powers. But the Frankfurt School is indebted in particular to two *new* meanings of critique, in which the heritage of the Enlightenment has been transplanted to new theoretical formations and refashioned to new needs. These have their source in German Idealist philosophy. It is imperative to distinguish between these two new senses.

In the first sense, critique denotes reflection on the conditions of possible knowledge: the potential capacities of human beings to engage their faculties of knowing, speaking, and acting. Critique in this vein has its rudiments in Kant. In the *Critique of Pure Reason*, Kant set out to answer the question: What are the conditions of our knowledge through which modern natural selection between competing ideas is possible, and how far does this knowledge extend? He wished to fix the range of invariable subjective conditions which both make any theory in natural science possible and enforce limits on that theory. Since we always perceive the world as a world of ordered things, it must be our faculty of perception itself which produces order out of the variety of impressions. The faculty of perception produces not indeed reality itself but the mode in which reality appears to us. Things are 'constituted' by us in the sense that we can know them only through certain synthetic forms or 'categories' which are necessarily and universally implanted in the human subject by the very nature of our mode of being-in-the-world, that is, through the Transcendental Ego, an archetype of reason to ground empirical findings phenomenally.

In the twentieth century, a heightened activity in language studies has led to a reconstruction of Kant's paradigm. Students of language and the philosophy of consciousness now endeavor to apprehend the generative nature of linguistic rules in themselves; here the mastery of the rules - the emergence of a competent human subject who is able to operate the rules - becomes a secondary issue. Wittgenstein's analysis of the construct of 'following a rule'; Chomsky's concepts of 'generative rules' and 'linguistic competence'; Lévi-Strauss's 'Kantianism without a transcendental subject' - these all have contributed to this development. The conditions which render language, cognition, and action plausible are being radically reconstructed in post-capitalist societies which are unclear of their self-images, in particular where capital growth is rapidly reaching the zero point because the anticipated returns are being dissipated to assuage social demands of the public arena, however diminished its pluralism of competing social interests.

The term critique acquires a second new significance. Here it denotes reflection on a system of constraints which are humanly evoked: distorting pressures to which individuals, or groups of individuals, or the human race as an entity, succumb in their process of self-transformation. This sense found its premier vindicator in Hegel. In the *Phenomenology of Mind*, Hegel articulated a concept of reflection which presents the ideal of liberation from coercive illusions. This idea was dramatically and archetypically portrayed and interpreted in the section of the *Phenomenology* which treats of the bonded relation between Master and Slave. The applications to date are universal, not only for the various species of philosophy but for the whole of the human condition, whatever its mode of production, ideology, or brand of politics. Consciousness, in the end, is decided in its specificity by the deadly game of the encounter of egos in a condition of 'scarcity', which can be defined in several ways, not just in an economic sense, which was Marx's ultimate drawback.

Without explicitly invoking the idea of a critique, Freud proposed what was in effect a new procedure of critical reflection. The constraints this reflection peers through are highly resistant to examination because their weight is convoluted and weighted from within the 'unconsciousness'. Freud's 'subject' is trammeled under this compulsive pressure of tabooed patterns of behavior and perception; he deludes himself about his own motivations; he conspires, through internalization of alienated power relations in the family, to impose his 'bad will' on others in his life space. Only by comprehending these illusions of bondedness to instincts emptied of their erotic content can one, as it were, free oneself from oneself. We liberate ourselves from the internalized conflicts which blinded us in our self-awareness and psychically impaired our cognitive faculties and critico-practical dispositions. Critique is here grounded in a specific experience, which is set down in Freud's psychoanalysis, in Hegel's *Phenomenology of Mind*, and in Marx's critique of ideology. The experience of emancipation by means of critical insight resides, at least in part, in the fact that these relationships of the institutionalized other have not been demystified of an 'aura' of sanctity and consequently cast a pall of the 'forbidden' in the search for self-identity.

It is perhaps practical to refer to the first type of critique as 'reconstruction' and the second as 'criticism'. There are at least three critical differences between *reconstruction* and *criticism*.

First, reconstruction (as advocated, e.g., by Kant) undertakes to grasp anonymous systems of rules which can be followed by any subject, conditional on having the requisite skills. Criticism (as expounded by Hegel or Freud) is brought to bear on something not anonymous but particular; it studies the conditioning of an individual's identity or the identity of a group. It engenders the explicit allusion to a subject.

Second, reconstruction is premised on data which are considered to be objective, like sentences, actions, or cognitive insights; these are the conscious operations of the human actor. Criticism, in comparison, is brought to fruition by laying bare objects of experience whose 'objectivity' is called before the bar of reason. Criticism supposes that there is a degree of built-in deformity which imitates reality. It strives to remove this distortion and thereby to make possible the liberation of what has been perverted. This entails the impetus toward emancipation.

Third, reconstruction explains what is deemed to be 'real' knowledge; for example, the knowledge we must appropriate if we are to operate rules competently and conversantly. Criticism aims at changing or even expunging the conditions of what is deemed to be a false consciousness. Thus reconstruction, by spelling out in detail the rules we follow implicitly, may lead to a broadened range and greater sophistication in our theoretical knowledge. It may do this without necessarily altering our practical conduct. Criticism, on the other hand, renders transparent what had erstwhile been obscured, and in doing so initiates a process of self-reflection, in individuals or groups, shaped to attain liberation from the domination of past inhibitions and proscriptions. Here a change in practice is indicated for a constitutive transformation in theory.

In addition to assimilating the general Enlightenment understanding of critique as oppositional thinking, the Frankfurt School has applied the idea to the dominant mainstream political and social science theories supportive of the political context, which often exercises a censoring function over dissident thought. The Frankfurt School has brought forth and committed to normative action the idea of critique in both of these new senses - without perhaps always making the fact of this dual purpose clear to its public. They have employed the term to denote reflection on the conditions of possible knowledge, and they have cultivated this sense to denote the analysis of the constraints to which classes of individuals are subject. Habermas in recent years has concentrated his research design on a social ontological Being philosophy of language and the study of law and the social structures that support it.

This range of meanings had its rudiments in a *Weltanschauung* which formed around 1770 when the theology of history was superseded by the German philosophy of history. At this juncture the role of the 'subject' of history, previously occupied by God, was imputed to Mankind, and the history of Humanity was now read as the result of a single purpose performed by this single agent. It might be objected that the idea of Mankind as a collective subject is merely the projection onto a fictive entity of a real subjectivity found only in the human individual. The point was made by Marx in his attack on the Young Hegelians. He spurned as naked Idealism their contention that the unified efforts of individuals in the course of world history could be construed as the 'self-production of the species'. Yet he himself took the stance that world history is 'the production of mankind through human work'. This still appeared to imply the hypostatization of 'man', or the human species, as the 'subject' of history for which he had taken to task the Young Hegelians.

The idea of a subject of history reappears in a different guise with the thesis that the emergence of capitalism has produced in the proletariat an agent by whom its own 'negativity', analyzed first as self-alienation and later as the fetish value of surplus value, can be surmounted.

Horkheimer, Adorno, Marcuse, and Habermas all eschew ingredients in the German philosophy of history. They no longer believe, with Marx, that the truth of their theory will be validated primarily by the historical action of the proletariat. They no longer believe, with Hegel, that progress, however it might be delineated, is underwritten by a logic of history. But they are hesitant to forsake their roots in the myth of enlightenment - the perspective of history as one all-encompassing process in which a historical subject consummates its essence. Hence the faculties originally ascribed by Kant to the consciousness of his transcendental subject are transposed by the early Horkheimer to the human species. On this interpretation, Kant's *Critique of Pure Reason* had marked a new terrain, although inadvertently and hence in a stilted presentation. The desired project is for a future society which would become truly productive of its own dormant potentials - the Frankfurt School thesis - given a 'minimal' material base for an infrastructure of the envisualized social institutions. Placed now in a possible future, this rational society, the goal of which is posited to be 'really invested in every man', would be enabled to attain concretely what Kant's transcendental subject could accomplish only formally: to change and pacify chaos into a rational order.

In Marcuse, the Enlightenment legacy assumes the form of what has been deftly called a bifocal perspective of history, constituted by the force of Eros which is being broken down by capitalism (1955, pp. 88, 97-8). It is bifocal in the sense that all spheres of experience are circumscribed by two dimensions. The first is the regulative order, whether political, economic, or sexual. The second incarnates human purposes. This second dimension is fleshed out practically, in undertakings to transform that medium; intellectually, in concepts which transcend the facts imposed by that order; and, passively, in the desires and ambitions which are stymied and rendered quiescent by it.

In the last instance, Habermas often claims that there is an interest (he sometimes refers to it as a 'deep-seated anthropological interest') in emancipation. The subject with this interest is the human species; for Habermas, also, the subject of history, in that last instance, is Mankind. It is true that he has more recently denied as fictive the notion of a 'human species which constitutes itself as the subject of world history' (Habermas and Luhmann,

1971, p. 179). Yet he persists in arguing (in a style reminiscent of Horkheimer's interpretation of Kant) that what found disfigured expression in that fiction was the intention (to whom precisely that intention is to be inferred becomes clouded) of controlling the development of societies by institutionalized and politically effective public dialogue. Then, in the past two decades, he performed his 'linguistic turn'. Since language by nature is ultimately and politically self-referential in terms of subject and object reconciliation, Habermas's project has collapsed in the last decade of the twentieth century.

The specific tenets propounded by the Frankfurt School are best presented negatively by locating the spheres in which they diverge from their selected paradigm, Marx's *Critique of Political Economy*. The divergences are fourfold. From the beginning, there is a 'turnover' conceptually from the infrastructure (the modalities of capitalist production) to the superstructure (the modalities of rationalization and legitimation) in determining the primary problematic not only for a theory of knowledge but for a political redress of those social structures no longer productive of human weal. Then the critique of political economy is displaced by the critique of instrumental rationality: the Aladdin's lamp of the technocrats. Next, the system of needs is reinterpreted through a partial incorporation of Freud. Last, Marx's philosophical anthropology is reviewed by drawing on the literature of hermeneutics in order to arrive at a 'critical phenomenology', which now subsumes the study of society's norms and laws. The question is what can be redeemed from the bourgeois moral code.

Marx was able to interpret the categories employed to vindicate those selfsame conditions. Concepts such as labor, commodity, exchange value, and the like, justify what existed through recourse to discursive theses, offer at the same moment an Archimedean point for firmly lodging Marx's own ideology-critique: the vehicle of a possible disjuncture between claim and reality galvanizes theory to attack these new problematic areas radically.

The central piece on the mantle of the latest development in critical theory pivots on a radically new issue brought about by a technological revolution. German fascism and organized capitalism together sundered the liberal economy and its attendant ideology from rationality to the degree that the subject was dimmed (in the perception of theorists) in his interaction with his corresponding object world. The field of the subject became measurably naturalized, giving rise to an unprecedented positivism with 'brave new worlds' to be administered without the human actors. Merely to recapitulate the Marxian critique of the 'fetishism of commodities' with respect to the old situation of classical-liberal capitalism has no point. The jaded analysis of the free and competitive market is an anachronism; both features missed the new facets of domination. Moreover, it was fascism which first divulged the decisive political power through public administration; it was organized capitalism which, by systematically developing the media, revolutionized the conditions of production in the superstructure. But not only in the superstructure itself, for, as organized capitalism began to achieve a stabilized equilibrium, underwritten by the state, the corporations which shaped consciousness permeated all other sectors of production, and the denial of human needs tended to shift from the economic mechanisms of the labor market to the social/psychological imperatives of the leisure market, the manipulation of consumption. But German fascism and organized capital did have one matter in common: they both broke down the boundary line between the public and private domains which had been the watermark of the liberal phase of capitalism. Both political propaganda and marketing psychology plumbed the private areas of individual life to exploit personal conflicts or to imbue artificial needs in the mass mind to support a particular system. By obfuscating the distinction between the private and the institutionalized, the authorities made it more difficult to separate internal desire and external suggestion. The superstructure was more deeply implemented in the individual substructure. It was this outcome which highlighted the capacity of ideologies to purge themselves of systems of theoretical and explanatory concepts, for the 'truth' was not to be the issue. It became possible to attenuate the 'ideological distance' between concepts and the circumstances to which concepts referred, to the detriment of the already 'given' circumstances. But this was precisely the 'space' within which Marx's classical ideology critique ruminated during the more 'leisurely' lulls in the crises of capitalism.

The Frankfurt School responded by extending ideology critique into the domain of social psychology. They endeavored to view simultaneously the combined effects of 'objective historical' conditions and 'subjective natural' conditions. Needs were no longer to be construed as natural and invariant; they were referred back to specific historical situations. This factor brought to the foreground the question how and where social conditions and their supportive norms were acculturated by the individual. The family was perceived as the psychological agent of society; through its process of socialization, economic processes were reinforced by conversion into psychic controls. The Frankfurt School located a pivotal element in fascism within the psychology of the individual citizen, the so-called 'authoritarian personality', and they strove through inquiry to demonstrate how authoritarianism was inculcated in and through the family unit, even to this very day.

The Frankfurt School thus turned to weighing the self-reinforcing qualities in the infrastructure. The result was a sharper divergence from Marx, who had believed the supportive political conditions of material production under capitalism to be self-annihilating. He contended that the mechanism propelling the movement of history was the contradiction between the forces of production and the relations of production. The forces of production are dependent on the generation of scientific knowledge and technical equipment and expertise, and on the organization of labor. The relations of production are pinpointed in the property relations and how surplus value is expropriated from labor power. In Marx's perspective, the bourgeoisie could reproduce its dominance only by constantly creating more powerful methods of production. But the relations of production are not transformed at the same rhythm and they become shackles on the further advance of the forces of production to serve human needs. The complexity of this situation brings about contradiction, so the system which then stands condemned for its lack of efficiency, effectiveness, and rudimentary humanity and justice that in turn belie the elaborate constitutions of the bourgeois democracies. But, in the understanding of the Frankfurt School, the unprecedented increase in the forces of production has produced an opposite effect from that prefigured by Marx. It has become a power to reinforce the status quo. For now, the existing relations of production can be represented as that form of organization which is technically necessary for a rational society; all problems can be made to seem reducible to technical adjudication. This signals that, once they have attained the peak of development, the forces of production stand in a revolutionized relationship to the relations of production. Previously, they offered fuel for a critique of the power structure of society; now they provide a basis for its legitimation.

The change is illuminated in the *Dialectic of Enlightenment*. Horkheimer's and Adorno's point of departure is the antagonism between two notions of reason. Practical reason is recovered in the liberation from externally imposed compulsion and it implies the good life, both private and collective, of individuals and citizens. Instrumental reason is located in the technical control of nature. This tension appears intellectually in the natural sciences and practically in modern technology. In the course of time, the second type of reason has elided the power of the first in constituting our social arrangements. What people have learned from nature enables them to use it wholly to dominate it and other people. The technical domination of nature implicates an intrinsic process in human heteronomy: intellectually, in the rational human sciences, and practically, in the continually refined administration of humanity by means of a social organization which reduces their life vistas to a dull, paleological routine of behavior. The Enlightenment is said to have metamorphosed into positivism; to serve capital; to become totalitarian; and to split off into fascism where crisis conditions preponderate. Horkheimer and Adorno have replaced the critique of political economy by the critique of instrumental reason. Elements from Marx are assimilated but also re-situated and recombined in their theory of knowledge. Marx tied the precept of commodity exchange with a specific social system of property. Horkheimer and Adorno now perceive it as the most complete articulation of instrumental rationality. The recommended reconciliation of the two concepts of reason is a utopia whose appeal has been entirely alien to the human mind to date.

Marcuse wants to impart a revolutionary impulse to critical theory through a revitalized power of the 'negative'. An attack is launched on technical rationality. Thus, in *Eros and Civilization*, Marcuse offers a revision of Freudian psychoanalysis as a replacement for the now dampened economic argument, and the concept of 'instinctual repression' here plays for Marcuse a role analogous to that of 'economic exploitation' in Marx. The primary conflict is outlined as taking place between technical rationality and latent human needs. Marcuse revises Freud's diagnosis by contending that the repressions so far characteristic of all human civilizations stem from the special conditions which have until now predominated in the evolution of culture: the need to master nature in the struggle against scarcity. If this portrayal is borne out, then the repressive organization of instinctual life is attributable to factors which emerge not from the inherent quality of the instincts but from specific historical conditions in which the instincts so far have had to be condensed to assure phylogenetic recapitulation of the species according to the ontogenetic exigencies of historical imperatives.

Thus the 'reality principle' is not universal. It is culturally specific to an economy of scarcity. But, in a civilization which tends to remove material scarcity, repression is allegedly 'surplus repression', that is, in excess of that necessary for reproducing a particular society. But other social and psychological wants can replace these fundamental material needs to wreak havoc and dissension in the social order. Marcuse envisions a 'psychic Thermidor' which has been incorporated by late capitalist culture to palliate general dissatisfactions with the substitute of the 'instilled' needs of consumer goods and services to create a pseudo-consensus. In this manner, Marcuse claims to validate his project to articulate on scale the political and sociological substance of Freud's meta-psychology, since psychological categories have become, in this interpretation, 'political categories'. But we can see that Marcuse has a clouded view of the distinctively political. The basic ingredients of Marcuse's insight into domination were in fact founded on the overly simple identification of his indicators of fascism, monopoly capitalism, totalitarianism, and technology, the parameters of his matrix being fixed before the Second World War.

The situation is complicated by the fact that technology has become an instrument and competitor of politics. On the one hand, science and technology have become crucial instruments of political action; on the other, they have an institutional modus operandi of their own and so have become a new generator of authority and power in society. Those directly involved in political action have to take into account this new dimension of reality and, to some extent defer to its authority. But whether as instrument or competitor, it has the effect of devaluing the distinctively political.

The last innovation of critical theory, best put forth by Habermas, reorients the issue of alienation by joining the lists of hermeneutics to find an allied terminology for critique. Habermas sharply distinguishes between instrumental and communicative action. In instrumental action, we encounter objects whose model is physical bodies in motion; in principle, they are overtly manipulable through directly applied action. In communicative action, we encounter objects whose model is speaking and acting subjects; in principle, they can be meaningfully delved into through a constellation of symbols taking on a kaleidoscope of forms corresponding to the situation. The contrast is between instrumental reason, which is interested in the domination of nature, and understanding, which is interested in communication without the desire of domination. The distinction has both practical and theoretical implications.

The practical upshot of the matter affects the sketch for a theory of politics. Habermas wants to restore the 'ideal' of the political, taken from the idealization of the Greek *polis*. In the *polis*, the slaves were subject to the necessity of labor, hence freeing the citizens to participate in political forums to shape the normative climate; in contemporary society, the place of the slaves could hypothetically be taken by automation (although it assumes a homogeneous rationality in society far different from that in Greek antiquity, particularly the heyday of the Athenian Empire). But Habermas argues that a scientific-technological society could be rational only if development and technology were subject to public control - which assumes an inordinately high level of scientific culture in the working masses free from coercion. He feels the goal must be worked for by constituting a dialogue among people about the values which organize their lives - although the institutional mechanisms are begged off for the moment, leaving us with a kind of naive objective idealism about how to help people come to govern themselves democratically and by just and reasonable standards.

What would the institutions look like, in which would be realized these speculations of Habermas, that sometimes quash empirical contingencies? There is a reasonably founded indictment that his work has culminated in the historicization of consciousness - an objective idealism - which in outline resembles Hegel much more than Marx. Indeed, the political element in Habermas has been so toned down that a drift toward conservatism could well be in the offing. Still, unlike Horkheimer and Adorno, he gives credence to a practical reason which could characterize a society, not only a practical reason for separate individuals 'heroically' overcoming adverse circumstances in their singularity. And, unlike Marcuse, he understands the content of utopia as the creation of an ideal situation of public discussion in which communicative distortions are *aufgehoben*. But locked into his own hermeneutic circle of inner dialogue, we must look for transcendence beyond Habermas, whose conceptual powers appear to be diminishing. Because his categories play arbitrarily with how he preconceives empirical contingencies, his theoretical range has been telescoped, if not outright manipulated to fit his utopian norms. But these transcendental norms are cast between categorical abstractionism and an empirical netherworld. Those aroused to political indignation about social injustice will not find their will steeled by an archaic mode of speculative reason so very idiosyncratically sketched by Habermas.

We may further consider Habermas's position by returning to Freud. For Freud, in fact, conceived a new hermeneutics: the study of texts, of which the dream is the paradigm, in which messages are by an 'inverted phenomenology' systematically subdued and altered. In this instance, the distortions and deletions are the 'intentional' result of the author of the text, so that his or her own product becomes incomprehensible in the de-realized social context. On the collective level, Nazi Germany provides a model for the study of a pseudo-community which has undergone desymbolization of its previously rich Weimar culture because of political immaturity and societal underdevelopment which could not adapt to its historically conditioned crises to reproduce capital at a moderated pace to maintain the traditional order. Psychoanalysis, aside from the interesting insights which can be made into psycho-history with modified meta-psychological concepts, may be perceived as a kind of linguistic analysis which treats systematically distorted communications - a position which has been amplified at some length by Alfred Lorenzer. To view it in this manner, Habermas's theory is initiated by the ideal of a smoothly flowing and functional language game which rests on a backdrop of consensus. He contends that his consensus is based on the mutual recognition of various kinds of validity claims which are implied in all speech acts - for instance, the claim that the utterance is comprehensive. When one or more such claims become problematic, the background consensus is called into question, and claims which were once only implicit, are called to the forefront in a public inquiry. Such 'discourses' entail the supposition by the participants that they are discussing problems under conditions which assure that the consensus attained will mark the force of the better argument and not of constraints on discussion. They are in an 'ideal situation of verbal communication' (1973, p. 25). Habermas strives to depict this absence of constraint formally: the structure of communication can be said to be free from constraint only when there is an effective equality of chances (presuming at least formal 'equality' in knowledge) for all the voluntary participants to partake in due course in the dialogue. This equality of chances would be necessary to optimize an outcome whereby because all have exercised their 'rights', then all have to assume a collective political responsibility for the sanctions of the 'worked through' situation. Hence the requirements of the ideal speech situation are such that the conditions for ideal discourse are inextricably associated with the conditions for ideal social life. *Between Facts and Norms* (1996) elaborates further on these themes.

Herein lies the bond between the theory of communicative competence and the theory of politics. The ideal and the real must be bridged by some institutional format in some political province if they are to be sensible and realizable. What are the political units of analysis? In the event of an intractable conflict of interests, how does one handle secessionists? Is there to be a yardstick of 'repressive tolerance' applied for some individuals who cannot articulate their interests cogently and hence by defaulting on a consensus are hindering the formulation of an immediately needed policy? Not delving into the marginal areas where there is a potential for dissensus, Habermas, however unsuspectingly, risks alienating total power to an agency which can set itself up to be the embodiment of the general will and, even inadvertently, resort to coercion in the compelling name of 'Truth'.

Habermas believes that a form of social life in which autonomy and responsibility are possible is augured in the structure of speech itself. Here, however, because of his idealism, he does not look at the reverse side of the coin - the historical materialist argument. Consider, for example, the situation of Mihailo Marković, who, in conjunction with the 'Praxis Eight' during the late 1970s and early 1980s, speaks out the truth in spite of the constraints of the authorities. These speech acts, then, because of the clarity of his outspokenness, become a part of material reality and transform it from within through theoretical elegance, and substantiated practically by moral example, which first unfolded during his guerrilla activities against the Nazis in his youth. Here the *whole* life experience is involved in a political struggle for freedom. Language analysis cannot be the end or the chief means but mainly a political means toward another means to create a universal consensus while immersed in conflict against bureaucrats. Involvement such as Marković's means *commitment* at personal risk which is far removed from the position of the language analysts, who, even given their truths, must substantialize their findings in concrete political terms and critico-practical activity. If reality is to be inverted and reified, practical reason and its reasoners must sally forth to protect even their own threatened interests; otherwise, their authority will be silenced. In the Serbian government of the mid-1990s, he is a decision-maker fighting against the possibilities of resurgent German interests intruding into the Balkans. As of 1992, he took up his position as an independent intellectual, hoping while working for a Velvet Revolution. There is a real fear of a Berlin-Teheran alliance in the area which could detonate a world war. On this point, Habermas is silent. Why? When will *logos* become praxis?

This whole matter of critical theory, then, is not just a matter of dispassionate inquiry, for its very radical findings exhort action, but, in fact, a program has been noticeably missing to date. The Frankfurt School has epitomized this debacle. In this way, the theory of communicative competence may be perceived to take the place of the analysis of the work process, once Marx's philosophical anthropology had been 'bracketed out' of the new operational rules. But this then leaves us in a domain of theory which no longer has the full urgency of critique in the genre of Marx's programmatic *Theses on Feuerbach*. Theory without critique reverts swiftly to a blind ideological defense of the status quo.

The Frankfurt School has had many running theoretical debates with their natural adversaries. The critical rationalism of Popper and Albert was the direct heir to the logical positivism which had flourished in Vienna in the 1920s in the group of philosopher-scientists and mathematicians known as the Vienna Circle, among the most prominent of which were Carnap and Popper himself. Like the critical theorists, the logical positivists have seen themselves as performing an educative role in the battle against irrational beliefs which can strangle collective life. Where their ways parted was in their belief that ideological assertions could be measured by scientific methods, hence by exactly those criteria of 'instrumental reason' which were anathema to the Frankfurt School. Critical Rationalism sought to reserve the name of 'knowledge' and 'science' for the results of those operations which were to be found in the evolution the modern natural sciences. Specifically, it became moored in Popper's principle of 'falsifiability', according to which only those statements can be considered as empirically authenticated about which one could say by what empirical methods of the same genre they could be refuted.

The progress of knowledge was believed to be underwritten socially by a controlled method of critical testing: proposing trial solutions to scientific problems and subjecting these solutions to criticism and the consequent elimination of error. The attitude of the intellectual whose convictions are inspired by controlled scientific thinking is to offer the paradigm toward which a well-organized education might lead society as a whole to its own enlightenment. It is the duty of intellectuals to work toward this end, in which the regulative function of violence is replaced by the regulative ideal of rational criticism. The politics thus sensed is a kind of rational social experiment. Hence Popper's *The Open Society and Its Enemies* was both a counter-example and a criticism of the *Dialectic of Enlightenment*. Popper and Albert have repeatedly charged the Frankfurt School of being now and again seized by paroxysms of irrationalism of a quasi-totalitarian ilk, a serious charge which has not yet been seriously answered.

There is a contour to this quarrel which can be traced. (1) Popper and Adorno employ the terms 'contradiction' and 'critique' in two entirely different ways. For Popper, problems arise because a contradiction is observed between our existing knowledge and existing facts. The method of the social sciences, as of the natural sciences, rests on the quest for solutions to these problems; it is the control of the tentative quest for solutions by the most trenchant possible critique of hypotheses. Thus, for Popper, critique alludes to a formal method of testing scientific propositions. For Adorno, the problem is not something rudimentarily epistemological, but alludes to a problematic condition of the social world. He cites as evidence the contradiction between the concepts of a liberal regime, which implies freedom and equality, and the true content of these categories under liberalism, in which inequality of relations between people is tied to social power and position of a quasi-hereditary character. The problem here is not a logical contradiction which could be corrected through more refined hypotheses, but one which can be remedied only by modifying the structural condition of society itself.

(2) Habermas then posed another objection to Popper's idea of a critical test. He contended that no system of basic concepts comparable to that established for the investigation of moving bodies and observable events is in principle possible in the study of society. This is because societies are differently constituted as objects of possible knowledge. They form a grid of intentional actions and statements about observable events. The inquirer must gain access to the data through an understanding of meanings. Instead of controlled observation, which underwrites the anonymity of the observing subject and assures the 'reproducibility' of experimental 'events', there is a participation in the dialogue between investigator and investigated, in which reciprocal interaction occurs, subject to a range of interpretations which is never exact. Here the paradigm is no longer the observation but the dialogue in which all must be held equally morally responsible: a naive psychological reductionism.

(3) What Habermas calls 'interest' cannot be experienced as such; it is an interest in which no one may be borne out to be interested in any empirically proven manner. The claim that natural science is informed by 'interest in possible technical control' can only be understood in the sense that this interest is the condition of the possibility of natural science. He is claiming that it is not merely the emergence and continued existence of science, but also its procedure and methodological structure which must be elaborated by such an interest. If this claim is to be validated, it must be demonstrated that there is a systematic relationship between, on the one hand, the logical structure of natural science, and, on the other hand, the pragmatic structure of the possible

social applications, even by the state, of the information generated by various tiers of the ensemble of social relations and the forces of production. In discussions of the meaning of models for scientific theories, it has been demonstrated adequately that natural science models are not merely an instrument of theory construction but an indispensable element of theory itself – an element which imprints on theory an intelligibility substantially independent of prediction and which adduces its essentially explanatory value. Habermas has too sharply dichotomized instrumentalized reason in antithesis to communicative competency. In terms of an operational overlap, there is a sufficient coincidence of the instrumental and the practical to merit a more moderated inquiry, thus, for the moment, forgoing the invocation of a 'transcendental ego'.

Habermas reworked psychoanalysis as his original model in elucidating the construct of an emancipatory social science. In psychoanalysis, the speech and actions of the patient are understood as a system of symbols whose meaning must be rebuilt after a demythicizing procedure undergone by the patient. The problem is largely one of reconstructing meaning which has become unintelligible even to the author. The analyst undertakes to accomplish this end by leading the patient through a 'trial', the scourging of self-reflection with the 'healthy' alter ego in the physician in order that the patient may become conscious of his or her errant ways and previously expressed needs and passions. The ability follows to acknowledge that these needs and motives are one's own, and recognize their value and normative dimensions. Habermas contends that this model can and should be applied to society as a whole. But this contractual and market arrangement gives far superior advantage to the physician, who might very well be induced to employ manipulation to force the client to be free. The client comes as a supplicant, and, not so ironically, the highly technical knowledge of the physician-entrepreneur provides a handsome surplus value in exchange not for 'recognition' but for parceled out expertise prorated by session.

The role of social theorists is to render autonomy to those to whom they speak by helping them understand their own situation in the social world as meaningful in their whole context. Individual self-reflection is woven by the dialectic of emancipation into a society for its own self-education. For the analyst, the patient is not supposed to be an object of coercion, but a subject who is to be 'assisted to emancipation'. Precisely this common purpose, however, is lacking in social conflicts. What obtains there is a condition of reciprocal resistance, with violence always a potential. For any ruling class, the endeavor to wrench freedom from an administered and controlled social condition must appear as an (irrational) peremptory challenge to the rule it exercises over other classes. And can it now be any clearer that Habermas is the 'arch-bourgeois intellectual', plagued by the amphiboles of a de-dialecticized reason? Too, according to his theory of language, we can all be friends if we act in *good faith*! We do so precisely because of humankind's dual nature: eros and thanatos are in perpetual struggle.

Why the continued interest in critical theory? The first reason is *methodological*. It relates necessarily to the idea of critique a reflection on that which is to be critiqued, that is, false consciousness and its reificatory mechanisms, which affect the conditions of knowledge of the social world. The critical theorists contend that no system of rudimentary concepts, comparable to the basic concepts of proven methods in the natural sciences for the investigation of moving bodies and observable events, is in principle possible in the examination of society, since societies, being systems of communicative action, are differently constituted as objects of possible practical knowledge.

The second reason is necessarily and sufficiently *political*. It is tied to the notion of critique as an analysis of constraints imposed by the historically variable structures of the social world. There is a circle whereby, contradictorily, society is made increasingly dependent on alienated applied science, and then scientific criteria are appealed to in order to resolve whether the social world is to be rationally ordered. The genuine answer can only emerge from those who are not immersed in protecting their own material interests and power. So we look now for a critical theory beyond the Frankfurt School, which, though no longer organizational in form, leaves us with a body of knowledge awaiting further cultivation by a new breed of 'engaged' theoretical practitioners and support by a skilled politicized constituency.

In the realm of the blind, the one-eyed individual will be king. This is the dilemma of Enlightenment reason and its advocates. Yes, it sees, but not self-consciously or multi-dimensionally. In politics, this 'pure' reason cannot manage the Dionysian eruptions of repressed historical memories. Compulsively we repeat the same errors as historical actors with half-baked theories in need of 'heroic' deeds to revitalize the human project.

Postface

The stifled cry inscribed on the memorial at Yad Vashem for the martyred six million Jews of the Nazi Behemoth does not serve the truth - to reveal, not simply to document. In out own administered society, there is a tendency to immolate truth to short and pithy programmatic statements. We must stand vigil against the seduction of adulterating the integrity of truth by vitiating its contents for the abstract form of the computer printout. This tendentiousness leads us to autocratism wherever concrete arguments are debased to the pseudo-concrete. The pseudo-concrete begets non-events where words in 'texts' receive 'special treatment' to reduce them to mere signs which remind one of the infamous sign over the entrance to Auschwitz: 'Labor liberates'. Lest we all be Jews taken unaware, I refer the readers of this volume to Fredric Jameson's caveat on the 'form' to which truth must aspire:

> Nowhere is the hostility of the Anglo-American tradition toward the dialectical more apparent, however, than in the widespread notion that the style of these works is obscure and cumbersome, indigestible, abstract - or, to sum it all up in a convenient catchword, *Germanic*. It can be admitted that it does not conform to the canons of clear and fluid journalistic writing taught in the schools. But what if those ideals of clarity and simplicity have come to serve a very different ideological purpose, in our present context, from the one Descartes had in mind? What if, in this period of overproduction of printed matter and the proliferation of methods of quick reading, they were intended to speed the reader across a sentence in such a way that he can salute a readymade idea effortlessly in passing, without suspecting that real thought demands a descent into the materiality of language and a

consent to time itself in the form of the sentence? In the language of Adorno - perhaps the finest dialectical intelligence, the finest stylist, of them all - density is itself a conduct of intransigence: the bristling mass of abstractions and cross-references is precisely intended to be read in situation, against the cheap facility of what surrounds it, as a warning to the reader of the price he has to pay for *genuine thinking*. The resolute abstractness of this style stands as an imperative to pass beyond the individual, empirical phenomenon to its meaning: abstract terminology clings to its object as a *sign* of the latter's incompleteness in itself, of its need to be replaced in the context of the totality. I cannot imagine anyone with the slightest feeling for the dialectical nature of reality remaining insensible to the purely formal pleasure of such sentences, in which the shifting of the world's gears and the unexpected contact between apparently unrelated and distant categories and objects find sudden and dramatic formulation. It is not, I would like to emphasize, a question of *taste*, any more than the validity of dialectical thinking is a question of *opinion*; but it is also true that there can be no reply to anyone choosing to discuss the matter in those terms. (1971, pp. xiii-xiv)

But Theodor Adorno tells us that today we are in the age 'after Auschwitz', where a transvaluation of all values has occurred in our totally administered society. The pessimistic tones in the passage below from *Negative Dialectics* should goad us to redeem critique by whatever struggle is necessary.

Once again, the dialectical motif of quantity recoiling into quality scores an unspeakable triumph. The administrative murder of millions made of death a thing one had never yet to fear in just this fashion. There is no chance any more for death to come into the individuals' empirical life as somehow conformable with the course of that life. The last, the poorest possession left to the individual is expropriated. That in the concentration camps it was no longer an individual who died, but a *specimen* - this is a fact bound to affect the dying of those who escaped the administrative measure.

Genocide is the absolute integration. It is on its way whenever men are leveled off - 'polished off', as the German military called it - until one exterminates them literally as deviations from the concept of their total nullity. Auschwitz confirmed the philosopheme of pure identity as death. ... Absolute negativity is in plain sight and has ceased to surprise anyone. Fear used to be tied to the *principium individuationis* of self-preservation, and that principle, by its own consistency, abolished itself. What the sadists in the camps foretold their victims, 'tomorrow you'll be wiggling skyward as smoke from this chimney', bespeaks the indifference of each individual life that is the direction of history. Even in his formal freedom, the individual is as fungible and replaceable as he will be under the liquidators' boots.

But since, in a world where law is universal individual profit, the individual has nothing but this self that has become indifferent, the performance of the old, familiar tendency is at the same time the most dreadful of things. There is no getting out of this, no more than out of the electrified barbed wire around the camps. Perennial suffering has as much right to expression as a tortured man has to scream; hence it may have been wrong to say that after Auschwitz you could no longer write poems. But it is not wrong to raise the less cultural question whether after Auschwitz you can go on living - especially whether one who escaped by accident, one who by rights should have been killed, may go on living. His mere survival calls for the *coldness*, the *basic principle* of *bourgeois subjectivity*, without which there could have been no Auschwitz; this is the drastic guilt of him who was spared. *By way of atonement* he will be *plagued by dreams* such as that *he is no longer living at all*, that he was sent to the ovens in 1944 and his *whole existence* since has been *imaginary*, an *emanation* of the *insane wish of a man killed twenty years earlier*. (1973b, pp. 362-3; emphasis mine)

Exploring the uniqueness of Auschwitz, Habermas supports my concluding remarks in the following poignant statement:

But since that moral catastrophe doesn't the survival of all of us stand under the curse in, attenuated form, of having merely escaped? And doesn't the fortuitousness of unmerited escape establish an intersubjective liability - a liability for distorted life circumstances that grant happiness, or even mere existence, to some only at the cost of destroying the happiness of others, denying them life and causing them suffering? (1989, p. 252)

In the spirit of 'friendship', I call and implore this reading public to struggle in unison to realize that the nature of critique as a matter of common concern: a concern to tear down the notional 'electrified barbed wire' to unify 'good will' with social science theory formation. Then we can no longer say that 'after Auschwitz you could no longer write poems'. In these kinds of value judgments lie the very preconditions for a 'radical' politics, one which plumbs the roots of things to better our society. If such events come to pass, we will no longer have to complain about the loss or alienation of the 'golden era' of classical Greek antiquity. Our own lived experience, then, will be a practically truthful one.

Appendix 1: Black nationalism and emancipation

What is the situation of the African American citizen in the United States today? Not good. The truth of this assertion is evident simply from economic indicators of equality. What are the problems, and how can they be remedied?[1]

We must first look at the ghettoes, the reservations for the poor masses who have become a caste with the looks of a permanent underclass. There has been a lack of progress since the 1960s. There are even significant income differentials between black men and women, resulting in power disparities which undermine family solidarity. Black women are paid more for doing the same work as their black male counterparts. In fact, black women make the same money as their white female peers. This discrimination against the male causes friction between the genders and undermines race solidarity in the quest for freedom. The popular, distorted perception and media portrayal of black men as innately dangerous hinders employment efforts. There is a strong correlation between unemployment and violence; in fact, if unemployment is factored out, white and black people would be equally violent (or non-violent as the case may be). Further progress could be made if we had serious gun control.[2] But there is an economic reason that in part explains the presence of masses of marginalized men: they are needed as a reservoir of cheap labor for the temporary needs of industries, businesses, and farms. The manufacturing system, once the largest source of employment and upward mobility and status for the blue collar male, is now dead. Capital and its jobs have moved abroad.

The traditional answer has been higher education. But how do you get the qualifications requisite for college? The public school systems are a disaster because it is too late to instill a work ethic by the time children reach school age. They already are psychologically traumatized by their racist environment. Even those blacks and whites eventually getting college degrees often do not find work appropriate to the level of their education. Successful black males must be a role model for inner city youth and sponsor efforts on their behalf to raise their expectations and performances. Too, they must open their checkbooks beneficently as an act of grace and thankfulness to have escaped the fate of their brethren. When you have self-esteem, you do not need drugs and you can acquire the high technology skills and critical thinking necessary to adapt to a rapidly changing world.

Programmatic suggestions

1. Higher education, if keyed into providing meaningful degrees with a linkage with the job market, must be the first priority of black youth. Affirmative action is invariably stigmatizing, and a date must be set for terminating it once the gates of the top academies have been opened. We would then shift to an achievement orientation to measure human worthiness. Every other ethnic group has gone this route without claims for preferential treatment. This 'exceptionalism' leads to social frictions within and outside the academy. The other route for upward social mobility, organized crime, must be forsaken because it destroys the fabric of the communities where it is ensconced as a parasite. Nonetheless, it undeniably creates monetary opportunities that the larger society to date has denied to inner city youth.

2. There must be industrialization of the ghettoes by creating tax-free economic spheres of opportunity for private entrepreneurs who would train these groups of the underprivileged. There should be an emphasis on high technology and the health service industries, which are high paying and promote personal pride.

3. There must be black and white coalitions of voters as in the 1960s to define radically common issues of interest.

4. The idea of legalizing drugs has to be considered; if you cannot beat the dealers, do an end run around them. We have the example of prohibition of alcohol to serve as a historical example. It was revoked.

5. Black nationalism and black capital are needed to develop the sense that one is a somebody who counts and is worthy of love.

6. The government should issue tax credits to black-owned businesses and educational credits and cash grants to indemnify blacks for their historical suffering. Each black person should get seventy thousand dollars over a twenty-year period. It is an investment in which the costs will be more than regained with enhanced productivity and the social peace which goes with true equality of the races. The total is less than $100 billion dollars per year.[3]

This restitution is a bargain in comparison to the cost of the Cold War, which we won decisively by perseverance. The historical model for such a radical action is what the Germans did for the Jews and Israel in the compensatory payments called *Wiedergutmachung*. The Germans gave the Jews a new start. This legislation in the United States could eliminate the economic legacy of racism by having African Americans fully employed. Americans will recover the monies in tax dollars and social tranquility.

7. On a limited scale, we can transform public schools into military schools where the primary values are discipline, honor, and competent performance, better known as the Protestant work ethic. The government could socially engineer a social outcaste into a military caste with social standing. This radical action would be a step toward true equality. Too, military training in conjunction with academic studies teaches 'hard' skills which are transferrable to the private business sphere.

8. Let us set up work camps instead of prisons for young offenders except murderers and other psychopathic types. Criminal records would be expunged on their finishing a tour of duty. Status would follow closely on being members of either a work brigade or the above mentioned military profession. Service would be exchanged for social status.

9. Congress and the President should issue a formal Declaration of Apology to the black nation for the institution of slavery. It would clear the national conscience. A constitutional amendment would denounce overt racism as a crime against humanity with serious penalties equivalent to those for treason. Such a declaration, in conjunction with the above revolutionary reforms, would bring our nation to a new birth innocent of our blood debt toward African Americans.

10. The country now needs an Economic Bill of Rights guaranteeing universal health care, a guaranteed minimum yearly income, free higher public education, and an overhaul of the university system, as human rights which go hand-in-glove with a progressive and democratic nation where the bottom line is not the almighty God, the dollar. Rather, we should create an ethical society

where all participate, particularly at the neighborhood level. Individuals can make a difference in their own habitat because it is in their self-interest. Collectively, then, these individual self-interests benefit the general interest.

There has been a steady deterioration in the purchasing power of the middle class over the past generation. We seem to be heading toward a two-class society: rulers and ruled. To undo this threat to the stability of democracy, moderate independent white voters would find it in their interest to integrate the black underclass into the mainstream. The combined forces of production from this coalition of workers would provide the enhanced efficiency of labor power to generate the necessary and fair taxes to underwrite government programs to educate 'average' Americans for the technical and social skills requisite to survive in the world economy where only the 'fittest' survive in the struggle for existence. At the same time, we could win back Americans to a sense of commitment to fighting for a workable democracy because the current alienation from the political system deprives us of the feedback needed for the government legitimacy, authority, and communicative competency necessary to engender novel public policies in adapting to a hostile and changing world environment. The time is now for patriotic and responsible action and not further demoralizing rhetoric from the professional political class.

Notes

1. An earlier form of this essay was presented as a lecture in the Intellectual Heritage Program at Temple University, December 12, 1994.

2. The American right seems to have an inordinate number of criminal psychiatric cases. The predisposition toward indiscriminate shooting and bombing of innocent, unarmed civilians are deducible from a genetic sexual incompetence. The Big Bang explosion in Oklahoma City displaces the orgasm. Subliminally, they have been unconsciously induced to organically repress their traumatic memories of premature ejaculation or impotence by compensating with an ideology of violence and machismo. They cite a constitutional right to bear arms, but do not want to pay taxes because the government which protects their rights to organize and exercise their free speech is the enemy; they love God, yet they kill in the name of the Lord. Love thy neighbor apparently is a precept that is not in their Bible. These 'civil libertarians' with borderline personalities are born to kill precisely because their manhood is merely a physical definition and their minds are that of psychopathic children. There is a castration complex at work in which Oedipal guilt is the root cause. These people resent women because of

jealousy: they wish they did not have a penis because they doubt their virility. We have at hand a new phenomenon, an emasculated male version of 'penis envy'. The whole philosophy of the Republican Party is built on an organic repression of suppressed homosexual instincts. The National Rifle Association and its agents, the embodiment of true Republican respect for our polity and life itself, are only the symbolic representation of a primal anal aggression at the national level. It is directed against imaginary enemies, like African males, before whom they feel deeply shamed in not matching their alleged sexual prowess, particularly with white women. Whatever the merits and demerits of the O.J. Simpson case, he proves that the real issue is the taboo of having had white women. Of course, Simpson is merely a symbol of a mythic construct which is in large part fictional and racist. White males cannot admit their own inferiority complex, for to concede such an elementary truth would violate the brotherhood of the primal horde and to confess that the ultimate transgression of our society is miscegenation. These whites band together out of weakness in a collective denial of their obvious ambiguous sexuality. What results is a perverted, because regressed, anal eroticized political philosophy in promoting law and order; stinginess in budget cuts hurting children, the most helpless in our society; and a meanness of spirit reflecting an arrested psychosexual personality development. Republican Senators openly sell their vote to Big Business lobbies: a vote for a Board seat when out of politics. Democrats collude, too, but with better rationalizations, indicating a residual social conscience.

So shit, however amorphous, is the irreducible ontogenetic unit of behavioral analysis in character formation and reaction not only to thoughts of dirt but to the perverse infantile sexuality associated with it. Defense mechanisms allow for its ultimate socially acceptable emergence into a sublimated Republicanism. This provides the *Urstuff* for future psychoanalytic research and dissertations. Social science analysis has taught us that shit has a deep, unconscious totemic significance which ultimately has to be tabooed to preclude its periodically surfacing to the conscious. The nexus between dirt and aggression is inextricable and hence cannot be acknowledged, for the awareness of it would cause unbearable anxiety and the ego's loss of self-esteem. Social scientists know all too well the connection binding fear of dirt and the fascination with one's own waste materials, whose ideational manifestations are denied by being projected onto the black nation. There is a *Schadenfreude* entailed in all these centuries of tormenting the black nation. This deep, dark joy in seeing others suffer at your hands is the consequence of an anal sadism which must be suppressed in social science research and repressed at the individual level; otherwise, a revolutionary situation could explode the accumulation of racial tensions building over this interminable time period. We would then stand shamed and ostracized by the world at large before which we hold ourselves to be the ultimate model of rectitude.

At the deepest level of analysis, there is a love of disorder constitutive of an idealized homosexuality in the Republican fraternity. When the Republicans talk tough about 'welfare mothers', they remorselessly target a powerless and defenseless minority group in order to enhance their own sense of insecurity toward a forgotten masculine identity. The Republicans make much ado about the loss of our democratic civic culture and community sensibility. There is the stink of hypocrisy in these pious utterances. This toughness extends further to the mindless accruing of property and companies, much like infants playing with their feces as a form of creation before toilet training when they learn that they really are not godheads.

Again, these substitute gratifications compensate for a sense of phallic inferiority in being unable to treat and psychologically accept women equally and caringly and the forbidden desire to emulate the mythopoetically constructed black male's sexual conquests. It is fortunate that these anal characteristics cannot be inherited by their children. At least, then, there is hope for future generations. With advances in sexual education and its technologies the phallocentric epistemology of laissez faire capitalism will evolve into true genital love and more mature political conduct, which will take into account the responsibilities entailed in fashioning a pragmatic democratic civic culture of mutual respect and recognition, once called common courtesy. That is why Republicans most fear sex education in the public schools. Their inalienable right to be ignorant, which they confuse with piety and an indignantly proclaimed patriotism, cannot be passed onto their progeny, threatening the lever of power over the minds of generations to come and their own sense of legitimacy and authority.

One can imagine some inventive graduate student writing a thesis on the genealogy of a concept whose full flavor and odor can only be expressed by a compound German word: *Sheisskraft*. In a thought experiment, Nietzsche would have appreciated the oxymoron and the fact that it penetrates through to conservative society's resentments and infantile frustrations. The shame of obsessing on shit results in a reaction formation to the nihilistic will to power (so the power to shit over others asymmetrically and uninhibitedly emerges paradoxically into our contemporary culture of shamelessness). Everything then is relative in a poststructuralist, postmodern world because all values have been transvalued into monetary terms by the global capitalist revolution. Structural changes in the world economy have outrun our moral capacity to deal with the implications for everyday behavior. These insecurities are the breeding ground of violent groups who are trying to reestablish a grip on reality. With the theme of shit (money is its sanitized symbol), the associated 'disgusting' behavioral traits have been projected onto the black nation, whose humanity, creativity, affect, and sensitivity of just accepting their own beautiful black being are precisely what whites secretly resent and envy. Whites denigrate these virtuous qualities of which they are frigidly incapable of expressing through the defense mechanisms of the denial of forbidden thoughts with their consequent projection onto an out-group. The sexual economy of racism lies in both tabooed desire and economic exploitation, shamelessly. The sexual economy of America engenders erotic gratification of a substitute nature and generates obscene super-profits which are redundant because not fairly distributed. These causal connections in our sexual economy explains, in part, our basic biases and their benefits. Prejudice pays. Nonetheless, Black is Beautiful.

An analogous critique can be applied to the Democratic Party and the American Association of University Professors. They have managed the Machiavellian art of speaking out of both sides of their mouths. They speak in the name of minorities, while those who manage the party and the university are so elitist as to be exclusive of any sincere motivation to recruit from the underclasses and share their power with people they despise as intellectually and morally inferior. What makes them contemptible is the fact that they have the universal culture and the social scientific research data to know better, yet not the character to effect a radical, if not revolutionary, change to finish the work of 1776, 1787-1789, and 1865. Their resistance stems from a terminal intellectual narcissism and oral sadism which does not allow them to carry on a dialogue with anyone outside the party's brain trust or the academy on the grounds that they do not have the proper credentials. There is the holy terror of mass-producing words while being the privileged mandarins who define which terms empower people. In the end, there is a cannibalism in which the world is consumed by fashionable ideologies of the left: feminism, sexual orientation studies, mechanistic class analysis, the new historicism, poststructuralism, and a host of other reductionist fads that reify consciousness rather than set standards to perceive the general interest above partisan issues. Their language is so esoteric as to be exclusive of others because there are no institutional linkages to provide for friendship and ordinary language analysis in the vernacular of the common folk. Have you ever seen a teamster and an academic communicate on common grounds to provide role models for working class and minority group members? In actuality, their interests are antagonistic at the university level. Academia intimidates the oppressed and is in fact part of the problem in the ultra-specialization and articulation of interest group politics. The professoriate mistakes thoughts and dreams for concrete policies, fantasies for political praxis, and redundant verbiage for reality. Lately, the Republicans have tested their political will quite successfully by tapping into the collective nihilism and racism of the masses to prevent the government from delineating any significant legislation and orchestrating it through Congress.

Without a rigorous collective self-analysis by all the parties and their patrons and agents to induce a national catharsis of all these negative and infantile emotions, we are doomed. We then have a gridlocked two-party system and an isolated imperial presidency which do not understand how to communicate competently within the system, let alone listen to ordinary citizens. The day is at hand where the notion of upward class mobility based on a higher level of education, as the undergirding of a viable democracy, will be antiquarian and quaint. Furthermore, the majority of American voters, at a preconscious level of thought, have seceded from the electoral process by nonparticipation. The penultimate game of democracy may already have been lost.

It may be time for the citizens to look toward countercultural political forms to articulate their needs and live out their lives in a self-fulfilled manner. These countercultural units, like the 'religious' ashrams in India and the better examples of the socialist kibbutzim in Israel, could accommodate many alternative lifestyles in a tolerant and creative social democratic parallel society. It would be therapeutic and morally instructive to learn that intellectual and manual labor are not mutually exclusive activities as we build democracy, reclaim nature as our common human heritage, and enhance the consciousness of our species. And, yes, we can build a democracy which goes beyond class privileges and their attendant fraudulent and sanctimonious attitudes: superiority and an elitist script in which the home of a nation's language is built on the straw materials of symbolic doublespeak. We talk a pseudo-language of equality (e.g., the Contract with America), but actual political events belie the democratic rhetoric, and bread and circuses for the masses only reinforce public cynicism. Can America wake up from its dream state? Or is reality testing, the touchstone of an operational and legitimate nation-state, defunct?

3. We should bluntly address this sixth point. How should we pay for what only can be described as American crimes against humanity since 1776, inaugurated by the Declaration of Independence with its 'over-determined' double standards applied against out-groups? The majority of adults, including blacks and women, had no legal standing or even recognition for their labor services at that revolutionary time. To redeem that forsaken promissory note, at this juncture of our history, the United States should unilaterally renounce its debt to the Japanese banks. Banks, business firms, and government (the Ministry of International Trade and Industry) have systematically waged economic war on us for the past two decades by unfair market practices, causing our government and major corporations to borrow monies on a ruinous

scale. The bureaucracy (the civil service) connives in a flagrant manner with the system of exclusionary trade structures called *keiretsu*. The President in unison with a joint session of Congress should compensate ourselves for our losses by renouncing in toto the principal and interest. Writing off our debt in exchange for our trade losses would close out the account by balancing the minuses and pluses.

Basically, we are a bankrupt nation-state which cannot pay its bills. Consequently, the multi-racial middle class has been paying in taxes the difference, and only in part. As its purchasing power radically declines, this middle class becomes alienated from government, and the latter loses its legitimacy and authority. If we are not to become the Argentina of North America and become a quasi-feudal structure of government run by an anti-democratic economic elite, we must take a revolutionary step in revitalizing a demoralized and financially besieged middle class. Without that middle class mobility, there can be no true equality of the races, because it must be based on economic parity.

Of course, the world's banks would revoke all lines of credit. Such a response would be therapeutic since we would be compelled then to spend within our means and 'option out' false needs from our acquisitive, collective mind set. Again, the United States could emerge as the productive, not addictive nation in both its domestic and foreign spheres of influence. We would be forced to apportion our limited means to attain realizable goals, affirmed by the *demos*. The outcome would be a multidimensional middle class with gender equality and the liquidation of the caste system based on color. Together, we will build 'the city on the hill'.

Appendix 2

At Temple University, in the heart of one of the worst ghettoes in the United States, North Philadelphia, I have been involved in an interesting thought experiment with a practical intent. Dr. Stephen C. Zelnick, Director and one of the authors of the Intellectual Heritage Program here, has helped create an interdisciplinary program uniting all the disciplines of the undergraduate curriculum. There is an intellectual integrity and purpose at Temple University which only the smaller, so-called elite institutions are usually in a position to practice. All students initially are required to take a writing course, so that inextricable dialectic between cogent writing and clear thought culminates in praxis. Then, in consecutive semesters, students take the courses Intellectual Heritage 51 and 52. These courses explore the building blocks of world civilization with the 'classic' texts which define historical periods from ancient epochs to the capitalist era. Ideas necessarily undergo changes by natural selection. They either improve or die as modified ideas come to birth (initially as neologisms for revolutionary situations).

'Democratic capitalism', since 1776, has created a global unity in terms of either accepting or rejecting hegemonic ideology. Ideas are engines which drive our culture, institutions, public policies, and ultimately, privately held value systems. Students learn to discriminate between 'good' and 'bad' books, the seminal from the trivial. There are criteria of excellence which transcend political considerations, even though what is actually read boils down to bargaining among competing interest groups.

My own favorite unit in the program, 'The Revolutionary Thinkers', includes Marx, Darwin, and Freud. Marx understood how political revolution can overthrow *anciens régimes* which no longer have legitimacy and authority. Darwin basically crowned science with his theory of evolution, in which religion received a serious rebuff, as a dogma in its formulation of creationism, and as an institution in its ideology of conservatism. It now functions strictly as a handmaiden for the forces of reaction. Freud, of course, showed how religion is an infantile expression of neurotic conflict. I have found his *Introductory Lectures on Psycho-Analysis* to be the ne plus ultra in instructing medical and lay audiences on the innermost and largely unconscious 'secrets' of the psyche. Our memories have to be 're-educated'.

Any lay person or student can learn key issues of mental health hygiene. Insanity is the last taboo of our society, one which people feel very uncomfortable discussing frankly. With intensive discussions (climaxing in group therapeutic encounters in the classroom) of precepts of repression, sexual neurosis, aggression, the reality principle, and similar topics, I teach my students how to help others in distress and come to self-understanding through self-analysis. These issues are critical at a very fundamental level. For instance, all students know they must get jobs in a 'dog-eat-dog' world. There are no euphemisms for work and death in their mutually defining necessity and inevitability. In the spring 1995 semester I was instrumental in deterring (for the moment) two suicidal students from committing an irrevocable act of self-destruction. These situations compel a conscientious teacher to be an activist outside the classroom and reach out into the community at large, not only as a matter of professional responsibility but to be a human being, meaning ultimately having to make social commitments to others *caringly*. You are your brother's and sister's keeper.

The Intellectual Heritage Program helps de-reify the technical division of labor at the university, which, of course, is situated in the more general context of the social division of labor. We have faculty meetings in which engaged teachers enlighten each other on how best to improve instructional methodologies for greater rapport with the students. In the end, too, friendships for a lifetime are formed, from colleagues to gratified students, who really do appreciate not only excellent teaching but the highly involved interpersonal contact. In this manner, we are all empowered to transform ourselves collectively. Mutual respect and recognition in a common language community allow all to educate their opinions where there is a global unity in the particularistic, articulated diversity of members from the whole spectrum of society. So long as there is no hidden political agenda, this good faith approach to learning leads to a common purpose: constituting a community where there is the peace of all loving all subliminally and aggressive instincts are redirected to an empirically verifiable soul force. This strategy is but one among many to redeem an errant Enlightenment reason whose illumination has been dimmed in the slaughterhouse of history in its twentieth-century workings. Take heart. The owl of Minerva takes flight at Temple University.

Appendix 3

Stephen C. Zelnick

Ronald J. Schindler's book holds back little. He is Jeremiah (his middle name) railing against the times. His voice is scholastic (pedantic, at times); his voice is fervent and personal. He hates these latter days of capitalist ignorance - the last wild party, renewed each day with frenetic exhaustion. He has contempt for the academy and its comfortable, parasitic relation to our evil times. There is pain everywhere in this book, as well as a ghastly Germanic playfulness.

How did this book come to be? I offer an invented history which, if not literally true, traces what lies behind this strange book. Schindler completed this book many, let's say twenty years ago. It was his doctoral thesis and, like all such documents, was essentially earnest and very respectful toward its subject and its learned audience. The doctoral thesis is meant to be a ticket of entry to academic employment. While it is certainly some sort of profound study of something or other, it is also the bulkiest portion of the job resume. And such was Schindler's book - weighted down with footnotes, many of them in foreign tongues (some requiring special fonts to print) and in a voice without passion or personality.

But there are no jobs in the field of political science, especially for theorists, and even more especially for theorists who study Marxian writers. Never mind that young Schindler has a passion to teach, a passion to make his touch with the world and with history through other human beings. The door is shut - except for the Scholar Gypsy, roaming from one institution to another, knitting a life together with part-time jobs which pay him a good deal less than he would earn driving a hack through the broken streets of the city.

Like so many other earnest young scholar-teachers, Schindler lives on bad pay and hopes for the opening he knows deep down will never open. Unlike others, Schindler works on his book, and it begins to grow into something strange and terrible. Like Dorian Gray's picture, Schindler's book becomes deformed, but also vivid and passionate and candid, without remorse.

The politeness toward the Academy disappears, year after dreadful year, as it becomes clear that there will never be a place for Schindler, while for lesser people with little to give there are happy times and power and the satisfactions of real homes and hearths. Schindler becomes the Bohemian Scholar, living in his cold garret, brewing revenge. Where once the target of his thesis was capitalist business, the state, politics, culture in a general sense, now, increasingly, the academy itself is the target. Even his blessed Frankfurters become implicated as comfortable thinkers, whose fashionable pronouncements, rather than shaking the world as it miserably is to its roots, are taken as the next wave of articles and conferences and t-shirts. The Frankfurters themselves are wrapped snug in their buns, stuffed into endowed chairs, with the added relish of corporate-style salaries. And Schindler lets them have it.

The world Schindler sees is falling apart, even as the GNP rockets skyward and a whole new class of hipster financiers with coke up their noses become the inheritors of the tradition of puritan thrift and responsibility. The cities descend into the jungle, the young are abandoned and re-tooled into prime markets for neon goodies, learning is tested by focus groups, the priests are groping the acolytes, hospital emergency rooms look like battlefield hospitals. Third-world diseases run rampant in the ghettoes of the wealthiest and most technically proficient nation the world, and everywhere one listens, there are lies, lies, lies.

There was time when the Academy fostered a rough gang of lie killers and sometimes truth-tellers, too. But, try as he can, Schindler cannot find them. Instead, university faculty seem to have shrunk into themselves and their specialties and to have turned their backs on the world and its problems. Already fat with comfy salaries, perks, and the blessing of lifetime employment no matter what, university faculty have punked out on their own best traditions.

Jeremiah turns his angry, wrathful spirit on the house which spurned him. The book becomes harsher, less accommodating, a bitter truth-telling. What were once neatly etched paragraphs, lining up texts, their analysis, and subtle parsing - these paragraphs begin to explode, evolve, transform, mutate. They begin to hum with anger, sarcasm, spite, and a strange kind of joy of liberation, as Schindler gets down below the foundations.

One has to admire the tenacity of this Jeremiah. So many of his generation of scholar/teachers have sunk into gloom and irony - a shrug: what can one do? But Schindler does not go quietly. He knows what he wants to do. He wants to take his disappointments and make an advantage of them. Won't invite me into the happy world of a university department, a tenure track, the lifetime imprisonment of a career? Good. I will use this catastrophe in my life to my own advantage. I will teach as a noble calling, not a job. I will write the truth, without remorse or apology. My judge will be God and not a tenure committee.

And this is Schindler. He arrives at his university at 5:55 in the morning, long before the great Teacher/Scholars. He works with his students, spending hard half-hours with them, pushing them to do their best, easing them into a respect for the classics (Locke, Marx, Wordsworth, Darwin, Freud) and a growing respect for themselves. The modern university is not supposed to help the young to maturity and reason; like all else in modern society, it is supposed to distract them from the life of the mind. Well, Schindler isn't having any. He is persistent. His smile and pleasantries mask an iron courage, a will to do what is right and noble and just, to affirm himself before the highest bar of judgement - the Good, True, and Beautiful.

His book, too, is the real thing, once one learns how to read it. Perhaps this fictional account shines some light into the book and its passions. I should say, I think I know all this about the book and Schindler because we have, in many respects, traveled the same path. I have drawn my battle line with the times in building academic programs which persist in the real thing. I am in love with the idea of the Academy, so I, too, hate what it has become. I come to work at 7:30 a.m. and stay all day to do what I can. Several revolutions which should have happened and which were necessary for the emergence of our humanity have not happened. Still, this pre-history is not yet over. There is still work to do for men and women who keep their vision clear and occasionally lose their tempers but not their wits.

Intellectual Heritage Program
Temple University

Afterword

David Lamb

I was very pleased to accept the invitation to write an afterword for Ronald Schindler's excellent book. This book is not merely about the central theory of the Frankfurt School; it is in many ways an intellectual biography of considerable stature. I share many of the attitudes expressed here concerning the role of philosophy in social policy and the role of the university philosopher. Many of my generation were attracted to philosophy during the 1960s in the belief that it offered a mode of discourse critical of both its own positivist background and the social values expressed by the Cold War protagonists. Democratic capitalism appeared to be morally bankrupt, the wealthy nations upheld Third World tyrants whilst Soviet socialism was a caricature of the values it proclaimed. The New Left of the 1960s adopted a critical standpoint but its sectarianism and surrealism rendered it ineffective. Within a decade intellectuals of the New Left became the administrators and bureaucrats of higher education.

The foremost tradition of critical theory in the post-war period was the Frankfurt School. This is Schindler's starting point. He addresses the work of Adorno and Horkheimer, then Habermas and his followers. Yet the Frankfurt School today, argues Schindler, exemplifies the plight of the modern intellectual; removed from political engagement, involved in discursive form without content, postulating critique without risk. Despite the radical critique of modern capitalism the Frankfurt School has not avoided the tendency for its own theories and critiques to become commodities in the university market place. There is a need, says Schindler, to provide new conceptual tools which are essential for the viability of any radical left movement. Trapped within the institutions and bureaucracies of higher education, exponents of Frankfurt critical theory are unable to do this.

But what can dialectical thought and the dialectical method accomplish? There is a great deal of misery and frustration in the world. Both national and global mismanagement are obvious and discontent is widespread. But how can this discontent be articulated, and how can radical change be effected? Schindler's book is an attempt to answer this question. There is no easy way, and he does not avoid the difficult task of reconstructing critical theory from its origins. He traces the origin of dialectical critical though in Hegel's *Phenomenology* and Marx's Hegelian legacy. He reconstructs Marx's historical materialism and takes the reader through the development of Habermas's critical programme. Whatever the verdict may be on Schindler's criticisms, no one can fail to be impressed by his erudition and appreciation of great thinkers of our epoch. But he does not pull any punches. Whilst Habermas clearly emerges as the best exponent of critical theory to date, Schindler reminds us of its failure to predict the implosion of Soviet socialism. It is necessary, argues Schindler, to go beyond the limitations of Habermas's theory; to this end he develops the method of phenomenological hermeneutics.

Schindler has also provided a critique of the modern philosopher. In recent years there has been a healthy flowering of diverse philosophical fields, embracing analytic philosophy, applied philosophy, hermeneutics, continental philosophy, and the revival of many old traditions - all of which was unthinkable thirty years ago when the universities of England and the US appeared to be committed to linguistic analysis of one form or another. Yet in another sense this diversification has revealed its downside whilst specialising in their own subfields many philosophers find it difficult to converse with each other; teaching and administration commitments occupy so much time that very few tenured philosophers have opportunity to conduct research beyond their narrow subfield. There is no arena for a more universal critique; we are told of an information revolution that will transform our attitudes and life-styles, with knowledge disseminated world-wide at the speed of light, yet its critical impact is negligible, its content banality, bureaucracy, and paperwork.

Schindler is not merely critical of the modern intellectual; he is angry, and this anger is manifest throughout the whole book, exploding in the Appendix where his wrath is directed at the political establishment. He is angry over the waste of a generation of intellectuals and teachers for whom modern academia has no place; he is angry with the cosmetic programmes of affirmative action and political correctness, which occupy the attention of the radical left but do no real service for equality and the fight against racism. Schindler belongs to that growing number of intellectuals which he describes as 'Gypsy Scholars', the untenured university teachers, underpaid, undervalued, existing on short-term contracts with little hope of future security. I have read his book. I know how he feels. I have been there myself. But Schindler is not merely angry; he has a constructive project. His involvement with the Intellectual Heritage

Program at Temple University, North Philadelphia is an example of an alternative vision for higher education, a fusion of theory and practical issues, breaking down barriers between the academy and the community. Schindler is not alone; other 'Gypsy Scholars' are searching for truths and developing teaching programmes within and yet outside the traditional universities. Survival is hard, but outside the academy is a restless population with a hunger for truth.

Bibliography

Ackroyd, Peter (1996), *Blake: A Biography*, Knopf: New York.
Adams, Robert M. (1994), Review of *The Western Canon: The Books and School of the Ages* by Harold Bloom, *New York Review of Books*, Vol. 41, No. 19, Nov. 17, pp. 4-6.
Adorno, Theodor W. (1967), *Prisms*, trans. Knut Tarnowski and Frederic Will, foreword Trent Schroyer, Northwestern University Press: Evanston, Ill.
Adorno, Theodor W. (1973a), *The Jargon of Authenticity*, trans. Knut Tarnowski and Frederic Will, foreword by Trent Schroyer, Northwestern University Press: Evanston, Ill.
Adorno, Theodor W. (1973b), *Negative Dialectics*, trans. E. B. Ashton, Seabury: New York, reprint 1995.
Adorno, Theodor W. (1974), *Minima Moralia: Reflections from Damaged Life*, trans. E.F.N. Jephcott, New Left Books: London.
Adorno, Theodor W. (1983), *Against Epistemology: A Metacritique - Studies in Husserl and the Phenomenological Antinomies*, trans. Willis Domingo, MIT Press: Cambridge, Mass.
Adorno, Theodor W. et al. (1950), *The Authoritarian Personality: Studies in Prejudice*, ed. Max Horkheimer and Samuel Lowerman, American Jewish Committee Publication 3, Norton: New York.
Adorno, Theodor W. et al. (1976), *The Positivist Dispute in German Sociology*, trans. Glyn Adey and David Frisby, Heinemann: London.
Ahlers, Rolf (1975), 'How Critical Is Critical Theory? Reflections on Jürgen Habermas', *Cultural Hermeneutics*, Vol. 3, No. 2, pp. 119-36.
Allport, Gordon W. (1955), *Becoming: Basic Considerations for a Psychology of Personality*, Yale University Press: New Haven, Conn.

Allport, Gordon W. (1958), *The Nature of Prejudice*, Doubleday: Garden City, N.Y.
Althusser, Louis (1969), *For Marx*, trans. Ben Brewster, Random House: New York; Penguin: London.
Althusser, Louis (1971), *Lenin and Philosophy and Other Essays*, trans. Ben Brewster, New Left Books: London.
Althusser, Louis (1972), *Politics and History: Montesquieu, Rousseau, Hegel, and Marx*, trans. Ben Brewster, New Left Books: London.
Althusser, Louis (1992), *The Future Lasts Forever: A Memoir*, ed. Olivier Corpet and Yann Moulier Boutang, trans. Richard Veasey, New Press: New York.
Althusser, Louis and Balibar, Etienne (1970), *Reading Capital*, trans. Ben Brewster, Pantheon: New York.
Anderson, Perry (1974a), *Lineages of the Absolutist State*, New Left Books: London; Humanities Press: Atlantic Highlands, N.J.
Anderson, Perry (1974b), *Passages from Antiquity to Feudalism*, New Left Books: London; Humanities Press: Atlantic Highlands, N.J.
Anderson, Perry (1976), *Considerations on Western Marxism*, New Left Books: London.
Applebome, Peter (1995), 'John Hope Franklin, the Last Integrationist: On his eightieth birthday, the distinguished historian reflects on the circular sweep of race relations in America', *New York Times Magazine*, April 23, Sec. 6.
Applebome, Peter (1996), 'Can Harvard's Powerhouse Alter the Course of Black Studies? In the mix: celebrity and substance', *New York Times Education Life*, Nov. 3, Sec. 4A, pp. 24-8.
Arato, Andrew and Gebhardt, Elke, eds. (1978), *The Essential Frankfurt School Reader*, intro. Paul Piccone, Urizen: New York.
Arendt, Hannah (1959), *The Human Condition*, Doubleday: Garden City, N.Y.
Arendt, Hannah (1963), *Eichmann in Jerusalem: A Report on the Banality of Evil*, Penguin: New York.
Arendt, Hannah (1965), *On Revolution*, Viking: New York.
Arendt, Hannah (1973), *The Origins of Totalitarianism*, new ed. with added prefaces, Harcourt Brace Jovanovich: New York.
Arendt, Hannah (1977-78), *The Life of the Mind*, Vol. I, *Thinking*, Vol. II, *Willing*, Harcourt Brace: New York.
Arendt, Hannah (1978), *The Jew as Pariah: Jewish Identity and Politics in the Modern Age*, Grove Press: New York.
Arendt, Hannah (1979), *Hannah Arendt: The Recovery of the Public World*, ed. Melvyn A. Hill, St. Martin's: New York.
Arendt, Hannah (1994), *Essays in Understanding, 1930-1954*, ed. Jerome Kohn,

Harcourt Brace: New York.

Arendt, Hannah and Jaspers, Karl (1995), *Correspondence: 1926-1969*, ed. Lotte Kohler and Hans Saner, trans. Robert Kimber and Rita Kimber, Harcourt Brace: San Diego, Calif.

Arendt, Hannah and McCarthy, Mary (1995), *Between Friends: The Correspondence of Hannah Arendt and Mary McCarthy, 1949-1975*, ed. and intro. Carol Brightman, Harcourt Brace: New York.

Arvon, Henry (1973), *Marxist Esthetics*, trans. Helen R. Lane, intro. Fredric Jameson, Cornell University Press: Ithaca, N.Y.

Ash, Timothy Garton (1995), 'Prague: Intellectuals and Politicians', *New York Review of Books*, Vol. 42, No. 1, Jan. 12.

Axelros, Kostas (1976), *Alienation, Praxis, and Techné in the Thought of Karl Marx*, trans. Ronald Bruzina, University of Texas Press: Austin.

Bachelard, Gaston (1968), *The Philosophy of No: A Philosophy of the Scientific Mind*, trans. G. C. Waterson, Orion: New York

Bailyn, Bernard, ed. (1993), *The Debate on the Constitution: Federalist and Antifederalist Speeches, Articles, and Letters During the Struggle over Ratification, Part One, September 1787 to February 1788, Part Two, January to August 1788*, Library of America: New York.

Baran, Paul A. and Sweezy, Paul M. (1966), *Monopoly Capital: An Essay on the American Economic and Social Order*, Monthly Review Press: New York.

Barbour, Ian G. (1974), *Myths, Models, and Paradigms: A Comparative Study in Science and Religion*, Harper and Row: New York.

Barlett, Donald L. and Steele, James B. (1996), *America: Who Stole the Dream?* Andrews and McNeel: Kansas City, Mo.

Barthes, Roland (1967), *Writing Degree Zero and Elements of Semiology*, trans. Annette Lavers and Colin Smith, Beacon Press: Boston.

Barthes, Roland (1972), *Mythologies*, trans. Annette Lavers, Hill and Wang: New York.

Bateson, Gregory (1972), *Steps to an Ecology of Mind*, pref. Mark Engel, Ballantine: New York.

Baudrillard, Jean (1975), *The Mirror of Production*, trans. Mark Poster, Telos Press: St. Louis.

Becker, Ernest (1967), *Beyond Alienation: A Philosophy of Education for the Crisis of Democracy*, George Braziller: New York.

Bell, Daniel (1976), *The Cultural Contradictions of Capitalism*, Basic Books: New York.

Bell, Quentin (1995), *Bloomsbury Recalled*, Columbia University Press: New York.

Benhabib, Seyla and Dallmayr, Fred (1990), *The Communicative Ethics*

Controversy, MIT Press: Cambridge, Mass.

Benjamin, Walter (1969), *Illuminations*, trans. Harry Zohn, ed. Hannah Arendt, Schocken: New York.

Benjamin, Walter (1973), *Understanding Brecht*, trans. Anna Bostock, intro. Stanley Mitchell, New Left Books: London.

Bennett, William J., ed. (1993), *The Book of Virtues: A Treasury of Great Moral Stories*, Simon and Schuster: New York.

Berger, Peter L. and Luckmann, Thomas (1966), *The Social Construction of Reality: A Treatise in the Sociology of Knowledge*, Anchor: New York.

Bernstein, Richard J. (1971), *Praxis and Action: Contemporary Philosophies of Human Activity*, University of Pennsylvania Press: Philadelphia.

Bernstein, Richard J. (1976), *The Restructuring of Social and Political Theory*, Harcourt Brace Jovanovich: New York and London.

Bernstein, Richard J. (1983), *Beyond Objectivism and Relativism: Science, Hermeneutics, and Praxis*, University of Pennsylvania Press: Philadelphia.

Bernstein, Richard J. (1991), *The New Constellation: The Ethical-Political Horizons of Modernity/Postmodernity*, MIT Press: Cambridge, Mass.

Berra, Tim M. (1990), *Evolution and the Myth of Creationism: A Basic Guide to the Facts in the Evolution Debate*, Stanford University Press: Stanford, Calif.

Bettelheim, Bruno (1979), *Surviving, and Other Essays*, Knopf: New York.

Bhaskar, Roy (1975), *A Realist Theory of Science*, Leeds Books: Leeds.

Binswanger, Ludwig (1973), *Being-in-the-World: Selected Papers of Ludwig Binswanger*, ed. Jacob Needleman, Basic Books: New York.

Black, Max (1962), *Models and Metaphors: Studies in Language and Philosophy*, Cornell University Press: Ithaca, N.Y.

Blackburn, Robin, ed. (1973), *Ideology in Social Science: Readings in Critical Social Theory*, Vintage: New York.

Blake, William (1995), *Selected Poems*, intro. Christopher Moore, Gramercy: New York.

Bleicher, Josef (1980), *Contemporary Hermeneutics: Hermeneutics as Method, Philosophy, and Critique*, Routledge: London.

Blitz, Mark (1981), *Heidegger's* Being and Time *and the Possibility of Political Philosophy*, Cornell University Press: Ithaca, N.Y.

Bloch, Ernst (1971), *On Karl Marx*, Herder and Herder: New York.

Block, Robert (1995), 'The Madness of General Mladić, *New York Review of Books*, Vol. 42, No. 15, Oct. 5, pp. 7-9.

Bloom, Allan (1987), *The Closing of the American Mind: How Higher Education Has Failed Democracy and Impoverished the Souls of Today's Students*, Simon and Schuster: New York.

Bloom, Harold (1992), *The American Religion: The Emergence of the Post-Christian Nation*, Simon and Schuster: New York.

Bloom, Harold (1994), *The Western Canon: The Books and School of the Ages*, Harcourt Brace Jovanovich: New York.

Bochénski, J. M. (1963), *Soviet Russian Dialectical Materialism (Diamat)*, trans. Nicolas Sollohub, Reidel: Dordrecht.

Bochénski, J. M. et al., eds. (1972), *Guide to Marxist Philosophy: An Introductory Bibliography*, Swallow Press: Chicago.

Böhm-Bawerk, Eugen Von and Hilferding, Rudolf (1975), *Karl Marx and the Close of His System and Böhm-Bawerk's Criticism of Marx*, 'Appendix: On the Correction of Marx's Fundamental Theoretical construction in the Third Volume of Capital' by Ladislaus von Bortkiewisz, trans. Paul M. Sweezy, Merlin Press: London.

Bolough, Roslyn Wallach (1979), *Dialectical Phenomenology: Marx's Method*, Routledge: Boston.

Boorstin, Daniel J. (1992), *The Creators: A History of Heroes of the Imagination*, Random House: New York.

Bork, Robert H. (1996), *Slouching Towards Gomorrah: Modern Liberalism and American Decline*, Regan/HarperCollins: New York.

Borneman, Ernest, ed. (1976), *The Psychoanalysis of Money*, Urizen: New York.

Boulding, Kenneth E. (1970), *A Primer on Social Dynamics: History as Dialectics and Development*, Free Press: New York.

Bowen, Catherine Drinker (1986), *Miracle at Philadelphia: The Story of the Constitutional Convention, May to September, 1787*, intro. Henry Steele Commager, Little, Brown: Boston.

Bowles, Samuel and Gintis, Herbert (1976), *Schooling in Capitalist America: Educational Reform and the Contradictions of Economic Life*, Basic Books: New York.

Braudel, Fernand (1994), *A History of Civilizations*, trans. Richard Mayne, Allen Lane/Penguin: New York.

Braverman, Harry (1974), *Labor and Monopoly Capital: The Degradation of Work in the Twentieth Century*, foreword Paul M. Sweezy, Monthly Review Press: London.

Breines, Paul, ed. (1972), *Critical Interruptions: New Left Perspectives on Herbert Marcuse*, Herder and Herder: New York.

Brontë, Charlotte and Brontë, Emily (1995), *The Complete Novels*, Gramercy: New York.

Brown, Bruce (1973), *Marx, Freud, and the Critique of Everyday Life: Toward a Permanent Cultural Revolution*, Monthly Review Press: New York.

Brown, Norman O. (1969), *Life Against Death: The Psychoanalytic Meaning*

of History, Wesleyan University Press: Middletown, Conn.
Brown, P. L. (1975), 'Epistemology and Method: Althusser, Foucault, Derrida', *Cultural Hermeneutics*, Vol. 3, No. 2, August, pp. 147-63.
Buber, Martin (1970), *I and Thou*, trans. Walter Kaufmann, Scribner: New York.
Buck-Morss, Susan F. (1977), 'T. W. Adorno and the Dilemma of Bourgeois Philosophy', *Salmagundi*, No. 36, Winter, pp. 76-98.
Bullock, Alan (1991), *Hitler and Stalin: Parallel Lives*, Knopf: New York.
Burleigh, Michael (1994), *Death and Deliverance: 'Euthanasia' in Germany, 1900-1945*, Cambridge University Press: Cambridge.
Butler, Judith (1990), *Gender Trouble: Feminism and the Subversion of Identity*, Routledge: New York.
Campbell, Norman (1952), *What Is Science?* Dover: New York.
Carver, Terrell, ed. (1991), *The Cambridge Companion to Marx*, Cambridge University Press: New York.
Cassirer, Ernst (1946), *The Myth of the State*, foreword Charles W. Hendel, Yale University Press: New Haven, Conn.
Chappell, Vere, ed. (1994), *The Cambridge Companion to Locke*, Cambridge University Press: New York.
Childers, Joseph and Hentzi, Gary, eds. (1995), *The Columbia Dictionary of Modern Literary and Cultural Criticism*, Columbia University Press: New York.
Chomsky, Noam (1977), *Language and Responsibility: Based on Conversations with Mitson Ranat*, Pantheon: New York.
Churchman, C. West (1948), *Theory of Experimental Inference*, Macmillan: New York.
Clecak, Peter (1973), *Radical Paradoxes: Dilemmas of the American Left, 1945-1970*, Harper and Row: New York.
Cohn, Norman (1996), *Warrant for Genocide: The Myth of the Jewish World Conspiracy and the Protocols of the Elders of Zion*, Serif: London.
Coleman, Fred (1996), *The Decline and Fall of the Soviet Empire: Forty Years That Shook the World, from Stalin to Yeltsin*, St. Martin's: New York.
Colletti, Lucio (1972), *From Rousseau to Lenin: Studies in Ideology and Society*, trans. John Merrington and Judith White, New Left Books: London.
Colletti, Lucio (1973), *Marxism and Hegel*, trans. Lawrence Garner, New Left Books: London.
Connerton, Paul, ed. (1976), *Critical Sociology: Selected Readings*, Penguin: New York.
Cook, Daniel J. (1973), *Language in the Philosophy of Hegel*, Mouton: The Hague.
Cowell, Alan (1995), 'German Scholar Unmasked as Former SS Officer', *New*

York Times, June 1, p. A3.
Coyle, Martin, Garside, Peter, Kelsall, Malcolm, and Peck, John, eds. (1991), *Encyclopedia of Literature and Criticism*, Routledge: Detroit.
Cropsey, Charles (1977), *Political Philosophy and the Issues of Politics*, University of Chicago Press: Chicago.
Cumming, Robert Denoon, ed. (1965), *The Philosophy of Jean-Paul Sartre*, Modern Library: New York.
Curran, Stuart, ed. (1993), *The Cambridge Companion to British Romanticism*, Cambridge University Press: New York.
Dallmayr, Fred R. (1976), 'Phenomenology and Critical Theory: Adorno', *Cultural Hermeneutics*, Vol. 4, No. 3, July, pp. 367-405.
Dallmayr, Fred and McCarthy, Thomas, eds. (1977), *Understanding and Social Inquiry*. Notre Dame University Press: Notre Dame, Ind.
Danto, Arthur C. (1975), *Jean-Paul Sartre*, Viking: New York.
Darwin, Charles (1975), *The Origin of Species*, intro. Philip Appleman, Norton: New York.
Darwin, Charles (1979), *Darwin*, 2nd ed., ed. Philip Appleman, Norton: New York.
Darwin, Charles (1996), *The Darwin Reader*, 2nd ed., ed. Mark Ridley, Norton: New York.
Dawidowicz, Lucy S. (1977), *The Jewish Presence: Essays on Identity and History*, Holt, Rinehart, and Winston: New York.
Dawkins, Richard (1996), *Climbing Mount Improbable*, Norton: New York.
De Cresigny, Anthony and Minogue, Kenneth, eds. (1975), *Contemporary Political Philosophers*, Dodd, Mead: New York.
DeGeorge, Richard T. and DeGeorge, Fernande M., eds. (1972), *The Structuralists: From Marx to Lévi-Strauss*, Doubleday Anchor: Garden City, N.Y.
Deleuze, Gilles and Guattari, Felix (1977), *Anti-Oedipus: Capitalism and Schizophrenia*, Viking: New York.
Demick, Barbara (1996), 'Scientology Throws Germany into a Panic: Politicians and others deem it a dangerous cult. Even Tom Cruise has come under scrutiny', *Philadelphia Inquirer*, August 9, pp. A1, A3.
Denby, David (1996), *Great Books: My Adventure with Homer, Rousseau, Woolf, and Other Indestructible Writers of the Western World*, Simon and Schuster: New York.
Dennett, Daniel C. (1995), *Darwin's Dangerous Idea: Evolution and the Meanings of Life*, Simon and Schuster: New York.
DeParle, Jason (1994), 'Daring Research or "Social Science Pornography"? Charles Murray: the incendiary conservative theorist sees America dividing into high- and low-I.Q. societies, largely for genetic reasons. Blacks,

poor whites and other scholars are likely to contest that fate', *New York Times Magazine*, Oct. 9, Sec. 6.

Derrida, Jacques (1994), *Specters of Marx: The State of the Debt, the Work of Mourning, and the New International*, trans. Peggy Kamus, intro. Bernd Magnus and Stephen Cullenberg, Routledge: New York.

Deutscher, Isaac (1971), *Marxism in Our Time*, ed. Tamara Deutscher, Ramparts Press: Berkeley, Calif.

Diagnostic and Statistical Manual of Mental Disorders (1994), 4th ed., American Psychiatric Association: New York.

Dickens, Charles (1982), *Four Complete Novels: Great Expectations, Hard Times, A Christmas Carol, A Tale of Two Cities*, Random House: New York.

Dinnage, Rosemary (1996), 'The Survivor', Review of *Bettelheim: A Life and a Legacy* by Nina Sutton, *New York Review of Books*, June 20, pp. 10-14.

Dobb, Maurice H. (1963), *Studies in the Development of Capitalism*, International Publishers: New York.

Dobb, Maurice H. (1973), *Theories of Value and Distribution Since Adam Smith: Ideology and Economic Theory*, Cambridge University Press: London.

Domhoff, G. William (1967), *Who Rules America?* Prentice-Hall: Englewood Cliffs, N.J.

Domhoff, G. William (1970), *The Higher Circles: The Governing Class in America*, Vintage: New York

Domhoff, G. William and Ballard, Hoyt B., eds. (1968), *C. Wright Mills and the Power Elite*, Beacon Press: Boston.

Donald, David Herbert (1995), *Lincoln*, Simon and Schuster: New York.

Douglass, Frederick (1942), *Douglass, Autobiographies: Narrative of the Life* [1845]; *My Bondage and My Freedom* [1855], *Life and Times* [1881], ed. Henry Louis Gates, Jr., Library of America: New York.

Drabble, Margaret, ed. (1995), *The Oxford Companion to English Literature*, rev. ed., Oxford University Press: New York.

Draper, Theodore (1996), *A Struggle for Power: The American Revolution*, Times/Random House: New York.

Dreifus, Claudia (1994), 'Chloe Wofford Talks About Toni Morrison: A year after winning the Nobel Prize, the author explains her dual identities, defends William Faulkner's racial politics, and champions a literature not written for white people', *New York Times Magazine*, Sept. 11, Sec. 6.

Dworkin, Ronald (1996), 'The Curse of American Politics', *New York Review of Books*, Oct. 17, pp. 19-24.

Eagleton, Terry (1976a), *Criticism and Ideology: A Study in Marxist Literary Theory*, New Left Books: London.

Eagleton, Terry (1976b), *Marxism and Literary Criticism*, University of California Press: Berkeley.
Edwards, Richard C., Reich, Michael, and Weiskopf, Thomas E., eds. (1972), *The Capitalist System: A Radical Analysis of American Society*, Prentice-Hall: Englewood Cliffs, N.J.
Elkins, Stanley and McKittrick, Eric (1993), *The Age of Federalism: The Early American Republic, 1788-1800*, Oxford University Press: New York.
Ellison, Ralph (1947), *Invisible Man*, Vintage International: New York.
Emmanuel, Arghiri (1972), *Unequal Exchange: A Study of the Imperialism of Trade*, trans. Brian Pearce, comments Charles Bettelheim, Monthly Review Press: New York.
Engels, Friedrich (1935), *Socialism: Utopianism and Scientific, with the Essay on 'the Mark'*, trans. Edward Aveling, International Publishers: New York.
Engels, Friedrich (1939), *Herr Eugen Dühring's Revolution in Science (Anti-Dühring)*, trans. Emile Burns, ed. Clemens P. Dutt, International Publishers: New York.
Engels, Friedrich (1940), *Dialectics of Nature*, trans. and ed. Clemens P. Dutt, pref. J.B.S. Haldane, International Publishers: New York.
Engels, Friedrich (1942a), 'Letter to Conrad Schmidt, 27 October, 1890', *Karl Marx and Frederick Engels: Selected Correspondence, 1846-1895*, trans. Dona Torr, International Publishers: New York, pp. 482-3.
Engels, Friedrich (1942b), 'Engels to J. Bloch, 21 September', *Karl Marx and Frederick Engels: Selected Correspondence, 1846-1895*, trans. Dona Torr, p. 476.
Engels, Friedrich (1942c), *The Origin of the Family, Private Property and the State: In the Light of the Researches of Lewis H. Morgan*, trans. Alan West, intro. Eleanor Burke Leacock, International Publishers: New York.
Engels, Friedrich and Marx, Karl (1969), *Germany: Revolution and Counter-Revolution*, ed. Eleanor Marx, International Publishers, New York.
Enzensberger, Hans Magnus (1974), *The Consciousness Industry: On Literature, Politics, and the Mind*, ed. Michael Roloff, Seabury: New York.
Erikson, Erik H. (1963), *Childhood and Society*, Norton: New York.
Erikson, Erik H. (1969), *Gandhi's Truth: On the Origins of Militant Nonviolence*, Norton: New York.
Essick, Robert N. (1994), *William Blake at the Huntington*, ed. Diana Murphy and Mark Greenberg, foreword Edward J. Nygren, Henry Abrams: San Marino, Calif.
Esterson, Aaron (1972), *The Leaves of Spring: A Study in the Dialectics of Madness*, Penguin: Harmondsworth.
Fanon, Frantz (1963), *The Wretched of the Earth*, trans. Constance Farrington,

pref. Jean-Paul Sartre, Grove Press: New York.
Fanon, Frantz (1967), *Black Skin, White Masks*, trans. Charles Lam Markmann, Grove Press: New York.
Farr, Judith, ed. (1996), *Emily Dickinson: A Collection of Critical Essays*, Prentice-Hall: Englewood Cliffs, N.J.
Febvre, Lucien and Martin, Henri-Jean (1976), *The Coming of the Book: The Impact of Printing, 1450-1800*, trans. David Gerard, ed. Geoffrey Howell-Smith and David Wootton, 'Manuscripta' by Marcel Thomas, New Left Books: London.
Feuerbach, Ludwig (1986), *Principles of the Philosophy of the Future*, trans. Manfred Vogel, intro. Thomas Wartenberg, Hackett: Indianapolis, Ind.
Feyerabend, Paul (1975), *Against Method: Outline of an Anarchistic Theory of Knowledge*, New Left Books: London.
Fichte, Johann Gottlieb (1970), *Fichte: 'Science of Knowledge' (Wissenschaftslehre), with the First and Second Introductions*, trans. and ed. Peter Heath and John Lachs, Appleton Century Crofts: New York.
Fichte, Johann Gottlieb (1987), *The Vocation of Man*, trans. Peter Preuss, Hackett: Indianapolis, Ind.
Fichte, Johann Gottlieb (1994), *Introduction to the Wissenschafstlehre and Other Writings, 1797-1800*, trans. and ed. Daniel Breazeale, Hackett: Indianapolis, Ind.
Figes, Orlando (1997), *A People's Tragedy: A History of the Russian Revolution*, Viking Penguin: New York.
Finkelman, Paul, ed. (1995), *His Soul Goes Marching On: Responses to John Brown and the Harpers Ferry Raid*, University of Virginia Press: Charlottesville.
Fischer, David Hackett (1994), *Paul Revere's Ride*, Oxford University Press: Oxford.
Fischer, George, ed. (1971) *The Revival of American Socialism: Selected Papers of the Socialist Scholars Conference*, Oxford University Press: New York and London.
Fodor, Nandor and Gaynor, Frank, eds. (1958), *Freud: Dictionary of Psychoanalysis*, pref. Theodor Reik, Fawcett: Greenwich, Conn.
Foucault, Michel (1971), *The Order of Things: An Archaeology of the Human Sciences*, Pantheon: New York.
Foucault, Michel (1972), *The Archaeology of Knowledge*, trans. A. M. Sheridan Smith, Tavistock: London.
Foucault, Michel (1977) *Language, Counter-Memory, Practice: Selected Essays and Interviews*, ed. Donald Brouchard, trans. Donald Brouchard and Sherry Simon, Cornell University Press: Ithaca, N.Y.
Frankel, Boris (1974), 'Habermas Talking: An Interview', *Theory and Society*,

Vol. 1, No. 1.
Frankfurt Institute of Social Research (1972), *Aspects of Sociology*, trans. John Viertel, pref. Max Horkheimer and Theodor W. Adorno, Beacon Press: Boston.
Frankl, Viktor (1962), *Man's Search for Meaning*, rev. ed., Simon and Schuster: New York.
Frankl, Viktor (1969), *The Will to Meaning: Foundations and Applications of Logotherapy*, New American Library: New York.
Frankl, Viktor (1978), *The Unheard Cry for Meaning: Psychotherapy and Humanism*, Simon and Schuster: New York.
Franklin, Benjamin (1986), *Benjamin Franklin's Autobiography: Authoritative Texts, Backgrounds, Criticism*, ed. J. A. Leo Lemay and P. M. Zall, Norton: New York.
Freire, Paolo (1970), *Pedagogy of the Oppressed*, trans. Myra Bergman Ramos, foreword Richard Shaull, Seabury: New York.
Freire, Paolo (1973), *Education for Critical Consciousness*, Seabury: New York.
Freud, Sigmund (1947), *Leonardo da Vinci: A Study in Psychosexuality*, trans. A. A. Brill, Vintage: New York.
Freud, Sigmund (1949), *An Outline of Psychoanalysis*, trans. James Strachey, Norton: New York.
Freud, Sigmund (1950), *Totem and Taboo: Some points of Agreement Between the Mental Lives of Savages and Neurotics*, trans. James Strachey, Norton: New York.
Freud, Sigmund (1956), *Delusion and Dream and Other Essays*, ed. Philip Roth, Beacon Press: Boston.
Freud, Sigmund (1959), *On Dreams*, trans. James Strachey, Norton: New York.
Freud, Sigmund (1959), *Group Psychology and the Analysis of the Ego*, trans. James Strachey, intro. Peter Gay, Norton: New York.
Freud, Sigmund (1959), *Inhibitions, Symptoms, and Anxiety*, trans. Alix Strachey, ed. James Strachey, intro. Peter Gay, Norton: New York.
Freud, Sigmund (1960a), *The Ego and the Id*, trans. Joan Riviere, ed. James Strachey, intro. Peter Gay, Norton: New York.
Freud, Sigmund (1960b), *Jokes and Their Relation to the Unconscious*, trans. and ed. James Strachey, intro. Peter Gay, Norton: New York.
Freud, Sigmund (1961a), *Five Lectures on Psycho-Analysis*, trans. and ed. James Strachey, intro. Peter Gay, Norton: New York.
Freud, Sigmund (1961b), *Civilization and Its Discontents*, trans. James Strachey, intro. Peter Gay, Norton: New York, 1961.
Freud, Sigmund (1961c), *Leonardo da Vinci and a Memory of His Childhood*, trans. Alan Tyson, ed. James Strachey, intro. Peter Gay, Norton: New York.

Freud, Sigmund (1962), *Three Essays on the Theory of Sexuality*, trans. James Strachey, intro. Steven Marcus, ed. note J. D. Sutherland, Basic Books: New York.

Freud, Sigmund (1965), *Introductory Lectures on Psycho-Analysis*, trans. James Strachey, intro. Peter Gay, Norton: New York.

Freud, Sigmund (1966a), *On the History of the Psycho-Analytic Movement*, trans. Joan Riviere, rev. and ed. James Strachey, intro. Peter Gay, Norton: New York.

Freud, Sigmund (1966b), *New Introductory Lectures on Psycho-Analysis*, trans. James Strachey, intro. Peter Gay, Norton: New York.

Freud, Sigmund (1967), *Moses and Monotheism*, trans. Katherine Jones, Vintage/Random House: New York.

Freud, Sigmund (1978), *The Question of Lay Analysis*, trans. and ed. James Strachey, intro. Peter Gay, Norton: New York.

Freud, Sigmund (1996), *The Interpretation of Dreams*, trans. A. A. Brill, Gramercy: New York.

Friedlander, Saul (1997), *Nazi Germany and the Jews*, Vol. 1, *The Years of Persecution, 1933-1939*, HarperCollins: New York.

Friedrich, Carl Joachim (1963), *The Philosophy of Law in Historical Perspective*, 2nd ed., University of Chicago Press: Chicago.

Fromm, Erich (1965), *Escape from Freedom*, Avon: New York.

Fromm, Erich (1966), *Marx's Concept of Man*, with a translation from *Marx's Economic and Philosophical Manuscripts* by T. B. Bottomore, Frederick Ungar: New York.

Fromm, Erich (1970), *The Crisis of Psychoanalysis*, Fawcett: Greenwich, Conn.

Fromm, Erich (1973), *The Anatomy of Human Destructiveness*, Holt, Rinehart, and Winston: New York.

Gabel, Joseph (1975), *False Consciousness: An Essay on Reification*, trans. Margaret A. Thompson with Kenneth A. Thompson, intro. Kenneth A. Thompson, Harper and Row: New York.

Gabel, Joseph (1976), 'Utopian and False Consciousness', *Telos*, Vol. 29, Fall.

Gadamer, Hans-Georg (1976), *Hegel's Dialectic: Five Hermeneutical Studies*, trans. P. Christopher Smith, Yale University Press: New Haven, Conn.

Gadamer, Hans-Georg (1989), *Truth and Method*, 2nd ed., trans. and ed. Garrett Barden and John Cumming, rev. Joel Weinsheimer and Donald G. Marshall, Crossroad: New York.

Gandhi, Mohandas K. (1956), *The Gandhi Reader: A Source Book of His Life and Writings*, ed. Homer A. Jack, Grove Weidenfeld: New York.

Garaudy, Roger (1967), *Karl Marx: The Evolution of His Thought*, trans. Nan Apotheker, International Publishers: New York.

Garaudy, Roger (1970), *The Crisis in Communism: The Turning-Point of*

Socialism, trans. Peter Ross and Betty Ross, Grove Press: New York.

Garrow, David J. (1994), 'Justice Souter Emerges: Once the stealth nominee, he has become an intellectual leader - and the Supreme Court has become politically unpredictable', *New York Times Magazine*, Sept. 25, Sec. 6.

Gay, Peter (1995), *The Bourgeois Experience, Victoria to Freud*, Vol. 4, *The Naked Heart*, Norton: New York.

Geller, Ernest (1994), 'The Last Marxists: Pretensions, Illusions and Achievements of the Frankfurt School', *Times Literary Supplement*, No. 4773, Sept. 23.

Gilbert, G. M. (1947), *Nuremberg Diary*, New American Library: New York.

Gilbert, Martin (1996), *The Boys: The Story of 732 Young Concentration Camp Survivors*, Henry Holt: New York.

Gill, Stephen (1989), *William Wordsworth: A Life*, Oxford University Press: Oxford.

Gillan, Garth Jackson (1976), 'Toward a Critical Conception of Semiotics', *Cultural Hermeneutics*, Vol. 3, No. 4, July, pp. 407-27.

Godelier, Maurice (1972), *Rationality and Irrationality in Economics*, trans. Brian Pearce, New Left Books: London.

Goldhagen, Daniel Jonah (1996), *Hitler's Willing Executioners: Ordinary Germans and the Holocaust*, Knopf: New York.

Goldmann, Lucien (1971), *Immanuel Kant*, trans. Robert Black, New Left Books, London.

Goldmann, Lucien (1973), *The Philosophy of the Enlightenment: The Christian Burgers and the Enlightenment*, trans. Henry Maas, MIT Press: Cambridge, Mass.

Goldmann, Lucien (1976), *Cultural Creation in Modern Society*, trans. Bart Grahl, intro. William Mayrl, Telos Press: St. Louis.

Goldmann, Lucien (1977), *Lukács and Heidegger: Towards a New Philosophy*, Routledge: London.

Goldschmidt, Tijs (1996), *Darwin's Dreampond: Drama in Lake Victoria*, trans. Sherry Marx-Macdonald, MIT Press: Cambridge, Mass.

Goodhart, C. B. (1996), 'Misunderstanding Yugoslavia', Letter, *London Review of Books*, Vol. 18, No. 1, June 6, p. 4.

Gorz, André (1973) *Socialism and Revolution*, trans. Norman Denny, Doubleday Anchor: Garden City, N.Y.

Gould, Stephen Jay (1995), *Dinosaur in a Haystack: Reflections in Natural History*, Harmony Books: New York.

Gouldner, Alvin W. (1970), *The Coming Crisis of Western Sociology*, Basic Books: New York.

Gouldner, Alvin W. (1973), *For Sociology: Renewal and Critique in Sociology*

Today, Basic Books: New York.

Gouldner, Alvin W. (1976), *The Dialectic of Ideology and Technology: The Origins, Grammar, and Future of Ideology*, Seabury: New York.

Grahl, Bart and Piccone, Paul, eds. (1973), *Towards a New Marxism: Proceedings of the First International Telos Conference, October 8-11, 1970, Waterloo, Ontario*, intro. Paul Piccone, Telos Press: St. Louis.

Gramsci, Antonio (1957), *The Modern Prince and Other Writings*, trans. Louis Marks, International Publishers: New York.

Gramsci, Antonio (1971), *Selections from the Prison Notebooks*, trans. Quintin Hoare and Geoffrey Nowell Smith, International Publishers: New York.

Greene, David (1950), *Greek Political Theory: The Image of Man in Thucydides and Plato*, University of Chicago Press: Chicago.

Greenfield, Liah (1992), *Nationalism: Five Roads to Modernity*, Harvard University Press: Cambridge, Mass.

Greenhouse, Linda (1995), 'By 5-4, Justices Cast Doubts on U.S. Programs That Give Preferences Based on Race', *New York Times*, June 13, pp. A1, D25.

Greenspan, Ezra, ed. (1995), *The Cambridge Companion to Walt Whitman*, Cambridge University Press: New York.

Guinier, Lani (1994), 'Who's Afraid of Lani Guinier? Here's what she thinks: The majority should rule, but even the minority sometimes gets a turn. What's so scary about that?' *New York Times Magazine*, Feb. 27, Sec. 6.

Gurwitsch, Aron (1966), *Studies in Phenomenology and Psychology*, Northwestern University Press: Evanston, Ill.

Gurwitsch, Aron (1974), *Phenomenology and the Theory of Science*, Northwestern University Press: Evanston, Ill.

Gutting, Gary, ed. (1994), *The Cambridge Companion to Foucault*, Cambridge University Press: New York.

Habermas, Jürgen (1970a), *Toward a Rational Society: Student Protest, Science, and Politics*, trans. Jeremy J. Shapiro, Beacon Press: Boston.

Habermas, Jurgen (1970b), 'Summation and Response', *Continuum*, Vol. 8, No. 1, Spring-Summer.

Habermas, Jürgen (1971), *Knowledge and Human Interests*, trans. Jeremy J. Shapiro, Beacon Press: Boston.

Habermas, Jürgen (1973), *Theory and Practice*, trans. John Viertel, Beacon Press: Boston.

Habermas, Jürgen (1975), *Legitimation Crisis*, trans. and intro. Thomas McCarthy, Beacon Press: Boston.

Habermas, Jürgen (1976), 'Communication and Emancipation', *On Critical Theory*, ed. John O'Neill, Seabury: New York.

Habermas, Jürgen (1979), *Communication and the Evolution of Society*, trans. Thomas McCarthy, Beacon Press: Boston.
Habermas, Jürgen (1983), *Philosophical-Political Profiles*, trans. Frederick G. Lawrence, MIT Press: Cambridge, Mass.
Habermas, Jürgen (1984), *The Theory of Communicative Action*, Vol. 1: *Reason and the Rationalization of Society*, Beacon Press: Boston.
Habermas, Jürgen (1986), *Autonomy and Solidarity: Interviews with Jürgen Habermas*, ed. and intro. Peter Dews, Verso: London and New York.
Habermas, Jürgen (1987a), *The Theory of Communicative Action*, Vol. 2: *Lifeworld and System: A Critique of Functionalist Reason*, Beacon Press: Boston.
Habermas, Jürgen (1987b), *The Theological Discourse of Modernity: Twelve Lectures*, trans. Frederick G. Lawrence, MIT Press: Cambridge, Mass.
Habermas, Jürgen (1988), *On the Logic of the Social Sciences*, trans. Shierry Weber Nicholsen and Jerry A. Stark, MIT Press: Cambridge, Mass.
Habermas, Jürgen (1989a), *The New Conservatives: Cultural Criticism and the Historians' Debate*, trans. Shierry Weber Nicholsen, MIT Press: Cambridge, Mass.
Habermas, Jürgen (1989b), *The Structural Transformation of the Public Sphere: An Inquiry into a Category of Bourgeois Society*, trans. Thomas Burger with Frederick Lawrence, MIT Press: Cambridge, Mass.
Habermas, Jürgen (1990), *Moral Consciousness and Communicative Action*, trans. Christian Lenhardt and Shierry Weber Nicholsen, intro. Thomas McCarthy, MIT Press: Cambridge, Mass.
Habermas, Jürgen (1992), *Postmetaphysical Thinking: Philosophical Essays*, trans. William Mark Hohengarten, MIT Press: Cambridge, Mass.
Habermas, Jürgen (1993), *Justification and Application: Remarks on Discourse Ethics*, trans. Ciaran P. Cronin, MIT Press: Cambridge, Mass.
Habermas, Jürgen (1994), *The Past as Future*, interview by Michael Haller, trans. Max Pensky, foreword Peter Hohendahl, University of Nebraska Press: Lincoln.
Habermas, Jürgen (1996), *Between Facts and Norms: Contributions to a Discourse Theory of Law and Democracy*, trans. William Rehg, MIT Press: Cambridge, Mass.
Habermas, Jürgen and Luhmann, Niklas (1971), *Theorie der Gesellschaft oder Sozialtechnologie*, Suhrkamp: Frankfurt am Main.
Halberstam, David (1993), *The Fifties*, Villard: New York.
Harrington, Michael (1976), *The Twilight of Capitalism*, Simon and Schuster: New York.
Harrington, Michael (1980), *Decade of Decision: The Crisis of the American System*, Simon and Schuster: New York.

Hart, James D. (1995), *The Oxford Companion to American Literature*, 6th ed., rev. Phillip W. Leininger, Oxford University Press: New York.

Hegel, Georg Wolfgang Friedrich (1929), *Hegel's 'Science of Logic'*, 2 vols., trans. W. H. Johnson and L. G. Struthers, intro. Viscount Haldane of Cloan, Allen and Unwin: London; Humanities Press: New York.

Hegel, Georg Wolfgang Friedrich, *Hegel: Selections*, ed. Jacob Loewenberg, Scribner: New York.

Hegel, Georg Wolfgang Friedrich (1956), *The Philosophy of History*, trans. J. Sibree, pref. Charles Hegel and J. Sibree, new intro. C. D. Friedrich, Dover: New York.

Hegel, Georg Wolfgang Friedrich (1964), *Hegel's Political Writings*, trans. T. M. Knox, intro. A. A. Pelczynski, Oxford University Press: Oxford.

Hegel, Georg Wolfgang Friedrich (1965), *Hegel: Texts and Commentary: Hegel's 'Preface' to His System in a New Translation with Commentary on Facing Pages, and 'Who Thinks Abstractly?'*, trans. and ed. Walter Kaufmann, Doubleday: Garden City, N.Y.

Hegel, Georg Wolfgang Friedrich (1967a), *Hegel's 'Philosophy of Right'*, trans. and foreword T. M. Knox, Oxford University Press: London.

Hegel, Georg Wolfgang Friedrich (1967b), *The Phenomenology of Mind*, trans. J. B. Baillie, Harper and Row: New York.

Hegel, Georg Wolfgang Friedrich (1970), *On Art, Religion, Philosophy: Introductory Lectures to the Realm of Absolute Spirit*, ed. J. Glenn Gray, Harper and Row: New York.

Hegel, Georg Wolfgang Friedrich (1971a), *Early Theological Writings*, trans. T. M. Knox with Richard Kroner, University of Pennsylvania Press: Philadelphia.

Hegel, Georg Wolfgang Friedrich (1971b), *Hegel's 'Philosophy of Mind': Being Part Three of the Encyclopaedia of the Philosophical Sciences*, trans. William Wallace; *Together with the 'Zusätze' in Boumann's Text (1845)*, trans. A. V. Miller, foreword J. N. Findlay, Oxford University Press: London.

Hegel, Georg Wolfgang Friedrich (1974), *Hegel's 'Lectures on the History of Philosophy'*, 3 vols., trans. E. D. Haldane and Frances H. Simson, Routledge: London, 1892; reprint Humanities Press: New York.

Hegel, Georg Wolfgang Friedrich (1975a), *Hegel's 'Logic': Being Part One of the Encyclopaedia of the Philosophical Sciences*, trans. William Wallace, Oxford University Press: London.

Hegel, Georg Wolfgang Friedrich (1975b), *Lectures on the Philosophy of World History. Introduction: Reason in History*, trans. H. B. Nisbet, intro. Duncan Forbes, Cambridge University Press: Cambridge.

Hegel, Georg Wolfgang Friedrich (1975c), *Natural Law: The Scientific Ways* of *Treating Natural Law, Its Place in Moral Philosophy, and Its Relation to the Positive Sciences of Law*, trans. John R. Silber, University of Pennsylvania Press: Philadelphia.

Hegel, Georg Wolfgang Friedrich (1977), *Phenomenology of Spirit* (1807), trans. A. V. Miller, foreword J. N. Findlay, Oxford University Press: Oxford and New York.

Hegel, Georg Wolfgang Friedrich (1988), *Introduction to* The Philosophy of History, *with an Appendix from* The Philosophy of Right, trans. Leo Rauch, Hackett: Indianapolis, Ind.

Hegel, Georg Wolfgang Friedrich (1991), *The Encyclopaedia of Logic*, Part I of the *Encyclopaedia of Philosophical Science with the Zusätze*, trans. and intro. T. F. Geraets, W. A. Suchting, and H. S. Harris, Hackett: Indianapolis, Ind.

Heidegger, Martin (1962), *Being and Time*, trans. John Macquarrie and Edward Robinson, Harper and Row: New York.

Heidegger, Martin (1982), *The Basic Problems of Phenomenology*, trans. and intro. Alfred Hofstadter, Indiana University Press: Bloomington.

Heilbrunn, Jacob and Michael Lind (1995), 'On Pat Robertson', *New York Review of Books*, Vol. 42, No. 7, April 20, pp. 67-71.

Heiss, Robert (1975), *Hegel, Kierkegaard, Marx: Three Great Phlosophers Whose Ideas Changed the Course of Civilization*, trans. E. B. Garside, Dell: New York.

Heller, Agnes (1975), 'Towards a Sociology of Knowledge of Everyday Life', *Cultural Hermeneutics*, Vol. 3, No. 1, May, pp. 7-18.

Herrnstein, Richard J. and Murray, Charles (1994), *The Bell Curve: Intelligence and Class Structure in American Life*, Free Press: New York.

Hobbes, Thomas (1958), *Leviathan: Parts One and Two*, 1651, intro. Herbert W. Schneider, Macmillan: New York, 1958.

Hobsbawm, Eric J. (1973), *Revolutionaries: Contemporary Essays*, Random House: New York.

Hobsbawm, Eric J. (1994), *The Age of Extremes: A History of the World, 1914-1991*, Pantheon: New York.

Hoffman, Rhonda (1994), 'Bringing *Schindler's List* to Life', *Jewish Times*, Vol. 19, No. 2, April 7, pp. 34-5.

Holmes, Steven A. (1995), 'As Affirmative Action Ebbs, a Sense of Uncertainty Rises', *New York Times*, July 6, pp. A1, A14.

Holz, Hans Heinz, Kofler, Leo, and Abendroth, Wolfgang (1975), *Conversations with Lukács*, ed. Theo Pinkus, MIT Press: Cambridge, Mass.

Horkheimer, Max (1972), *Critical Theory: Selected Essays*, trans. Matthew J. O'Connell et al., intro. Stanley Aronowitz, Herder and Herder: New York, 1972.

Horkheimer, Max (1974), *Critique of Instrumental Reason*, trans. Matthew J. O'Connell et al., Seabury: New York.

Horkheimer, Max and Adorno, Theodor W. (1995), *Dialectic of Enlightenment*, trans. John Cumming, Continuum: New York.

Howard, Dick (1972), *The Development of the Marxian Dialectic*, Southern Illinois University Press: Carbondale.

Howe, Irving, ed. (1976), *Essential Works of Socialism*, Yale University Press: New Haven, Conn.

Hughes, H. Stuart (1977), *Consciousness and Society: The Reorientation of European Social Thought, 1890-1930*, rev. ed., Vintage: New York.

Hughes, Robert (1993), *Culture of Complaint: The Fraying of America*, Oxford University Press: New York.

Husserl, Edmund (1962), *Ideas: General Introduction to Pure Phenomenology*, Collier: New York.

Husserl, Edmund (1970), *The Crisis of European Sciences and Transcendental Phenomenology*, intro. David Carr, Northwestern University Press: Evanston, Ill.

Hyppolite, Jean (1969), *Studies on Marx and Hegel*, trans. John O'Neill, Basic Books: New York.

Hyppolite, Jean (1974), *Genesis and Structure of Hegel's 'Phenomenology of Spirit'*, trans. Samuel Cherniak and John Heckmann, Northwestern University Press: Evanston, Ill.

Ihde, Don (1977), *Experimental Phenomenology: An Introduction*, Putnam: New York.

Ilyenkov, E. V. (1977), *Dialectical Logic: Essays on Its History and Theory*, Progress Publishers: Moscow.

Israel, Joachim (1971), *Alienation: From Marx to Modern Sociology, a Macrosociological Analysis*, Allyn and Bacon: Boston.

Jacoby, Russell (1975), *Social Amnesia: A Critique of Conformist Psychology from Adler to Laing*, intro. Christopher Lasch, Beacon Press: Boston.

Jaeger, Werner (1945), *Paideia: The Ideals of Greek Culture*, Vol. 1, *Archaic Greece: The Mind of Athens*, 2nd ed., Oxford University Press: New York.

Jameson, Fredric (1971), *Marxism and Form: Twentieth-Century Dialectical Theories of Literature*, Princeton University Press: Princeton, N.J.

Jameson, Fredric (1976), 'Ideology of the Text', *Salmagundi*, Nos. 31-32, Fall/Winter, pp. 204-46.

Jay, Martin (1973), *The Dialectical Imagination: A History of the Frankfurt School and the Institute of Social Research, 1923-1950*, foreword Max Horkheimer, Little, Brown: Boston.

Jay, Martin (1993), *Force Fields: Between Intellectual History and Cultural*

Critique, Routledge/Chapman and Hall: New York and London.
Joffe, Josef (1996), 'Goldhagen in Germany', *New York Review of Books*, Nov. 28, pp. 18-21.
Johnson, Frank (1975), 'Psychological Alienation: Isolation and Self-Estrangement', *Psychoanalytic Review*, Vol. 62, No. 3, Fall, pp. 369-405.
Johnson, Hugh (1993), *Pocket Encyclopedia of Wine, 1994*, Fireside: New York.
Jones, Ernest (1961), *The Life and Work of Sigmund Freud*, ed. and abr. Lionel Trilling and Steven Morris, Basic Books: New York.
Jung, Haw Yol, ed. (1972), *Existential Phenomenology and Political Theory*, Henry Regnery: Chicago.
Kafka, Franz (1930), *The Castle*, trans. Willa Muir and Edwin Muir, homage by Thomas Mann, Schocken: New York.
Kafka, Franz (1952), *Selected Stories of Franz Kafka*, intro. Philip Rahv, Modern Library/Random House: New York.
Kafka, Franz (1956), *The Trial*, trans. Willa Muir and Edwin Muir with E. M. Butler, Knopf, New York.
Kainz, Howard P. (1976), *Hegel's 'Phenomenology', Part I: Analysis and Commentary*, Studies in the Humanities No. 12, University of Alabama Press: University.
Kamenka, Eugene (1969), *Marxism and Ethics*, pref. W. P. Hudson, Macmillan: London; St. Martin's: New York.
Kant, Immanuel (1983), *Perpetual Peace and Other Essays*, trans. Ted Humphry, Hackett: Indianapolis, Ind.
Kant, Immanuel (1990), *Critique of Pure Reason*, trans. J. M. D. Meiklejohn, Prometheus Books: Buffalo, N.Y.
Kaplan, Morton (1971), *On Historical and Political Knowing: An Inquiry into Some Problems of Universal Law and Human Freedom*, University of Chicago Press: Chicago.
Karol, K. S. (1974), *The Second Chinese Revolution*, trans. Mervyn Jones, Jonathan Cape: London.
Kaufmann, Walter (1974), *Nietzsche: Philosopher, Psychologist, Antichrist*, 4th ed., Princeton University Press: Princeton, N.J.
Keane, John (1975), 'On Tools and Language: Habermas on Work and Interaction', *New German Critique*, Vol. 6, Fall.
Kendall, Walter (1975), *The Labour Movement in Europe*, Allen Lane: London.
Keneally, Thomas (1982), *Schindler's List*, Penguin: New York.
Keniston, Kenneth (1965), *The Uncommitted: Alienated Youth in American Society*, Delta: New York.
Kerlinger, Fred N. (1973), *Foundations of Behavioral Research*, 2nd ed., Holt Rinehart: New York.

Kettler, David (1975), 'Political Theory, Ideology, Sociology: The Question of Karl Mannheim', *Cultural Hermeneutics*, Vol. 3, No. 1, May, pp. 69-80.

Kierkegaard, Søren (1954), *Fear and Trembling and The Sickness unto Death*, trans. Walter Lowrie, Princeton University Press: Princeton, N.J.

Kissinger, Henry (1994), *Diplomacy*, Simon and Schuster: New York.

Koch, Sigmund (1981), 'The Nature and Limits of Psychological Knowledge: Lessons of a Century qua "Science"', *American Psychologist*, Vol. 36, No. 5, March, pp. 257-70.

Kockelmans, Joseph J. and Kisiel, Theodore (1970), *Phenomenology and the Natural Sciences*, Northwestern University Press: Evanston, Ill.

Kohlberg, Lawrence (1981), *The Philosophy of Moral Development*, Harper and Row: San Francisco.

Kojéve, Alexandre (1969), *Introduction to the Reading of Hegel: Lectures on the 'Phenomenology of Spirit'*, assembled Raymond Queneau, trans. James H. Nichols, Jr., ed. Allan Bloom, Basic Books: New York.

Kolakowski, Leszek (1968), *Toward a Marxist Humanism*, trans. James Zielonko Peel, Grove Press: New York.

Kolchin, Peter (1993), *American Slavery: 1619-1877*, consulting ed. Eric Foner, Hill and Wang: New York.

Korsch, Karl (1963), *Karl Marx*, Russell and Russell: New York.

Korsch, Karl (1970), *Marxism and Philosophy*, trans. Fred Halliday, New Left Books: New York.

Kracauer, Siegfried (1947), *From Caligari to Hitler: A Psychological History of the German Film*, Princeton University Press: Princeton, N.J.

Kracauer, Siegfried (1948), 'Psychiatry for Everything and Everybody: The present Vogue - and What Is Behind It', *Commentary*.

Krieger, Leonard (1957), *The German Idea of Freedom: History of a Political Tradition*, University of Chicago Press: Chicago.

Kuhn, Thomas S. (1970), *The Structure of Scientific Revolutions*, 2nd enlarged ed., University of Chicago Press: Chicago.

Lacan, Jacques (1977), *Ecrits: A Selection*, Norton: New York.

Laing, Ronald D. (1965), *The Divided Self: An Existential Study in Sanity and Madness*, Penguin: Harmondsworth.

Laing, Ronald D. (1967), *The Politics of Experience*, Ballantine: New York.

Lakatos, Imré and Musgrave, Alan, eds. (1970), *Criticism and the Growth of Knowledge*, Cambridge University Press: Cambridge.

Lana, Robert E. (1976), *Assumptions of Social Psychology*, Irvington: New York.

Landgrebe, Ludwig (1981), *The Phenomenology of Edmund Husserl*, Cornell University Press: Ithaca, N.Y.

Lang, Berel and Williams, Forrest, eds. (1972), *Marxism and Art: Writings in Aesthetics and Criticism*, David McKay: New York.
Lasch, Christopher (1995), *The Revolt of the Elites and the Betrayal of Democracy*, Norton: New York.
Lauer, Quentin (1958), *Phenomenology: Its Genesis and Prospect*, Fordham University Press: New York.
Lechte, John (1994), *Fifty Key Contemporary Thinkers: From Structuralism to Postmodernity*, Fordham University Press: New York.
Lecourt, Dominique (1975), *Marxism and Epistemology: Bachelard, Canquilhem, and Foucault*, trans. Ben Brewster, foreword to Part One Georges Canquilhem, New Left Books: London.
Lefebvre, Henri (1968), *Dialectical Materialism*, trans. John Sturrock, Jonathan Cape: London.
Lefebvre, Henri (1969), *The Explosion: Marxism and the French Revolution*, Monthly Review Press: New York.
Lefebvre, Henri (1971), *Everyday Life in the Modern World*, trans. Sasha Rabinovitch, Harper and Row: New York.
Lefkowitz, Mary (1996), *Not Out of Africa: How Afrocentrism Became an Excuse to Teach Myth as History*, Basic Books: New York.
Leiss, William (1976), *The Limits to Satisfaction: An Essay on the Problems of Needs and Commodities*, University of Toronto Press: Toronto.
Lemann, Nicholas (1995), 'Taking Affirmative Action Apart', *New York Times Magazine*, June 11, Sec. 6.
Lenin, Vladimir Ilyich (1972), *Collected Works*, Vol. 1, *Philosophical Notebooks*, trans. Clemens Dutt, ed. Steward Smith, Progress Publishers: Moscow.
Lenin, Vladimir Ilyich (1975), *The Lenin Anthology*, ed. Robert C. Tucker, Norton: New York.
Lentricchia, Frank and McLaughlin, Thomas, eds. (1990), *Critical Terms for Literary Study*, University of Chicago Press: Chicago.
Lerner, Michael P. (1973), *The New Socialist Revolution: An Introduction to Its Theory and Strategy*, Dell: New York.
Lichtheim, George (1973), *Collected Essays*, Viking: New York.
Lifshitz, Mikhail (1973), *The Philosophy of Art of Karl Marx*, trans. Ralph B. Winn, Pluto Press: London.
Lind, Michael (1995a), 'Reverend Robertson's Grand International Conspiracy Theory', Review of *The New World Order* by Pat Robertson, *New York Review of Books*, Vol. 42, No. 2, Feb. 2, pp. 21-25.
Lind, Michael (1995b), *The Next American Nation: The New Nationalism and the Fourth American Revolution*, Free Press: New York.
Lind, Michael (1996), *Up from Conservatism: Why the Right Is Wrong for*

America, Free Press: New York.
Lipset, Seymour Martin (1979), *The First New Nation: The United States in Historical and Comparative Perspective*, Norton: New York.
Litt, Edgar, ed. (1969), 'Education and Political Enlightenment in America', *The New Politics of American Policy*, ed. Litt, Holt, Rinehart, and Winston: New York.
Locke, John (1952), *The Second Treatise of Government*, ed. Thomas P. Peardon, Macmillan: New York.
Long, Priscilla, ed. (1969), *The New Left: A Collection of Essays*, intro. Staughton Lynd, Extending Horizons Books, P. Sargent: Boston.
Löwith, Karl (1967), *From Hegel to Nietzsche: The Revolution in Nineteenth-Century Philosophy*, trans. David E. Green, Doubleday: New York.
Löwith, Karl (1995), *Martin Heidegger and European Nihilism*, ed. Richard Wolin, trans. Gary Steiner, Columbia University Press: New York.
Luijpen, William A. (1960), *Existential Phenomenology*, Duquesne University Press: Pittsburgh.
Lukács, Georg (1970), *Lenin: A Study on the Unity of His Thought*, MIT Press: Cambridge, Mass.; New Left Books: London.
Lukács, Georg (1971), *History and Class Consciousness: Studies in Marxist Dialectics*, trans. Rodney Livingstone, MIT Press: Cambridge, Mass.
Lukács, Georg (1972), *Political Writings, 1919-1929: The Question of Parliamentarianism and Other Essays*, trans. Michael McColgan, ed. Rodney Livingstone, New Left Books: London.
Lukács, Georg (1973), *Marxism and Human Liberation: Essays on History, Culture, and Revolution*, ed. E. Jan Juan, Jr., Dell: New York.
Lukács, Georg (1975), *The Young Hegel: Studies in the Relations Between Dialectics and Economics*, trans. Rodney Livingstone, Merlin Press: London.
Lundberg, Ferdinand (1968), *The Rich and the Super-Rich: A Study in the Power of Money Today*, Bantam: New York.
Luttwak, Edward (1996), 'Buchanan Has It Right', *London Review of Books*, Vol. 18, No. 9, May 9, pp. 6-8.
Luxembourg, Rosa (1974), *Selected Political Writings*, trans. William D. Graf, ed. Robert Looker, Grove Press: New York.
Lyotard, Jean-François (1984), *The Postmodern Condition: A Report on Knowledge*, Theory and History of Literature, Vol. 10, trans. Geoff Bennington and Brian Massumi, foreword Fredric Jameson, University of Minnesota Press: Minneapolis.
Lyotard, Jean-François (1993), *Toward the Postmodern*, ed. Robert Harvey and Mark S. Roberts, Humanities Press: Atlantic Highlands, N.J.
Machiavelli, Niccolo (1995), *The Prince*, ed. and trans. David Wotton, Hackett:

Indianapolis, Ind.

MacPherson, C. B. (1974), *The Political Theory of Possessive Individualism*, Oxford University Press: New York.

Madison, James, Hamilton, Alexander, and Jay, John (1987), *The Federalist Papers*, ed. Isaac Kramnick, Penguin: New York.

Magner, Denise (1997), 'A "Tenured Radical" Takes Aim at the Inequities in Academe: Cary Nelson's book says graduate students are exploited and liberal professors are complicit', *Chronicle of Higher Education*, May 16, pp. A10-12.

Magnus, Bernd and Higgins, Kathleen, eds. (1996), *The Cambridge Companion to Nietzsche*, Cambridge University Press: New York.

Maitan, Livio (1976), *Party, Army and Masses in China: A Marxist Interpretation of the Cultural Revolution and Its Aftermath*, trans. Gregor Benton and Marie Colletti, New Left Books: London.

Malcolm X (1964), *The Autobiography of Malcolm X*, with Alex Haley, intro. M. S. Handler, Ballantine: New York.

Malia, Martin E. (1994), *The Soviet Tragedy: A History of Socialism in Russia, 1917-1991*, Free Press: New York.

Malthus, Thomas Robert (1976), *An Essay on the Principle of Population*, ed. Philip Appleman, Norton: New York.

Mandel, Ernest (1970), *An Introduction to Marxist Economic Theory*, intro. George Novack, Pathfinder Press: New York.

Mandel, Ernest (1975), *Late Capitalism*, trans. Joris DeBres, New Left Books: London.

Mannheim, Karl (1936), *Ideology and Utopia: An Introduction to the Sociology of Knowledge*, trans. Louis Wirth and Edward Shils, Harcourt, Brace and World: New York.

Mannheim, Karl (1993), 'The Problem of Knowledge', *From Karl Mannheim*, ed. Kurt H. Wolff, intro. Volker Meja and David Kettler, Transaction Books: New Brunswick, N.J.

Marcuse, Herbert (1960), *Reason and Revolution: Hegel and the Rise of Social Theory*, with 'A Note on Dialectic', Beacon Press: Boston.

Marcuse, Herbert (1964), *One-Dimensional Man: Studies in the Ideology of Advanced Industrial Society*, Beacon Press: Boston.

Marcuse, Herbert (1966), *Eros and Civilization: A Philosophical Inquiry into Freud*, rev. ed., Beacon Press: Boston.

Marcuse, Herbert (1968), *Negations: Essays in Critical Theory*, trans. Jeremy J. Shapiro, Beacon Press: Boston.

Marcuse, Herbert (1972a), *Counterrevolution and Revolt*, Beacon Press: Boston.

Marcuse, Herbert (1972b), *Studies in Critical Philosophy*, trans. Joris DeBres, New Left Books: London.

Marković, Mihailo (1974a), *The Contemporary Marx: Essays on Humanist Communism*, intro. and foreword Ken Coates, European Socialist Thought Series 3, Spokesman Books: Nottingham.

Marković, Mihailo (1974b), *From Affluence to Praxis: Philosophy and Social Criticism*, foreword Erich Fromm, Ann Arbor Paperbacks, University of Michigan Press: Ann Arbor.

Marković, Mihailo (1976), Report, conference on 'Dynamics of Growth in a Finite World', Philadelphia, Nov. 20.

Marković, Mihailo (1982), *Democratic Socialism*, St. Martin's: New York.

Marković, Mihailo and Petrović, Gajo, eds. (1979), *Praxis: Yugoslav Essays on the Philosophy and Methodology of the Social Sciences*, Reidel: Boston.

Markus, György (1975), 'The Marxian Concept of Consciousness', *Cultural Hermeneutics*, Vol. 3, No. 1, May, pp. 19-28.

Marx, Karl (1947), *The German Ideology*, Parts I, III, ed. R. Pascal, International Publishers: New York, 1947.

Marx, Karl (1963) *The Poverty of Philosophy*, intro. Frederick Engels, International Publishers: New York.

Marx, Karl (1964a), 'Critique of Hegel's Dialectic', *Karl Marx: Early Writings*, trans. T. B. Bottomore, foreword Erich Fromm, McGraw-Hill: New York.

Marx, Karl (1964b), *Pre-Capitalist Economic Formations*, trans. Jack Cohen, ed. Eric J. Hobsbawm, International Publishers: New York.

Marx, Karl (1964c), *Class Struggles in France: 1848-1850*, intro. Frederick Engels, International Publishers: New York, 1964.

Marx, Karl (1967a), *Writings of the Young Marx on Philosophy and Society*, trans. Lloyd D. Easton and Kurt H. Guddat, Doubleday Anchor: Garden City, N.Y.

Marx, Karl (1967b), *Capital: A Critique of Political Economy*, Vol. 1, *The Process of Capitalist Production*, Vol. 2, *The Process of Circulation of Capital*, Vol. 3, *The Process of Capitalist Production as a Whole*, trans. Samuel Moore and Edward Aveling, ed. Frederick Engels, International Publishers: New York.

Marx, Karl (1970), *A Contribution to the Critique of Political Economy*, ed. Maurice Dobb, International Publishers: New York.

Marx, Karl (1971), *The Grundrisse*, trans. David McLellan, Harper Torchbooks, Harper and Row: New York.

Marx, Karl (1972a), 'Contribution to the Critique of Hegel's *Philosophy of Right*: Introduction', *The Marx-Engels Reader*, ed. Robert C. Tucker, Norton: New York.

Marx, Karl (1972b), *Economic and Philosophic Manuscripts of 1844*, trans.

Martin Milligan, *The Marx-Engels Reader*, ed. Robert C. Tucker, Norton: New York.

Marx, Karl (1972c), 'Theses on Feuerbach', *The Marx-Engels Reader*, ed. Robert C. Tucker, Norton: New York.

Marx, Karl (1973a), *Capital: A Critique of Political Economy*, Vol. 1, *The Process of Production*, trans. Martin Nicolaus, Vintage: New York.

Marx, Karl (1973), *Grundrisse: Foundations of the Critique of Political Economy*, trans. Martin Nicolaus, Random House Vintage: New York.

Marx, Karl (1975), *Early Writings*, trans. Rodney Livingstone and Gregor Benton, intr. Lucio Colletti, Random House Vintage: New York.

Marx, Karl and Engels, Frederick (1942), *Karl Marx and Frederick Engels: Selected Correspondence, 1846-1895*, trans. Dona Torr, International Publishers, New York.

Marx, Karl and Engels, Frederick (1948), *The Communist Manifesto*, International Publishers: New York.

Marx, Karl and Engels, Frederick (1964), *The German Ideology*, trans. R. Ryasanskaya, Progress Publishers: Moscow.

Marx, Karl and Engels, Frederick (1968), *Selected Works*, International Publishers: New York.

Marx, Karl and Engels, Frederick (1972), *The Marx-Engels Reader*, ed. Robert C. Tucker, Norton, New York.

Marx, Karl, Engels, Frederick, and Lenin, Vladimir Ilyich (1974), *On Historical Materialism: A Collection*, International Publishers: New York.

Marx, Werner (1975), *Hegel's 'Phenomenology of Spirit': Its Point and Purpose - A Commentary on the 'Preface' and 'Introduction'*, trans. Peter Heath, Harper and Row, New York.

Marx, Werner (1976), 'Habermas' Philosophical Conception of History', *Cultural Hermeneutics*, Vol. 3, No. 4, July, pp. 335-47.

Matlock, Jack F., Jr. (1996), 'The Struggle for the Kremlin', *New York Review of Books*, Vol. 48, No. 13, Aug. 8, pp. 28-34.

May, Rollo (1969), *Love and Will*, Dell: New York.

May, Rollo, ed. (1969), *Existential Psychology*, Random House: New York.

May, Rollo, Angel, Ernest, and Ellenberger, Henri F., eds. (1958), *Existence: A New Dimension in Psychiatry and Psychology*, Basic Books: New York.

Mazlish, Bruce (1976), *The Revolutionary Ascetic: Evolution of a Political Type*, Basic Books: New York.

McCarthy, Thomas (1978), *The Critical Theory of Jürgen Habermas*, MIT Press: Cambridge, Mass.

McGurrin, Martin (1981), Private communications, Philadelphia Office of Mental Health.

McMillen, Liz (1997), 'Judith Butler Revels in the Role of Troublemaker: She challenged ideas of gender and helped create queer theory; now she moves to defend free speech,' *Chronicle of Higher Education*, May 23, pp. A14-15.

McNamara, Robert S., with VanDeMark, Brian (1995), *In Retrospect: The Tragedy and Lessons of Vietnam*, Vintage: New York.

Meehan, Johanna, ed. (1995), *Feminists Read Habermas: Gendering the Subject of Discourse*, Routledge: New York.

Mehring, Franz (1962), *Karl Marx: The Story of His Life*, trans. Edward Fitzgerald, new intro. Max Shachtman, Ann Arbor Paperbacks, University of Michigan Press: Ann Arbor.

Mejo, Volker (1975), 'The Sociology of Knowledge and the Critique of Ideology', *Cultural Hermeneutics*, Vol. 3, No. 1, May, pp. 57-68.

Memmi, Albert (1975), *The Colonizer and the Colonized*, trans. Howard Greenfield, intro. Jean-Paul Sartre, Beacon Press: Boston.

Merleau-Ponty, Maurice (1962), *The Phenomenology of Perception*, trans. Colin Smith, Routledge: London.

Merleau-Ponty, Maurice (1963), *The Structure of Behavior*, Beacon Press: Boston.

Merleau-Ponty, Maurice (1968), *The Visible and the Invisible: Followed by Working Notes*, trans. Alphonso Lingis, ed. Claude Lefort, Northwestern University Press: Evanston, Ill.

Merleau-Ponty, Maurice (1969), *Humanism and Terror: An Essay on the Communist Problem*, trans. John O'Neill, Beacon Press: Boston.

Merleau-Ponty, Maurice (1973a), *Adventures of the Dialectic*, trans. Joseph Bien, Northwestern University Press: Evanston, Ill.

Merleau-Ponty, Maurice (1973), *Consciousness and the Acquisition of Language*, Northwestern University Press: Evanston, Ill.

Mészáros, István (1970), *Marx's Theory of Alienation*, Merlin Press: London.

Mészáros, István, ed. (1971), *Aspects of History and Class Consciousness*, note from Georg Lukács, Routledge: London.

Miliband, Ralph and Saville, John, eds. (1974), *The Socialist Register 1974*, Merlin Press: London.

Miller, James E., Jr. (1992), *Leaves of Grass: America's Lyric-Epic of Self and Democracy*, Twayne: New York.

Mills, C. Wright (1956), *The Power Elite*, Oxford University Press: London.

Minkowski, Eugene (1970), *Lived Time: Phenomenological and Psychopathological Studies*, trans. Nancy Metzel, Northwestern University Press: Evanston, Ill.

Misgeld, Dieter (1976), 'Critical Theory and Hermeneutics', *On Critical Theory*, ed. John O'Neill, Seabury: New York.

Morawski, Stefan (1974), *Inquiries into the Fundamentals of Aesthetics*, foreword Monroe Beardsley, MIT Press: Cambridge, Mass.
Morgan, Ted (1994), 'The Hidden Frenchman: Caught after decades of hiding, Paul Touvier presented a "Schindler defense" - that actually he was saving Jews. The story, and fate, of the last war criminal', *New York Times Magazine*, May 22, Sec. 6.
Morrison, Toni (1977), *The Song of Solomon*, Plume: New York.
Morrison, Toni (1982), *Sula*, Plume: New York.
Natanson, Maurice (1969), *Essays in Phenomenology*, Nijhoff: The Hague.
Natanson, Maurice, ed. (1973), *Phenomenology and the Social Sciences*, 2 vols., Northwestern University Press: Evanston, Ill.
Nee, Victor and Peck, James, eds. (1975), *China's Uninterrupted Revolution: From 1840 to the Present*, intro. Victor Nee and James Peck, Pantheon: New York.
Neu, Jerome, ed. (1991), *The Cambridge Companion to Freud*, Cambridge University Press: New York.
Newton, Isaac (1995), *Newton*, ed. I. Bernard Cohen and Richard S. Westfall, Norton: New York.
Niebuhr, Gustav (1995), 'Baptist Group Votes to Repent Stand on Slaves', *New York Times*, June 21, pp. A1, B7.
Nietzsche, Friedrich (1967), *The Will to Power*, trans. Walter Kaufmann and R. J. Hollingdale, ed. Walter Kaufmann, Vintage: New York.
Nietzsche, Friedrich (1968), *The Portable Nietzsche*, trans. Walter Kaufmann, Viking: New York.
Nietzsche, Friedrich (1977), *A Nietzsche Reader*, trans. R. J. Hollingdale, Penguin: London.
O'Connor, James (1973), *The Fiscal Crisis of the State*, St. James Press: London.
Ollman, Bertell (1971), *Alienation: Marx's Conception of Man in Capitalist Society*, Cambridge Studies in the History and Theory of Politics, Cambridge University Press: Cambridge.
O'Neill, John (1972), 'Public and Private Space', *Sociology as a Skin Trade: Essays Towards a Reflexive Sociology*, Harper: New York.
O'Neill, John, ed. (1976), *On Critical Theory*, Seabury: New York.
Oshinsky, David (1996), 'Alger Hiss and the Intellectuals: Meaning of an Enduring Controversy', *Chronicle of Higher Education*, Dec. 20, pp. B6-7.
Ousby, Ian, ed. (1993), *The Cambridge Guide to Literature in English*, foreword Doris Lessing, Cambridge University Press: Cambridge.
Outhwaite, William (1994), *Habermas: A Critical Introduction*, Stanford University Press: Stanford, Calif.

Paci, Enzo (1972), *The Function of the Sciences and the Meaning of Man*, trans. Paul Piccone and James E. Hanson, Northwestern University Press: Evanston, Ill.

Paine, Thomas (1994), *Collected Writings*, ed. Eric Foner, Library of America: New York.

Palermo, James (1975), 'Pedagogy as a Critical Hermeneutic', *Cultural Hermeneutics*, Vol. 3, No. 2, Aug., pp. 137-46.

Palmer, Richard E. (1969), *Hermeneutics: Interpretation Theory in Schleiermacher, Dilthey, and Gadamer*, Northwestern University Press: Evanston, Ill.

Parini, Jay and Millier, Brett T., eds. (1993), *The Columbia History of American Poetry*, Columbia University Press: New York.

Parker, Peter, ed. (1995), *A Reader's Guide to Twentieth-Century Writers*, pref. Frank Kermode, Oxford University Press: New York.

Pepper, Stephen C. (1970), *World Hypotheses: A Study in Evidence*, University of California Press: Berkeley.

Petrović, Gajo (1967), *Marx in the Mid-Twentieth Century*, Doubleday: New York.

Piaget, Jean (1971a), *Insights and Illusions of Philosophy*, World: New York.

Piaget, Jean (1971b), *Psychology and Epistemology: Towards a Theory of Knowledge*, Penguin: New York.

Pirsig, Robert M. (1974), *Zen and the Art of Motorcycle Maintenance: An Inquiry into Values*, Bantam: New York.

Pirsig, Robert M. (1991), *Lila: An Inquiry into Morals*, Bantam: New York.

Pivčević, Edo, ed. (1975), *Phenomenology and Philosophical Understanding*, Cambridge University Press: Cambridge.

Plato (1992), *The Republic*, trans. G.M.A. Grube, rev. C.D.C. Reeve, Hackett: Indianapolis, Ind.

Plekhanov, Georgi (1974), *The Development of the Monist view of History*, 3rd ed., Progress Publishers: Moscow.

Poe, Edward Allen (1985), *Works of Edgar Allen Poe*, Random House: New York.

Popper, Karl (1959), *The Logic of Scientific Discovery*, Basic Books: New York.

Poster, Mark (1975), *Existential Marxism in Postwar France: From Sartre to Althusser*, Princeton University Press: Princeton, N.J.

Poulantzas, Nicos (1973), *Political Power and Social Class*, trans. Timothy O'Hagan, New Left Books: London.

Poulantzas, Nicos (1974), *Fascism and Dictatorship: The Third International and the Problem of Fascism*, trans. Judith White, ed. Jennifer O'Hagan and Timothy O'Hagan, New Left Books: London.

Poulantzas, Nicos (1976), *The Crisis of the Dictatorships: Portugal, Greece,*

Spain, trans. David Fernbach, New Left Books: London.
The Protocols of the Meetings of the Learned Elders of Zion (1934), trans. Victor E. Marsden, Noontide Press: Newport Beach, Calif.
Radzinsky, Edvard (1996), *Stalin: The First In-Depth Biography Based on Explosive New Documents from Russia's Secret Archives*, trans. H. T. Willetts, Doubleday: New York.
Rakove, Jack N. (1996), *Original Meanings: Politics and Ideas in the Making of the Constitution*, Knopf: New York.
Rasmussen, David M. (1975), 'The Symbolism of Marx: From Alienation to Fetishism', *Cultural Hermeneutics*, Vol. 3, No. 1, May, pp. 41-75.
Rasmussen, David M. (1973), 'Between Autonomy and Sociality', *Cultural Hermeneutics*, Vol. 1, No. 1, April, pp. 3-45.
Rasmussen, David M. (1976a), 'Advanced Capitalism and Social Theory: Habermas on the Problem of Legitimation', *Cultural Hermeneutics*, Vol. 3, No. 4, July, pp. 349-66.
Rasmussen, David M. (1976b), 'Editorial Note', *Cultural Hermeneutics*, Vol. 3, No. 4, July, p. 333.
Ravets, Jerome R. (1971), *Scientific Knowledge and Its Social Problems*, Oxford University Press: New York.
Rawls, John (1971), *A Theory of Justice*, Belknap Press of Harvard University Press: Cambridge, Mass.
Rawls, John (1993), *Political Liberalism*, Columbia University Press: New York.
Reich, Wilhelm (1970), *The Mass Psychology of Fascism*, trans. Vincent R. Carfagno, Farrar, Straus, Giroux: New York.
Reich, Wilhelm (1972), *Sex-Pol: Essays, 1929-1934*, trans. Anna Bostock, Tom DuBose, and Lee Baxandall, ed. Lee Baxandall, intro. Bertell Ollman, Vintage: New York.
Reid, Herbert G. (1974), *Up the Mainstream*, David McKay: New York.
Reid, Herbert G. and Ihara, Randal H. (1976), 'Ideology Critique and Problems of Student Consciousness in the United States', *Cultural Hermeneutics*, Vol. 3, No. 3, March, pp. 217-44.
Reid, Herbert G. and Yanarella, Ernest J. (1974), 'Toward a Post-Modern Theory of American Political Science and Culture: Perspectives from Critical Marxism and Phenomenology', *Cultural Hermeneutics*, Vol. 2, No. 2, Aug., pp. 91-166.
Reiman, Jeffrey H. (1972), *In Defense of Political Philosophy: A Reply to Robert Paul Wolff's 'In Defense of Anarchism'*, Harper Torchbooks, Harper and Row: New York.
Remnick, David (1993), *Lenin's Tomb: The Last Days of the Soviet Empire*, Random House: New York.

Remnick, David (1996), 'Hammer, Sickle, and Book', *New York Review of Books*, Vol. 43, No 9, May 23, pp. 45-51.

Remnick, David (1997), *Resurrection: The Struggle for a New Russia*, Random House: New York.

Revel, Jacques and Hunt, Lynn, eds. (1995), *Histories: French Constructions of the Past*, trans. Arthur Goldhammer, New Press: New York.

Reynolds, David S. (1995), *Walt Whitman's America: A Cultural Biography*, Knopf: New York.

Ricoeur, Paul (1970), *Freud and Philosophy: An Essay on Interpretation*, trans. Denis Savage, Yale University Press: New Haven, Conn.

Ricoeur, Paul (1971), 'The Model of the Text: Meaningful Action Considered as a Text', *Social Research*, Vol. 38.

Ricoeur, Paul (1973), 'Ethics and Culture: Habermas and Gadamer in Dialogue', *Philosophy Today*, Vol. 17.

Ricoeur, Paul (1974), *The Conflict of Interpretations: Essays in Hermeneutics*, ed. Don Ihde, Northwestern University Press: Evanston, Ill.

Rieff, David (1995), *Slaughterhouse: Bosnia and the Failure of the West*, Touchstone: New York.

Riegel, Klaus F. (1979), *Foundations of Dialectical Psychology*, Academic Press: New York.

Roazen, Paul (1974), *Freud and His Followers*, Meridian, New American Library: New York.

Robertson, Pat (1991), *The New World Order*, Word Publishing: Dallas.

Robinson, Jancis (1996), *Jancis Robinson's Wine Course*, Abbeville Press: New York.

Rockmore, Tom (1976), 'Radicalism, Science, and Philosophy in Marx', *Cultural Hermeneutics*, Vol. 3, No. 4, July, pp. 429-49.

Rogin, Michael (1996), 'How Dirty Harry Beat the Ringo Kid', Review of *John Wayne: American* by Randy Roberts and James Olson, *London Review of Books*, Vol. 18, No. 9, May 9, pp. 3, 5.

Romanyshyn, Robert (1970), "Theoretical-Empirical Analysis of White Attitudes Toward Blacks and Black Attitudes Toward Whites: A Phenomenology of Attitudes," dissertation, Duquesne University.

Roper, Robert (1996), 'Fathers and Heroes: A Legacy of Resistance', *Philadelphia Inquirer Magazine*, June 16, pp. 18-22.

Rorty, Richard (1979), *Philosophy and the Mirror of Nature*, Princeton University Press: Princeton, N.J.

Rorty, Richard (1987), 'Thugs and Theorists: A Reply to Bernstein', *Political Theory*, Vol. 15, No. 4, Nov., pp. 564-80.

Rosen, Stanley (1974), *G.W.F. Hegel: An Introduction to the Science of Wisdom*, Yale University Press: New Haven, Conn.

Rosenberg, Tina (1996), 'Essay: In the Shadow of Goebbels', *New York Times Book Review*, Vol. 101, No. 22, June 2, pp. 26, 27.
Rothgeb, Carrie Lee, ed. (1973), *Abstracts of the Standard Edition of the Complete Psychological Works of Sigmund Freud*, pref. Bernard D. Fine, International Universities Press: New York.
Rousseau, Jean-Jacques (1964), *The First and Second Discourses*, trans. Roger D. Masters and Judith R. Masters, ed. Roger D. Masters, St. Martin's: New York.
Rousseau, Jean-Jacques (1974), *The Social Contract or Principles of Political Right*, with *On Political Economy*, rev. ed. trans. Charles M. Sherover, New American Library: New York.
Rousseau, Jean-Jacques (1987a), *The Basic Political Writings*, ed. and trans. Donald A. Cress, intro. Peter Gay, Hackett: Indianapolis, Ind.
Rousseau, Jean-Jacques (1987b), *On the Social Contract*, ed. and trans. Donald A. Cress, intro Peter Gay, Hackett: Indianapolis, Ind.
Rousseau, Jean-Jacques (1992), *Discourse on the Origin of Inequality*, trans. Donald A. Cress, intro. James Miller, Hackett: Indianapolis, Ind.
Ryan, Alan (1994), Review of *The Bell Curve: Intelligence and Class Structure in American Life* by Richard J. Herrnstein and Charles Murray, *New York Review of Books*, Vol. 41, No. 19, Nov. 17, pp. 7-11.
Rychlak, Joseph F. *A Philosophy of Science for Personality Theory*, Houghton Mifflin: Boston.
Sartre, Jean-Paul (1953), *Existential Marxism*, trans. Hazel E. Barnes, intro. Rollo May, H. Regnery: Chicago.
Sartre, Jean-Paul (1956), *No Exit and Three Other Plays*, Vintage: New York.
Sartre, Jean-Paul (1963), *Search for a Method*, trans. Hazel E. Barnes, Random House: New York.
Sartre, Jean-Paul (1967), *Existential Psychoanalysis*, trans. Hazel E. Barnes, intro. Rollo May, Regnery: Chicago.
Sartre, Jean-Paul (1973), *Being and Nothingness: An Essay on Phenomenological Ontology*, trans. Hazel E. Barnes, Washington Square Press: New York.
Sartre, Jean-Paul (1974), *Between Existentialism and Marxism*, trans. John Matthews, New Left Books: London.
Sartre, Jean-Paul (1976), *Critique of Dialectical Reason*, Vol. 1, *Theory of Practical Ensembles*, trans. Alan Sheridan-Smith, ed. Jonathan Rée, New Left Books: London.
Schacht, Richard (1975), *Hegel and After: Studies in Continental Philosophy Between Kant and Sartre*, University of Pittsburgh Press: Pittsburgh.
Schacht, Richard (1994), *The Future of Alienation*, University of Illinois Press: Urbana.
Schaff, Adam (1963), *A Philosophy of Man*, Dell: New York.

Schaff, Adam (1970), *Marxism and the Human Individual*, trans. Olgried Wojtasiewicz, intro. Erich Fromm, ed. Robert S. Cohen, McGraw-Hill: New York.

Schemo, Diana Jean (1994), 'Good Germans: "Honoring the Heroes, and Hiding the Holocaust"', *New York Times*, June 12, Sec. 4.

Schindler, Ronald Jerome (1978), 'The Frankfurt School Critique of Capitalist Culture: The Implications for Modern-Day Social Science Theory and the Counterpoint of Revisionist Marxist Thought', Ph.D. dissertation, University of Pennsylvania.

Schindler, Ronald Jerome (1984a), *The Crisis of American Sciences and Quasi-Transcendental Phenomenology*, 2 vols., Scholastic Monograph Series, Wyndham Hall Press: Bristol, Ind.

Schindler, Ronald Jerome (1984b), *Power Politics and Applied Ethics: A Study of the Research and Evaluation Section of the Philadelphia Office of Mental Health*, Foundations Press: Notre Dame, Ind.

Schindler, Ronald Jerome (1996), *Applied Social Sciences in the Plutocratic Era of the United States: Dialectics of the Concrete*, Avebury: Aldershot.

Schmidt, Alfred (1971), *The Concept of Nature in Marx*, trans. Ben Fowkes, New Left Books: London.

Schneider, Michael (1975), *Neurosis and Civilization: A Marxist/Freudian Synthesis*, trans. Michael Roloff, Seabury: New York.

Schneider, Peter (1995), 'The Sins of the Grandfathers: How German Teen-Agers Confront the Holocaust, and How They Don't', *New York Times Magazine*, Dec. 3, Sec. 6.

Schrag, Calvin O. (1980), *Radical Reflection and the Origin of the Human Sciences*, Purdue University Press: West Lafayette, Ind.

Schroyer, Trent (1973), *The Critique of Domination: The Origins and Development of Critical Theory*, Braziller: New York.

Schütz, Alfred (1970), *On Phenomenology and Social Relations: Selected Writings*, ed. Helmut R. Wagner, University of Chicago Press: Chicago.

Schütz, Alfred (1967), *The Phenomenology of the Social World*, Northwestern University Press, Evanston, Ill.

Scott, Luci (1994), 'Survivor: Jews saved Schindler from going on trial in Nuremberg', *Jewish Times*, Vol. 19, No. 4, April 21, p. 12.

Selsam, Howard and Martel, Harry, eds. (1963), *Reader in Marxist Philosophy: From the Writings of Marx, Engels, and Lenin*, International Publishers: New York.

Sevé, Lucien (1978), *Man in Marxist Theory and the Psychohistory of Personality*, Humanities Press: Atlantic Highlands, N.J.

Shea, Christopher (1996), 'Debating the Uniqueness of the Holocaust', Review of *Is the Holocaust Unique: Perspectives in Comparative Genocide* ed.

Alan Rosenbaum, *Chronicle of Higher Education*, Vol. 42, No. 38, May 31, pp. A6, 7, 12.
Shelley, Percy Bysshe (1994), *Selected Poems*, Random House: New York.
Simonds, A. P. (1975), 'Mannheim's Sociology of Knowledge as a Hermeneutic Method', *Cultural Hermeneutics*, Vol. 3, No. 1, May, pp. 81-104.
Simopoulos, V. (1975), 'The Existential Hero: Schizophrenic or the Forerunner of a New Affectivity', *Psychoanalytic Review*, Vol. 62, No. 3, Fall, pp. 429-36.
Smith, Adam (1993), *An Inquiry into the Nature and Causes of the Wealth of Nations*, ed. Laurence Dickey, Hackett: Indianapolis, Ind.
Smith, Barry and Smith, David Woodruff, eds. (1995), *The Cambridge Companion to Husserl*, Cambridge University Press: New York.
Smith, Jean Edward (1996), *John Marshall: Definer of a Nation*, Holt: New York.
Soboul, Albert (1975), *The French Revolution, 1787-1799: From the Storming of the Bastille to Napoleon*, trans. Alan Forrest and Colin Jones, Random House: New York.
Solzhenitsyn, Aleksandr I. (1973), *The Gulag Archipelago, 1918-1956: An Experiment in Literary Investigation*, Harper and Row: New York.
Sorel, Georges (1950), *Reflections on Violence*, trans. T. E. Hulme and J. Roth, intro. Edward A. Shils, Collier-Macmillan: London.
Specter, Michael (1994), 'Why Russia Loves This Man: The primitive, populist, powerful appeal of Vladimir Zhirinovsky and the Russian extremists', *New York Times Magazine*, June 19, Sec. 6.
Specter, Michael (1996), 'The Wars of Alexandr Ivanovich Lebed: Part democrat, part dictator, the volatile Russian general is battling with Kremlin rivals and his own political contradictions. But with Yeltsin in failing health, he is the man Russians overwhelmingly want right now as their next leader', *New York Times Magazine*, Oct. 13, Sec. 6.
Spiegelberg, Herbert (1972), *Phenomenology in Psychology and Psychiatry: A Historical Introduction*, Northwestern University Press: Evanston, Ill.
Spiegelberg, Herbert (1975), *Doing Phenomenology: Essays On and In Phenomenology*, Nijhoff: The Hague.
Spiegelberg, Herbert (1976), *The Phenomenological Movement: A Historical Introduction*, 2 vols., Martinus Nijhoff: The Hague.
Stace, W. T. (1955), *The Philosophy of Hegel: A Systematic Exposition*, Dover: New York.
Stannard, David E. (1996), 'The Dangers of Calling the Holocaust Unique', *Chronicle of Higher Education*, Vol. 42, No. 47, Aug. 2, pp. B1-2.
Stojanović, Svetozav (1973), *Between Ideals and Reality: A Critique of Socialism*

and Its Future, trans. Gerson S. Sher, Oxford University Press: London.
Stowe, Harriet Beecher (1995), *Uncle Tom's Cabin*, Barnes and Noble: New York.
Strong, Tracy B. (1975), *Friedrich Nietzsche and the Politics of Transfiguration*, University of California Press: Berkeley.
Styron, William (1979), *Sophie's Choice*, Random House: New York.
Szasz, Thomas (1969), *Schizophrenia: Sacred Symbol of Psychiatry*, Basic Books: New York.
Szasz, Thomas (1974), *The Myth of Mental Illness: Foundations of a Theory of Personal Conduct*, rev. ed., Harper and Row: New York.
Tarnas, Richard (1991) *The Passion of the Western Mind: Understanding the Ideas That Have Shaped Our World View*, Ballantine: New York.
Taylor, Telford (1992) *The Anatomy of the Nuremberg Trials: A Personal Memoir*, Knopf: New York.
Therborn, Göran (1976), *Science, Class, and Society: On the Formation of Sociology and Historical Materialism*, New Left Books: London; Humanities Press: Atlantic Highlands, N.J.
Thompson, John B. and Held, David, eds. (1992), *Habermas: Critical Debates*, MIT Press: Cambridge, Mass.
Thurow, Lester (1996), *The Future of Capitalism: How Today's Economic Forces Shape Tomorrow's World*, William Morrow: New York.
Timpanaro, Sebastiano (1975), *On Materialism*, trans. Lawrence Garner, New Left Books: London; Humanities Press: Atlantic Highlands, N.J.
Timpanaro, Sebastiano (1976), *The Freudian Slip: Psychoanalysis and Textual Criticism*, trans. Katie Soper, New Left Books: London.
Tocqueville, Alexis de (1969), *Democracy in America*, ed. J. P. Mayer, trans. George Lawrence, Harper and Row: New York.
Tucker, Robert C. (1990), *Stalin in Power: The Revolution from Above, 1928-1941*, Norton: New York.
Tudge, Colin (1996), *The Time Before History: Five Million Years of Human Impact*, Scribner: New York.
Twain, Mark (1992), *The Adventures of Huckleberry Finn* (1884), Book of the Month Club: New York.
Ulam, Adam B. (1989), *Stalin: The Man and His Era*, rev. ed., Beacon Press: Boston.
Unger, Robert Mangabeira (1975), *Knowledge and Politics*, Free Press: New York.
Vajda, Mihaly (1975), 'Truth or Truths', *Cultural Hermeneutics*, Vol. 3, No. 1, May, pp. 29-39.
van den Heuvel, William J. (1996), 'The Holocaust Was No Secret: Churchill knew. We all knew, and couldn't do anything about it - except win the

war', *New York Times*, Dec. 22, Sec. 6, pp. 30-31.
Vásquez, Adolfo Sánchez (1973), *Art and Society: Essays in Marxist Aesthetics*, trans. Maro Riofrancos, Monthly Review Press: New York.
Vásquez, Adolfo Sánchez (1977), *The Philosophy of Praxis*, trans. Mike Gonzalez, Merlin Press: London.
Wallerstein, Immanuel (1974), *The Modern World-System: Capitalist Agriculture and the Origins of the European World-Economy in the Sixteenth Century*, Academic Press: New York.
Wann, T. W., ed. (1964), *Behaviorism and Phenomenology: Contrasting Bases for Modern Psychology*, University of Chicago Press: Chicago.
Washburn, Katherine and Thornton, John, eds. (1996), *Dumbing Down: Essays on the Strip-Mining of American Culture*, Norton: New York.
Weber, Bruce (1997), 'Swift and Slashing, Computer Topples Kasparov', *New York Times*, May 12, pp. A1, B4.
Weber, Max (1976), *The Agrarian Sociology of Ancient Civilizations*, trans. R. I. Frank, New Left Books: London, 1976.
Wellmer, Albrecht (1971), *Critical Theory of Society*, trans. John Cumming, Herder and Herder: New York.
Wellmer, Albrecht (1976), 'Communication and Emancipation', *On Critical Theory*, ed. John O'Neill, Seabury, New York.
West, Cornel (1993), *Keeping Faith: Philosophy and Race in America*, Routledge: New York and London.
West, Cornel (1994), *Race Matters*, Vintage: New York.
Wetter, Gustav A. (1973), *Dialectical Materialism: A Historical and Systematic Survey of Philosophy in the Soviet Union*, trans. Peter Heath, Greenwood Press: Westport, Conn.
White, Stephen K., ed. (1995), *The Cambridge Companion to Habermas*, Cambridge University Press: New York.
Whitman, Walt (1992), *Selected Poems*, intro. Christopher Moore, Gramercy: New York.
Wiedmann, Franz (1968), *Hegel: An Illustrated Biography*, trans. Joachim Neugroschel, Pegasus Books, Western Publishing: New York.
Wiesel, Elie (1960), *Night*, trans. Stella Roadway, foreword François Mauriac, pref. Robert McAfee Brown, Bantam: New York.
Wiggershaus, Rolf (1994), *The Frankfurt School: Its History, Theories, and Political Significance*, trans. Michael Robertson, MIT Press: Cambridge, Mass.
Wills, Garry (1978), *Inventing America: Jefferson's Declaration of Independence*, Vintage: New York.
Wills, Garry (1992), *Lincoln at Gettysburg: The Words That Remade America*, Touchstone: New York.

Wilson, Edmund (1993), *The Sixties*, ed. and intro. Lewis M. Dabney, Farrar, Straus and Giroux: New York.

Wilson, Edward O. (1992), *The Diversity of Life*, Harvard University Press: Cambridge, Mass.

Winch, Peter (1958), *The Idea of a Social Science and Its Relation to Philosophy*, Routledge: London.

Wolff, Kurt H. and Moore, Barrington, Jr., eds. (1967), *The Critical Spirit: Essays in Honor of Herbert Marcuse*, Beacon Press: Boston.

Wolff, Robert Paul, Moore, Barrington, Jr., and Marcuse, Herbert, eds. (1969), *A Critique of Pure Tolerance*, Beacon Press: Boston.

Wolin, Richard (1992), *The Terms of Capitalist Criticism: The Frankfurt School, Existentialism, Postructuralism*, Columbia University Press: New York.

Wolin, Sheldon (1960), *Politics and Vision*, Little Brown: Boston.

Wollheim, Richard (1971), *Sigmund Freud*, Viking: New York.

Wood, Gordon S. (1992), *The Radicalism of the American Revolution*, Knopf: New York.

Woodring, Carl and Shapiro, James, eds. (1994), *The Columbia History of British Poetry*, Columbia University Press: New York.

Woolf, Virginia (1957), *A Room of One's Own* (1929), foreword Mary Gordon, Harcourt Brace: New York.

Wordsworth, William (1993), *Selected Poems*, intro. Christopher Moore, Gramercy: New York.

Wright, Georg Henrik von (1971), *Explanation and Understanding*, Cornell University Press: Ithaca, N.Y.

Wright, Richard (1993), *Native Son*, ed. Arnold Rampersad, HarperCollins: New York.

Yalom, Irvin D. (1980), *Existential Psychotherapy*, Basic Books: New York.

Young-Bruehl, Elisabeth (1996), *The Anatomy of Prejudices*, Harvard University Press: Cambridge, Mass.

Zahar, Renate (1974), *Frantz Fanon: Colonialism and Alienation: Concerning Frantz Fanon's Political Theory*, trans. Wilfried F. Feuser, Monthly Review Press: New York.

Zaner, Richard and Ihde, Don (1975), *Phenomenology and Existentialism*, Putnam: New York.

Zeidner, Lisa (1996), 'Essays Look into Troubled Psyche of American Society', Review of *Dumbing Down: Essays on the Strip-Mining of American Culture*, ed. Katherine Washburn and John F. Thornton, *Philadelphia Inquirer Books*, June 16, p. Q5.